Born This Way

Science, Citizenship, and Inequality in the American LGBTQ+ Movement

JOANNA WUEST

The University of Chicago Press
Chicago and London

The University of Chicago Press, Chicago 60637
The University of Chicago Press, Ltd., London
© 2023 by The University of Chicago
Published 2023
Printed in the United States of America

30 29 28 27 26 25 24 23 22 21   1 2 3 4 5

ISBN-13: 978-0-226-82751-3 (cloth)
ISBN-13: 978-0-226-82753-7 (paper)
ISBN-13: 978-0-226-82752-0 (e-book)
DOI: https://doi.org/10.7208/chicago/9780226827520.001.0001

Library of Congress Cataloging-in-Publication Data

Names: Wuest, Joanna, author.
Title: Born this way : science, citizenship, and inequality in the American
    LGBTQ+ movement / Joanna Wuest.
Description: Chicago : The University of Chicago Press, 2023. | Includes bibliographical
    references and index.
Identifiers: LCCN 2022056001 | ISBN 9780226827513 (cloth) | ISBN 9780226827537 (paperback) |
    ISBN 9780226827520 (ebook)
Subjects: LCSH: Gay liberation movement—United States—History. | Sexual minorities—
    Civil rights—United States—History. | Gender identity—United States. |
    Biopolitics—United States. | Identity politics—United States.
Classification: LCC HQ76.8.U5 W84 2023 | DDC 306.76/60973—dc23/eng/20230111
LC record available at https://lccn.loc.gov/2022056001

♾ This paper meets the requirements of ANSI/NISO Z39.48-1992
(Permanence of Paper).

Born This Way

Contents

Introduction 1

PART I **Origins**

1. **The Science of Civil Rights**
The Rise and Demise of Sexual Deviancy 31

2. **Desire in the Throes of Power**
Gay Liberation, Psychiatry, and the Politics of Classification 51

3. **"Why Is My Child Gay?"**
The Liberal Foundations of Born This Way 69

4. **Immutability before the Gay Gene**
Biology and Civil Rights Litigation 90

PART II **Evolutions and Adaptations**

5. **Rise of the Gay Gene**
Science, Law, Culture, and Hype 107

6. **From Pathology to "Born Perfect"**
Marriage Equality and Conversion Therapy Bans 135

7. **The Scientific Gaze in Transgender and Bisexual Politics** 160

Conclusion: Beyond Born This Way
Fluid Desires, Fixed Identities, and Entrenched Inequalities 190

Acknowledgments 207
Notes 211
Index 275

Introduction

In 2021 during the sweltering heat of the hottest Pride Month on record—or any June in the contiguous United States for that matter—Lady Gaga commemorated the ten-year anniversary of her electro-pop sensation *Born This Way*.[1] That album, rife with references to DNA and predestiny, actually borrowed its name from a disco-era gay liberation anthem titled "I Was Born This Way."[2] The record's themes and triumphal spirit seemed to forecast an impending torrent of civil rights victories. Just months after the album's initial release, the Department of Defense would repeal its discriminatory "Don't Ask, Don't Tell" policy, a cause for which Gaga had repeatedly campaigned.[3] A few months before that, the Obama administration's Justice Department had refused to defend the Defense of Marriage Act, which by 2013 would be deemed unconstitutional.[4] *Born This Way*'s refrain about the right to live as our authentic selves put to melody a sentiment that so often attended these reforms: our sexual and gender identities owe their origins to something encoded deep down within ourselves.

By the twenty-first century, the idea that our desires precede our own self-recognition of them had become a mainstay in the LGBTQ+ advocacy movement. In dozens of legislatures and courthouses, the National Center for Lesbian Rights has promoted its "Born Perfect" anti-conversion-therapy campaign, fit with a not-so-terribly subtle rainbow-hued fingerprint logo.[5] And in *Obergefell v. Hodges* (2015), the Supreme Court's historic ruling that made same-sex marriage the law of the land, Justice Anthony Kennedy put judicial weight behind the theory. "Psychiatrists and others recognized that sexual orientation is both a normal expression of human sexuality and immutable," the justice wrote. "Far from seeking to devalue marriage," a gay couples' "immutable nature dictates that same-sex marriage is their only real path to this profound commitment."[6]

Today biology reverberates across campaigns to thwart those Republican Party state legislators and their Christian conservative backers who would proscribe clinicians from treating trans youth and exclude trans athletes from sex-segregated sports. These fights and others like them are almost always framed in the language of ontology. Medical experts take the witness stand to opine on a trans youth's "true" sex—that is, one which conforms to a gender identity rooted in the brain, blood, or genes—and to counter the social conservative denial that there could be an organic basis for such abomination. In true reactionary form, clinical-esque terms like "irreversible damage" and "rapid onset gender dysphoria" have become choice phrases for equal rights opponents.[7] They incite concerns of a contagious "gender ideology" that corrupts the brains—and then bodies—of susceptible teenagers.

For anyone familiar with American LGBTQ+ history, or the history of moral panics more broadly, these current controversies are likely to arouse memories of prior civil rights struggles. Over half a century ago, queer people were met with similar charges of contagion, oftentimes for the crime of merely congregating in bars and on street corners. During the country's eugenics craze, so-called sexual and gender deviants were worthy candidates for castration, sterilization, and electroshock therapy, all in the name of the nation's good health. Then, just as now, those scapegoats for society's ills searched for a medical means of sanitizing their urges and predilections. They sought out sympathetic scientists who could calm their compatriots' anxieties, to explain that there was nothing to fear, that they were neither sick nor deranged. They were perhaps simply born that way.

The Scientific and Medical Foundations of American LGBTQ+ Advocacy

The central claim of this book is that the natural sciences and mental health professions have been foundational to American LGBTQ+ advocacy. Since the first modern gay and lesbian social movement organizations formed in the wake of World War II, reformers have leveraged scientific evidence and authority to justify rights expansions and social acceptance. Whether queer rights advocates have depicted themselves as "sick citizens"—mentally ill but in need of state reprieve nonetheless—or of sound body and mind, plagued only by a lack of legal protections, they have done so with the assistance of reform-inclined scientists and clinicians.

No mere metaphor or clever campaign slogan, the "gay gene" and other "born this way" tales of evolution and human nature are both the stuff of serious scientific inquiry *and* politics. This book answers a series of questions about the conjoined nature of science and politics, and about how the born this way ideology took shape and for what ends. It explores what mix of political, legal, and economic incentives compelled first the search for a means of combating the mental illness model of homosexuality and, later, the hunt for a biological origins story. It examines the relationships that interlace the modern interest-group advocacy movement with the realms of psychology, psychiatry, behavioral genetics, endocrinology, and neuroscience. That we now conceive of LGBTQ+ identities as discrete, stable, and relatively innate extends from how tightly entwined the fight for equal rights and the science of sexuality and gender have become.[8] The letters that make up the movement's ever-expanding acronym parallel Darwin's famous finches, each one resplendently unique, all the while belonging to a tidy taxonomy that accounts for the difference.

Born This Way is at once a celebratory and cautionary story, one that delineates a minority rights movement's impressive victories, its powerful and persuasive allies, and its inherent limitations. Its immediate task is to tell a story about the LGBTQ+ rights movement, the scientific study of human difference, and the biopolitical character of citizenship that formed at the nexus of the two. From there, it works to uncover some insight into something that we might call identity politics and the undergirding essentialist ideologies that are intrinsic features of that particular brand of minority rights advocacy. Though some of the problems with born this way politics will be familiar to those raised on queer theory skepticism, others concerning related threats to reproductive freedom, the administrative state, and procedural democracy are less known. In total, the book shows how, in bringing science to bear on civil rights struggles, LGBTQ+ advocates have transformed American politics and the epistemology of identity politics more broadly.

It is important to say from the outset that there is as of today still very little evidence for anything like a "gay gene" or a "transgender brain"—or any other neat biological source for gender identity or sexual orientation for that matter. Stripped of the media hype and political grandstanding, these studies tend to exhibit relatively humble explanations on the margins of an identity—a bit of genetic or hormonal influence may be present here or there, but nothing close to a definitive claim about etiology is generally offered. Furthermore, it is clear from public opinion data, psychological observation, and ethnographic field notes that many queer people do not adhere to the biological idea themselves.[9] This is not to say that gay and trans people choose their "lifestyle" or the direction of their desire. Human beings are, after all, highly complex biocultural beings whose traits are rarely reducible to the soundbite-level nuance of either-or contentions.[10] Ergo, even if a queer sense of self cannot be traced back to a primordial factor, there is considerable evidence (psychological, sociological, and personal) that desire cannot be easily eradicated by coercion, at least not without trauma or death.

That so many Americans have come to believe something to the contrary—either that such identities are fixed at birth or are entirely within one's ability to alter—is a central concern of this work. Throughout, the book examines the enduring fascination and contestation over biological theories of human difference, ones that can be best described as scientistic. By this I mean something slightly different than pseudoscience, the preferred term for a scientific paradigm erroneously insisting that it conforms to the reigning standards of professional scientific inquiry when it clearly does not.[11] Many biological studies of sexual orientation and gender identity pass that test in that they are conducted in elite academic institutions with grant moneys from reputable sources and adhere to the rigorous standards that regulate their given discipline.

I use the term "scientism" to refer to an ideologically weighty version of truth-seeking, one that feigns objectivity while being anything but.[12] Like the vulgar race science of the eugenicist Madison Grant or his reincarnated presence in Charles Murray, today's scientism is an ideology that adroitly naturalizes the world as it appears—in all its dazzling diversity and its horrific inequality—as the way it was meant to be. Born this way ideology has a far more mixed record than does twentieth-century eugenics, of course, and those differences and divergences are the subject of this chapter and many others in the present volume. But they do share a peculiar privileging of science as *the* means of knowing thyself and neighbor. This is crucial because it highlights the fundamentally political nature of how etiological theories were gestated in political movements, medical professional associations, biomedical funding streams, and legal campaigns. It also reveals how such scientific theories live on today in our collective imagination as much as anywhere else.[13]

And so, the remainder of this introduction previews born this way's evolution, beginning in the late nineteenth century and traversing its maturation throughout the mid- to late twentieth century. Along the way, it maps how bioessentialism became ascendant, and why its central premise that genetics, brain structures, and hormonal balances play the most determinative role in what it means to be a man or a woman, gay or straight, cisgender or trans, has become so hegemonic. It also examines the surprising adaptability of the born this way logic, which has long been critiqued for its rigidity and inability to capture nonbinary genders and sexual fluidity. Finally, the chapter delineates the class character of bioessentialist ideology, its susceptibility to revanchist right-wing attacks on scientific authority and minority rights, and its racial dimensions.

The Evolution of Born This Way

To tell the story of born this way's evolution is to spell out exactly how LGBTQ+ people won their—albeit fragmented—civil rights.[14] It is to fully account for the transformations in law, social movements, the science of human behavior and identity, and political economy that allowed LGBTQ+ advocates to dispel the myth of mental illness and to replace it with an alternative tale of biological origins.

On the matter of what scholars have come to call "biopolitical citizenship," the LGBTQ+ movement's reliance on scientific and medical authority has consequences for how the state, society, and individuals come to perceive and articulate conceptions of self and identity.[15] Since French philosopher Michel Foucault's adoption of the term, biopolitics has been the dominant framework through which political and social theorists have grappled with these varying and interwoven power relations and resultant subjectivities.[16] The academic work that generally flies under the banner of biopolitical citizenship studies is concerned with conflicts within the domain of public health and medical bureaucracies. Classic investigations have detailed the aftermaths of nuclear disasters as well as the racial politics of government-funded clinical trials.[17] The case of the American LGBTQ+ movement, however, demonstrates how certain identity-based interest groups have also used science and medicine both to contest their ill treatment and to undergird civil rights claims.

The modern governance of sexuality and gender has always relied upon scientific expertise to legitimate its rule. The punitive American sexuality regime, which existed in its most oppressive form from the late nineteenth to the mid-twentieth century—was characterized by interlocking and reinforcing public health regulations and criminal codes, all of which aimed to quash "deviant" behaviors like homosexuality, prostitution, and other so-called social maladies.[18] In the name of social hygiene, proscriptions against a wide variety of sexual behavior and gender presentation proliferated within bureaucracies and legislatures. They, too, were generally upheld by courts as proper exercises of state power.

In this sense, today's born this way ideology—and much of contemporary American politics today—is downstream from the Progressive Era, that period lasting roughly between 1890 and 1920, when the modern scientific study of difference became central to matters of statecraft and citizenship.[19] As policymakers constructed a sprawling bureaucratic apparatus to manage the economic complexities and social disarray associated with the Second Industrial Revolution, they drew heavily on medicine and the natural and social sciences for insight and authority.[20] The classic tensions between the administrative state and democratic rule, on the one hand, and the "fuzzy border between truth and power," on the other, were hallmarks of the era.[21] Adding to the democratic deficit, robber barons like the Rockefellers established charitable foundations that would fund the study, treatment, and control of social undesirables (i.e., the poor, racialized, and gendered subjects of the age's enormous inequalities).[22] The legal system was correspondingly transformed, as evinced by a 1923 Supreme Court ruling that directed lower court judges' evaluation of expert testimonies, which had proliferated as independent scientific authorities were asked to guide good governance.[23] Courts, federal agencies, and state bureaucratic boards would serve as key institutional venues for regulating aberrant sexualities, genders, and related social problems.

Accordingly, the first gay rights advocacy organizations fought fire with fire; they gradually chipped away at the scientific authority of their oppressors and banded together with a new cohort of sympathetic researchers. Beginning in the early 1950s, small sects of civil rights activists emerged, which soon formed the county's first national gay rights advocacy movement. From the very outset, homophile groups like the Mattachine Society and lesbian ones like the Daughters of Bilitis recruited allies in sexology and mental health to contest the reigning consensus that portrayed them as dangerously unwell (the term "homophile" itself was coined as a substitute for the pathology-laden "homosexual"). They drew strength from reformers like sex researcher Alfred Kinsey, whose survey-based studies had pulled back the curtain on sexual mores, exposing the fiction that Americans were typically "exclusively" heterosexual throughout their life spans.[24] In report after report, the Indiana University–based Kinsey Institute (which ironically drew from Rockefeller-funded foundations) found that same-sex attraction was a naturally occurring and benign variation on human sexuality.[25] Throughout the early decades of the gay and lesbian rights movement, activists translated their newfound friends' scientific studies into challenges to public health policies, employment regulations, and immigration restrictions, all of which took homosexuals to be noxious "social contagions" or even violent "sexual psychopaths."

These field-changing shifts in science and medicine aligned the interests of civil rights activists and reform-spirited mental health professionals. Within two decades, insurgent reformers transformed the American Psychiatric Association (APA) from the inside, culminating in the 1973 decision to declassify homosexuality as a pathological disorder in the influential *Diagnostic and Statistical Manual of Mental Disorders* (*DSM*).[26] As gay reformers took aim at their clinical oppressors, splinters within both the mental health profession itself and academic psychology were undermining the authority of the psychoanalytic old guard that had sustained the pathological thesis. Both the young liberal psychiatrists who had cut their teeth in the cultural revolutions of the 1960s and closeted queer clinicians despised the APA leadership for its political conservativism, while proponents of both behavioral psychology and a biomedical approach to clinical care launched attacks on psychoanalysis for its purported lack of rigor. Homosexuality's declassification was ultimately downstream from these intra-scientific disputes, which played a decisive role in revising the *DSM*.

Gay and lesbian rights leaders would emerge from the fight at the APA and other conflicts in medical professional associations with deep ties to those in the highest echelons of mental healthcare, many of whom were becoming more biomedically disposed by the day. As early as the late 1960s, the consensus on pathology was corroding while jurists and policymakers were becoming increasingly amenable to alternative ontological explanations. Major developments in liberal social movement politics, the scientific study of mental health and human behavior, and the political economy of biomedicine illustrate how born this way took its now-familiar shape.

For one, a new crop of liberal advocates began organizing into what would soon become the sleek and professional nonprofit interest groups and legal operations that we know today, including the National Gay Task Force, the Human Rights Campaign, Parents and Friends of Lesbians and Gays (PFLAG), and Lambda Legal. The nonprofit foundation model is itself a Progressive Era philanthropic invention.[27] Pioneered both as a tax haven for donors and a unique tool for policy intervention, interest groups such as 501(c)(3) organizations have become a staple of postwar American politics.[28] This corporate-driven, tax-write-off style of interest-group politics has only ramped up with the displacement of labor unions and other mass membership organizations for those groups that generate advocacy through low-lift charitable giving.

Drawing from their homophile ancestors, these liberal nonprofits refined the idea that gays and lesbians were akin to any other ethnic or religious minority group seeking integration into the existing pluralist order. This ideology allowed movement representatives to speak what it claimed to be the authentic voice of a relatively homogeneous queer constituency, one that desired freedom from discrimination above all other demands. In the words of the sociologist Rogers Brubaker, this is the process by which a group becomes a social category.[29] It dissolves the difference between a historically contingent group like the largely urban-dwelling, middle-class gay and lesbian advocates and the taxonomic distinction signified by born this way.[30] Influenced in part by the budding religious right's insistence that homosexuality was an immoral "choice," movement leaders also adopted the era's rhetoric of family values, promising that a modicum of equal rights and social tolerance was in no way a back door into a second sexual revolution. In this light, sexual orientation could be posited as having had very little to do with sexual activity itself. Rather, it was an *essence*.

At the same time, the science of sexuality itself began to shift away from a psychoanalytic paradigm, which had long cast homosexuality as the result of social determinants including poor upbringing by effeminate fathers and overbearing mothers, and toward a biological one. This was not simply due to a new generation's rejection of the APA old guard's conservative impulses, but rather a consequence of changes that scale all the way up to the structure of the American economy.[31] Midway through the twentieth century, the revolution in DNA research and biomedical technologies erupted. In the wake of the traditional domestic manufacturing sector's decline, both the federal government and private capital directed investments into medical and bio-agricultural technologies, many of which had lucrative industrial uses.[32] These investment projects were facilitated by deregulatory reforms that eliminated strictures on collaborations among private investor and government-funded academics and allowed for the patenting of genetically modified organisms. Such relationships between biotech entrepreneurs and academic researchers set new norms for partnerships, which drove both Wall Street speculation and the cultural spectacle of bioreductivism. In this sense, the search for sexual orientation's nature is in many ways an ideological derivative of the state and industry's own search for profits in a neoliberal political economy.

As a result, many mental health researchers picked up these biological methodologies and premises as a replacement for disgraced psychoanalytic ones. Fresh faces in the nascent fields of sociobiology, behavioral genetics, and neuroendocrinology further boosted bio-based theories of sexuality. This exalted place for biology did not itself predetermine a pivot to fixity. Theodosius Dobzhansky, one of the era's great evolutionary geneticists, protested too fine a separation between biological premises and sociocultural ones: "Man's biological evolution changes his nature; cultural evolution changes his nurture."[33] Despite this caution against an either-or mindset, many of this paradigm's practitioners—and certainly its celebrity popularizers—would come to equate biology with predestiny. This was particularly true for the study of sexuality as researchers moved beyond disclosing the invalidity of the pathological model and on to the much more difficult task of exploring its etiological truth.

These trends—that is, the creation of a new interest-group apparatus, developments within the mental health professions, and a sizable shift toward biology-based psychological research—converged to produce the hypothesis that gays and lesbians may be "born that way." For example, a legal stratagem document produced by advocates in the 1970s implored attorneys to "address the judge's curiosity" and to ask and answer questions such as: "What is lesbianism? What is homosexuality? What causes it?"[34]

As these scientific and political forces progressively wrapped together tightly like the twin strands of DNA's double helix, they coproduced even stronger assertions that homosexuality was an immutable, inborn identity—an intrinsic biological element of personhood that would inform the gay and lesbian narrative of their political peoplehood. Owing its origins to nearly $3 billion in federal funding and private investment, the Human Genome Project's sequencing efforts made the 1990s the era of "genomania."[35] This investment trickled down to academic disciplines like behavioral genetics, which infused massive amounts of grant money into a field that previously had received little federal money with which to work.[36] Prodded on by a rapt media eager to broadcast biological truths, researchers examined the human genome for everything from innocuous personality traits to pathological conditions like addiction—and then, of course, the "gay gene."[37] Far from being mere spectators to the event, LGBTQ+ movement leaders were present at the inception of these studies' research designs and played an outsize role in promoting and politicizing their findings.

That the gay gene can be traced back to relationships which began percolating as early as the 1950s should dispel the notion that the born this way narrative was a clever rhetorical invention or an opportunistic reach for a message that existed "out there," independent of social forces. To be sure, the LGBTQ+ movement relied enormously on its well-regarded expert allies to combat the religious right; however, it took conservatives several decades to unite around the narrative of "choice," as evinced by Ronald Reagan's 1978 remark: "Whatever else it is, homosexuality is not a contagious disease like the measles. . . . Prevailing scientific opinion is that an individual's sexuality is determined at a very early age and that a child's teachers do not really influence this."[38] Instead, the seed of "nature over nurture" was planted decades earlier. It was fertilized in the dialectical developments between the homophiles and their foes within the psychiatric establishment, local police departments and liquor boards, and Cold War anti-communism.[39] Rather than pressuring advocates to adopt bioessentialism as a defensive move, the social conservative insistence on "choice" was actually *reacting* to a force that had long been in motion.

Fit and Adaptation

To borrow a metaphor from biology, the LGBTQ+ movement has evolved to be far more *fit* for its terrain than has its adversaries. Courts, for instance, have come to expect a duel between competing experts, a fight that LGBTQ+ advocates come into with an upper hand.[40] Accordingly, such scientific evidence has featured prominently in campaigns and litigation to repeal military exclusion policies, to find a constitutional right to same-sex marriage, and to defend legislative bans on conversion therapy (which mental health professionals now call "sexual orientation and gender identity change efforts," or SOGICE). Having cultivated a legion of allied expert witnesses in psychology, psychiatry, behavioral genetics, endocrinology, and neuroscience, LGBTQ+ advocates promise courts that they alone possess the truth according to which they ought to adjudicate.[41] As the relationships between movement and scientific actors have deepened and compounded, those conservative researchers and clinicians who clung too tightly to the pathological model have been ousted from their professional homes; having been relegated to the pseudoscientific fringe, they are often dismissed by judges who find their expert witness testimonies to be nonrepresentative of their respective fields.[42]

As a result, the victories have piled up. Don't Ask, Don't Tell has been dead for over a decade, same-sex marriage is the law of the land, and bans on conversion therapy cover twenty states, the District of Columbia, Puerto Rico, and over eighty cities and counties.[43] Throughout the fights for marriage equality and against conversion therapy, mental health advocates flipped an old biopolitical script on queer parents and youth. Whereas such guardians and children were once seen as a social threat—in queer theorist lingo, they jeopardized *futurity* itself—the orthodoxy now claims that gay parents and families require tolerance and civil rights to flourish and to reproduce a happy and healthy nation. Absent these protections, a queer youth subjected to conversion therapy risks trauma and suicidality while a same-sex couple's children are emotionally and cognitively scarred by the state's misrecognition of their family. In this interpretation, equal rights not only fulfill the liberal promise of American constitutionalism—they are existential to the body politic itself.

These triumphs have come with their critics and consequences. Much ink has been spilled cataloging all the myriad ways that assimilable or "respectable" sexual and gender identities have constricted the bounds of representation, equality, and human flourishing. Surely science can assist in making representative images of identity (e.g., the professional-class white gay couple that desires civil rights protections, a life of domesticity and consumption, and a lower income-tax rate to boot) that swallow up incredibly heterogeneous groups of individuals.

That all aside, bioessentialist ideology has proven surprisingly adaptive to transgender and bisexual political identities. Contrary to lamentations that these marginalized persons would sit forever outside the born this way logic, the "B" and the "T" of LGBT have been remarkably cast as such.[44] For example, as mainstream gay and lesbian civil rights organizations have made trans legal rights a top priority, their attorneys have developed a legal strategy that makes use of the movement's biological firepower. In challenges to discriminatory bathroom ban policies, litigators have argued that neuroanatomical evidence suggests that gender identity is not only one factor in constituting biological sex (the others being chromosomes, gonads, and secondary-sex characteristics like bone structure and skin texture) but is instead the most important one.[45] Convincing courts that gender identity *is* sex itself is a clever legal maneuver through which to achieve protections under sex-based statutory civil rights laws like Title VII and IX as well as the Constitution's equal protection clause. This route bypasses a polarized and gridlocked Congress, which has stalled repeatedly on legislation like a gender-identity-inclusive Employment Non-Discrimination Act and its revamped version, the Equality Act.[46]

Notably, gender identity is neither volitional nor a product of culture according to this narrative. It is instead biological in nature and can be made legally legible with reference to biomedical studies, *DMS* diagnoses, and clinical observations. In a strange turn of events, social conservative opponents have countered with their own interpretation of the traditional feminist theory distinction between sex as biology and gender as culture.[47] In a 2017 Supreme Court brief challenging a transmasculine high school student's right to access the men's restroom, opponents of trans rights cited Judith Butler's *Gender Trouble* to make their point that "gender is a fluid concept with no truly objective meaning," something that is far too "fuzzy and mercurial" to equate with biological sex.[48]

As critics of bioessentialism have pointed out time and again, however, there is very little evidence that human beings possess a sexual or gender telos, one that unfolds naturally in accordance with some predetermined biological self.[49] In the words of political theorist Nina Hagel, such theories "may uphold untenable ideals of self-knowledge and self-congruence," which have a negative impact on children who vacillate in and out of varied modes of gender expressions.[50] There is some hope for change in that clinics have developed modules that better attend to experiences of fluidity and periods of questioning (e.g., a child who dresses themselves in one gendered garb one day and another the next is not deemed "inadequately" nonconforming).[51] However, when rigid conceptions of identity predominate in law, policymaking, and campaign rhetoric, they can foreclose the very possibility of gender fluidity or periods of questioning that may or may not lead a child or adult to adopt an LGBTQ+ identity.[52] Rather than nonconformity outright presenting the greatest obstacle, it is *uncertainty* with which the paradigm is incapable of comprehending.

Given the uptick in talk of gender fluidity and a renewed interest in the slippery spectrum of sexuality, one might expect that born this way's prowess has diminished. Maybe certainty has had its day. Maybe the next adaptation will entail something other than another letter added to the movement's moniker. Advocates might instead refashion sexuality and gender in a new, more pliable mode. This would be a significant shift from the early days of the Kinsey Institute, when researchers and their activist acolytes would attempt to peg the number of "exclusive heterosexuals" at somewhere around 10 percent of the US population. Since the 1970s, gay and lesbian rights leaders have used this scientific premise—along with statistical estimates of their exact number in the population—to assert that their assimilation would simply mean a static group exiting the closet.

The fact that LGBTQ+ advocates remain unable to acknowledge that their ranks may actually be expanding shows that adaptation has its limits. Survey data and demographic research suggest that millennials and "zoomers" are more likely than any generation before them to eschew standard sexual and gendered social scripts.[53] One could make a convincing case that rising rates of political protections and cultural visibility have influenced individuals in ways that conservatives have always feared and that liberals—being so wedded to biopolitical legitimation—could hardly afford to consider. When it is less dangerous and more socially acceptable to stray from long-standing social norms, there just might be more people who fit under the queer umbrella.

This secular trend has historical antecedents as well. Though same-sex relationships and gatherings certainly flourished before the twentieth century, what we know today as gay life was itself inconceivable prior to industrial capitalism, particularly the expansion of wage labor and the rise of modern cities.[54] The industrial economy allowed a critical mass of individuals— mostly men but some women too—to subsist outside the economic comforts and security of the nuclear family and to create for themselves communities, bar scenes, and cruising spots. These social arrangements and subcultures— once unthinkable in the family-dominated agrarian political economy— proliferated throughout the late nineteenth and early twentieth centuries as Americans moved off the pastures and into the cities.[55]

Despite recent data and gay history alike, LGBTQ+ advocates studiously avoid the hypothesis that environment has much to do with steady increases in identification. In its coverage of a 2021 study on high school students' gender diversity, Condé Nast's LGBTQ+-themed magazine *them* dismissed the notion that the world was becoming quantitatively queerer. "Experts believe it's not the case that the percentage of people who are transgender is not necessarily on the rise," the magazine reported. "Rather, as more language has developed for expansive gender identities, and LGBTQ+ visibility and acceptance have increased, more young people feel comfortable openly rejecting the limitations of cisgender identity at an earlier age than they would have otherwise."[56] The core premise here and in related advocacy messaging meshes well with bioessentialism, if not an epigenetic variant of its core logic: more tolerant environments allow for the expression of an underlying queer disposition.[57] We may soon find ourselves with tidy taxonomies and origins stories that treat every letter in an ever-expansive acronym like LGBTQQIP-2SAA as stable, discrete, and potentially innate.[58]

Neither commerce, culture, nor civil rights are turning the kids queer. The world is simply a nicer place than it once was, which has allowed everyone to live as they always would have in the absence of social hostility. This commonsense sentiment resonates with classical deterministic reasoning. It divorces a person's "true self" from its environment, rendering the two as wholly distinct entities separated by a metaphysical gulf. As the renowned evolutionary biologist Richard Lewontin has cautioned, this is not even an accurate description of how animals and plants express traits in new environments, let alone a plausible account of how intricate human behaviors and identities might spring into being.[59] To crib from literary theorist Walter Benn Michaels's writings on race and cultural pluralism, the form of identity with which we are left may be culturally inflected, but it is a closer cousin of its biological ancestor than we might assume. Though such identities may be "lost or stolen, reclaimed or repudiated," they are, in the last instance, taken as essences waiting to be realized.[60] And so, bioessentialism has exhibited a curious tenacity in our supposedly foundationless postmodern world.[61]

Biologically Linked Fates and the Ends of Identity

If the foregoing has emphasized matters of born this way's origins and persistence, we might then ask: Whose interests does a bio-backed theory of identity serve?

In light of the history of discrimination and the ongoing onslaught on trans rights, it is no wonder that advocates have sought refuge in the comfort of scientific authority and the legal pluralist approach to combating prejudice and discrimination. Threat is indeed a powerful motivator.[62] To combat harm, advocacy organizations and pro-LGBTQ+ politicians frame their leaderships as organically tied to an amorphously defined "queer community."

The leadership then pursues a narrowly legalistic civil rights strategy in a sort of one-size-fits-all model to preventing and ameliorating suffering.

In many respects, this is an apt enough description of the strengths and constraints imposed by the neat biologized account of LGBTQ+ identities. It sums up both its legal prowess—victories for antidiscrimination laws, for instance, could be easily understated—as well as its limited ability to redress the more basic material fact of economic exploitation, which can itself texture and compound the damage of discrimination. At the same time, this thesis misses something crucial. It neglects an element based in political economy.[63] That is, liberal identity-based social movements require essentialist narratives that ideologically cohere their respective group for both their defensive *and* offensive moves.

A sense of a *biologically linked fate* does this ideological work splendidly.[64] By this I mean that these interest-group spokespersons and self-anointed cultural representatives frequently perform acts of ventriloquism, ones that unite a belief about selfhood with a supposedly shared collective political interest—that is, a peoplehood. None of this is to suggest that queer people everywhere begin their morning by gazing into the mirror and seeing their desire reflected back at them, in their physiognomy or the blood trickling from a nick on their neck. It is also not to say that the average LGBTQ+ person perceives their own material interests as congruent with those national nonprofits that claim to speak on their behalf while bestowing workplace equality awards to billionaires like Amazon's Jeff Bezos who believe in antidiscrimination but not the right of workers to use the restroom. Indeed, the linked-fate logic works less through elite deception or false consciousness than it does by speaking for a population that is largely silent. Rancorous protests and political demonstrations aside, the vast majority of Americans are effectively silenced by their lack of political power, no matter their gender or sexual identity.

This fact is what allows a national LGBTQ+ rights leader to proclaim that queer people "argue very strenuously that their sexual orientation is very well defined and biological" (this begs the question of who made that self-conception possible) while the Human Rights Campaign lobbies GOP support for an antidiscrimination measure by offering to assist its attempt to privatize Social Security.[65] This heavily symbolic politics does little to serve the vast majority of LGBTQ+ Americans who exhibit lower rates of health insurance and higher rates of poverty in a country where being at the baseline already means living with high rates of debt, inadequate healthcare coverage, and at-will employment.[66] While vital, civil rights remedies and social tolerance are feeble means of confronting economic exploitation and widening gaps in the American social welfare state.

This is the mature political form of what LGBTQ+ interest-group leaders have achieved and what the born this way idea has sanctioned. It is what has made possible its assemblage of allies within professionalized liberal advocacy circles, the Democratic Party, and diversity-conscious corporate elites.[67] These forces often leverage diversity and inclusion against more egalitarian redistributive programs like universal healthcare or public housing. Biologically linked fate has done considerable ideological work for the LGBTQ Victory Fund's lobbying efforts to compel redistricting authorities to carve out gay populations as "communities of interest" in their electoral map drawing.[68] The most likely consequence would be to facilitate the elections of spokespersons who draw from and reinforce the notion that wealthy and business-friendly gay politicians (particularly those who would represent affluent, commercialized "gayborhood" urban districts) speak on behalf of a largely working-class queer constituency.[69]

To see how this directly serves a certain segment of capital class interests, we need look no further than the *Harvard Business Review*. In a 2013 issue on diversity in the workforce, a trio of corporate consultants observed that boosting "inherent diversity" metrics involving "traits you are born with, such as gender, ethnicity, and sexual orientation," is a surefire way to exploit "under-leveraged markets."[70] More recently, the corporate coffee giant Starbucks unveiled a line of "born this way"–branded charity drinks.[71] Corporate advocacy for LGBTQ+ rights in general has increased seemingly exponentially as newly formed industry groups like Freedom for All Americans and similar coalitions of multinational corporations, chambers of commerce, small businesses, and banks have put their weight behind antidiscrimination in state houses across the country.[72] Unless a rainbow-shaded corporate-class hierarchy paired with some important, yet highly constricted, civil rights wins are one's idea of the best of all worlds imaginable, then it is dire to take stock of what born this way and its social movement vehicles can and cannot do.

This political project is also buttressed by the fact that nonprofit LGBTQ+ interest groups and public health organizations alike are encouraged by grant funders (both public and private) to compulsively collect demographic data that count the number and condition of various identity categories.[73] Amassing these figures and estimates is occasionally imagined as a social justice end in itself, thus spurring an endless cycle of pinpointing a range of disparities in health outcomes, housing rates, and income (just to name a few).[74] Today, the notion that disparities measured at the level of group difference are *the* most significant indicators of inequality has become the lifeblood of identity-based organizations. The liberal invocation of disparity statistics is what allows a class-skewed representative group to tell a constituency—presumed to possess a single united interest—"this impoverishment or violence happens to people just like you, it could even happen to you, and you need us to stop it."[75]

One might protest that organizations like the Trevor Project have made the case against unduly homogenizing the LGBTQ+ population and for taking an intersectional approach that involves collecting data on poor trans youths of color.[76] It is, of course, noble work to concern oneself with the needs of LGBTQ+ youths who exhibit extraordinarily high rates of suicidality. The Trevor Project's leadership has even gone so far as to advocate for increased public mental health services. Might an intersectional approach remedy the flaws of born this way politics?

There are good reasons to be doubtful. Racial justice rhetoric aside, there is a fundamental contradiction at the heart of this project. The Trevor Project may be staffed by those concerned with the lack of mental health resources, yet its donor base—which includes anti-healthcare-reform insurance and pharmaceutical companies like Aetna, Gilead, Anthem, and Bristol Myers Squibb—thwarts its ability to achieve those measures. Even more, the intersectional logic deployed here rests on the premise that the oppressed group's identity (trans youths of color) and its relative conditions of immiseration are the metric by which to measure injustice.[77] This emphasis on "the least of us" is morally righteous but ill-equipped for the kind of mass coalitions that have historically won the kinds of social welfare reforms (e.g., universal single-payer healthcare and public housing) that are actually necessary to ameliorate the ills of inequality. I think it is not too cynical to say that we ought to measure the Trevor Project's ability to commit to this public-goods vision through a longer-term assessment to see which way the wind will actually blow. Given that rising rates of gay civil rights and social tolerance have been, for half a century now, essentially the inverse of rates of economic equality and labor power, there is scant reason to be hopeful.[78]

Finally, liberal nonprofits are not the only ones who place their faith in political appeals to marginality. For decades now, some left-wing critics of bioessentialism and liberal identity politics have posited that the spread of nonconforming identities themselves will lead to broader egalitarian transformations in society and government.[79] Throughout the women's and gay liberation movements of the late 1960s and early 1970s, radical interpretations of Freud prophesized the impending demise of both heterosexuality and homosexuality. These gay liberationists looked on the horizon for a utopian state of free bisexual expression and emancipatory social arrangements (e.g., communal living and childcare, open relationships, less-gendered divisions of social reproductive labor, etc.).[80] This "disruptive identities" thesis persists today among self-styled radicals in academic departments and small sectarian activist groups.[81] The inherently adaptive nature of bioessentialist ideology—as well as capital's embrace of queer inclusivity—should finally put to rest this hopeful, yet naive notion that just because an identity is articulated as transgressive, unsettling, resistive, disruptive, or revolutionary means that it has a transformative political potential.[82]

Inverted Pluralism and the Politics of Uncertainty

As if the foregoing discussion was not enough to rethink born this way politics, even its limited utility as a defense against right-wing assaults has begun to abate. Its approach to equality is presently proving to be a rather shoddy safeguard against right-wing revanchism and threats to civil rights, reproductive freedoms, state power, and democracy itself.

Opponents of LGBTQ+ civil rights have reoriented their strategy, preferring at times to bypass questions of ontology and essentialism in favor of a "competing" or "conflicting" rights narrative.[83] Wielding First Amendment religious liberty and free speech doctrine, the right has pitched itself as the standard bearer of pluralism. In a brilliant maneuver to avoid charges of unconstitutional animus against sexual and gender minorities, conservatives have framed themselves as casualties of secular liberalism, which has trampled on the rights of Christian traditionalists who have refused to bake wedding cakes for same-sex couples or to photograph their wedding celebrations.[84] Cis women are also frequently portrayed by this crowd as unduly harmed by reforms that allow trans women access to sex-segregated bathrooms, shelters, and prisons.[85] In this way, right-wing forces have inverted pluralism for inegalitarian ends; they have done so by casting themselves as victims of a totalitarian insistence on tolerance for sexual and gender minorities.[86]

Conservative attorneys, policymakers, and think tanks have also leveraged a politics of uncertainty to undermine the biopolitical claims of equal rights advocates. Taking inspiration from the tobacco and oil industries' campaigns against cancer research and climate change, respectively, they have argued that physicians and biologists are not as certain as they seem about the nature of LGBTQ+ identity or the proper healthcare regimen for trans youth.[87] This strategy of denialism functions through incessant calls for "additional research" and a minimization of legal or regulatory action.[88]

In the courts, the notion of medical uncertainty has been levied against conversion therapy bans, trans healthcare access, and reproductive freedoms. In these cases and others like them, right-wing litigators and judges have erroneously framed certain abortion procedures, conversion therapy, and trans youth's access to puberty blockers as either unsafe or dangerously untested and, therefore, open to whatever actions conservative lawmakers wish to take.[89] Since 2020, Republican-controlled states have worked aggressively to criminalize transition-related healthcare for minors by labeling gender-affirmative care as "child abuse."[90] In defending these draconian laws, attorneys for states like West Virginia have leveraged federal evidentiary standards to exclude gender clinicians' testimonies on the basis that they improperly characterize transgender identity as inalterable.[91]

Today, fearmongering about "trans trenders" and trigger-happy gender clinicians is everywhere. As dozens of states have begun to limit and even criminalize transition-related healthcare for minors with bills like the "Save Adolescents from Experimentation Act," shock jocks like HBO's nominally liberal Bill Maher have loudly denounced trans healthcare as "experimenting on children."[92] A 2022 report issued by the conservative think tank Center for the Study of Partisanship and Ideology claimed that social media and the "Great Awokening" have led depressed and anxious teenagers to medicate their mental illnesses with hormone therapies and social gender transitions.[93] The *New York Times* has carried water for these critics, reciting the social media contagion hypothesis to explain the sudden rise in trans identification.[94] Most striking of all, a handful of dissenters within well-renowned transgender medical associations like the World Professional Association for Transgender Health (WPATH) have vocalized fears that "part of the rise in trans identification among teenagers could be a result of what they called 'social influence,' absorbed online or peer to peer."[95] Marci Bowers (slated to be the next WPATH president) and former WPATH board member Erica Anderson went so far as to endorse far-right journalist Abigail Shrier's book *Irreversible Damage: The Transgender Craze Seducing Our Daughters*, while blasting healthcare providers for allegedly overprescribing hormone blockers to minors.[96]

Foundational to this criticism is a concern for the distinction between who is trans and who is merely a "trender." These conjurers of doubt exploit the fact that LGBTQ+ advocates have long assured a degree of what seems now to be an unattainable certainty about the messy contingency and malleability of sex and gender—a promise that one really could discern who is *really* gay or which child is *truly* trans. For this reason, detransition narratives of regret take the spotlight in conversations, which—while important on their own terms—are cynically used to rationalize rollbacks of healthcare access and civil rights. This conservative reaction to trans visibility has taken the form of a new social contagion theory, one that echoes the early religious right's claim that gays and lesbians target children because they need to "recruit" to reproduce.

Shrouded by the veil of concerns for women, children, and Christian traditionalists are a cohort of right-wing dark-money funders who eagerly egg
on a culture war for their own benefit. This corporate anti-statist movement
led by those like Charles Koch, the DeVos family, and the Bradley Foundation has been waging a protracted war on regulation and social welfare in part
through proxy campaigns against everything from the rights of transgender
youth to critical race theory.[97] These are the same corporate leaders that have
funded Federalist Society campaigns for judicial appointments and have mobilized elected officials to attack the scientific expertise that inform policies
like the Environmental Protection Agency's climate regulations and local,
state, and federal COVID-19 public health measures.[98] Dark-money conservatives have also funneled millions into litigation groups like the Becket
Fund for Religious Liberty, the Alliance Defending Freedom, and the Heritage Foundation, which have inverted religious free exercise doctrine to allow
wealthy Christian-owned nonprofits like Hobby Lobby to deny reproductive
healthcare to their employees and to grant Catholic child welfare and adoption agencies the right to deny taxpayer-funded services to queer couples.[99]
Such groups have worked to move "fetal pain" research in from the fringe,
thereby providing a (dubious) medical reason to grant citizenship protections
to gestating fetuses—a move that would go far beyond simply overturning
Roe v. Wade (1973).[100] Altogether, these long-sighted titans of industry make
up a neoliberal authoritarian political front, one defined by its weaponization
of what Colin Crouch has termed "politicized pessimistic nostalgia" to scapegoat minority populations in its pursuit of a governing regime that guarantees
an upward redistribution of wealth and life chances.[101]

The most lamentable development in this whole affair has not just been
the inefficacy of LGBTQ+ advocates and other civil rights nonprofits in combating this tendency, but rather their complicity in it.[102] In 2020 a coalition of
liberal interest groups headed up by the Human Rights Campaign (HRC), the
American Civil Liberties Union (ACLU), and the National Association for
the Advancement of Colored People (NAACP) sided with Koch group Americans for Prosperity (AFP) in its challenge to a California donor transparency
law.[103] It is understandable that these groups fought to protect the NAACP's
hard-won judicial precedents that once shielded its supporters from vigilan-
tes and state officials alike who got their hands on a civil rights groups' donor
rolls. Today, however, the decision to back the AFP has far more to do with
these liberal organizations' own self-interest in loosened restrictions on big
donor-backed advocacy outfits. The Supreme Court's June 2021 ruling in favor of this peculiar bipartisan alliance says much about the strange bedfellows
that the neoliberal state has made.

Undoubtedly, right-wing dark-money operations advance the interests of a far more sinister group than do these liberal nonprofits.[104] Intentions aside, liberal social movements would do well to take the long view of what such bipartisan sanctioning of this kind of anti-democratic effort is fueling. As government loses its very legitimacy to regulate the economy and to enforce civil rights protections, so, too, do queer advocates lose the policies, statutes, judicial doctrines, and venues in which scientific authority has spoken with such a powerfully persuasive voice.

Race, Science, and Reification

Though I have alluded to matters of race throughout these introductory remarks, such matters merit a few additional observations. First, critics of born this way frequently invoke the term "homonormative" to denote how the ideology has overwhelmingly served the interests of a white, middle-class, and gender-normative crowd. While the neologism has some historically delimited descriptive value, it mistakenly attributes an eternal racialized essence to what is a very particular and contingent rationalization.

The homonormative distinction falsely casts the racial character of the late twentieth-century gay gene discourse as endemic, rather than a reflection of the class composition of the advocacy movement's wealthiest, most politically powerful leaders and donors of that moment.[105] It is somewhat unsurprising that the homonormative critique has enjoyed such a long shelf life. As a result of the LGBTQ+ movement's upper-class stratum that has historically been disproportionately white and gender-normative, the born this way narrative has tended to be put into service of their interests—it reflects back their own image and posits it as total. It thus reifies the status quo as natural.

In the past several years, however, the liberal movement has begun to forefront race in its advocacy and image. Mainstream LGBTQ+ organizations now highlight trans women of color in their policy positions and rhetoric, all while preserving their foundational commitments to bioessentialism.[106] Those purporting to be once-marginalized queer people's representatives have been brought into E. E. Schattschneider's infamous "heavenly chorus" of the liberal advocacy realm's "pluralist heaven," a choir that continues to sing "with a strong upper-class accent."[107]

Thus, the "homonormative" nature of the queer rights movement's white racial hue is a legacy of its bourgeois character and its tight relationship to a business and political elite. What is notable is that the movement has not done nearly as much to reform its class nature even in light of its clear recognition that it has historically elided its working-class and poor members; this is because that element is more deeply constitutive of the enterprise itself. Bio-essentialist ideology can be deployed to describe whatever phenotypical blend of persons that the movement wants to make as its face, but given entrenched neighborhood patterns of segregation, the decimation of the labor movement and federal employment programs that had previously chipped away at racial disparities in employment and earnings, and other extant racially textured social conditions, these advocacy groups will persist in underrepresenting the interests of a racialized working-class and poor population.[108]

That said, there does exist a connection between the ongoing rebirth of race science in the domains of population genetics and biomedicine and the LGBTQ+ movement's own investment in biomedical technologies and logics.[109] The ancestry DNA home-testing firm 23andMe, for instance, has since 2012 collected data on the "genetics of sexual orientation," thereby exemplifying how tightly coiled neo-race science and born this way have become.[110] More broadly, there is a disturbing tendency as of late to entertain biological theories of human difference. As the concluding chapter spells out in a detailed assessment of the contemporary bioessentialist paradigm, liberal advocates of equal rights and supposedly enlightened academics have as of late succumbed to neo-race-scientific premises.[111] The tendency to taxonomize is rampant *and* bipartisan.

This liberal identitarian capitulation to race-scientific logic has diminished the ability of some civil rights groups to adequately critique even the vilest research. Condemning Stanford University psychologist Michal Kosinski's infamous "gaydar" should not have taken much effort. In 2018 Kosinski and coauthor Yilun Wang announced that their facial recognition software could distinguish between straight subjects and self-identified gays and lesbians. Relying on the premise from prenatal endocrinology that takes gays and lesbians to exhibit "gender-atypical facial morphology, expression, and grooming styles," Kosinski and Wang's algorithm accurately categorized male subjects 81 percent of the time and female ones 74 percent (notably, the work has since been debunked).[112] Not only has this work rehabilitated Cesare Lombroso's criminal physiognomy for the twenty-first century, but Kosinski has shown a profound lack of responsibility in handling authoritarian leaders who have been enticed by his results. As reported by *The Guardian*, Kosinski took meetings with top members of Russian President Vladimir Putin's government including then prime minister Dmitry Medvedev.[113]

One might expect LGBTQ+ advocates to have taken issue with these foreboding political implications. At the very least, Kosinski and Wang's gender-normative hypotheses might have set off some alarms. Instead, the Human Rights Campaign and Gay and Lesbian Alliance Against Defamation

(GLAAD) settled on a diversity-centric reproach. In their joint press release, a bullet-point list of the study's flaws began with the contention: "The study did not look at any non-white individuals."[114] The study drew solely from "a small subset of out white gay and lesbian people on dating sites" and, therefore, did not encompass the broad array of "people of color, transgender people, older individuals, and other LGBTQ people who don't want to post photos on dating sites."[115] The historical illiteracy in a claim that physiognomy is repugnant when it neglects nonnormative genders and racial minorities is breathtaking. Given the record of Gilded Age eugenics and the adaptability of the born this way thesis, future research may prove fully capable of incorporating these so-called unaccounted for traits and identities. Mix Kosinski's techno hubris with a repressive regime's incentive to smoke out social undesirables with little regard for the science's actual veracity, and you get a door swung wide open to persecution.

Just what that persecution could look like and who its victims might be is to be determined. The neoliberal political order's present legitimation crisis is ripe for the kind of sex panics that previous crises have produced.[116] If there is any truth to Stephen Jay Gould's dictum that "resurgences of biological determinism correlate with periods of political retrenchment and destruction of social generosity," we would do well to guard against the scapegoating that so often attends such unequal times.[117] The GOP's war on trans youth is just one symptom of this resurgent pathologizing. As Arlene Stein's classic account of an economic downturn in 1990s Oregon documented, queer people have before been cast as wealthy cosmopolitans seeking "special rights," making them ripe for reproach as the presumably cis-het working class and poor suffered.[118] Both the January 6th insurrectionist Senator Josh Hawley and the hordes of QAnon-rapt disciples, for instance, make little distinction between shadowy globalist cabals of sex pests and minorities seeking their civil rights.[119] In its 2022 platform, the Texas Republican Party followed suit in denouncing homosexuality as "an abnormal lifestyle," gender-affirming surgery as "medical malpractice," and conversion therapy as a legitimate medical intervention for clients of any age.[120] Eliding the difference between pathological and benign is itself a long tradition in the history of American sex panics as is the propensity to police sexual and gender morality as a solution to broader social ills.[121]

Some skepticism is warranted on this front. Public opinion data indicate a clear secular trend in LGBTQ+ support both among masses and political elites, but that is not guaranteed to remain a constant, especially in our increasingly crisis-prone political economy.[122] Again, it is necessary to conceive of bio-tinged ideologies as rationalizing devices and not as distractions or the products of sheer conspiratorial machinations. The latter two notions are hall-marks of a far more paranoid left-wing critique of the gay gene that hears in every bioessentialist utterance a eugenic wish.[123] Scientific authority and epis-temologies can inform the creation of a liberal pluralist group defined by a shared essence as much as they can be wielded to single out, oppress, or exter-minate a group on similar grounds. The devil is in the details of that dialectic.

If queer people are not blamed for presently entrenched and expanding inequalities, however, someone else will likely be. Sky-high levels of inequal-ity encourage those across the ideological spectrum—from the most tepidly liberal to the most virulently neo-fascist—to go in search of natural causes.[124] In line with Gould's musings on the matter, there is a suspicious correlation between early industrial capitalism's widespread inequality and that era's eu-genics programs; others, too, have detected a link between the advent of neo-liberalism and the popularity of sociobiology and evolutionary psychology's most reductively rationalizing stories.[125] These expeditions time and again lead to explanations that reify measures of intelligence, income, and race into natural human kinds—that is, biologically heritable traits presenting limits that a society must build around rather than against.

The fact that such excuses for our age of inequality could very well then let queer people largely off the hook (at least, that is, for their desires and gen-dered expressions proper) prompts a final reflection on terminology. It is for this reason that Richard Lewontin admonished those who affix the misnomer "race science" to each and every one of those ideological reifications.[126] His terse statement is worth reproducing below:

> In America, race, ethnicity, and class are so confounded, and the reality of so-cial class so firmly denied, that it is easy to lose sight of the general setting of class conflict out of which biological determinism arose. Biological determin-ism, both in its literary and scientific forms, is part of the legitimating ideology of our society, the solution offered to our deepest social mystery, the analgesic for our most recurrent social pain.[127]

The future is uncertain, so much so that we should not pretend to know the specific content and referents of an ascriptive ideology prior to its birth. As with desire, contingency abounds.

Outline of Book

The bulk of *Born This Way* is organized into two parts. Part I, titled "Origins," explores how early gay rights activists allied with medical reformers to com-bat the pathological thesis and how, in doing so, they laid the groundwork for the born this way ideology to come. It begins with a chapter on the homophile and lesbian organizations of the 1950s and 1960s, which made inroads with Kinsey Institute researchers and others sympathetic to their plight. These initial relationships proved immensely influential in civil rights efforts across an array of state and federal bureaucratic agencies, courts, and legislatures. In criminal, employment, administrative, and immigration cases, these scientists and medical practitioners combated the government's expert witnesses and citations to studies buttressing the view that homosexuals presented predatory and contagious threats. While these scientific and legal arguments involved relatively modest claims about what homosexuality *was* intrinsically (they focused much more on what homosexuality was *not*—i.e., a social contagion or psychotic state), they created important institutional ties that would generate bioessentialist ones in a subsequent moment.

In turning from these tussles across state institutions, chapter 2 examines intra-movement developments in gay liberation politics as well as intradisciplinary ones in the fields of psychiatry and psychology. The Stonewall Riots of 1969 witnessed the birth of many new variants of queer social movement politics. A slew of gay liberation, lesbian separatist, Black lesbian feminist, and transsexual organizations formed and joined the ranks of the New Left social movements. Unlike even the most militant homophiles of the 1960s, these radicals sought to undermine the distinction between heterosexuality and homosexuality entirely. They, too, outright rejected collaborating with medical professionals who they believed would only buttress a liberal pluralist mode of assimilation that would thwart their aims of transforming society into a utopia of "polymorphous perversity."

Just as these tensions were brewing in the activist realm, there were also deep disagreements in the mental healthcare profession and the academic study of human behavior and the mind. These ultimately played out in fights at the American Psychiatric Association and similar professional associations, which led to a proxy war between gay rights activists and liberal reformers on one side and a conservative psychoanalytic old guard on the other. The final sections of the chapter recount how these two camps clashed repeatedly and how the *DSM* was ultimately cleansed of the pathological thesis. The future leaders of the incipient modern liberal gay and lesbian rights movement would emerge from the APA fights with even richer ties to scientific and medical experts than ever before.

Chapter 3 then examines the formation of modern equal rights interest groups and details the structural and ideological developments in gay and lesbian politics that made them so amenable to the biological narrative. It also looks to how scientific discoveries, novel medical technologies, expanded capital investments in biotechnologies, and an increase in federal funding for such work incentivized researchers to explore the conjectured biological nature of sexual orientation. This coincidence of the broader biological turn in the sciences, and the advent of the modern gay and lesbian interest-group model came to jointly produce a bioessentialist ideology, one that would develop and mature in laboratories, courtrooms, and the campaign trail throughout the late 1980s and early 1990s.

Chapter 4 focuses on how early forms of the biological thesis were brought into state and federal courts and how a civil rights strategy and doctrinal incentives reinforced—but importantly did not by themselves engender—a commitment to scientific expertise and biological narratives in equal rights and citizenship claims. In cases involving discrimination against parents and teachers and challenges to sodomy bans, groups like Lambda Legal and their allies in the ACLU became increasingly wedded to arguments that gay and lesbian identities were the products of biological phenomena. The chapter serves as a corrective to assumptions that the reach for such studies and expert testimonies was motivated entirely by a quest to demonstrate sexual orientation's immutability per equal protection clause case law.

The three chapters that comprise part II, "Evolutions and Adaptations," track how the born this way ideology and its opposition have evolved through policy domains and doctrinal disputes. Many of these transformations have been clearly salutary—they have led to protections for same-sex couples who wish to marry, transgender persons who fear harassment when using the restroom, and queer youths who face the trauma of a conversion therapist's office. Other aspects of these developments are a cause for concern, particularly as escalating right-wing threats have proven to be quite adaptive themselves.

Chapter 5 covers the late 1980s and early 1990s as the bioessentialist narrative matured with the announcement of that era's infamous gay gene and gay brain studies. The chapter delineates how the movement popularized and politicized genomic, neurological, and hormonal studies and made minor celebrities out of their authors. As support for the gay gene thesis and the liberal pluralist politics it served gained traction, contenders from across the ideological spectrum emerged. On the right, those like the Heritage Foundation and the Family Research Council amplified the voices of "ex-gays" and their therapists, all of whom mobilized the rhetoric of "choice" and "lifestyle" in the face of the ascendant "by nature" narrative. On the left, groups like ACT UP and Queer Nation as well as university-based social theorists insisted that bioessentialism reflected neither their own self-conceptions of desire nor their political aims. The chapter closes on the surprising longevity of the gay gene thesis, which has outlasted the hype of genomania.

Chapter 6 recounts a not-so-distant past when marriage bans and conversion therapies were well-regarded in the realms of psychiatry and psychoanalysis; in fact, they were deemed essential to preserving everything from the well-being of children to the maintenance of the nuclear family itself. The chapter documents the interwoven developments of these decades-long transformations in mental health care and the political coalitions on the right and the left that brought these intra-scientific disputes into fights for marriage equality and conversion therapy bans. It concludes with an assessment of what has been won throughout the same-sex marriage and conversion therapy fights and how conservatives have begun to roll back these nascent wins with disingenuous appeals to pluralism.

Chapter 7 tells the story of how bioessentialist ideology adapted to integrate bi and trans identities into the gay and lesbian movement. The chapter begins with a brief history of bisexuality and transsexuality extending back to the nineteenth century. It moves then to an examination of trans legal claims in employment discrimination, prisoners' rights cases, bathroom bill fights, and trans youth and sports participation cases. Throughout, it tracks how transgender legal and political claims to identity were depicted as a bioessentialist variant of "sex" in the law, social movement rhetoric, and culture. The latter part of the chapter takes up lesser-known developments in the biopolitics of bisexual identity, focusing especially on how contentious scientific authority has been in bisexual activist circles as well as how bisexual health disparities became a central concern of the LGBTQ+ movement. Paralleling the conclusion of the previous chapter, chapter 7 closes with conservatives' dual attack on trans rights, one that emphasizes medical "uncertainties" about trans healthcare regimens and the supposed pluralist imperative of balancing Christian traditionalist concerns with trans rights ones.

Finally, the book concludes with a long chapter on the state of bioessentialism today. The conclusion commences from the seeming paradox of the sudden surge of sexual fluidity and gender flexibility, on the one hand, and the resilience of biological accounts of sex, gender, race, and class, on the other. To make sense of this enigma, I collect and examine narratives of essence as they have popped up in genome-wide association studies (GWAS), neo-race science studies, and fringe theories of transgender social contagions and mental illness. What I uncover is the branching off into new "species" of non-binaristic gendered expressions and sexual predilections, each of which can ultimately be traced back to the trunk of some essentialist ideology (be it biological, biocultural, or simply cultural). Inspired as I am by the cultural anthropologist Roger Lancaster's own desire for a materialist-minded queer theory—and his caution that such an approach precludes an ending "with all the loose ends tied up: a pat statement about the human condition, a mystery solved, the theoretical equivalent of a happy ending"—this final chapter is as speculative as it is summative.[128]

However tenacious the essentializing tendency on both the right and the left remains, the book does not close on predestination. As such, I conjecture that the promise of social democracy presents a political alternative to the present legitimation crisis, one that would at once curb conservative witch-hunts and the liberal anxieties that generate these various tales of human difference. It might get us a bit closer to resolving the tension between what it is that we might be able to know with regards to scientific inquiry versus what it is that we often hubristically think that we can know—or perhaps what is deemed existential to know. Contrary to more typical state-phobic ruminations on biopolitics, one might actually be able to *use* the state in many ways to undermine these and other biopolitical by-products of our highly unequal and unstable political order. Or so, that is my hope for a world that goes beyond born this way.

PART I

Origins

The Science of Civil Rights:
The Rise and Demise of Sexual Deviancy

One of the earliest recorded debates over science's role in gay rights advocacy was duked out in 1965 across the pages of the lesbian activist journal *The Ladder*. In three back-to-back issues, the research director of the country's first lesbian political organization, Florence Conrad, an alias for the economist Florence Jaffy, squared off with the DC-based activist Frank Kameny, who was fast becoming a gay civil rights icon. Their dispute took place during a bleak era when gays and lesbians were still routinely denounced as mentally ill, public nuisances, and predators.

Representing a more cautiously conservative position, Conrad argued that advocacy groups should accept assistance from mental health professionals— even those who would diagnose them as mentally ill—as long as those experts supported decriminalization efforts. She implored her fellow activists to heed the fact that "ours is a science-oriented society, and scientists are God to most people."[1] Where Conrad expressed deference, Kameny embodied defiance. In his riposte titled "Emphasis on Research Has Had Its Day," he argued that gay men and women ought to define their own sense of self, and that the so-called experts who labeled them "ill-adjusted" or just outright ill ought to be eschewed entirely.

Kameny's position soon won the day as local and regional gay rights organizations issued statement after statement condemning not only the notion that a cure was possible or desirable, but also the idea that medicine ought to have—or even *could* have—the last word on the meaning of gay and lesbian identities. By the mid-1960s, the sexual revolution had emboldened equal rights advocates to cast off scientific authority and to define themselves, unaided and unencumbered by a medical community that still saw queer people as ill, if not pitiable.

Though the terms of the Conrad-Kameny debates obscure this point, Kameny was actually one of the most influential boosters of reformist trends in science and mental health. Moreover, Kameny was simply keeping with tradition. From their very outset in the 1950s, gay and lesbian rights advocacy groups began seeking out allies to contest the most pernicious effects of the reigning consensus that portrayed them as dangerously unwell. Throughout the 1960s, Kameny and his like-minded acolytes deepened their relationships with new thinkers and leaders in sexology, psychology, and psychiatry who aimed to vanquish the practices and paradigms upon which the pathological model rested. Time and again, Kameny and company brought these authoritative voices into courts, bureaucracies, and to the American people at large to make the case for tolerance.

What follows is an account of how an alliance of organized gays and lesbians came to work in tandem with reformist scientists and clinicians to coproduce a new logic of homosexuality as natural and benign, a conception of identity that was at once scientific and political. While this is somewhat well-trodden ground, I retell these moments in social movement, legal, and medical history with an eye toward what these decades portended for "born this way" politics. In doing so, this opening chapter lays the foundation for how gay rights advocates came to fashion a liberal pluralist orientation—one that depicted gays and lesbians as just one minority cultural group among many in American society—and fought for their civil rights by translating a new science of sexuality into law, policy, and public opinion. But before turning to these early triumphs, one must first inquire: From where did these sexologists, gay rights reformers, and vice patrols emerge in the first place?

We "Other Progressives"

Probing the nature of sexuality and gender is not a practice exclusive to the present era. Medical fascination and public health intrigue concerning supposed deviations from the norm trace at least as far back as the nineteenth century. In Germany and the United States especially, researchers, social reformers, and government officials alike became entranced with novel medical instruments, scientific theories of human populations, and their implications for governance.[2] This *scientia sexualis*—the term that Michel Foucault famously used to denote the modern clinical study of sexuality—became a matter of cultural, medical, and political obsession.[3]

By the advent of the Progressive Era, a clinical model of sexual and gender difference had displaced an archaic moral discourse as the dominant mode of categorizing—and often criminalizing—such transgressions.[4] The first sexologists were a heterogeneous bunch; they conducted their taxonomic work from a variety of evolutionary, epidemiological, and psychogenic perspectives. The German jurist and sexologist Karl Ulrichs, for instance, took what he called "sexual inversion" to be a mostly congenital condition. Others like psychiatrist Richard von Krafft-Ebing, whose approach attracted many admirers in the United States, blended biological and environmental factors in pure Lamarckian fashion.[5] Placing blame on modernity's stresses and their adverse impact on the species, Krafft-Ebing described what he called "*psychopathia sexualis*" as having socially acquired a degenerative neuropathological disorder.[6] Still others like Sigmund Freud's American disciples saw homosexuality as psychogenic maladaptation to childhood trauma or other psychic injury.[7]

During the early twentieth century's highwater mark for American eugenics, elected officials and bureaucrats clutched sexology reports in hand while frantically denouncing homosexuality's threat to race, nation, and the capitalist political order.[8] That the sodomite was no simple criminal but rather a distinct biological abnormality—and a hazardous one at that—became orthodoxy.[9] Presidents including Teddy Roosevelt and Woodrow Wilson along with eugenics' popularizers like Charles Davenport and Madison Grant fretted about lower-class and racialized sex predators, miscegenation, lesbianism and the degraded state of the heterosexual marriage, and the perils of Anglo-Saxon "race suicide." In pursuit of interventions, state and local governments often teamed up with private foundation funders to study the causes and solutions to these problems of public health and "social hygiene."[10] Notably, this obsession with nonconformity did not always lead down a eugenic route; for a brief moment in the interwar period, American and German metropolitans frequented nightclub "pansy" shows and treated homosexuality with an attitude of equanimity and mirth.[11]

World War II and its aftermath proved to be a catalyst for queer cultures as soldiers who had engaged in covert same-sex relations and relationships abroad returned home en masse.[12] The incidence of sexual activity among American troops was so great that the military and federal bureaucracy developed an array of new surveillance practices and institutions to track, categorize, treat, and discipline the deviants within their ranks.[13] Though military psychiatrists occasionally urged accommodation for these servicemen, back stateside the burgeoning pockets of gay urban dwellers were met by a wave of repression spurred by the advent of the Cold War. A national witch-hunt led by Republican Senator Joseph McCarthy cast the New Deal regime as a haven for communist sympathizers and sexual degenerates.[14] Throughout the hysteria of what became known as the Lavender Scare and similar localized sex panics in cities and states, homosexuality was equated with psychopathology, street crime, and communism. All of this threatened to stomp out gay life just as it had begun to bloom.

The Birth of the Homophile Movement:
Identity, Culture, and the Clinic

The homophile movement, which lasted roughly from 1951 to the late 1960s, was the first instantiation of modern gay rights advocacy in the United States. While there were more short-lived civil-rights-styled organizations before it—the Chicago-based Society for Human Rights was formed in 1924 only to crumble after several months under the weight of obscenity charges—the Mattachine Society represented the first long-lasting, politically mobilized, and eventually national constituency of gay and lesbian Americans. Founded in 1950 as a secretive sect of gay men in Los Angeles, the Mattachine originally tasked itself with studying and advocating for gay men in a period of Cold War right-wing revanchism.[15]

Harry Hay and a small group of fellow defectors from the Communist Party of the United States (CPUSA) formed the Mattachine Society in part because they had no place else to go. Though the Bolsheviks had decriminalized sodomy shortly after taking power, Stalin had recriminalized sex between persons of the same gender in 1934, rebuking such behavior as a symptom of "bourgeois decadence."[16] American communists adopted a strict prohibition against homosexuality among party members not only in fealty to the Soviets but also as a defense against McCarthyism.[17] Conscious of the risks they bore, Hay and his comrades met covertly in clandestine cell structures as they quietly devised their appeal for civil rights.

The Mattachine leadership spent their early years theorizing the nature of the homosexual as an oppressed cultural minority similar to their "fellow minorities [like] the Negro, Mexican, and Jewish people."[18] Though the early Mattachine entertained diagnoses of homosexuality as a contagion or the symptom of a "deviant" or "disturbed" state of mind, they ultimately settled on a sociological approach. Drawing from a mix of Marxist theories of class consciousness, an ironic twist on Stalin's own writings on the national minority question, and their personal experiences as advocates for racial civil rights, they determined that gay men and lesbians constituted a class "in itself" (as an objective and identifiable social group) that had the potential to become a class "for itself" as a coalesced constituency.[19] They, too, were inspired by the writings of those like Friedrich Engels and historical anthropological accounts on gender and sex, and accordingly understood the modern heterosexual monogamous family unit as contingent rather than a universal or primordial form; ergo, gay men and women were not diseased or congenitally abnormal, but instead they were simply innocuous deviations from a regnant social norm.[20] Indeed, Hay's adoption of the term "homophile" was an attempt to distance the Mattachine from the medicalized term "homosexual."

Sex researcher Alfred Kinsey's wildly popular studies on human sexuality also shaped the early homophile sense of self. Published in 1948 and 1953, respectively, Kinsey's volumes on male and female sexuality exposed the façade of America's prudishly Victorian public face.[21] The zoologist-turned-sexologist revealed that criminalized and socially proscribed behavior like adultery, sodomy, fellatio, and cunnilingus were, in fact, commonplace. In some of the studies' most scandalous results, Kinsey's team reported that over a third of American men had engaged in sex with other men and that nearly 10 percent of American men and women engaged in homosexual behavior exclusively. In recounting Kinsey's influence, Hay remarked that the 1948 volume on male sexuality was frequently tucked under his arm alongside informational pamphlets on the Mattachine Society. (Hay presumably valued Kinsey more for his anti-pathological stance than his spectrum account of sexuality, the latter of which seemed to cut against the minority model.)[22]

Although Kinsey's work was a boon for the early homophiles, the sexologist's influence and infamy were in some sense a double-edged sword. Kinsey offered the victims of sex panics some respite as he testified against Lavender Scare era criminal codes.[23] He stressed that homosexuality was a natural variant of human sexuality, which he portrayed as nodes on a spectrum rather than a strict binary between the acceptable and the abnormal. However, Kinsey's startling findings led to heightened public concerns over the pervasiveness of homosexuality. His results made it easier than ever to imagine furtive queers lurking in every corner of a society once presumed to be safely straight.[24]

Neither deviant nor as minuscule in number as they had once believed, homophiles took comfort in knowing that there were likely thousands of other queer Angelenos to be mobilized for the cause. The Mattachine first crawled out of the shadows and into the city's sunlight when member Dale Jennings became a victim of police entrapment in the summer of 1952.[25] On the eve of his trial, the Mattachine distributed flyers and drafted press releases to the media demanding Jennings's release. Though their pleas to the media and city officials went unheeded, their willingness to advocate publicly as homophiles earned them financial contributions and legal advisement from silent supporters.

During his trial, Jennings made the dangerous declaration that he was indeed a homosexual. Rather than deny his desire or grovel for a plea deal,

Jennings affirmed the Mattachine's message that homosexuality was a benign and natural form of sexual desire and activity. This risky decision to concede his status and to denounce oppressive and police tactics as cruel and nonsensical provided a necessary spark to the Mattachine's political program (it certainly behooved their cause that Jennings walked away from a hung jury as a free man). As the pretrial propaganda and transcripts of Jennings's trial testimony spread throughout Southern California, the organization began to expand rapidly, growing to nearly one hundred discussion groups and over two thousand members by 1953.[26] A decade and a half before the Stonewall generation would boisterously chant "out of the closets and into the streets," the homophiles began to do just that.

Sexology, Mental Health, and the Politics of Tolerance

As the Mattachine Society grew, tensions fomented between a new caucus of reformers called the "Fifth Order" and the Hay-led leadership. Upon seizing control of the Mattachine at a pair of conventions in 1953, the reformers established a more transparent and democratic organization.[27] They also adopted a softer public image, one less triumphantly gay than the Jennings orientation and devoid of its Marxian vestiges, both of which were deemed liabilities during the height of Senator McCarthy's communist witch-hunts.[28] In the words of Fifth Order member Marilyn Rieger, equal citizenship might be best realized "by integrating . . . not as homosexuals, but as people, as men and women whose homosexuality is irrelevant to our ideals, our principles, our hopes and aspirations."[29]

This change in political orientation was accompanied by parallel shift in scientific thought. Some newer Mattachine members were sympathetic to the pathological model and the belief that—even if homosexual activity did not merit a jail sentence—they required psychiatric instruction. The most socially conservative-minded among the homophiles drew from a neo-Freudian paradigm that predominated in postwar American psychology.[30] Having gained prominence and institutional footholds in both military and public health bureaucracies throughout WWII, psychiatry and psychoanalysis possessed the resources and cultural clout to frame the "homosexual menace" as a contagion to be cured.[31] These clinicians and theorists castigated Kinsey's results and his normative takeaways, positing instead that the prevalence of loveless heterosexual intercourse and homosexuality alike were social maladaptations produced by the stresses of modernity.[32] In the first edition of the *Diagnostic and Statistical Manual of Mental Disorders* published in 1952, the American

Psychiatric Association entrenched this perspective in clinical care by listing homosexuality as "sociopathic personality disturbance."[33]

In the wake of the conservative reformers' victory, the Mattachine frequently invited proponents of the pathological model to speak to its membership and to publish in its journal, the *Mattachine Review*. Among the most widely read of these researchers was the sociologist Donald Webster Cory—a pseudonym for the closeted Edward Sagarin—who owned a covert gay mail-order book company and penned his own popular account of homosexuality.[34] Cory's 1951 *The Homosexual in America* combined a history and partial defense of those with same-sex desires with a foreword by psychologist Albert Ellis, who maintained that "exclusive" homosexuality was a sign of a neurosis.[35] Though the two disagreed over the extent to which therapy might "adjust" homosexuals to a heterosexual lifestyle—Cory wrote that the drive itself was "virtually as ineradicable as if it involved the color of one's skin or the shape of one's eyes," and Ellis retorted that the multiplicity of homosexuality's causes contradicted this belief in "the natural inherency and compulsivity of homosexual drives"—they shared in the view that homosexuals had been long unduly persecuted.[36]

The message that homosexuals were merely "sick citizens" struck a chord with a membership dominated by middle-class white men, many of whom had much to lose if they were found out. At the height of this attitude's resonance, Chair Ken Burns gave a 1956 convention speech insisting that preventing the spread of homosexuality was a key goal of the Mattachine.[37] Several years later in a letter to Kinsey's collaborator Wardell Pomeroy, member Curtis Dewees wrote, "I regret that there is no group working for the homosexual in this country similar to the National Council of Alcoholism or the National Family Council on Drug Addiction."[38] Just like the tendency to overindulge was once deemed sinful, homosexuality also moved from the realm of the moral to the medical. Although it is easy today to chide those like Burns and Dewees for apparent self-loathing, many in the Mattachine trusted the clinic to furnish both political and therapeutic solutions to their suffering.

The pathological model was, however, not without its opponents. The homophile-run ONE Inc.—a nonprofit that splintered from the Mattachine following the 1953 change in leadership—frequently condemned backers of pathology in the pages of its eponymous journal. *ONE*'s editors regularly ran articles such as "I Am Glad I Am Homosexual" and takedowns of clinicians who would rather treat than endorse homosexuality.[39] Internal fights raged within the Mattachine over the mental illness model, as evinced by a 1954 proposal that would have established strict guidelines for any clinician seeking referrals from the organization.[40] Finally, by 1958 the *Mattachine Review* took a firm stance against the efficacy and ethics of reparative therapy.[41] By the end of the decade, a final break with pathology was imminent.

As the largely male membership of the Mattachine continued to deliberate the gay male condition, newly formed lesbian advocacy groups like the Daughters of Bilitis (DOB) wrestled with similar questions about pathology and etiology. Founded in San Francisco in 1955 by a small group of middle-class white women, the DOB worked to "promo[te] the integration of the homosexual into society" through public education and penal reform.[42] Optimistic in scientific authority's role to generate understanding and compassion, the DOB funneled its members into sexological studies and devoted much of its in-house journal, *The Ladder*, to discussing the latest in sex research and clinical care. At one point, the DOB even distributed a survey among its membership that would have created a ready-made database for future research.[43]

In its early years, the DOB often endorsed conservative theories on the nature of homosexuality, some of which were closely tied to the pathological model. *The Ladder* routinely printed the opinions of psychoanalysts and sexologists who depicted lesbianism as an impediment to "full happiness" and even a suspicious correlate of violent crime.[44] Readers of *The Ladder* often wrote into the journal to express their own—at times, shockingly disparaging—perspectives on lesbian sexuality.

Before long, reformist voices began to gain influence in *The Ladder*. Three years after its founding, the journal published an interview with psychotherapist Alice LaVere, who advised against treating lesbianism as a mental disturbance, and in 1959 DOB research director Florence Conrad criticized psychoanalytic accounts that frequently portrayed lesbians as innately irresponsible and immature.[45] Eventually, the Daughters of Bilitis came to argue against—in the words of national officer Sten Russell—that "ancient heterosexual viewpoint that homosexuality is simply a matter of *choice*, as easily changed as an old shirt."[46] An official statement in 1959 declared that it is "generally established by the experts in the field that the *cause* of homosexuality is still an unknown quantity [and] that it is a process of development and *not a matter of choice*."[47] By the end of the 1950s, the DOB leadership had joined the Mattachine in the view that homosexuality was of a natural, benign, and relatively fixed quality.

"Gay Is Good": Liberal Pluralism and Gay Rights

The 1960s ushered in a new kind of gay politics, one that styled itself in the mold of other midcentury liberal pluralist movements for minority legal rights and social assimilation. Inspired by the demands and rhetoric of the civil rights movement and riding the wave of the sexual revolution, a more militant breed of homophile overtook an ossified and enervated old guard in the Mattachine. No longer willing to consider themselves inferior or ill, the militant homophiles embraced their sexualities, emphatically affirming gay identity with a trademark slogan: "gay is good."[48]

One of the central figures in the Mattachine's metamorphosis was Frank Kameny. A Harvard-trained astronomer working for the US Army Map Service, Kameny was terminated in 1957 when an investigation revealed that he had been arrested for lewd conduct the previous year.[49] While at first Kameny fought his legal battles against the Civil Service Commission (CSC) alone, he was soon introduced to members of the New York City Mattachine Society (MSNY) who provided him with the names of those in Washington, DC, interested in forming a homophile organization of their own. Having already attained some prominence in the DC gay bar scene as an entertainment organizer, Kameny and a handful of disciples founded the Mattachine Society of Washington (MSW) in the summer of 1961.[50] Driven by a strategy of aggressive legal campaigns and direct actions, Kameny's MSW took a sharp turn from the pleading respectability politics that had characterized the post-Hay Mattachine. Throughout its first few years, the chapter engaged in protests and additional lawsuits against the CSC, the DC police, and even the US Congress, the last of which had rescinded MSW's permit to fundraise as a nonprofit.[51]

The liberal militants also challenged the hunkered-down, defensive crouch of those homophiles still committed to the pathological model. Shortly after its founding, the MSW became the first chapter to declare that homosexuality was not a sickness but instead a "preference, orientation, or propensity, on par with, and not different in kind from, heterosexuality."[52] In July 1964, Kameny gave a speech to the national Mattachine membership in which he invoked Martin Luther King Jr. and urged a repudiation of the idea that homosexuality was immoral, an illness, or anything other than a desire and identity to be donned pridefully.[53] The following year, a slate of militants wrested control of the moribund national Mattachine from a conservative faction that had been beholden to reparative therapy's promise. While the MSW was ousting its ancestors from their seats of power, the Daughters of Bilitis's conservative leadership was also met with a militant insurgency. Upon replacing *The Ladder*'s founding editorial team, Barbara Gittings began publishing more critiques of the pathology school.[54]

Sensing a need for regional and national networks to direct their political activity, the leaderships of the MSW, MSNY, DOB of New York, and the newly

formed Janus Society of Philadelphia founded the East Coast Homophile Organizations in 1963 and the North American Conference of Homophile Organizations (NACHO) in 1966. In these coalitions, new tensions erupted between those like the more libertine Clark Polak of the Janus Society, who
wished to place sexual freedom at the center of the movement's message, and
Kameny, who emphasized themes of status, preference, and orientation.[55]
Though pugnacious in his equal rights advocacy, Kameny's MSW retained
some strategically traditional practices such as male and female dress codes
for protests.[56]

Ultimately, the latter won out as these liberal pluralist advocacy outfits
settled on the frame that gay men and women constituted a discrete class of
sexual minorities deserving of civil rights.[57] Taking a firm stance against calls
for conversion, the 1968 NACHO convention adopted the position that "the
homosexual in our pluralistic society has the moral right to be a homosexual"
and that just as Catholics and Jews are "free of insolent and arrogant pressures
to convert to the prevailing Protestant Christianity," the homosexual must be
free to live without suffering penalties for living out a homosexual identity
and life and without the "pressures to convert to the prevailing heterosexuality."[58] Perhaps the most characteristic element of the late homophile movement's pluralism is evinced in the Annual Reminder, a Fourth of July protest
at Independence Hall in Philadelphia held annually from 1965 to 1970.[59] As a
flyer for one Annual Reminder declared, "The principles of the Declaration of
Independence [must] now be extended to all Americans," including the once-
maligned homosexual minority.[60]

Against Psychopathology: Reforms in Sexology, Psychology, and Psychiatry

As the homophile movement came to rebuff psychopathological renderings
of sexuality, those researchers and mental health practitioners who had grown
suspicious of the consensus view began to work alongside these activists. These
relationships between scientific and political actors were symbiotic in nature:
as the sexual revolution kicked off and the "gay is good" message spread, the
agendas of sympathetic scientists attracted enthusiastic research participants
and—at times—interlocutors. Homophile movement members lent their own
bodies and psyches to the construction of a competing medical paradigm—
one that might discredit theories of illness, contagion, and choice.

In 1952 the Mattachine's original leadership had founded an educational
nonprofit appendage called the Mattachine Foundation, which in subsequent
years would help plug the homophile movement into clinical research.[61]

One of the foundation's earliest and most consequential collaborations was with UCLA psychologist Evelyn Hooker, who was horrified by the sexual oppression that she witnessed while training in Nazi Germany and traveling throughout Stalin's Soviet Union.[62] Later while teaching psychology at UCLA, she befriended a gay student who humanized homosexuals by exposing Hooker to Los Angeles's gay night life. Although Hooker declined an offer to sit on the Mattachine Foundation's board of directors (this level of partnership would become the norm decades later, though at the time it may have appeared uncouth), she began working closely with its leadership and drew from its membership for her research.

The relationship paid off quickly, as Hooker's 1956 and 1957 studies provided compelling evidence against the personality disorder thesis. Hooker's clinical trials demonstrated that homosexuals and heterosexuals had similar rates of mental pathology.[63] In explicating the significance of her findings for mental healthcare, Hooker emphasized the positive benefits of "coming out."[64] She also castigated previous studies for failing to hypothesize how social factors such as employment and housing discrimination, stigma, and violence may have contributed to higher measures of mental illness among homosexual research subjects.

Hooker's studies represented only a fraction of those that had begun to critically interrogate the psychoanalytic illness model. The infamous "anti-psychiatry" psychiatrist Thomas Szasz was an early critic of his own discipline's tendency to diagnosis presumed diseases of the mind, including homosexuality.[65] Paralleling Michel Foucault's skepticism of clinical inquiry's ever-expansive claims to social knowledge, Szasz sought to undermine the rationalizing role that psychiatry had come to play in society. He saw clinicians as stewards of ideology who could cordon off aberrant behavior with a range of diagnoses and curative regimens.[66] In 1965 Szasz took on homosexuality directly in an essay titled "Legal and Moral Aspects of Homosexuality," in which he argued against classifying exclusive heterosexuality as the natural tendency of human beings.[67] He also explicitly denounced criminal codes and reorientation schemes as inherently punitive and destined to fail in their function to quell desire.

Others in medicine and mental health began to work closely with the homophiles in ways that cultivated additional alliances and medical clout for reformers. The physician-turned-ethnographer Martin Hoffman's 1968 book *The Gay World* became immensely popular for its message of tolerance.[68] Much like Hooker, Hoffman's investigations led him to realize that any social ills associated with homosexuality likely resulted from gay men and women having been made pariahs and outcasts. Even the rare psychoanalyst occasionally defected from the pathological thesis. Hendrik Ruitenbeek cast suspicion on the illness model and called for future studies to be undertaken by sociologists rather than clinicians based on the assumption that the former were less interested in diagnosing and treating their subjects of study.[69]

These reform studies eventually came to displace reports on the medical model in homophile journals and magazines. In some instances, editors or prominent organization members would correct these scientists for not going far enough to root out pathology. In 1966 the Mattachine's C. A. Tripp wrote into *The Ladder* to criticize psychiatrist Judd Marmor for inaccuracies and perceived affronts in the edited volume *Sexual Inversion*.[70] Though Marmor was fast becoming a well-positioned ally of the movement (Marmor would soon become president of the American Psychiatric Association), Tripp reproached Marmor for including essays by those like psychoanalyst Irving Bieber, who remained wedded to the view that a cure for homosexuality was possible, even desirable.[71] Tripp also criticized Marmor for conflating homosexuality with transgressive gender identities, thereby equating gay male identity with femininity. Committed to a particular style of gay assimilation, those like Tripp were loath to be associated with transvestites, cross-dressers, and others who did not conform to a heteronormative gender presentation.

It was not uncommon for homophile leaders to be in direct communication with researchers in discussions about how to challenge discriminatory laws. Kameny, for instance, had a long-standing correspondence with Alfred Kinsey's Indiana University–based research institute. Kinsey Institute director Paul Gebhard even described the relationship as "a cooperative venture rather than the usual scientists-and-the-object-under-the-lens" approach.[72] Richard Inman, founder of the Florida chapter of the Mattachine Society, also kept close contact with Kinsey Institute–affiliated researchers including Gebhard as he fought against an oppressive state legislature. In one letter to Gebhard, Inman wrote that the institute's advocacy against Florida's Criminal Sexual Psychopath bill had been "the key factor" in defeating that measure.[73]

What is especially revealing about Inman's letters with Gebhard and others at the Kinsey Institute are how frequently they involved conversations about homosexuality's etiology. In one extended exchange on the subject from 1966, Inman and a group of prominent Kinsey Institute researchers shared their musings on the question of causality. In response to Dr. Walter Alvarez's remark that "most of you were born with it," Inman laid out a skeptical view toward that notion of biological heredity. He explained:

> Studies of genetics as applied to the ancestry of homosexuals might be good and might indeed develop more evidence that heredity is a factor, or even a major force, as to why some persons become homosexuals, and why others do

not. This would, to some extent, result in evidence to show that "homosexuals are born that way and can't help what they are." From the point of view of the homosexual, who is attempting through the Homophile Movement, to educate the public not to discriminate against him, such evidence would be a possible key towards solving of some of the problems. But I think the addition of the "sickness" through hereditary theory, without some additional evidence[,] is a very dangerous course to take.[74]

Though Gebhard "agree[d] that the odds are against homosexuality being genetic," it is striking how Inman's conflicted attitude toward this theory foreshadowed debates concerning the "gay gene's" political utility and scientific validity.[75] While Inman saw some promise in a born this way frame, those homophiles who were well-read in sexology knew that an earlier pathological model had itself been founded upon the assumption that homosexuals were congenitally marred.[76] Accordingly, most homophiles kept their eyes trained on pathology and its associated treatment protocols.

Contesting the American Sexuality Regime

The post-WWII era was a pivotal moment when oppressive legal sanctions and a repressive psychiatric regime remained largely undisturbed, yet ripe for reform. When the homophiles began orchestrating challenges to its many facets, the American sexuality regime was already vulnerable. The homophiles rode reform trends, including a new bipartisan penchant for deinstitutionalizing the country's asylums and psychiatric wards, which had long housed supposedly incorrigible sexual psychopaths.[77] They, too, benefited from constitutional developments such as the Supreme Court's opinion in *Griswold v. Connecticut* (1965), which erected a legal barrier between the state and certain private sexual behaviors, as well as First Amendment cases that reduced the US Postal Service's ability to regulate obscenity.[78] In its own successful Supreme Court challenge to obscenity laws, ONE Inc. cleverly argued that its magazine was a vehicle for understanding "the problems of [sexual] variation," a task it accomplished through columns by scientists and mental health practitioners.[79] With the aid of their expert allies in the Kinsey Institute, homophile advocates strove to further fissure the cracks that had begun to form in a series of challenges to state liquor board clampdowns on gay and lesbian bars, federal employment hiring exclusions, and discriminatory immigration law standards.

Among the first legal fights pursued by the homophiles were a series of bureaucratic and judicial challenges to state liquor regulations in California, New Jersey, New York, and Florida. After the repeal of national Prohibition with the Twenty-First Amendment in 1933, the states were returned their original jurisdiction over the regulation of alcohol per their state police powers—that is, the power to regulate on behalf of their citizenry's health, safety, and morals. Laws and administrative regulations against vague targets like "lewd conduct" and sodomy were passed during the height of eugenic aspirations. As such, the public health risk of homosexual contagion provided the justification and authority for policies that promised to root out a dangerous and deviant clientele (even though the deviancy rhetoric was mostly pretextual, masking a more fundamental concern with urban disorder and blight).[80]

The first cases levied against the vice squad were fought not by homophiles themselves, but instead by bar owners who had lost their liquor licenses for allegedly having created safe havens for gay and lesbian customers. The California Board of Equalization revoked the liquor license of the gay-friendly Black Cat Café upon deeming the bar "a disorderly house for purposes injurious to public morals" that harbored "persons of known homosexual tendencies."[81] In a 1951 judicial appeal of the agency's decision, the California Supreme Court ruled in favor of the Black Cat. In differentiating the bar's catering to gays and lesbians from illicit activity itself (such as that which occurs in a brothel), the court reasoned that a business should not lose its license for simply serving queer customers, at least without evidence of actual criminal behavior.[82]

While this ruling was made on behalf of restaurant owners rather than civil rights proper, the court's ruling and legal rationale invigorated subsequent homophile challenges. In its decision, the California Supreme Court had made a key distinction between homosexuality as a status (a protected category in places of public accommodation) and unprotected homosexual behavior. Problems plagued the application of this precedent: illegal behavior could be construed as something as innocuous as two men holding hands.[83] Still, the legal distinction was an inspiration to reformers. If one could divorce homosexual status from conduct, the argument could be made that the mere presence of homosexuals in a public place did not present a social hazard.

Sensing that there were more state-level victories to be won, the Mattachine Society and the Society for Individual Rights began funding similar cases in other states and defending the California precedent from the threat of rollback. These efforts paid off as a coalition of homophile organizations and bar owners defeated a state legislative attempt to thwart the 1951 ruling. In the 1959 *Vallerga v. Department of Alcoholic Beverage Control*, the California Supreme Court reiterated the status versus conduct distinction in striking down an amendment to the California Business and Professions Code, which had sought to punish bars that had the reputation of being "resorts for illegal possessors or users of narcotics, prostitutes, pimps, panderers, or sexual perverts."[84]

As legal battles over the burgeoning gay bar scene proliferated, they evolved into conflicts over the scientific and medical accuracy of the mental illness model. In a 1955 New Jersey Alcoholic Beverage Control (ABC) hearing, the owner of a bar introduced expert testimony that homosexuality was not a contagion and that gay or lesbian patrons would not adversely affect the health or morals of heterosexual customers.[85] In 1967 the Mattachine Society funded a state court appeal to this bureaucratic ruling and provided testimony by Dr. Wardell Pomeroy, a renowned sexologist who had coauthored the famous Kinsey studies. Pomeroy's testimony proved influential as the New Jersey Supreme Court took his evidence to legitimate the California Supreme Court's rationale in *Vallerga*.[86] Notably, the court also chastised the state liquor authority for not providing its own scientific expert witness to back up its claims of contagion. Though homophile advocates were not always so lucky—that same year, a Florida court sided with the state's psychiatric experts against the Sunshine State's sole Mattachine chapter—these early defenses of the gay bar scene and assaults on the pathological model introduced considerable ambiguity over just what these strictures on service were intended to regulate.[87]

After the Lavender Scare: The Fight for Federal Employment

In litigation spearheaded by Frank Kameny, the Mattachine Society of Washington spent the 1960s making steady legal gains against discrimination in federal employment. The MSW's decade-long campaign against the Civil Service Commission endeavored to topple employment restrictions that had ramped up in the early days of the Lavender Scare. In 1953 following both the investigations of the House Subcommittee on the Employment of Homosexuals and Other Sex Perverts in Government and FBI Director J. Edgar Hoover's crusade against "sexual deviants" in the federal bureaucracy, President Eisenhower issued Executive Order 10450, which established a strict security clearance procedure for employment in civil service. As a means of implementing these policy changes, the CSC developed new protocols for identifying employees with "any criminal, infamous, dishonest, immoral or notoriously disgraceful conduct, habitual use of intoxicants to excess, drug addiction, or sexual perversion" that might be used to coerce them into divulging national security information.[88] Bolstered by a waning McCarthyism and the rise of new judicial protections for private sexual behavior, homophiles scored victories against the CSC policy by undermining the validity of the pathological perspective upon which it rested.[89]

Having been dismissed from federal civilian employment in 1957 for lewd conduct, Kameny's initial appeal to the CSC was based on a denial of his homosexuality. His request for reinstatement featured a letter from his psychiatrist Benjamin Karpman, a neo-Freudian who had testified on behalf of the DC sexual psychopath law a decade earlier and whom Kameny had convinced to declare him "cured" of his perverted predilections.[90] Kameny's strategic reliance on the pathological model was, however, short-lived. Upon losing his appeal and subsequently founding the MSW, Kameny implored the federal courts to overturn the entire CSC employment framework.[91]

Although Kameny's 1961 appeal was unsuccessful, the DC Circuit Court soon ruled in favor of the MSW in a series of subsequent cases. These rulings steadily diminished the power of the CSC to terminate federal employees solely on the basis that they identified or were identified by a criminal sex-related charge as a homosexual. In the first of these cases, *Scott v. Macy*, secretary of the MSW Bruce Scott sued CSC chair John Macy Jr. after Scott was fired from the Department of Labor.[92] The DC Circuit's Chief Judge David Bazelon ruled in Scott's favor, arguing that the CSC had based its decision on an impermissibly vague standard (Scott had been hit with a nebulous charge of "unspecified homosexual conduct") that flew in the face of constitutional due process guarantees. Bazelon was himself a key nexus between science and the law. Throughout the mid-twentieth century, the judge was renowned for incorporating insights from the latest research in psychiatry and medicine into his jurisprudence, as exemplified by his innovative approach to insanity defenses.[93]

Four years later, the homophiles won an even more dramatic ruling against the CSC standards in the 1969 case *Norton v. Macy*.[94] In that case, the MSW funded an appeal for NASA employee Clifford Norton, who had been dismissed after an arrest for cruising. Arguing against the notion that Norton was a weak degenerate and liable to buckle under the threat of communist blackmail, the MSW asserted that there was no causal connection between a gay man's ability to perform his duties and his sexual behavior outside of work. Writing for the DC Circuit Court once again, Bazelon accepted this argument and stressed the MSW's distinction between the kinds of immoral conduct that the CSC had a rational reason to enforce and the mere status of a person as a homosexual or the nature of his private sexual behavior. In enshrining the distinction in a new judicial standard, Bazelon constructed the "rational nexus test," which differentiated a benign conception of homosexuality from the assumption that any and all non-heterosexual behavior was a sign of a pathological condition.[95]

In the *Scott* case, Bazelon observed that researchers and clinicians had become internally divided over the nature and dangers of "homosexual conduct." To demonstrate the incoherence of the government's legal designation, Bazelon juxtaposed quotes from the 1950 Senate Subcommittee's reference to medical and psychiatric testimonies on sexual perversion with evidence from a 1947 paper by medical professor and psychoanalyst Clara Thompson, who characterized such terms as having become underspecified referents, "a kind of wastebasket into which are dumped all forms of relationships with one's own sex."[96] Bazelon, too, reached for the Kinsey study, which revealed that at least 37 percent of the American male population would engage in homosexual conduct at least once in their lifetimes. In his opinions for the *Scott* and *Norton* cases, the judge reasoned that excluding one-third of the male population from federal employment would pose a larger threat to the functioning of the government than would allowing them to take federal jobs.[97]

Bazelon was not alone in his nuanced application of science to federal policy, nor was his reformist perspective confined to his own judicial bench. In 1967 the National Institute of Mental Health Task Force on Homosexuality brought together a mix of state officials and leading researchers in sexology and psychiatry, many of whom were among the homophile movement's collaborators. Chaired by Evelyn Hooker, the task force was charged with reviewing "the current state of knowledge regarding homosexuality in its mental illness aspects and [making] recommendations for programming and policing reforms."[98] The report, which was completed in October 1969 and heralded as an American "Magna Carta for homophiles," recommended a vast reconfiguration of federal and state policy. The task force concluded that because the mental illness model was outdated and effectively meaningless, discrimination in policing and employment was unwarranted and an undue abrogation of civil rights. Though the Nixon administration deemed the report "too tolerant and too liberal" and withheld official publication until 1972, the task force's report would prove influential in future strikes against the pathological model in law and public policy.[99]

The Sexual Psychopath in Immigration Law

The legal struggle against sexual psychopath classifications in immigration law brought together a broad coalition including the Philadelphia-based Homosexual Law Reform Society (HLRS), the New York ACLU, Frank Kameny, and scientific opponents of the illness model.[100] Throughout the first half of the twentieth century, federal immigration law provided for the deportation of aliens charged with crimes of "moral turpitude," a catch-all provision that included same-sex sexual behavior. By the 1950s, the moral turpitude test had proven inefficient as it relied upon a patchwork of state and municipal legal

codes to define its content. As cities and states began to liberalize their various laws against sodomy and lewd conduct—such efforts were propelled in
part by the American Law Institute's newly drafted Moral Penal Code, which
called for decriminalization—federal immigration standards became even
more fragmented and confused.[101] As a remedy, Congress passed the 1952
McCarran-Walter Act, a sweeping immigration law, which included a revised
"psychopathic personality" provision to replace the moral turpitude one.[102]
To impose some degree of in-house uniformity, this provision directed Public
Health Services (PHS) psychiatrists to work with the Immigration and Naturalization Services (INS) in assessing immigrants suspected of sex crimes.[103]

The first judicial challenge to the McCarran-Walter Act was brought not
by a homophile advocate but instead by the Swiss immigrant George Fleuti
acting on his own accord. Throughout his deportation hearings, Fleuti's psychiatrist and resident psychiatrists from the PHS dueled over whether his 1958
arrest for cruising was indicative of a "psychopathological personality."[104] In
a 5–4 ruling, the Supreme Court balked on the question of whether the provision was unconstitutionally vague, but did let stand a Ninth Circuit ruling
that struck against the statute's language for possessing no accepted meaning
within the psychiatric profession.[105] In response, Congress quickly amended
the statute with more precise language classifying those "afflicted [with] sexual deviation" as grounds for denial of naturalization and deportation.[106]

That same year, Clive Michael Boutilier, a Canadian citizen residing in
the United States, was denied citizenship after disclosing a history of same-
sex sexual behavior. Sensing an opportunity to take another shot at the
McCarran-Walter Act's restrictions, the Homosexual Law Reform Society
partnered with the New York ACLU to challenge the law on behalf of Boutilier.[107] The HLRS collected expert testimonies from top practitioners and researchers including sexologists John Money and Harry Benjamin as well as
the famed anthropologist of sex and gender Margaret Mead in a brief that
differentiated homosexuality from psychopathology.[108] Although the Second Circuit's majority opinion ruled in favor of the INS, Judge Leonard Page
Moore penned a dissent drawing from these reformist trends. Presaging a
similar rationale in Bazelon's *Norton* opinion, Moore posited that it could not
possibly be the case that Congress had intended to exclude all immigrants
who at one point had engaged in same-sex behavior given, according to Kinsey's 1948 volume, that such a rule would disqualify over a third of the American male population for naturalization.[109]

In an attempt to bypass the budding controversies within scientific and
clinical circles, the INS argued that the revamped psychopath provision did
not signify so much a strict *medical* definition as it did a *legal* distinction.[110]

Sidestepping the fact that Boutilier had provided two independent psychiatric reports at odds with the diagnosis of the INS's special inquiry officer, the agency appealed to a sense of conventional social mores rather any strict adherence to scientific objectivity.[111] Once again, Judge Moore's dissent reveals how the law obfuscated rather than clarified how and why a person might be classified as a psychopath. Moore reasoned that the law's language "suggests a careful and particularized analysis by distinguished psychiatrists to determine whether [the] appellant was so disturbed as to be 'afflicted with psychopathic personality,'" when in fact the PHS and INS had simply glanced at Boutilier's criminal past, given him a quick look over, and deemed him an incorrigible psychopath.[112]

In response to the government's defense, Boutilier's attorneys highlighted the absurdity of the agency's discursive dodge and pressed on the fact that the law was based on an outdated, highly contested scientific opinion. The homophile coalition's appeal to the Supreme Court characterized the new legal distinction as being just as ambiguous and ill-defined as its predecessor.[113] Boutilier's team raised questions such as who is a homosexual and how can one define a homosexual?[114] They contended that Boutilier might not even be a homosexual at all because he had sex with women as well as with men. Here, Kameny advised Boutilier's legal team to press even further by calling into question the INS's use of a seemingly binaristic status claim—one is either a sexual psychopath or a conforming heterosexual—derived from a catalog of various kinds of sexual conduct, much of which did not fall along such a neat dichotomous distinction.[115] Not only was the law incoherent, they claimed, but the logic upon which it rested was hopelessly circular. Though the Supreme Court ruled against Boutilier and deferred to Congress's ostensible intent to bar all "sexual deviants," Justices William O. Douglas and Abe Fortas dissented by documenting the inconsistencies in the INS's psychiatric expert pronouncements and by citing those like Kinsey, Ruitenbeek, and Freud approvingly.[116]

The 1960s ended on a paradox. While the CSC was at this same moment refusing to acknowledge that homosexuality could be rendered as a protected legal status independent of an outlawed behavioral component, the INS defended the notion that a person could indeed be a homosexual as a matter of status or condition.[117] The Supreme Court, Congress, and the INS had little idea that construing homosexuality as a legal status lent, in Margot Canaday's words, "authority to a burgeoning gay rights movement that base[d] its claims on a legal-political conception of homosexuals as potentially good citizens."[118] In its persistent attack on the illness model, the homophile movement exposed the illogical and inconsistent way in which that model's suppositions

had been used to justify legal prohibitions and restrictions. By the end of the
1960s, the scientific consensus was corroding, legal and constitutional ave-
nues for future civil rights claims were being charted, and a slowly yet steadily
growing number of state officials and judges were becoming more amenable
than ever to alternative explanations for diverse sexual desires and identities.
Having dealt pathology a series of legal, scientific, and cultural blows, the homophiles and their allies in science and medicine entered the next decade
prepared to go in for the kill.

2

Desire in the Throes of Power: Gay Liberation, Psychiatry, and the Politics of Classification

In the wake of the Stonewall Riot of 1969, a slew of radical gay, lesbian separatist, Black lesbian feminist, and transsexual organizations joined the ranks of the New Left social movements. Wielding Molotov cocktails lit by a burning desire to transcend their forebearers' liberal pluralist politics, groups like the Gay Liberation Front (GLF) promised an alternative to incremental reform. In stark contrast to the straitlaced white male, middle-class homophile movement, those like POC trans activist Marsha P. Johnson are said to have been the true instigators of the era's rebellion. Unlike even the most militant homophiles, these radicals sought to upend the distinction between heterosexuality and homosexuality entirely. They envisaged an imminent future of unrestrained libidos, a sexually fluid society where gender and sexuality could be expressed outside of the repressive institutions of marriage and psychiatry.

Gay liberation has been occasionally recalled as the first organized refusal of science and medicine's dominion over sexuality and gender.[1] Unlike those in the Mattachine Society who would gladly employ the resources of whatever authority might pronounce gay sexuality as harmless, these radicals aimed to displace such authority, castigating it as undue, intrusive, and, most importantly, counterproductive to their ultimate political aims. The liberationists—a diffuse group of self-styled radicals drawing from the New Left student movement, bohemian circles, and other countercultural communities—rejected such influence as an impediment to their far more expansive vision for desire. They feared that any cooperation with scientific experts—any small concession to the authority of another—would sap the strength from their fusillade. And so, when an opportunity arose to work alongside reformers within the American Psychiatric Association (APA) in the early 1970s to topple the pathological model for good, the liberationists balked. Better to be on the margins of society, they surmised, than to collaborate with the enemy.

This chapter serves as a corrective to the standard account of gay liberation. For all of the romanticism that so often attends histories of gay liberation, stories that rely on "reform or revolution" and "science vs. self-definition" formulations are more hagiographic than they are an accurate depiction of gay politics from 1969 to 1973. For one, the liberationists did not actually denounce all scientific arguments, but rather only those that naturalized the sharp distinction between a heterosexual majority and a homosexual minority. They frequently invoked anthropological and biological evidence to posit sexuality's true unencumbered form, one that might at last be unchained from modern social mores. In fact, the liberationists opposed only *certain* taxonomic schemas while imposing their own classificatory system of properly political ways of living out one's sexuality and gender.

Moreover, the liberationists were far from unified. They also lacked a coherent plan and the ability to chart a different path for gay politics even if they did.[2] During this time, a wide range of gay and lesbian advocates engaged in sustained pressure campaigns at the annual conferences of organizations like the APA and the American Medical Association (AMA). There, opponents of the pathological model confronted psychiatrists, psychologists, and physicians who met to discuss the treatments of sexual deviance.[3] In fact, many of the most cautiously conservative homophile organizations to the most ostentatiously combative liberationist ones participated in rancorous, impassioned pleas and demands to cease treating same-sex attraction as a mental disturbance.[4]

The second half of the chapter pivots from intra-movement politics to the intra-disciplinary rivalries within psychiatry and psychology that culminated in the APA's 1973 decision to declassify homosexuality as a disorder. The gulf between liberation and homophile politics did, in fact, matter a great deal to the APA changes and the future of gay rights—just not the way that it is frequently remembered.

The story of declassification has more to do with how homophile leaders rode a wave of larger conflicts and reforms in mental healthcare, the most important of which expanded into an all-out assault on psychoanalysis. Ironically, it was the homophiles and not the radicals who wound up working alongside New Left reformers within the APA and a handful of covertly queer clinicians who positioned themselves against the illiberal psychoanalytic old guard. Gay rights leaders also worked alongside others in the field of cognitive behavioral therapy and biomedical psychiatry proponents, both of whom cared less about demedicalizing homosexuality and far more about discrediting the psychoanalysts who had for decades controlled the APA.

The decision that gays and lesbians had to make, in other words, was not whether to infuse their work with an accommodationist or liberatory spirit throughout the fights against the APA and institutions like it. Instead, the available option was to steer these various reformers to knock out homosexuality's medicalization as those forces bulldozed through the rest of the psychoanalytic tradition. Homosexuality's declassification was ultimately downstream from these intra-scientific disputes.

"The End of the Homosexual"

Gay liberation was premised on the hope that we might all be much freer than we are. Cribbing from a mix of women's liberation writings and Freudo-Marxism, the liberationists saw their identities as the products of a socially imposed repression.[5] They posited that their own predilections and practices were simply those parts of human sexuality that the reigning straight society had squeezed out and relegated to the realm of the aberrant. As such, the liberationists struggled to overcome that repression—not just for themselves, but for the libido of all.

Much like how women's liberation theorists depicted patriarchy as a durable set of social institutions rather than a simple psychic prejudice, the New Left gays depicted heterosexism as a human-made structure. In the early years of radical feminism, writer-activists like Kate Millett and Shulamith Firestone penned best-selling books cautioning that the integration of women into the status quo was impossible because society necessitated their subordination.[6] Liberal feminist outfits like the National Organization for Women (NOW) were considered insufficient—counterrevolutionary even—to achieving deeper transformations in gender relations. In this view, both second-wave liberal feminism and the '60s sexual revolution offered the false freedoms of civil rights and consumer goods. Rather than mere reform, the liberationists demanded fundamental changes to wage labor and domestic labor, reproductive care, and culturally prescribed gender roles. A corollary of this perspective was that women and queers alike did not even exist as natural categories outside of their history of oppression and exploitation. Women were subordinated on the basis of their role in reproduction whereas gays and lesbians were defined by their refusal to take part in that affair. Though these processes of differentiation touched on nature, they were seen as irreducibly social.

The Frankfurt school's Herbert Marcuse was perhaps one of the greatest influences on gay liberation and the New Left writ large. By the time of the Stonewall Riots, Marcuse had earned himself the nickname of "guru to the New Left" for providing student radicals and self-styled militants with an analytic that conjoined a critique of political economy with a Freudian analysis of repression and sexual transformation.[7] Throughout his own best-selling works like *Eros and Civilization* and *One-Dimensional Man*, Marcuse illustrated how capitalist society had corrupted libidinal instincts, channeling them away from the pursuit of pleasure and toward capitalist productivity.[8] Women's liberation theorists like Firestone joined Marcuse in portraying sexism, heterosexism, and the natural ethos of productive work as the pillars of the social order.[9] Liberation would thus entail a reactivation of once-subordinated pleasures and the creation of new communal relationships, neither of which patriarchal capitalist society could condone.

Liberationists latched on to this starry-eyed vision of sexuality's central role in refashioning, in Marcuse's words, "the human body [as] an instrument of pleasure rather than labor."[10] GLF member and political scientist Dennis Altman expounded this promise of remaking the social, which would decimate sexual and gender binaries and sprout new modes of desire and being. One of the key claims of Altman's 1971 *Homosexual: Oppression and Liberation* was that the "end of the homosexual" would be achieved through the adoption of gay identities and relationships that would expose the repressive nature of capitalist social relations.[11] This was no utopian outlook, either. Altman and others believed that American society was on the precipice of being replaced by more emancipatory impulses and social arrangements. Inspired by Freud, Altman promised that the polymorphously perverse society was in sight; an unrestrained sex instinct, one that had not yet been narrowed down to mere heterosexual genital pleasure, might be our future rather than our past.[12] In contrast to Marcuse's warnings against repressive desublimation—a concept that he used to describe the false promises of the sexual revolution's commodification of the erotic, which transformed the nature of repression without transcending it—Altman and his ilk were much more optimistic about the radical potential of their sexual selves.[13]

Emancipation did require some effort. Rather than engage in civil rights campaigns, however, the liberationists favored consciousness-raising activities and theatrical protests. Former Daughters of Bilitis leader-turned-cofounder of the Gay Liberation Front Martha Shelley made the case for a politics of self-renewal in her seminal 1970 essay, "Gay Is Good."[14] In a reframe of the homophile-inspired slogan, Shelley interpreted the homosexual as the negation of the heterosexual, a figure who might dialectically abolish the conditions that had generated that tension-laden duality. Addressing an imagined audience construed as straight, Shelley scolded those who had "managed to drive your own homosexuality down under the skin of your mind." The GLF wanted "not for you to tolerate us, or to accept us, but to understand us.... [We] want to reach the homosexuals entombed in you, to liberate our brothers and sisters, locked in the prisons of your skulls."[15] Like Altman, Shelley saw homosexual identity as a pit stop en route to the liberation of all.

Across the pond, the GLF's London chapter housed a number of influential activist-theorists. Among them was Jeffrey Weeks, whose 1972 essay "Ideas of Gay Liberation" integrated racial and sexual oppression into a critique of liberal pluralism.[16] Weeks distinguished the GLF's multi-front approach to the homophile one, which he condemned for naturalizing gay identity as white, middle class, and largely male.[17] "What's the use of having equality with straights if we are still imprisoned by class, racial, and sex divisions?" Weeks asked rhetorically in making a pitch for a united New Left coalition.[18] Though the liberationists were divided over the roots of heterosexism—those inspired by Firestone claimed that sexism, racism, and capitalist exploitation alike originated in the sexual division of labor, whereas others like the Chicago-based Third World Gay Revolution and the Combahee River Collective would describe regimes of oppression as distinct and interlocking— they shared in the belief that assimilation could only slightly ameliorate those suffering from oppression rather than deal with the rot through revolutionary struggle.[19]

Gay liberation newspapers also propagated revolt against liberal pluralism. In a 1970 article for the New York–based paper *Come Out!*, GLF member Jim Fouratt rebuked the hetero-homo dichotomy as a symptom of a "culture [that] has created these artificial categories defining human sexuality, to protect and to perpetuate the institutions and systems in power whose end result is only to dehumanize life."[20] Others writing in papers like *Gay Community* perceived the distinction itself as perpetuating an "oppressive duality," one that could only serve as a "barrier to liberation."[21] In Altman's words, sexual identity could only be made useful if it was at once "joyful, spontaneous, and erotic," untethered by taxonomies, which had historically functioned to ossify its object.[22]

Against Expertise

Gay liberationists were highly suspicious of scientific expertise and classifications, especially those that reinforced naturalistic conceptions of a heterosexual majority and a homosexual minority. Given the liberationist investment in consciousness-raising as a tactic and its faith in the power of language, the

very act of self-definition as "naturally" homosexual was anathema. They often perceived even those scientists most sympathetic to their plight as representatives of an establishment class that would prefer to rationalize rather
than to reform the degraded social order. Liberationist manifestos, meeting
minutes, organizational statements of purpose, and correspondence spell out
a mix of skepticism and outright hostility that they harbored against these researchers, mental health practitioners, and all others who would prefer to address them cloaked in a white lab coat.

In a widely circulated 1970 essay, "Refugees from Amerika: A Gay Manifesto," Carl Wittman of the Gay Liberation Front of Los Angeles (GLF-LA)
confronted naturalistic theories of sexuality and gender head-on. Wittman
posited that "nature leaves undefined the object of sexual desire" precisely
because "the gender of that object is imposed socially."[23] The endeavor to
distinguish between sexual desire's aim (multiple and malleable) and object (defined through gendered social markings) is reminiscent of a Freudian logic that Wittman and others in the GLF-LA's Red Butterfly caucus had
encountered in their studies of Freudo-Marxism.[24] Neither homosexuality
nor heterosexuality could be meaningfully described as "genetic," Wittman
protested, because the neat distinction between the two was the result of historically contingent social processes.[25] Reciting Wittman's sentiment, a GLF
chapter in Hartford reiterated that "what a person does should not constitute
a complete social classification."[26]

Beyond the manifestos, the GLF frequently rebuffed scientific authority in
their organizational mission statements. In its 1970 "Statement of Purpose,"
the GLF-LA announced that it would "refuse to engage in discussion of causation, 'Sickness' (A LIE), degrees of sexuality, or any other such Establishment
Hang-Ups."[27] Though the chapter's opposition to pathology is unremarkable,
the strike against "causation" and "degrees of sexuality" was unique to the gay
liberationists. Even talk of the Kinsey-inspired spectrum of sexuality—itself
a challenge to binaristic assumptions—was deemed suspect. Whether sexology pitched homosexuality in terms of a blunt dualism or as nodes on a continuum made little difference. Both preserved "exclusive homosexuality" and
"exclusive heterosexuality" as poles for a paradigm that they sought to upend.

In their opposition to the mental illness model, the GLF went much further than the Mattachine in their near-total denouncements of the mental
health profession. They were not alone in their mistrust. The radical psychiatrists of the New Left such as R. D. Laing and Thomas Szasz claimed that diagnoses ranging from sexual deviancy to schizophrenia were clinical means of
social control.[28] Just as this cohort of mental health professionals saw reason
itself as a social imposition on the psyche—the mad were a mere symptom of

modernity—GLF members fashioned themselves as the victims of "oppression sickness" who suffered from "stress resulting from the oppression of homosexuals in our society."[29] They inverted the clinical view in explaining that the depression many homosexual patients experienced was the result of their mistreatment. If mental health professionals were to assist at all in liberation, it would necessarily be a subordinated one. The GLF-LA, for instance, recommended that these experts "utilize their skills for the sexual liberation of all people" by reprimanding their colleagues and clearing a space for gay men and women to define themselves. According to a GLF handout titled "A Brief Essay on Bullshit Expertise," any attempt to claim expertise over another was antithetical to their agenda.[30]

Though this spirit of self-definition peppered GLF leaflets and mission statements, some members made use of scientific evidence occasionally, particularly anthropological evidence that squared with their thesis on contemporary sexual norms. In one long essay authored by members of the Red Butterfly cell, liberationists discussed anthropologist Clellan S. Ford's and zoologist Frank A. Beach's studies on the abnormality of exclusive homosexuality and heterosexuality.[31] They also cited work on the sexual habits of primates that might illuminate, in their own words, "the genetic bases of our own behavior." Rather than using the genetic argument to fix any one modern pattern of desire as natural, the Red Butterfly appealed to evidence that unmasked the incredible plasticity of sexuality. They, too, cited studies on human sexual behavior and relationships in prisons to buttress their view on sexuality's malleability.

In at least one instance, a prominent GLF member invoked a "by nature" account to counter the more homophobic elements of the New Left and those in communist organizations who still adhered to the Stalinist view of homosexuality as bourgeois decadence. In a 1971 statement, the GLF's Craig Hanson reprimanded those he termed "Marxist-Leninist heterosexuals" who believed that abolishing the capitalist mode of production would inevitably lead to the demise of homosexuality. Without citing specific evidence, Hanson claimed, "There is growing evidence that homosexuality has a biological rather than an environmental basis. Eliminating capitalism will not eliminate homosexuality."[32] Though Hanson's overall argument relied heavily on the Firestonian concepts, the allure of nature was apparently too great to resist.

For the most part, though, GLF chapters and others in the liberation orbit only brought science to bear on questions of desire and identity when they reinforced claims to autonomy and the looming gay horizon. In one case, a GLF chapter in St. Louis squared its radical ethos with a citation to the Kinsey Institute estimate that up to 10 percent of the population was exclusively homosexual. Instead of treating that estimate as a static figure, the GLF–St. Louis saw that figure as ascending upward.[33] The Minnesota-based Fight Repression of Erotic Expression (FREE) also found a way to meld Kinsey Institute research to political self-determination. In one informational pamphlet, FREE cited Wardell Pomeroy, whose research suggested that "the homosexual" was itself a social category, one that could not be pinned down to one or another psychological or physiological factor. This, FREE argued, was evidence that gay identity ought to be "defined by Gay people" and that "Gay Power is needed to secure and to protect identity."[34]

Catalytic Classifications: The Inverted Taxonomies of Gay Liberation

Despite this commitment to autonomy and self-determination, the liberationists wound up placing significant strictures on the proper way to enact the catalytic potential of gay and lesbian identities. The radical refusal of prevailing scientific taxonomies did not preclude the liberationists from exercising their own variety of identitarian policing over how exactly the artificial homosexual-heterosexual divide might be overcome. In pitting their project against their assimilation-minded homophile counterparts, the liberationists ironically sketched out their own taxonomies of human nature and difference. As the editorial collective of the New York GLF's paper *Come Out!* indicated, gay identity was an imperative. "Gay Liberation has to be. There can be no life in this country without it. All women and men must be liberated. All women and men must be gay."[35]

Having been kicked out of the women's liberation movement for being gay and having left the gay liberation movement for its misogyny, lesbian feminists depicted lesbian identity as a political choice and the only means by which the heterosexist social order might be eroded.[36] This separatist ideology was based in the belief that such self-categorization was a means of cultivating resistance, one that might work dialectically to undermine those institutions and prejudices that made such identification necessary in the first instance. Accordingly, groups like Radicalesbians, Gay Women's Liberation, and the UK-based Counter-Psychiatric Group denounced clinical attempts to classify and make inert a sexuality that was inherently volitional and dynamic.[37]

GLF-style liberationists and separatist lesbian feminist ones both agreed that while bisexuality was a fact of life, bisexual *identity* was a political dead end. In charting out a path toward polymorphous perversity, liberationists often discussed bisexuality in terms of an innate human disposition that had become socially denied. They cited everyone from Freud to Kinsey to Masters and Johnson on desire's intrinsically multidirectional nature. Rather than encourage members to adopt bisexual identities, however, most liberationists decried bisexuality as carrying less radical potentiality than gay and lesbian identities. Though some prominent voices in liberation politics like Kate Millett, Martha Shelley, and the members of the Sexual Freedom League would adopt bisexual identities, they incurred condemnation for doing so.[38] Bisexuality was loathed by those lesbian feminists who saw the label as a threat to their own project of imploring women to bear a lesbian identity. Separatists did not believe that bisexuality—or any sexual or romantic encounter between a man and a woman—could be practiced ethically until social revolution had abolished gender and sex roles.[39] The "Gay Manifesto," too, had explained that while bisexuality could be a normatively desirable form of love and erotic expression, gay identity was much more antagonistic and threatening to heterosexuality.[40]

Transsexuality and drag personas were also subject to scrutiny. Some GLF chapters were willing to make room for transvestite and transsexual issues in their programs, as evinced in a GLF-LA list of demands that included a line on "the right to change sex or cross dress."[41] However, many among the lesbian feminist crowd especially denounced such gender transgression as form of sexist parody. Others like the Red Butterfly cell cautioned against surgical procedures, arguing that "'modification of sex' is a false concept. . . . We are philosophical materialists, rejecting the theological concepts of soul-body dualism, and therefore, we consider an injury to the body an injury to the real person."[42]

Founders of early trans organizations like Lee Brewster's Queens Liberation Front (QLF), Sylvia Rivera's and Marsha P. Johnson's Street Transvestite Action Revolutionaries, and Angela Douglas's Transvestite-Transsexual Action Organization also debated these questions of expertise and gender. In its coverage of a 1971 meeting of the National Transsexual Counseling Center where Douglas presented alongside a panel of lawyers, physicians, and welfare workers, the *Drag Queens* editorial team lamented the domineering medical perspective that perceived transsexuality not as a social identity, but rather a "disease for which there is no cure."[43] Elsewhere, drag queens associated with the QLF remarked that a drag queen is "many times more militant and flamboyant than his transvestite sisters because he plays around more with gender without hang-ups about masculinity or femininity."[44]

These debates over sexual and gender roles ironically led liberationists to construct their own normative hierarchies and taxonomies. In their attempts to prefiguratively achieve a more radically queer world and to discern the proper role that scientific and medical experts might play to help get them there, the liberationists ended up resembling their homophile brothers and sisters much more than they might have imagined. Rather than making a clean break with the liberal pluralist propensity to taxonomize, they reflected its radical mirror image.

Classified: Disciplinary Developments in Midcentury Mental Health

Far away from community center basement debates over gay liberation, another conflict over the meaning of homosexuality was being hashed out among mental healthcare professionals. Throughout the 1960s and into the 1970s, the fields of psychology and psychiatry were still dominated by those who had made their careers in classifying, diagnosing, and treating homosexuality as if it were a psychic affliction. Mid-twentieth-century American psychiatry in particular was heavily influenced by a domestic variant of the psychoanalytic tradition, which perceived homosexuality as a sign of sociopathology.[45] Sigmund Freud himself, of course, did not consider same-sex attraction to be pathological—a famous letter to a mother assured her that while her son might be a neurotic, his sexual appetites were no cause for concern.[46] The adaptational school that came to steer psychoanalysis through the 1940s, 1950s, and 1960s, however, adopted a pathological perspective that paralleled an earlier generation of sexologists with whom Freud had sparred.[47]

In the immediate postwar period, the theories and treatment guidelines of Freud's pupil and Columbia University professor Sandor Rado had come to prevail.[48] Inspired by the likes of Social Darwinian Herbert Spencer, Rado reformulated Freud's richer, more complex work on the multiple aims and objects of sexual experience into a more naturalistic reproductive account of normative heterosexual relations.[49] In this context, homosexuality was recast as a trauma-based response to some childhood injury or developmental disruption that produced a maladaptation. Unlike the nineteenth-century degeneration school of sexology that had located this maladaptation in physiology—for example, a congenital defect—the adaptationists focused on the psyche.[50] In 1952 this perspective was codified in the first edition of the *Diagnostic and Statistical Manual of Mental Disorders* (*DSM*), which labeled homosexuality a "sociopathic personality disturbance."[51]

This psychoanalytic "consensus" was always contested even at its midcentury peak. The adaptationists fought vigorously against Alfred Kinsey's influence in the years just before and after the *DSM* was compiled. Rado's adherents were whiplashed by Kinsey's claim that human sexuality sat on a continuum—each node from exclusive heterosexual to exclusive homosexuality a natural variation, no more praiseworthy or condemnable from the next—rather than a binary separating health from harm.[52] However, Kinsey's findings were often a double-edged sword. The data showing that up to one-third of adult men had engaged in same-sex sexual behavior both exposed the absurdity of the strictly straight image of American culture while also bolstering attempts at curing deviations from the ostensible heterosexual norm. For some, this evidence for an epidemic of deviancy further justified efforts to clinically quell homosexuality.

American psychoanalysis soon found itself fighting a two-front war, one against the Kinsey normalizing project and another against a British variant of behavioral psychology.[53] As for the latter, British psychologist Hans Eysenck's experimental research purported to show that psychotherapeutic reorientation treatments were highly ineffective, barely performing above the base rate of doing nothing at all.[54] A homegrown strain of behavioral psychology also began to mount challenges to psychoanalysis, pitching itself as an empirically driven enterprise based in experimental methods and principles from the natural sciences such as biology and zoology.[55] Others like psychoanalytic apostate Aaron Beck infused behavioral psychology with findings from the cognitive revolution in neuroscience much to the same effect.[56] Throughout the 1960s, new professional institutions like the Association for the Advancement of Behavioral Therapies (AABT) formed to promulgate these therapeutic and theoretical alternatives to psychoanalysis.[57]

Far from egalitarians themselves, American behaviorists regularly pitched their reorientation therapies as scientifically sound substitutes for psychoanalytic ones. Whereas the psychoanalysts relied on self-report and analyst observations to measure an intervention's efficacy, the behaviorists used new physiological measurements to assess theirs.[58] Their instruments measured bodily arousal and blood flows to the genitals in order to determine whether patients had actually experienced true redirections of desire. Additionally, the behaviorists often depicted their therapeutic approach as more humane than psychoanalytic ones, which had come to be associated with barbaric shock therapy and induced vomiting treatments (despite the fact that many behaviorists used comparably painful techniques).[59] One of behavioral therapy's early evangelizers Gerald Davison pioneered the "orgasmic reorientation" method as a gentler version of conversion treatment.[60]

Feeling the barrage from the behaviorists and Kinsey-inspired reformers alike, New York Medical College professor of psychiatry Irving Bieber attempted to rejuvenate the embattled psychoanalytic reorientation paradigm with his 1962 *Homosexuality: A Psychoanalytic Study of Male Homosexuals*. In that work, Bieber accrued the analyst reports of 106 men who had undergone reparative therapy for their alleged "overt homosexuality" along with those from a control group of 100 heterosexual men. After nine years of sifting through patient reports, Bieber triumphantly announced that the study supported "a fundamental contribution of Rado on the subject of male homosexuality: A homosexual adaptation is a result of 'hidden but incapacitating fears of the opposite sex.'"[61] In a long conclusion, Bieber took aim at past and present challengers to his brand of psychoanalysis, including twins study pioneer Franz Kallmann, who had in the 1950s posited that genetic causes rather than environmentally induced adaptations may be the true culprit of the homosexual disposition.[62]

On the eve of what would become a multiyear struggle over the diagnostic criteria and therapeutic response to homosexuality that would span across numerous professional and medical associations, devotees of the pathology school continued their work with gusto. In 1965 psychiatrist and Bieber collaborator Cornelia Wilbur extended the lab's 1962 study to female homosexuality, finding that lesbianism was also the product of trauma, fear, and inadequately gender-normative parental figures.[63] The psychiatrist Charles Socarides, another close colleague of Bieber's, published his 1968 *The Overt Homosexual*, which continued to blame maternal influence for effeminate gay men.[64] Known for boasting his patient cure rate and his ferocious rebuke of sexual freedom, Socarides would come to make an ideal target for both the behaviorists as well as a rising socially conscious younger cohort of psychiatrists and analysts who had begun to bring New Left politics into the discipline.[65]

As challenges to the orthodoxy grew in volume and variety, pathology's pushers made an early rescue attempt by reclassifying homosexuality in the second edition of the *DSM*. In that 1968 update, homosexuality was relocated from a section on personality disorders to one on sexual deviations (among its new neighbors were pedophilia, fetishism, transvestitism, sadism, and masochism).[66] This was done in large part to deflect criticism that had emerged from psychologist Evelyn Hooker's research in the late 1950s uncovering no such evidence of psychopathology.[67] Whereas the 1952 edition reflected the ascendancy of psychodynamic theories within psychiatry, the 1968 update indexed the Freudians' slipping influence.

Not only was psychiatry embattled internally, but the psychoanalysts were beginning to cost the field precious federal funding, which the National Institute of Mental Health had constricted under the guise that much of psychodynamic psychiatry was unsound and unduly expensive. The real story has much more to do with deinstitutionalization (i.e., the end of asylums and other networks of publicly funded mental healthcare) as a broader social and fiscal phenomenon.[68] Despite the conniving of the *DSM-II* drafters to beat back those who had questioned the validity of psychodynamic interventions—both with regard to homosexuality specifically and therapeutic practice more broadly—the mental illness model's most ardent defenders were more unequipped than ever to reckon with the discontent that they would meet in a brewing war over homosexuality's classification and the future of mental healthcare. Wilbur, Socarides, and Bieber were positioned as poorly as any other cohort of those Thomas Kuhn termed "normal scientists" at the edge of a paradigm shift; the looming eclipse of their conversion treatments—no less than psychoanalysis as a whole—threatened their professional stature and their livelihoods.[69]

Declassified: The Politics of Reform

As psychiatry fissured over its Freudian legacy, both the homophiles and liberationists geared up to confront the mental health establishment. Just as the Mattachine Society and similar organizations had aligned with sympathetic researchers in its earlier civil rights battles, homophile leaders began collaborating with clinicians who sought to topple the mental illness model. In 1968 the Society for Individual Rights (SIR) sent a letter to the AMA requesting that it host an interdisciplinary panel discussion on homosexuality at its 1968 annual meeting. Rather than shun pathology's proponents, SIR asked for a session in which homophiles might communicate alongside "anthropologists, sociologists, psychologists, zoologists, and psychiatrists of the nonsickness, as well as the sickness school."[70] Similarly, members of the North American Conference of Homophile Organizations (NACHO) arrived at the 1968 AMA conference in San Francisco to challenge Socarides on his own turf.[71] Though unsuccessful in their initial attempts to speak alongside the conversion therapists themselves, NACHO continually demanded representation on future panels for its activists as well as a small yet influential reform cohort of psychologists and sexologists that included Hooker and several Kinsey Institute researchers.

Taking a different tack, the Gay Liberation Front persisted in drawing stark friend-enemy distinctions between themselves and the medical establishment. When the National Association for Mental Health issued a statement in 1970 advocating for decriminalization and therapeutic reform, the liberationists denounced the nonprofit for trespassing on their domain.[72] Decrying the report as measly "token liberalism," the GLF's Los Angeles chapter published a rejoinder that read:

WHO HAS GIVEN YOU THE RIGHT TO ESTABLISH THE DEFINITION OF OUR BEING? WHAT HOMOSEXUALS WERE CONSULTED CONCERNING THE VALIDITY OF YOUR POSITIONS? WHY WAS NO MENTION OF THE FEMALE

HOMOSEXUAL MADE? Homosexuals in America are at last standing up and demanding the right to define their own humanity. No longer will we stand by passively and allow you to tell us who we are.[73]

Other writings like the Chicago Gay Liberation Front's leaflets at the 1970 AMA conference posited that only "political organization and collective action" would bring about liberation and that, accordingly, all psychiatrists should "refer their homosexual patients to gay liberation." Echoing the radical psychiatrists, the GLF-Chicago explained, "Once relieved of patients whose guilt is not deserved but imposed, psychiatrists will be able to devote all their effort to the rich—who do earn their guilt but not their wealth, and can best afford to pay psychiatrists' fees."[74]

None of this precluded the liberationists from engaging medicine and mental health so long as they were the ones in charge. Unlike the homophiles who longed to sit beside and reason with their opponents on conference-sponsored panels, members of the GLF would redirect members of a disrupted meeting to form small discussion groups, which activists would then lead. At the 1970 Second Behavior Modification Conference, GLF members crashed a session on treatments to curb homosexual behavior, chanting things like "Medieval torture!"; "Barbarism!"; and "You're going to talk to us as you've never talked to homosexuals before—as equals!"[75] In the words of one GLF–Bay Area member at another protest, the sterile professional language and decorum "protected [clinicians] from emotional involvement" and allowed them to hide behind a "gibberishy vocabulary which translates humanity into 'scientifically' quantifiable and 'objective' terms."[76]

By the late 1960s, a few small groups of dissenters in psychiatry began planning quietly how to overtake the APA leadership. One such cabal of young liberal psychiatrists began meeting as the "Young Turks," which would soon formalize as the Committee for Concerned Psychiatry (CCP).[77] These New Left–inspired psychiatrists aimed to elect a slate of APA governing officials and instill a wide array of reforms (many of these concerned representation for women and racial minorities in the APA).[78] Among its targets was the mental illness model of homosexuality. At the same time, a group of discreet gay psychiatrists began meeting as the "GAYPA" with the intention of pushing the APA Committee on Nomenclature to scrub homosexuality from the *DSM*.[79]

After two years of attending the professional conference circuit in hopes of convening a public meeting, leaders of the Mattachine and SIR finally had some luck at the 1970 APA annual conference. There, SIR president Larry Littlejohn made inroads with the psychiatrist Kent Robinson, who agreed to facilitate a panel at the following year's meeting titled "Lifestyles of Non-Patient Homosexuals."[80] Making good on his promise—likely out of the fear that not doing so would lead to further protest activity and the cancellation of scheduled events—Robinson and the following year's conference organizers agreed to a number of panels at subsequent meetings.[81] These would place homophile leaders including Frank Kameny, Barbara Gittings, Del Martin, Lilli Vincenz, and Jack Baker in conversation with the reform-minded psychiatrist and future APA president Judd Marmor as well as the famed feminist psychiatrist Robert Seidenberg. That initial meeting in 1971 would spur an additional meeting at the 1972 conference.

The panel at the 1972 conference in Dallas—titled "Psychiatry: Friend or Foe to Homosexuals?"—was a forceful plea to the APA to reconsider its relationship to homosexual patients.[82] This time Gittings, Kameny, and Marmor were joined by psychiatrist and GAYPA member Dr. John Fryer, who hid behind the moniker "Dr. H. Anonymous" and cloaked himself in a Richard Nixon mask, oversize suit, and overcoat. Combining theatrics with a dead-serious panel presentation, Fryer introduced himself by declaring, "I am a homosexual. I am a psychiatrist," before imploring his colleagues to abandon the DSM's immoral and unscientific schema.[83]

The 1972 APA conference also witnessed the election of Marmor to vice president of the APA as well as the appointment of then-closeted psychiatrist John Patrick Spiegel to the board of trustees. Marmor's election was especially noteworthy as he had trained as a psychoanalyst only to become increasingly attracted to both behaviorist theories and those concerning the biological causes of homosexuality.[84] The APA victories would quickly compound. The following year, the CCP was successful in an unprecedented petition campaign to elect its handpicked candidate, Alfred Freedman, to the APA presidency.[85] In addition to being an all-around social-justice-oriented psychiatrist—among his reform projects were the creation of residency training programs for single parents and an opposition to the mental health field's complicity in death penalty proceedings—Freedman came out immediately against pathologizing homosexuality.

The spark that set reform into motion came from a covert hotel room meeting between gay rights advocates and high-ranking reform psychiatrist Robert Spitzer. Impressed by the newly formed Gay Activists Alliance's (GAA) organizing efforts and protests at the 1972 AABT conference, Spitzer sought their counsel for his work as the subcommittee chair on the APA's Committee on Nomenclature. Fortuitously, that committee had just been tasked with assessing the association's catalog of mental disorders. Spitzer met with members of GAYPA as well as GAA cofounder Ronald Gold, the latter of whom would give a speech at the 1973 APA conference titled "Stop It, You're Making Me Sick!" In an issue of that year's *American Journal of Psychiatry*, Spitzer and his fellow reformers published Gold's speech as part of a debate with Socarides and Bieber.[86] Shortly thereafter, Spitzer drafted a proposal to the nomenclature committee to evict homosexuality from its home among sexual disorders in the *DSM*.

Although Spitzer surely had sympathy for the plight of gays and lesbians, his eyes were trained on the larger goal of overhauling the entire *DSM*. While he had been instructed in the psychoanalytic tradition—he had even read Wilhelm Reich with an analyst mentor while in high school—Spitzer would become the architect of the 1980 *DSM-III*, an edition that barely resembled the old-school psychoanalytic nature of its previous two editions and that Spitzer declared as marking a "biological revolution."[87] In this sense, reforming the homosexuality diagnosis was merely sending in the shock troops. Spitzer's efforts would soon remake mental healthcare with reference to biomedicine's clearly defined disease categories and its psychometric scales and related forms of assessment. It would also gradually replace traditional psychotherapy with a slew of behavioral therapies that were briefer in duration (i.e., far cheaper for insurance companies and other payers) and pharmacological interventions that were far more profitable than talk therapy.[88]

In December 1973, newly inaugurated president Alfred Freedman and an APA Board of Trustees chock-full of reformist young bloods approved Spitzer's resolution on homosexuality with a 13–0 vote.[89] Within a month of the conference's end, the APA had put in place a process for the eventual elimination of the pathological diagnosis from the *DSM*. In its stead, Spitzer and others on the Council on Research and Development and Reference committees replaced the sexual deviation entry with a new, much more limited entry on "sexual orientation disturbance," which referred only to the subjective experience of distress with one's sexuality.[90]

Though Socarides and Bieber promptly sought a referendum vote on the APA Board of Trustees' 1973 decision, their counterstrike failed. Fifty-eight percent of 10,000 voting APA members favored retaining the changes to the *DSM*.[91] The following year, then AABT president Gerald Davison (alongside others like the openly gay graduate student Charles Silverstein) would put that organization on the path to reform.[92] In his convention address that year, Davison announced a total repudiation of his own conversion methods.[93] Others within organizations like the APA and the AABT would continue to research and advise conversion treatment, albeit with a narrower focus on "ego-dystonic homosexuality," which kept alive the notion that therapeutic intervention was appropriate for those experiencing unwanted or

otherwise personally deleterious same-sex desires.[94] In the interregnum between 1973 and the total eradication of homosexuality from the *DSM* in 1987,
those like Marmor would caution against conversion therapy for the very few
who found the experience of their same-sex desire to be unbearable.[95] Still,
prominent members—even presidents—of organizations like AABT including David Barlow and Steve Hayes would continue to conduct conversion
therapy research for homosexuals as well as "transsexuals."[96] Those who remained committed to the discredited deviance model would hunker down
in those institutions that still welcomed their perspective, first in organizations like the American Psychoanalytic Association—which would not adopt
an antidiscrimination policy until 1991—and then later in ex-gay groups positioned outside the boundaries of legitimate scientific inquiry and medical
treatment.[97]

After Classification: Enduring Alliances within the APA

The 1973 victory at the APA is a staple of American queer history for good
reason. It heralded a new era of reform within mental health, dealing a seis-
mic blow to pathology and the conversion therapy regime that had long gov-
erned the academic study and treatment of so-called aberrant sexualities.
The outcome of the war over nomenclature was a crucial redirect, a pivot
that aligned the interests of psychiatrists and psychologists with those of gay
rights advocates. In doing so, it ceded an unprecedented degree of authority
over the interpretation of sexuality to those who had been previously treated
as mere patients. Pathology was thus partially banished by a loose-knit group
that united insurgent behaviorists, disaffected psychoanalysts, young politically liberal psychiatrists, biomedical psychiatry's pioneers, and an assort-
ment of strategic gay rights activists.

   In all, the battle over the *DSM* created and nurtured long-lasting relationships between gay rights activists and mental health researchers and practitioners. Those like former GAA member and cofounder of the National
Gay Task Force, Bruce Voeller—himself a trained biologist—saw the coordinated activity at the APA as just the beginning of their joint efforts. Following the board of trustees' vote in late 1973, Voeller used his office as president
of the Task Force to propose a formal relationship with the psychiatric community that might have taken on state sodomy laws, military exclusion, and
the lack of national antidiscrimination laws.[98] Though the petition for an official channel was rejected by the APA, informal movement-academic relations
developed with alacrity. In subsequent years, the Task Force would accumu-
late new allies as the American Psychological Association and the American

Public Health Association came to oppose the pathological thesis, which in turn spurred coordinated actions for reform in government agencies including the US Public Health Service.[99]

Reading through APA discussions that spawned these emergent alliances, one might get the impression that homosexuality's declassification as a disorder shared some inheritance with the gay liberationists' longing to nix the term entirely. In the words of the reform psychiatrist Robert Stoller: "There *is* homosexual behavior; it is varied. There is no such *thing* as homosexuality. In that sense it should be removed from the nomenclature."[100] Despite the surface-level similarity between this kind of statement on disaggregating categories of deviant desire and Altman's "the end of the homosexual," the relationships forged throughout the APA fight would soon bring evolutionary theories and biomedical technologies to bear on the nature and origins of homosexuality as a thing in itself. Far from escorting out the traditional taxonomic thinking that demarcated a homosexual minority and a heterosexual norm, the next generation of researchers would reconstruct that binary with premises and evidence from the fields of genetics, endocrinology, and neuroscience. With the swift dissolution of the largest gay liberation groups and the rise of nonprofit liberal gay rights organizations, this reassertion of the sexual binary—imbued with biological substance—would soon take shape.

3

"Why Is My Child Gay?":
The Liberal Foundations of Born This Way

"Why is my child gay?" asked a popular piece of advocacy literature from the 1980s. By the late twentieth century, gay and lesbian civil rights campaigners could posit this question without fear of reproach for what *they* had ostensibly done to instill such a disposition in the youths under their care. They could reach into a bag of studies and sound bites by child psychologists, psychiatrists, sociologists, endocrinologists, geneticists, and neuroscientists, all of whom could verify that, in fact, no one was to blame. The overbearing mother, the effeminate father, the predaceous schoolteacher—these and other suspected sources of contagion were at long last being exonerated. A new consensus across these disparate fields came to downplay theories based in social and environmental causes, trading them for hypotheses about the fixed biological nature of homosexuality. In the course of this change, the whole concept of "blame" itself was cast as a misnomer. Steadily, the verdict on homosexuality's nature and origins moved from the Oedipal to the germ line.

This chapter details how transformations in civil rights politics, scientific funding streams, and the American economy made this possible. As for the gay and lesbian rights social movement, assimilation was the name of the game. The election-oriented Gay Rights National Lobby, the policy-focused National Gay Task Force, and the litigation-centric Lambda Legal were representative of a larger turn in American civic life away from federated mass membership organizations and toward the more donor-dependent professional advocacy firms and nonprofits that characterize interest-group politics today.[1] Gradually, the gay rights movement evolved from cramped basement meetings and being hamstrung by an austere volunteer-based staff into sleek, professional, and politically connected campaign operations.

Along with this change in structure, gay and lesbian interest groups morphed ideologically. Picking up where their homophile ancestors left off, these new organizations refined the notion that gays and lesbians were just one minority group among many others seeking to integrate into a pluralist America. Unlike their liberationist counterparts, these liberal civil-rights-oriented organizations stressed a stark division between queer and straight. Those like the family-support group Parents of Gays pioneered a new emphasis on family values—that is, a promise that queer couples could raise well-adjusted children in white picket-fenced suburban houses just the same as anyone else. Downplaying talk of sexuality itself (too lewd and threating), activists opted for a tamer logic of deeply rooted orientation.

By sanitizing their sexualities, gay rights advocates combated the rise of the religious right. This assemblage of Evangelical ministers like Jerry Falwell of the Moral Majority, former celebrities turned culture warriors like Anita Bryant, and free-market libertarian idealogues like Paul Weyrich and Joseph Coors sought to scapegoat gays and lesbians en route to their larger political aims.[2] In a striking parallel to the contemporary Republican Party's ongoing campaign against queer and queer-friendly teachers ("child groomers") and gender identity clinicians and sympathetic parents ("child abusers"), the religious right leveraged theories that continued to place blame on parents and other role models for children's adoption of the "wrong" type of gendered affect or sexual desire.[3]

Just as the social movement groups began to professionalize, discoveries in the natural sciences and transformations in the political economy of scientific funding generated fresh possibilities for the study of behavior and identity. Novel RNA and hormonal technologies, massive capital investments in biotechnologies, and an increase in federal funding for such work incentivized researchers to explore the biological nature of human difference. These developments had an immense impact on scientists and clinicians who had been studying sexuality for decades, including the gay rights movement's allies in the American Psychiatric Association (APA) and the Kinsey Institute. Many in the cognitive sciences and mental health fields were eager to trade in the discredited psychoanalytic theories that linked homosexuality to a child's upbringing environment. Newcomers in fields like sociobiology, behavioral genetics, and neuroendocrinology were also quick to pose questions about where same-sex desire might reside in the brain, blood, or genetic code. Though more nuanced thinkers cautioned against a vulgar "nature over nurture" mindset, this new paradigm's proponents and its pop science cheerleaders came to associate biology with fate.[4]

Thus, an arsenal of biological firepower fell into the hands of the gay and lesbian rights movement just at the moment it was seeking a new story for sexual identity. The following traces how both interest-group leaders and university researchers navigated these changes in political economy, gender norms, and biotechnologies. In doing so, the chapter reveals how these intertwined developments in science and civil rights heralded the born this way era to come.

Pluralist Politics and the Love of Expertise

Formed in 1973 out of remnant parts of the short-lived Gay Activists Alliance (GAA) and the last standing homophile organizations, the National Gay Task Force quickly became one of the preeminent gay and lesbian interest groups. Having grown weary of what they took to be gay liberation's inefficacies and its bloated political agenda, this group of GAA defectors and homophile veterans founded the Task Force as a national single-issue gay rights organization. Instead of targeting abstractions like "capitalism" and "patriarchy," theirs was a narrower and concrete program aimed at discrimination in housing, employment, and public accommodations.[5] Its founders traded the chaotic leaderless style that defined horizontalist organizations like the Gay Liberation Front for a centralized donor-driven operation that was worried more about its integration into the Democratic Party than it was about converting the capitalist soul of America.[6]

Among the Task Force's founding members were an all-star cast of former Mattachine Society leaders and the most pragmatic, policy-minded former GLF members. Those like Frank Kameny of the Mattachine Society of Washington, DC, and Barbara Gittings of the Daughters of Bilitis brought with them a combined thirty years' worth of experience in organizing and litigation. Most of the other original members—among them, Bruce Voeller, Ronald Gold, Jean O'Leary, Nathalie Rockhill, Arthur Bell, and Martin Duberman—had cut their teeth in the post-Stonewall years and in leadership positions of the GAA and Lesbian Feminist Liberation. Similar to Kameny and Gittings, this younger cohort of ex-radicals had spent their early organizing years in legislative politics, urging both New York City councilpersons and President Jimmy Carter to pass antidiscrimination statutes. Lastly, at the helm of the Task Force's board of directors sat physician and former New York City Health Services administrator Dr. Howard Brown, who had made history in coming out while serving in that municipal post.[7]

In a 1974 speech commemorating his youthful days in the GAA and imploring the group's current members to move beyond their own political adolescence, Ronald Gold presented the Task Force's perspective as the cure for the malady of "ideological purity."[8] Gold advocated for a civil rights politics

that would eschew issues of structural sexism, capitalist exploitation, and im-
perialist violence. This new liberal style would address the more immediate concerns of ordinary gays and lesbians who often found themselves fired
from work or evicted from their homes.

Like any good organizer, Gold sought to persuade his audience by finding some common ground. He assured them that "[along with] some of our
radical theorists, I am opposed to capitalism, racism and war, and I do see our
movement as part of a broad cultural revolution." However noble these projects were, Gold remarked, they could not feasibly be cohered into a singular
formidable movement. He beseeched his fellow activists to "accept the idea
that, if we aren't going to expend our energies by flagellating each other like a
pack of Trotskyites, gay liberation can mean moving together, gradually, in different personal directions." A gay political movement needed to be a home for
those ranging from "the radical theorist" to the "Minnesota Democratic Party
worker," even the "activist capitalist in San Francisco," who might fight together for the right to live whatever sexual or romantic life they might desire.[9]

Writing in an early issue of the Task Force's newsletter, the organization's
first president Bruce Voeller echoed the call for a pluralist touch, a queer politics sans a concern for class. Like Gold, Voeller praised "the largely coun-
terculture left who had been so effective in beginning our movement—that
group of people who dared to act and show the rest of us it worked." The time
had come, however, to transcend "blue denim elitism" and to welcome "the
many talented people with skill in public relations, law, media, legislation,
[and] fund raising . . . militant activists and more conservative" ones alike.[10]

In crafting its message, the Task Force swiftly put into service its APA and
Kinsey Institute allies. Throughout most of 1977, Voeller—who happened to
hold a PhD in biology—and Gold corresponded with Kinsey Institute director Paul Gebhard about the exact number of homosexuals living in the United
States.[11] Gebhard had been in the process of reworking the tabulations upon
which the original Kinsey volumes had relied, and the Task Force wanted to
ensure that its campaign literature reflected the most up-to-date figures. Having abandoned the "polymorphous perverse" notion that freedom from repression would open everyone to same-sex desires, these gay liberation apostates were keen on finding a static figure to advertise as the natural rate of
homosexuality in a population.

The Task Force also put their Kinsey connections to work in its antidiscrimination campaigns. In a joint effort with the ACLU and the National Organization for Women (NOW), the Task Force sought to shift the national conversation on sex abuse and predators away from homosexual men by demonstrating
that heterosexual male family members were responsible for the majority of

abuse.[12] In a letter responding to Voeller's request for help in combating the predator myth, Gebhard advised that the Task Force mention that no study has ever demonstrated a relationship between adult homosexuality and pedophilia, and that gay adults do not affect the sexualities of children who admire them as role models or authority figures.[13] Gebhard wrote, "The major causes of homosexuality are still being investigated, but we presently are in a position to say that role modelling with adults and seduction of children by adults are not among them."[14] Together, Gebhard's demographic figures and studies on child abuse bolstered the Task Force's liberal pluralist plan for reform.

Families without Influence

Founded in 1973, Parents of Gays (POG)—the progenitor of today's PFLAG—was established by the parents of gay liberation activist Morty Manford as an educational and equal rights advocacy resource for parents who wished to understand and support their gay and lesbian children. From the moment that Morty came out, Jeanne Manford and her husband had accepted their son's sexuality and his work in the GAA. But after Morty suffered a brutal beating at a protest, the Manfords saw an urgent need for straight society to take action. In a demand for parents to follow their children out of the closet, an early POG newsletter read: "IF THERE ARE MORE THAN 100,000 GAYS AND LESBIANS IN NEW YORK CITY—THERE SHOULD ALSO BE MORE THAN 200,000 PARENTS WHO HAVE 'COME OUT.'"[15] In 1982 Adele Starr, founder of the Los Angeles chapter, rechristened the organization as Parents and Friends of Lesbians and Gays (PFLAG) and incorporated its twenty chapters across the country as a nonprofit charitable organization.[16]

PFLAG inaugurated a new family-centric model of gay politics, one that was built both organizationally and ideologically around the family as a normative ideal. PFLAG leaders endeavored to reconcile homosexual identity with the nuclear family, that cherished private realm of intimacy, mutual support, and—in most instances—biology. Going against the grain of at least half a century of recurring sex panics, PFLAG insisted that the family was safe from perversion and that a family could keep its gay and lesbian loved ones in the fold without fear of soiling the clan. This contention that queer desire and family values could be made congruent served as a bulwark against the budding religious right's argument to the contrary.[17] In this vein, historian Heather Murray has described PFLAG as "activists [who] affirmed not only that they were simply loving parents but also that they were, in fact, socially conservative: their heterosexuality, marriages, and families were intact, and they were not particularly left-leaning or sympathetic to radicalism."[18]

While it may not be obvious what sinew united the donor-backed lobbying operations like the National Gay Task Force and PFLAG's family-support model, both were adaptations to major shifts in political economy and social relations. During this period, a bipartisan reemphasis on the family and the sacred place of the private sphere accompanied the advent of the postindustrial American economy.[19] A medley of neoliberal and neoconservative policymakers, united by their opposition to social welfare policies like Aid to Dependent Children, began sounding the alarm over what these social policies had wrought on traditional values and ways of life.[20] As evidence, they pointed frantically to single-mother households and rising divorce rates as an omen of the traditional family's impending total collapse. In a clever effort to undermine both welfare programs for single mothers and Keynesian fiscal policy that encouraged federal spending, the New Deal order was blamed for having wreaked a corroding influence on familial relations.

Though motivated in large part by class interests (industry leaders in banking, manufacturing, energy, and many other sectors had for decades sought to roll back the interventionist state), the uproar over the nuclear family's future was based in reality. This renewed national obsession with the family and its associated anxious defenses of heterosexuality were interwoven with—and were in many ways a *reaction to*—the destabilizing social ramifications of post-Fordism (that is, the decline of industrial manufacturing in the United States and the accompanied loss of the single-income, male-breadwinner household).[21] In other words, the brief moment when the male head of household who brought home the family wage to his wife and two kids was on its historical way out—and in a hurry. However, this had less to do with the welfare state alone and much more to do with broader changes in American industry and employment such as who could work (increasingly women as well as men) and under what conditions and for what wage (increasingly non-union and for less than one individual might hope to support a family).[22] In the face of these disruptions to the Fordist era status quo, this loose-knit coalition of reactionary forces attempted to nail it all back down in a hurry with cultural interventions like reduced welfare spending and anti-queer-family values campaigns.[23]

Having emerged in the midst of this embattled fight, PFLAG's ideology embodied a mixture of normative attachment to the family, a celebration of individual responsibility, and a denigration of welfare and government spending. The organization's early newsletters stressed equality of opportunity in statements like "the time is ripe to join together to appeal to the public conscience in order to achieve equal opportunities for our daughters and sons."[24] In a display of its suspicions of the social welfare state, PFLAG representative

Jean Smith wrote in a 1977 letter to *Newsweek*: "Depriving homosexuals of their civil rights is not only unconstitutional and inhumane but it means we will be adding twenty million homosexuals to our overburdened welfare rolls if we do not permit them to be productive individuals."[25] The middle-class concern with what Barbara Ehrenreich famously termed the "fear of falling" rings loudly here.[26] In an era defined by increasing competition and disappearing social safety nets, PFLAG members offered a bargain: suspend the societal rules against homosexual children in the heterosexual home, and we will assimilate seamlessly into the order of things.

In its blend of liberal tolerance and a traditionalist attitude toward family life, PFLAG differed in considerable ways from the homophile activism of the 1950s and 1960s as well as the gay liberation critics of "liberal paternalism" and "patriarchal institutions." While the early homophiles are often portrayed as quite cautious not to appear as lewd deviants, it is striking how much *more* they emphasized sexual behavior in comparison to PFLAG.[27] The homophile movement worked primarily on issues like police brutality in the bar scene and entrapment schemes in which cops poached those cruising for sex in public spaces.[28] Even the relatively conservative Society for Individual Rights called for the decriminalization of sodomy and all other sex laws (of course, with the exclusion of those protecting minors).[29] The homophiles focused so intensely on defending their male members against sex-based criminal charges that the lesbians in their ranks criticized what felt like a disproportionate attention to what were construed as gay men's issues.[30]

In contrast, PFLAG exercised strict message discipline as it fought back discriminatory measures with an unremitting appeal to family values. In the late 1970s, there were plenty of good reasons to do so. A conservative backlash against the movement's few early antidiscrimination legislative victories had spawned fearmongering about the need to protect defenseless schoolchildren from predatory gay schoolteachers. California state senator John Briggs justified his proposed discriminatory prohibitions on public employment by asserting that "one of the most fundamental interests of the State is the establishment and preservation of the family unit."[31] As PFLAG and the National Gay Task Force leaders prepared canvassers to go to war with Briggs and his celebrity supporters like Miss Oklahoma pageant star-turned-spokesperson for the religious right Anita Bryant, they encouraged door knockers to "be proud that you are good and loving parents . . . assure people that homosexuality is not a threat to the family unit."[32]

Ever so cautious in its rhetoric, PFLAG advocates swept aside references to sexual acts themselves, particularly when discussing child sexuality. The gay or lesbian child was often depicted as essentially asexual in that their

desire was conceived in terms of a deeply rooted selfhood rather than a specific sexual penchant or behavior. When spokespersons did resort to speaking about child sexuality in more explicit terms, they tended to make sharp
normative distinctions between those youths who deserved compassion and
those who undermined the fight for equality through their transgressions.
In a letter to journalist Dan Rather responding to a CBS News broadcast on
young gay men and prostitution, Florida chapter leader Jean Smith argued
that the latter were an unrepresentative group who engaged in the practice
"for fast, easy money."[33] Smith likely felt the pressure to combat the propaganda of those like Bryant's Save Our Children, which was just then lobbying
Dade County voters to repeal a newly passed antidiscrimination ordinance.
In what was an ultimately successful repeal effort, that campaign portrayed
queer children as degenerates, sullied by their encounters with unleashed
adult sex pests and then set loose onto the streets of suburban America. As
Smith downplayed the idea that young gays and lesbians might turn to sex
work after being evicted from their family homes (a common occurrence),
she maintained a strict separation between innocuous, well-behaved gay children and those she lambasted as "the few who discredit all homosexuals."[34]

    Though PFLAG's trepidations are not likely to strike most modern read-
ers as out of the ordinary, its rhetoric clashed with liberationist-inspired advocates who had backed youth legal rights to sexual autonomy. This latter
group had been inspired by Carl Wittman's influential "A Gay Manifesto,"
which included lines such as "Kids can take care of themselves, and are sexual
beings way earlier than we'd like to admit. . . . Those of us who began cruising in early adolescence know this, and we were doing the cruising, not being
debauched by dirty old men."[35] At the 1970 National Student Gay Liberation
Conference in San Francisco, delegates from a San Diego–based group stirred
controversy in calling for the abolition of laws that regulated adult sexual behavior without addressing youth-based ones. Dissenters drowned out the San
Diego contingent with rancorous cries that non-adults ought to be afforded
sexual autonomy as well.[36] In 1979 at a national gay rights conference in Washington, DC, the Gay Youth Caucus petitioned to revise age-of-consent laws
across the country as a means of enervating police power more generally.[37]

    At the most extreme end of this debate was the infamous pro-pederasty
group, the North American Man/Boy Love Association (NAMBLA). The organization's cofounder David Thorstad argued that the spirit of the "Stonewall generation" was one of "pleasure-affirming impulses" and that its message was that "sex is fun, homosexuality is fun, boy-love is fun, gay liberation
is a movement for everyone's sexual liberation."[38] While NAMBLA became
the subject of both police scrutiny and marginalization within gay rights cir-

cles almost immediately upon its inception, its founders were active in the GAA and held forums through that group to discuss the nuances of youth sexuality and the law.[39] As gay activism became more disconnected from these proponents of pederasty, Thorstad criticized PFLAG leaders specifically for what he believed was an undue defensive posture in response to those like Bryant and Briggs. By the late 1970s and the rise of the new gay rights movement, Thorstad lamented that activists had ceased "fighting to liberate youth [and instead] it became fashionable to argue that youth needed protection, especially from sex with men."[40]

Though PFLAG and the National Gay Task Force both might be fairly described as less concerned with dismantling sexual taboo than their gay liberation counterparts, much is missed in branding their politics as wholly defensive in nature. Rather, these early years demonstrate just how quickly this new breed of interest-group activism grew its ranks, allies, and political presence. Unburdened by the most unpopular demands of their forebearers and equipped with more money and resources than the Gay Liberation Front could have ever imagined, single-issue gay and lesbian rights groups took the pulse of the national mood and planned accordingly. As they became progressively more adept at this work, they discovered just how effective framing their appeals in biology could be.

To Essence from Environment: The Biological Turn in the Study of Sexuality

In the decade leading up to the 1973 APA reform, the pathological model and its concern with homosexuality's environmentally induced causes was gradually displaced by theories that entertained a multiplicity of causes—some of which were biological. Shortly after the 1973 declassification of homosexuality in the *DSM*, the search for biological determinants came to dominate mental health research and sexology more broadly as scientists considered the role of hormonal, genetic, and neuroanatomical factors. As the previous two chapters have delineated, this was in no small part the doing of gay rights advocates and mental health reformers who together toppled the APA's conservative leadership. However, that explanation begs the question: Where did all the funding and fervor for a biological narrative come from in the first place?

This turn to biology was in some ways a return to monocausal theories of human difference. These conceptions of homosexuality were commonplace throughout the late nineteenth and the early twentieth centuries as intellectuals and policymakers enamored with social hygiene programs and the promise of eugenics constructed taxonomies of sexual difference and gender nonconformity.[41] For a short interregnum following World War II and the horrific realization of where the taxonomic train could lead, the most intensely biodeterministic theories receded from view. But after a brief respite, psychiatry and psychology began to readopt monocausal explanations for traits including schizophrenia, sexuality, and many others.[42] These theories were driven by discoveries like DNA's double-helix form, neurohormones and receptors that linked the endocrine system to brain development, and complex chromosomal processes of sex determination.[43]

The return to a biological zeitgeist was in many ways just as political as was its momentary absence. The technological developments and capital investments that made this research possible were downstream from broader developments in the life sciences and their new place in a rapidly evolving US political economy. By the 1970s, reduced opportunities for investment in domestic manufacturing had begun to drive private investors and the state to expand into and exploit the life sciences.[44] During this period, new technologies like hormone assay techniques and recombinant DNA were developed to cut and splice gene fragments for both academic study and industrial use.[45] The National Institutes of Health and the National Science Foundation funding incentives encouraged social scientists to take up such ventures while the legislative and legal loosening of patent law and copyright regulations made such investments attractive to finance.[46] Laws like the Bayh-Dole Act of 1980 and the Technology Transfer Act of 1986 and a landmark Supreme Court decision in 1980 allowing patents for genetically modified organisms enabled private companies to reap returns by partnering with state-funded university researchers.[47] A promise was made to investors and the public alike: with the proper funding and financing, we could soon learn humankind's inner workings and the mysteries of our desires.

This neoliberal turn in the political economy of the life sciences coincided with the liberal turn in gay and lesbian interest-group politics in ways that were mutually reinforcing. At the nexus sat those reformist scientists and clinicians instrumental in reforming the APA. One of the most influential allies that advocates had made throughout the fight to demedicalize homosexuality was psychiatrist and physician Judd Marmor. Marmor stands out as one of the most high-ranking APA figures—he served as vice president and then president of the APA during and after the fight over homosexuality's classification—to be directly involved in pushing biological premises into mainstream psychological research. In reflecting back upon his own role in that battle, Marmor remarked that although he had helped move the APA in a more progressive direction that benefited the gay rights movement, it was the neo-Freudians and their family-based accounts of homosexuality that were actually unscientific and excessively political.[48]

An early skeptic of the pathological model, Marmor brought together a wide range of researchers and clinicians to wrestle with the question of etiology in his 1965 edited volume, *Sexual Inversion: The Multiple Roots of Homosexuality*.[49] That book featured eighteen accounts by scholars including Evelyn Hooker and other Kinsey reformist types as well as proponents of the mental illness thesis like psychoanalyst Irving Bieber. In his introduction to the eclectic collection, Marmor presented his multiple-causes thesis, which held that sexologists and therapists "are probably dealing with a condition that is not only multiply determined by psychodynamic, sociocultural, biological, and situational factors but also reflects the significance of subtle temporal, qualitative, and quantitative variables."[50]

In a section titled "The Question of the Biological Factor," Marmor reviewed studies by geneticists such as twin-studies popularizer and schizophrenia researcher, Franz Kallmann.[51] In 1952 Kallmann had conducted a twins study in which he solicited pairs of monozygotic (identical) and dizygotic (fraternal) twin pairs in addition to pairs of non-twin brothers and adoptive brothers to observe how many of the pairs contained two gay men. The assumption that undergirds this measure is that the monozygotic pairs (i.e., those with presumably identical genomes) will exhibit the highest concordance rate (i.e., proportion of pairs that share the observed trait) if there is a probable genetic basis to the pertinent trait.[52] Upon finding that his monozygotic twin pairs expressed full concordance for the measure of "overt homosexual behavior," Kallmann observed that psychodynamic theories likely "over-stress the importance of such precipitating or perpetuating factors as social ostracism, incompetence of a particular parent, or other potentially traumatizing experiences arising from the effect of uncontrolled imperfections in the structure of modern human societies" and, therefore, underplayed untapped biological explanations.[53] While Marmor ultimately found Kallmann's and similar studies to be lacking in methodological rigor—more pointedly, he suspected that Kallmann suffered from an "unconscious bias" and that his reputation for being a hard-line proponent of genetic determinism made his "scientific objectivity . . . open to question"—he did believe that evidence of a "chromosomal abnormality" might eventually be discovered as a determinant of homosexuality.[54]

In a second edited volume on sexuality published in 1980, Marmor reaffirmed the multiple-causes thesis. His preface began with a statement of faith: "It is my firm conviction that the complex issues surrounding the phenomenon of same-sex object-choice cannot be understood in terms of any unitary cause whether it be biological, psychological, or sociological." However, by this period Marmor appeared much more amenable to considering biological factors than he had been fifteen years prior. In reviewing the latest biological research, Marmor saw a "strong possibility that predisposing factors in at least some obligatory homosexuals may be due to intrauterine or early postnatal influence."[55]

Though Marmor was convinced that homosexuality's roots were at least somewhat biological in nature—in an interview conducted in 2002, the year before his death, he had come fully around to the biological account, stating: "We now know that, to a great extent, variations in sexual orientation are determined by the degree of androgenization of the fetal midbrain at a critical period of intrauterine development"—he was not himself a full-blown biodeterminist during this period.[56] In a 1985 editorial for the *Harvard Medical School Mental Health Letter*, he refused to even consider homosexuality as a "unitary phenomenon or singular 'condition,'" arguing that "different people with this [same-sex] sexual preference have different psychodynamic make-ups, different behavior patterns, and different life experiences."[57] Marmor did, however, open the door to increasingly biodeterministic conceptions of homosexuality by amplifying the voices of those pursuing this agenda, as well as by downplaying the theories of conservatives who sought to keep homosexuality situated in family dynamics. In that very same editorial, for instance, Marmor posited that the hypothalamic centers of the male brain might be a determinative factor in male homosexuality.[58]

Marmor was not the only psychodynamic-trained researcher to begin entertaining biological theories. Psychoanalyst Richard C. Friedman's 1988 *Male Homosexuality* was a landmark text that attempted to replace conservative neo-Freudianism with an updated biopsychosocial perspective. Though explicitly anti-deterministic in his outlook, Friedman implored his colleagues to consider how neuroendocrinological and genetic factors mixed with social ones.[59] That following year, former program chair for the American Psychoanalytic Association Richard Isay invoked biological research to discredit conversion therapy. In his 1989 book *Being Homosexual*, Isay encouraged analysts to help their gay analysands reckon with the psychic pain they endured in a homophobic society.[60] As Friedman's and Isay's works gained traction, the more orthodox psychoanalyst Charles Socarides would update his own work to explicitly counter the biological thesis (though to diminishing returns).[61]

Back at the Kinsey headquarters in Indiana, researchers were hard at work on the institute's long-awaited third installment on American sex life. In 1981 psychotherapist Alan P. Bell and sociologists Martin S. Weinberg and Sue

Kiefer Hammersmith published this work under the title *Sexual Preference: Its Development in Men and Women*.[62] Unlike the previous Kinsey studies that were more descriptive in nature, these researchers set out to test hypotheses, ranging from Bieber's family background thesis to a series of novel biologically informed ones. In a press release for *Sexual Preference*, the researchers touted that "parents have little influence on whether their children develop a homosexual orientation."[63] Bell, Weinberg, and Hammersmith explained to parents: "You may supply your sons with footballs and your daughters with dolls, but no one can guarantee that they will enjoy them." While this framing demonstrates that most researchers in the 1980s had not yet separated questions of gender identity and normativity from sexuality proper, they did exonerate parents from their conjectured roles in a child's sexuality. Most strikingly, the Kinsey team reached for genetic and hormonal explanations, stating that "homosexuality may arise from a biological precursor (such as left-handedness and allergies, for example) that parents cannot control."[64] Though they did not collect any original biological data of their own (the study was based mainly on interviews from the 1960s and 1970s), the researchers were emphatic in their denunciation of older psychoanalytic accounts and their belief that evidence of specific biological mechanisms was on the horizon.[65]

The results precipitated a mix of media intrigue, old-guard skepticism, and liberationist discontent. The press played its own part in hyping the biological speculations. In its coverage, the *San Francisco Chronicle* announced that the Kinsey team had discovered that "sexual preference is most likely the result of a deep-seated predisposition, probably biological in nature."[66] Lamenting the Kinsey Institute's turn to biology, C. A. Tripp, a former Kinsey-affiliated scholar who had worked closely with the Mattachine Society through the 1960s, saw *Sexual Preference* as an overcorrection, one that was too quick to toss nearly all psychological and social learning hypotheses, leaving only biological ones.[67] In a recognition of the study's controversial content, *Sexual Preference* coauthor Bell noted, "I expect the study to be condemned from both sides, by the radical gays for even looking into the subject and by the analysts who may say we're trying to paint a glowing picture of homosexuality . . . [b]ut we reported what people say, and it's all very consistent."[68]

As researchers in psychology and psychiatry were fast becoming receptive to biological causation, a new cohort of endocrinologists and neuroscientists began investigating the effect that hormones and brain development might have on sexuality's directionality. The notion that endocrine glands might regulate gender expression and sexual preference extends back to at least the late 1920s.[69] However, feuds between psychoanalysts and endocrinologists kept the two fields distant from one another for decades.[70] That began to change with Günter Dörner's 1976 *Hormones and Brain Differentiation*.[71] Based on results from experiments on castrated mice, Dörner posited that homosexual men had lower levels of testosterone and higher levels of estrogen than heterosexual men. As was common in endocrinology, Dörner's work did not distinguish gender nonconformity from homosexuality, but instead hypothesized a shared etiology tied up in sex hormones that regulated an individual's physiology and psychology. That theory itself was taken up quickly by those like Bell, Weinberg, and Hammersmith, who cited the Dörner study in *Sexual Preference*.[72]

In 1984 a research team led by psychoendocrinologist Brian Gladue and psychiatrists Richard Green and Ronald Hellman (notably, veterans of the 1973 APA fight) sought to put Dörner's sex-hormone hypothesis to a more rigorous test. Their study involved administrating Premarin—a strong dose of estrogen used to treat menopause and uterine bleeding—to self-identified homosexual and heterosexual men. They hypothesized that because Premarin caused women's luteinizing hormone (LM) levels to drop initially and then rise to double their baseline, homosexual men's baseline levels would rise as well. Endocrinology's focus on sex hormones led to an assumption that homosexual men were essentially a hybrid species between gender-normative heterosexual men and women. The results showed that although none of the seventeen heterosexual men experienced a rise in their LM baseline, nine out of fourteen of the homosexual men experienced a rise of about 35 percent, thus leading the researchers to conclude that hormonal factors had a causal impact on sexual orientation.[73] Upon this study's publication, Task Force executive director Virginia Apuzzo issued a statement on the study's political implications:

> Gay men and lesbians have maintained that sexual orientation is not a "choice," as it is often charged by those campaigning against lesbian and gay rights. If the SUNY [referring here to Gladue's university affiliation] study is valid, it would appear to support what we have said all along. And it would be yet another indication of the need for legislative and executive action to ensure protection against discrimination. If being gay or lesbian is biologically determined, then gay men and lesbians clearly deserve the same civil rights guarantees afforded people on the basis of skin color, gender, or age.[74]

Though the Task Force was keen on using the study to naturalize male sexual identity in a binaristic fashion (e.g., one is either straight or gay), Gladue, Green, and Hellman surmised that sexual orientation was more complicated. They were transparent about the fact that the study's sample included only "lifelong homosexuals." Citing the original Kinsey spectrum, which places individuals on a six-point scale ranging from exclusive heterosexuality to exclusive homosexuality, they suggested that less-than-exclusive homosexual men might respond differently to their treatment effects, and thus "whether a differential neuroendocrine response is present in men of less exclusive homosexual orientation is an open question."[75] For Gladue, Green, and Hellman, not every node of sexual orientation could be described by this *particular* study; however, it was possible that other biological mechanisms might.[76]

As new subdisciplines like sociobiology and behavioral genetics took shape, pioneers in these incipient paradigms applied their techniques to human sexuality.[77] In the late 1970s, the entomologist E. O. Wilson traded his interest in insects for the grandiose project of outlining an evolutionary theory for all of human culture and society.[78] As a progenitor of evolutionary psychology, the sociobiology school posits that common traits and behaviors in contemporary human life extend from deeper universal dispositions that formed long ago in the evolution of *Homo sapiens*. For example, traits like altruism or out-group animosity are assumed to possess some adaptive quality that can be traced back to their origins in hunter-gatherer societies.[79] In his 1975 *Sociobiology: The New Synthesis*, Wilson immediately applied his theory to homosexuality. In assessing previously published studies of macaques, Wilson observed that "pseudo-copulation rituals" among male members were not merely linked to pleasure-seeking activity; rather they functioned as an expression and maintenance of a complex hierarchical system.[80] Certain species of fish also had spawning patterns that could be rendered as a "transvestitism evolved to serve heterosexuality."[81] These and other queer oddities of the animal kingdom proved to Wilson that homosexuality owed its origins to some evolutionary adaptation. The idea has had a long shelf life as evinced by the persistent cultural fascination with rams, penguins, and other animals that engage in same-sex activity and parentage arrangements.[82]

It is not hard to see why Wilson's theory was attractive to gay rights supporters. His analyses of animal behavior and his later look into human sexuality freed gays and lesbians from accusations of corruption. To the contrary, Wilson posited, same-sex desire played a constitutive role in the very creation of human civilization. In an updated 1978 version of his grand theory, Wilson stated his homosexuality hypothesis more starkly than many of his contemporaries, writing: "The predisposition to be a homophile could have a genetic basis, and the genes might have spread in the early hunter-gatherer societies because of the advantage they conveyed to those who carried them."[83] He reasoned that while early homosexual men would not have passed on their genetic material through reproduction themselves, they might have "taken the roles of seers, shamans, artists, and keepers of tribal knowledge" that enabled their immediate relatives to survive and reproduce at higher rates and, thus, pass on these "gay genes."[84]

Sociobiologists were soon accompanied by the blossoming field of behavioral genetics, a loose interdisciplinary assemblage of geneticists, biologists, and psychologists. As historian of science Aaron Panofsky has recounted, the field owes its origins to geneticists who sought to reestablish ties with social scientists that had frayed in previous decades. Behavioral geneticists were best known for their bold bioreductive claims and the twin and sibling studies that they used to back them up. As they spread the gospel of their genetic methodology, they attacked those who harbored suspicions of bioreductivism as unscientific romanticists and reactionaries.[85] Though those like Wilson had only lukewarmly endorsed twin-study methodology as a limited means of assessing evolutionary claims—in 1978 Wilson had critiqued a twin study on homosexuality for "suffer[ing] from the usual defects that render twin analyses less than conclusive"—behavioral geneticists were enormously successful in establishing state-of-the-art twins databases and propagating their theories and techniques throughout the social sciences.[86] In fact, Wilson's own student James Weinrich came to publish an influential heritability study of homosexual and heterosexual brothers with his coauthor Richard Pillard, the first openly gay psychiatrist in the United States. For that 1986 paper, Pillard and Weinrich recruited a sample of fifty-one primarily homosexual men and fifty heterosexual men and demonstrated that the homosexual subjects were four times as likely to have a gay sibling compared to the heterosexual ones.[87] In a few short years, many more behavioral geneticists would confirm Pillard and Weinrich's conclusion that there was likely "a significant familial component to male homosexuality" and that it resided in the genome.[88]

Ideology Entwined

As theories of human difference were shifting heavily toward biology, the National Gay Task Force and PFLAG further deepened their relationships with familiar friends in the sciences while making many new ones along the way. Many researchers in the fields of psychology, genetics, neurology, and endocrinology were invited to national movement conferences, consulted in the creation of advocacy literature, and served as expert witnesses in political and legal fights. Gay and lesbian advocates leaned increasingly on studies indicating that queer parentage was not likely a significant causal factor in the development of child sexuality and that, as another Task Force pamphlet put it, "sexuality cannot be taught or learned."[89] As these researchers, practitioners, and gay rights leaders reticulated into new networks of collaboration and influence, a new way of seeing sexuality through the prism of biology came into focus.

Having worked in close concert with Marmor throughout the APA fight, Task Force leaders often cited the multiple-causes thesis in their messaging. In a 1979 pamphlet titled *Answers to a Parent's Questions about Homosexuality*, the Task Force explained:

> Most researchers agree that the causes of both homosexuality and heterosexuality are as yet unknown. All they *do* know is that all human beings are born with the capacity for both homosexual and heterosexual responses and that somehow, probably as a result of very early childhood experiences and possibly genetic, hormonal, and environmental factors, one or the other *capacity for human loving* and sexual response becomes the predominant sexual *preference* or *orientation*.[90]

In deflecting accusations that gay and lesbian adults preyed on and recruited children, the authors of this pamphlet also contended that "although most researchers now acknowledge that the causes of both homosexual and heterosexual orientation are not known, many of them believe that basic sexual orientation is set at a very early age, probably by the time a child begins school. They believe that these primarily affectional inclinations may not be recognized and acknowledged by an individual for many years, but they are nevertheless established in early children and do not radically change."[91] If a child's sexual orientation prefigured any exposure to the act of sex itself, then homosexuality was innocuous. Gay and lesbian adults could, therefore, be treated with love and support rather than suspicion and hostility.

At least in its early years, the Task Force could not be blamed for approaching research without nuance. In another pamphlet from 1979, this one called *Twenty Questions about Homosexuality*, Task Force leaders curiously rebuffed the simple question of "choice or nature." One passage read: "Behavioral scientists reject the notion that either heterosexual or homosexual orientation is a simple matter of choice. The vast majority also rule out constitutional, genetic, glandular, or hormonal factors, asserting that human sexuality is unfocused at birth and that the development of either homosexual or heterosexual preferences is a matter of complex learning and experience."[92] This quote appears—at least on the surface—to deny the biological account. Even more confusingly, it conflicts with the organization's other advocacy literature from the era, which had emphasized the natural aspects of homosexuality.[93] However, other sections of the *Twenty Questions* pamphlet show that this disconnect can be attributed to a belief that most etiological inquiries from the early to mid-twentieth century had been done in bad faith by biased researchers. Further, in a letter explaining the pamphlet's tone on the matter, Task Force board member Barbara Gittings stated that the real problem was that "the research has been badly done. The studies don't ask the legitimate question, What causes homosexuality?"[94] In all, this pamphlet does not signal so much a repudiation of biological evidence as it did a due skepticism about just who was pronouncing the biological thesis and for what ends.

Whereas the National Gay Task Force stepped more tepidly into the gene pool, PFLAG's leadership dove in headfirst. Throughout its advocacy pamphlets and statements to the press, PFLAG promoted the idea that homosexuality was "not a choice" but instead an endemic part of a person's constitution.[95] Writing to the *National Observer* in 1977, LA chapter leader Adele Starr criticized the paper for running an article titled "What If Your Child Is Gay?" which rested on the theory that parents were most responsible for instilling homosexuality in their children.[96] Starr complained that the paper did not reach out to opponents of this idea such as Evelyn Hooker and Judd Marmor, but instead chose to interview Irving Bieber, who clung to a pathological understanding of homosexuality even after the APA abandoned that model. If only journalists would contact these experts, Starr argued, they would see "another truth": "realization that is emerging is that it is natural for a gay person to be attracted to the same sex, just as it is natural for a non-gay person to be attracted to the opposite sex. It is not contagious. It is probably innate."[97] In a letter to CBS News, PFLAG executive committee member Lawrence Starr explained, "The consensus of professional opinion of psychologists is that sexual preference is determined in very early childhood, that environment has little influence in determining sexual preference and that probably ten percent of all persons are homosexual."[98] Rather than the result of poor upbringing or stray instances of "contamination," homosexuality was simply part of the natural ordering of human sexuality wherein a certain fixed proportion of the population was inherently gay.

PFLAG leaders also hounded the authors of popular advice columns to disseminate this theory—and to great effect. In 1977 Florida chapter leader Jean Smith wrote to Ann Landers of the "Ask Ann" advice column to assist Landers in better addressing the concerns of her readers who had found themselves raising gay children. Smith sent specific studies to Landers, noting: "I have articles stating that some psychiatrists suspect three factors: 1) genetic inclination, 2) personality makeup, 3) social stresses, and that some geneticists suspect biochemical or hormonal conditions already present at birth."[99] Several years later in 1981, Starr repeated this move in offering scientific resources to the author of the nationally syndicated "Dear Abby" column.[100]

Abby not only enthusiastically referred her readers to PFLAG in her next column on the topic, but she also referenced the scientific knowledge that Starr had provided in advice to a mother who was struggling with her young lesbian daughter's sexuality. Abby responded by dispelling myths about parental influences and reassured the mother that "sexual preference is not a matter of choice; it is determined at a very early age."[101]

From its beginnings, PFLAG had invited researchers to speak at its annual gatherings. Gradually, these talks shifted in focus from those who merely debunked the pathology model to adherents of the insurgent biological thesis. In those first national conferences, longtime movement allies like Evelyn Hooker gave presentations with titles like "Facts and Misconceptions about Homosexuality," which offered reassurance to PFLAG members that gays and lesbians were not mentally ill.[102] At a later meeting, sociologist and coauthor of *Sexual Preference* Martin Weinberg gave a presentation titled "Development of Sexual Orientation" modeled on his work that considered hormonal factors.[103] And in 1987, one of the most biologically laden of these presentations was delivered by June Reinisch, who had just been appointed director of the Kinsey Institute. Her talk, titled "Biological Factors in Psychosexual Development," highlighted the new director's efforts to move the Kinsey Institute in a biomedical direction, a commitment that was reflected in her decision to change the institute's name to the Kinsey Institute for Research in Sex, Gender and Reproduction.[104] In her work, Reinisch probed genetic, prenatal, and postnatal factors to explain gender differences in personality; she and her colleagues believed that hormonal fluctuations in utero were at the root of masculine and feminine behaviors in males and females, respectively.[105] Unsurprisingly, as gender differences were so heavily linked to homosexuality at this time, Reinisch saw a role for these prenatal factors in producing sexual as well as gender nonconformity.[106]

In addition to these conference presentations, PFLAG circulated advocacy literature that placed these expert opinions front and center. Its 1988 pamphlet titled *Why Is My Child Gay?* was intended to show "how experts in the field (scientists, researchers) answer the questions most commonly asked by parents and friends of gays and by homosexuals themselves."[107] The experts consulted here comprised the usual suspects: Judd Marmor, Alan Bell, Richard Green, Richard Pillard, June Reinisch, Martin Weinberg, James Weinrich, and Evelyn Hooker, all of whom had entertained the biological thesis to some degree. Out of the remaining three researchers, only one—the anthropologist Gilbert Herdt, who studied semiotics and gender in Papua New Guinea—questioned outright the biological approach to sexuality.[108] Among the other two were transsexuality and intersex sexologist John Money, who studied hormonal determinants in sex, gender identity, and sexuality; and Lee Ellis, a sociologist who researched the neurohormonal causes of aggression, a decidedly biodeterministic enterprise.

The most striking part of the document was its cover, which detailed a series of the conclusions offered by a consensus of the experts surveyed. The results began with a hedged statement granting that while "the exact causes of heterosexuality and homosexuality are unknown . . . [they are] likely to be the result of an interaction of several different factors, including genetic, hormonal, and environmental factors." Even more forcefully, a subsequent bullet point explained that "a biological (genetic, hormonal, neurological, other) predisposition toward a homosexual, bisexual, or heterosexual orientation is present at birth in all boys and girls."[109] This represents one of the clearest articulations of the biological thesis of the time. And while the fourth conclusion offered a caveat that "none of the contributing factors *alone* can cause homosexuality," the rest of the pamphlet stressed biological causes above all others.

A look to the individual statements given by the researchers confirms this biological bent. Each scientist was posed the prompt: "What is the basis of sexual orientation/which factor or factors drives most?"[110] Whereas Marmor offered his usual statement on multiple causes, most of the others replied with some restatement of the stronger biological thesis. Weinberg's response reiterated the premise that even if bisexuality and other degrees of sexuality did not fit neatly with biological studies focused on gays and lesbians at the far end of the Kinsey scale, other biological factors might explain those who did not fit the hetero-homo binary.[111] Bell, Ellis, and Money all gave answers that hinged on the link between gender nonconformity and homosexuality. Ellis's comment in particular stands out: "The most significant factors responsible for variation in sexual orientation appear to occur before birth." Ellis explained that the hypothalamus in the brain "not only appears to largely control sexual orientation, but has been shown to be organized differently for males and females (albeit to varying degrees, depending on the amount and timing of exposure to testosterone and other sex hormones)."[112]

Anticipating the queries and objections of incredulous readers, the pamphlet asked rhetorically, "Why ponder the questions? . . . Why analyze facts we cannot change?" PFLAG authors explained that some parents require "a means of coping with the fact that their child is gay in a heterosexual society— [the parents] seek to explore the origins, prevalence, and history of male homosexuality or lesbianism before they can accept their child's homosexuality or bisexuality as a reality." PFLAG offered a few more overtly political justifications as well. "Scientists [have] found evidence that homosexuality and heterosexuality may not be a matter of free choice," PFLAG observed, and the equal rights movement's future depended on combating the right-wing rhetoric of "choice" and "preference" with that of "sexual orientation."[113] Hence, the answer to "why is my child gay?" was perhaps an existential one.

The Shape of Sexual Identity to Come

Evolutionary biologist and social critic Richard Lewontin famously argued that neither the advent of nineteenth-century bioreductive accounts of human nature nor their late twentieth-century renaissance can be separated from the political and economic state of affairs from which they emerged.[114] Though Lewontin was primarily interested in how the unequal distribution of resources and life chances was legitimated by such ideologies, he saw evolutionary explanations for homosexuality as an exemplar of how the bioreductive paradigm mistook complex and contingent social phenomena for something written into the species long ago.[115] Like other simple stories about human behavior that became so popular throughout the late twentieth century, the assumption that the heterosexual-homosexual divide had an evolutionary basis came to overshadow more sociologically informed theories— both those that buttressed the psychoanalytic pathological model as well as the gay liberationists' Frankfurt school twists on Freud, the notion that desire could be unleashed.[116] Like any good bit of ideology, it came to sound like common sense.

The early leaderships of the National Gay Task Force and PFLAG had a strong affinity for this new crop of work. How could they resist an ideology so complementary to the liberal pluralist politics in which they sought to assimilate, particularly when it came with the backing of scientific authority and expertise? In the following decades, these developments in the life sciences, political economy, and the gay and lesbian interest-group world would further enmesh and mature into the "gay gene" studies of the Human Genome Project era and related latter-day bioessentialist ventures. In this sense, gay and lesbian rights advocates were among the first to incorporate the contemporary bioreductive ideology into their political project. But they were far from the only ones. Rather, they merely adopted the ideology while it was in its embryonic stage, just several years out from its evolution into a principal epistemology of our time.[117]

4

Immutability before the Gay Gene:
Biology and Civil Rights Litigation

When US Air Force Lieutenant Sharron Frontiero was denied spousal benefits for her husband based on an administrative rule that imposed more stringent requirements on a male partner's eligibility than those for wives, she sued the military for sex discrimination. In 1973 Frontiero won her case in a Supreme Court decision that declared such instances of discriminatory sex-based classifications antithetical to the Fourteenth Amendment's principle of constitutional equal protection.[1] Though unwilling to grant that women were a suspect class that merited strict scrutiny—that is, the highest judicial protection offered by the judiciary, typically reserved for categories like race, religion, and national origin—the court did raise its standard of discernment significantly. If sex were, as a court plurality ruled, "an immutable characteristic determined solely by the accident of birth," one that "frequently bears no relation to ability to perform or contribute to society," then very few legal distinctions between men and women could stand.[2]

For obvious reasons, those seeking to comprehend how and why biology was baked into gay rights litigation look to *Frontiero*'s influence, particularly the connection the court made between immutability and heightened judicial scrutiny.[3] If the path toward constitutional equal protection required evidence that sexual orientation was innate, "an accident of birth," then litigators would pursue such cases with bold pronouncements about sexuality's deep roots in the first few months of life, in utero, or even in an individual's genetic code. Whereas previous legal efforts had thoroughly addressed the question of pathology—a debate that touched on etiology in all sorts of ways but could be won without a robust origins story—the new equal protection doctrine appeared to necessitate more. For some civil rights lawyers, it appeared to beckon biology for proof.

The story here is a convincing one. After all, expert witness testimonies and citations to scientific papers became a staple feature of gay rights litigation throughout the 1970s and 1980s. And when the Supreme Court struck down the movement's right to privacy claims against anti-sodomy legislation in *Bowers v. Hardwick* (1986), equal protection became advocates' most plausible route to rights through the federal judiciary. Prior to *Hardwick*, bio-inflected narratives of ontology had diffused throughout gay rights litigation but were not nearly present in all cases. Shortly after that 1986 ruling, biology had become ubiquitous.

The problem with this account is that it is at best half true. For one, it elides the fact that legal arguments about bio-fixity were already widespread by the 1970s. In cases involving the right to privacy, freedom of speech, and even the First Amendment's prohibition on religious establishment, organizations like the National Gay Task Force, the ACLU, and the newly established Lambda Legal Defense and Education Fund enlisted their scientific and medical allies to give an evidentiary backbone to their various doctrinal appeals. Rather than serving as the primary catalyst, the immutability condition presented the most natural—but far from the only—legal channel through which to funnel biodeterministic representations of gay and lesbian personhood.

The following explores how the "born this way" narrative gestated in the movement's 1970s and 1980s civil rights strategy, and how legal institutional and doctrinal incentives reinforced—but importantly did not themselves engender—a commitment to that narrative. In examining cases involving gays and lesbians who were kicked out of their classrooms and charged with "crimes against nature," this chapter recounts how the movement's post-APA-reform allies took the stand as expert witnesses and contributed their studies to legal briefs. Those researchers and physicians did so in the hopes that the American judicial system would strike down discriminatory local and state laws, whether or not they did so by way of the equal protection clause.

Child Development Psychology and the Hardening of Gay Identity

Throughout the late twentieth century, gay rights litigators began carting their scientific and medical allies into courts—especially in custody cases and those involving adults who worked with children such as schoolteachers. They did so to assure judges and juries that homosexuality was neither a mental illness nor a communicable disease but rather a benign variant of normal human sexuality with its root in early childhood development. As early as 1970, homophile organizations had begun to argue before courts that no credible expert believed that there was a causal link between gay and lesbian parentage and queer children.[4] Buttressed by the APA's demedicalization of homosexuality—as well as a doctrinal shift in the courts away from a preference for maternal custody and toward a gender-neutral "best interests of the child" standard—gay rights advocates made legal headway.[5]

By the end of the decade, movement leaders were counseling attorneys to take the offense on ontology. In a 1979 document distributed among advocate attorneys, the National Gay Task Force implored litigators to "address the judge's curiosity" and to ask and answer questions such as "What is lesbianism? What is homosexuality? What causes it?"[6] The short pamphlet culminated in an extended bibliography on the conjectured causes of homosexuality, many of which explicitly challenged the notion that a gay or lesbian parent or teacher could be blamed for a child's sexuality. Fears concerning undue exposure or contagion, these psychologists and psychiatrists argued, were largely groundless in the face of new evidence that placed sexual orientation's etiology in very early childhood development or in utero.[7]

Cognizant of this paradigm shift, the pathological school's holdouts in mental healthcare reformulated their opposition to gay rights. The most recurrent theme in their own expert witness testimonials is one of caution: with the old consensus thrown into question and a relatively untested competitor in its place, civil rights reforms were premature at best. Now that the causes of sexual orientation were up for debate in a manner they had not been for decades, it was essential that the nation's vulnerable children were not among the first guinea pigs in a social experiment of tolerance. These researchers and practitioners insisted that young children teetering toward homosexuality be protected from the painful uncertainty and stress that the mere presence of an openly gay guardian or schoolteacher might have upon their delicate psyches. Even if such children wound up attracted to their same kind in adulthood, these researchers cautioned, uninvited or unanticipated contact with their gay adult counterparts might cause irreparable damage.

Trial court testimonies from this era's civil rights contests bear this out. In 1973 first-year middle-school teacher Joe Acanfora sued a Maryland school district for relieving him of his teaching duties at Parkland Junior High School. The school board moved Acanfora to an administrative position upon learning that he had been a member of a homophile student group while attending Penn State University.[8] Acanfora's case was assisted in part by the Washington Gay Activists Alliance (GAA), an organization that had ties to the Task Force's founding members including Frank Kameny (two years prior, the group had managed Kameny's failed congressional campaign). The Washington GAA saw Acanfora's case as an opportunity to enlist its expanding ranks of allied mental health professionals and sexologists.[9] Accordingly, much of the trial centered around a debate between Acanfora's team of expert witnesses, comprised of a professor of pediatrics Stanford Friedman, family psychiatrist William Stayton, and famed sexologist John Money, and the school board's own experts from the field of child psychology including psychiatrist Reginald Spencer Lourie and pediatrician Felix P. Heald.

Throughout the trial, Lourie and Heald testified that Acanfora's presence in the classroom threatened students with overburdensome stress, the risk of suicidality, and the possibility of contagion.[10] Quoting from a recent study published in the *Journal of the American Medical Association*, Heald noted that bisexual and homosexual teenage boys had much higher risks of attempted and completed suicide than their straight counterparts. Heald reasoned that Acanfora served as a constant reminder of their own tormented condition. This could manifest in severe "homosexual panics" in queer-inclined students. Lourie's testimony also warned against the harm that Acanfora might wreak upon his students. Drawing from similar studies, Lourie analogized Acanfora's removal from the classroom to the practice of mass immunization. While he admitted that the school board's action would likely only protect a very marginal number of students who entered the classroom with a preexisting anxiety about their sexualities, the child psychiatrist reasoned that "when we have inoculation programs on a preventive basis for millions of individuals when only a handful of individuals could be protected, we are preventing a relatively handful of contagious diseases that could be fatal or damaging."[11] Indeed, the schoolteacher's dismissal was rendered a literal public health intervention akin to inoculation, one that was presumed to affect the whole— Lourie admitted that most students would experience no distress and therefore would suffer the loss of their instructor for no purpose—for the benefit of the few.

Although both Lourie and Heald avoided depicting Acanfora's homosexuality as menacingly as their forebearers oftentimes characterized the sexual psychopath, they persisted in portraying homosexuality as suboptimum and infectious. Lourie classified adolescent homosexual behavior as generally indicative of a normal "transitional stage" of which most would outgrow. School boards must then give susceptible students a chance to reckon with their own conflicted desires independent of any external coercive agent that might make such attractions permanent. In recounting Lourie's testimony, the federal district court noted that shielding students from the influence of an openly gay instructor was necessary because "one cannot escape the cultural definition of homosexuality as abnormal and the need to give children the utmost opportunity to be essentially normal in this important phase of life."[12]

To counter these claims of contagion, Acanfora's attorney coaxed their expert witnesses to establish under what conditions and at what stage of maturity a child's sexuality takes shape. Overall, the strategy was to reveal just how small a temporal window there was to alter a person's sexual orientation. Acanfora's team tapped their star witness, John Money, for this task. In the 1950s, Money had made a name for himself with a series of papers on "gender acquisition," which construed a child's sense of both gender and sexuality as cemented before the end of the toddler years.[13] Since then, he had become world-renowned for his work on intersexuality and transsexuality.

When Money was asked by the court to summarize the thesis of his seminal 1971 *Man & Woman, Boy & Girl*, Money explained that the book explores "how a boy develops his concept of masculinity and a girl develops her personal identity concepts of femininity. [I]t traces this process from the genes to all the learning experiences up through adulthood."[14] Like many of his contemporaries, Money did not sharply differentiate intersexuality, transsexuality, sexual orientation, and gender identity from one another; rather, he posited that each person had a core gender role that was either male or female and that a person's gender presentation and sexuality were manifestations of that inner core. Somewhere between the age of eighteen months and five years, a child was *imprinted* with a "gender awareness" that was essentially irreversible.[15] Prior to this early period, Money believed that adults such as the child's parents might play some determinative role, but by school age—especially junior high school age—a person's core self was set in stone.[16] In their own testimonies, Friedman and Stayton deferred to Money on this version of the multiple-causes theory, recognizing that it was quickly becoming the new norm in the field.

Money and Stayton went beyond simply defending Acanfora from charges that he was causing his students undue anguish. They also laid out a blueprint for a gender-normative version of gay identity, one that might facilitate social tolerance and avoid future disputes over queer schoolteachers. A homosexual instructor who adopted the gender presentation and behaviors of his straight counterparts could actually serve as a positive role model to teenagers struggling with their own feelings. That is, as long as the schoolteacher avoided nonnormative gender expression and presented himself as a "non-monster-type, non-monstrous, freakish-type person, homosexual." Money added that "even if [a person] were going to be stuck with themselves as homosexually-inclined, they at least could be a constructive and participating member of the human race and not some kind of derelict, discarded monster that nobody would be able to accept and approve of, if they knew."[17]

Further expounding the noble homosexual caretaker archetype, Stayton testified that "my belief is that if there are good homosexual models in the society that [a child] has contact with that are responsible, well respected, capable people, and if there are heterosexual models that [the child] comes in contact with that are responsible, with the same qualifications, it seems to me that this will help the individual to be more comfortable . . . in dealing with [the child's] own personality and own sexual orientation."[18] Stayton accepted that some students would come into the classroom with extant same-sex attractions and that providing an acceptable gay role model could be to their benefit. Money agreed, stating that such a teacher might grant students "the courage to disclose their anxieties about themselves, sexually, instead of keeping them hidden where they become a source of continued destructive anxiety" and that "the tolerant acceptance of a respectable homosexual is a good lesson for these wise and sophisticated youngsters of teaching them the degree of tolerance that we could stand more of in our society."[19] Stayton himself went even further when asked by the defense if the prevention of homosexuality in children was a priority in child psychiatry. While acknowledging that the even relatively tolerant and reform-disposed National Institute of Mental Health (NIMH) Task Force had taken this line in the late 1960s, Stayton advised that prevention was misguided—likely impossible—and that practitioners ought to spend more resources caring for the psychic health of all children.

While federal district court Judge J. H. Young was convinced by much of the plaintiff's evidence and noted his own "special recognition" of Money's research, Young proceeded with caution. Noting that while "it is fair to state that factors present in the embryonic and early childhood stages appear to have the greatest impact," Young concluded that "the book is by no means closed on the possible behavioral and sociocultural impact" that a homosexual male teacher might have on his students. Even if mental health experts were coming to perceive the real social problem as "the cultural stigma and repression" that was meted out to gays and lesbians, Young gestured to the fact that the NIMH Task Force's report had recommended some preventive measures still be taken with school-age children.[20]

Young ultimately ruled against Acanfora's reinstatement based on Acanfora's decision to plead his case before the public on *60 Minutes*, deeming the segment an improper use of national media that was certain to disrupt his ability to teach without distraction. However, the judge found that Acanfora had indeed been the victim of unconstitutional discrimination. In the text of his decision, Young included a short section on the equal protection clause and suspect classification. He began by quoting from *Frontiero*, speculating that sexuality—like race, national origin, and sex—might also feature "an immutable characteristic determined solely by the accident of birth" and that it, too, might "bear no relation to ability to perform or contribute to society."[21] Presaging a line that the Supreme Court would take two decades later on gay rights, Young surmised that Acanfora's removal could not even survive a more limited rational basis review, as the school board's actions were fundamentally arbitrary.[22]

Later cases involving schoolteachers' rights would replicate these efforts to loosen the grip of that the pathological model and other social anxieties still held by the federal bench.[23] In a case involving an openly bisexual teacher that went all the way up to the Supreme Court before being denied certiorari in 1984, the National Gay Rights Advocates (NGRA) presented evidence from Alfred Kinsey and Judd Marmor in order to dispel her school board's fears. Though the NGRA lost that case, it did persuade a dissenting judge on the Sixth Circuit Court to cite the sexological reports as well as the 1973 changes to the *DSM* in his opinion lambasting discriminatory policies that kept queer people from remaining in their classrooms. Though sweeping judicial reform remained a few decades out, the discriminatory legal regime's empirical basis was eroding, and judges were taking notice.

Science and the Sodomy Cases

Beginning in the mid-1970s, state prohibitions against sodomy became major targets for civil rights groups. The National Gay Task Force, Lambda Legal, and the ACLU were confident that a window of opportunity was opening on the Supreme Court. Within a few years even, they imagined striking a constitutional blow that would knock down sodomy bans nationwide.[24] Their confidence was understandable. State legislative reform commissions and courts had been revisiting the policy implications and constitutional soundness of both the sexual psychopath laws passed between the 1930s and 1960s as well as older prohibitions on consensual sodomy from the eighteenth and nineteenth centuries.[25] State-sponsored policy studies, for instance, frequently uncovered how costly these laws were in practice. One California state legislative study of the Los Angeles Police Department's policies buttressed these calls for legal reform when its authors revealed that police entrapment was the primary cause of convictions under local and state sex laws.[26] This indicated to the legislature that the mayor and police were needlessly creating the "problem of homosexuality" themselves by engaging in overly aggressive surveillance tactics and behavior-inducing schemes that did little to encourage actual public health, safety, or morality.

Emboldened by these nascent reforms coupled with the Supreme Court's willingness to sweep out the vast majority of state laws on abortion in its 1973 decision *Roe v. Wade*, Bruce Voeller and several other Task Force members met with Supreme Court Justice William O. Douglas. In that meeting, they discussed how precedents like *Roe* and *Virginia v. Loving*'s (1963) invalidation of state bans on interracial marriage might achieve similar results in a sodomy case.[27] Unfortunately, the court took a different route in the Task Force's sponsored case, *Doe v. Commonwealth's Attorney of Richmond* (1976), by offering only a brief summary affirmance of the federal district court's earlier decision upholding a Virginia sodomy ban.[28] Repealing sodomy bans might require more time and effort than their opponents first thought.

This early setback, however, did not prevent Lambda Legal and the ACLU from persisting with their own challenges to sodomy's criminalization. In 1974 Lambda and the ACLU took on the case of Eugene Enslin, who had become the target of an entrapment scheme undertaken by Jacksonville detective Sam Hudson.[29] No neutral enforcer of the law, Hudson had admitted an intention to "run [Enslin] out of town" for his sexuality. Upon paying another man to proposition Enslin at an adult bookstore, Hudson arrested him under a North Carolina sodomy ban that proscribed same-sex sexual acts construed as "crimes against nature."[30]

Noting the woeful absence of "expert testimony in the fields of psychiatry, psychology, sociology, and theology" presented in the *Doe* case, Enslin's attorneys sought the aid of Kinsey Institute–affiliated sociologist Albert Klassen Jr. to construct a more thorough defense against the North Carolina law.[31] Klassen's testimony spanned the range of reformist scientific theories of his era.[32] He contended with the baseless assumption that homosexuals were motivated by insatiable sex drives and pedophiliac urges, and that tolerance for homosexuals would undermine the institutions of marriage and the heterosexual nuclear family. Klassen reassured the court that there was no evidence that children or adults could be "converted" to homosexuality or that the removal of criminal sanctions would result in a sudden proliferation of queer Americans. Citing the APA's 1973 changes to the *DSM* along with the NIMH Task Force report, he explained that forced rehabilitation was no longer seen by professionals as effective or appropriate.

Though the district court judge decided the case on the narrow grounds that *Doe* had settled the question of sodomy bans' constitutionality, Enslin's lawyers appealed to the Fourth Circuit—and then later to the Supreme Court.[33] In making an equal protection clause argument, the Enslin brief cited additional scientific evidence. It read that "although there is continuing debate and uncertainty in the scientific community concerning the causes of homosexuality, authorities are generally agreed that sexual orientation is determined early in life, and, once determined, is virtually impossible to alter."[34]

Lambda and the ACLU also cited First Amendment religious establishment case law to argue that religious bigotry, rather than any rigorous scientific conception of "nature," had motivated North Carolina's ban. Delving into comparative sociology and anthropology, Klassen held that US state sodomy laws were derived from Christian and Judaic scripture and theological pronouncements, whereas at least seventy-six other societies without such religious heritage condoned homosexuality.[35] A constitutionally sound secular definition of "nature" as written into the North Carolina ban on "crimes against nature" ought to be interpreted with reference to "considerations of a psychological, sociological, or medical basis" rather than theological doctrines of natural law or biblical interpretation. "The lack of any discussion of what constitutes unnatural sexual behavior in terms of modern scientific conceptions," Lambda and the ACLU concluded, constituted a clear violation of the establishment clause.[36] Though Enslin ultimately lost on appeal in 1978, his legal saga epitomizes the sentiment among gay rights litigators that scientific authority was on their side. In this sense, the fight for civil rights could be waged in part as a proxy war that pit scientific truth against religious-based prejudice.

In November 1979, the Texas Human Rights Foundation filed suit on behalf of Donald F. Baker against the state of Texas for its ban on homosexual sodomy. Though the original Texas law was decades old and proscribed a variety of behaviors—many of which were acts frequently performed by heterosexual married couples like fellatio, cunnilingus, and anal sex—the state legislature had in 1974 "reformed" its ban to single out gays and lesbians in particular. Baker was in many ways the model plaintiff for a challenge to something as taboo as sodomy. He was a thirty-five-year-old Dallas schoolteacher, a US Navy veteran, and an active churchgoer who happened to be romantically and sexually attracted to men.[37] After a years-long struggle with his sexuality that nearly led him to suicide, Baker exited the closet, reconciled his Christian faith with his sexual orientation, and became a leader in his local Dallas gay rights organization. Though Baker himself had not been arrested under the revised statute, his lawsuit highlighted the stigma and danger that gays and lesbians incurred by granting the police the authority to arrest persons for engaging in private consensual sexual activity. He contended that the ban encouraged police harassment in general and provided employers, landlords, and judges in child custody cases a statutory cover when they discriminated against gays and lesbians.[38]

Like Enslin, Baker challenged the state ban on constitutional privacy, religious establishment, and equal protection grounds. Leaning most heavily on the last of these, Baker asserted that the Texas statute had been reformed to expressly target gays and lesbians for a kind of sexual activity that remained legal for heterosexual couples. Based on the precedent set in *Frontiero*, Baker's team argued that the law merited heightened scrutiny as it targeted the *sex* of the person or persons involved in a sexual act to determine whether the activity was proscribed or lawful. In establishing discrimination against homosexuality as inherently linked to unconstitutional classifications based on sex, Baker could claim that gays and lesbians ought to be considered a quasi-suspect class under the equal protection clause, thereby meriting heightened judicial protection from onerous laws like the Texas one.

Baker's legal challenge rested heavily on the idea that gays and lesbians satisfied the immutability criteria spelled out in *Frontiero*. To make it stick in court, Baker's lead attorney, James Barber, reached out to the Task Force's Bruce Voeller for leads on a credible expert witness. Voeller in turn referred Barber to former APA president Judd Marmor, who at that time was becoming more convinced than ever by biological explanations. In his letter to Marmor, Barber wrote that he "would like to discuss with you the possibility of testifying as an expert witness on the psychiatric and behavioral aspects of homosexual conduct, to show that homosexuality is basically fixed and immutable at an early age."[39]

Marmor, along with the Kinsey Institute–affiliated sociologist William Simon, accepted Barber's request to serve as expert witnesses.[40] The two researchers presented as evidence the APA's changes to the *DSM* and similar stances taken by the American Anthropological Association, the American Bar Association, and the American Psychological Association declaring that homosexuality was not a disease or mental illness that could be "cured." Most notably, Marmor and Simon endorsed a much more biodeterministic view of sexuality than the norm in these testimonies. Writing for a Texas federal district court, Judge Jerry Buchmeyer wrote that Baker's witnesses demonstrated that

> "exclusive homosexuals" did not choose to be homosexuals. Obligatory homosexuality is not a matter of choice: it is fixed at an early age—before one even begins to participate in sexual activities—and only a small minority can be changed or "cured," if at all. Although there are different theories about the "cause" of homosexuality, the overwhelming majority of experts agree that individuals become homosexuals because of biological or genetic factors, or environmental conditioning, or a combination of these and other causes—and

that sexual orientation would be difficult and painful, if not impossible, to reverse by psychiatric treatment.[41]

Marmor's multiple-causes thesis can be seen on full display as well as his
gradual movement in the direction of biological determinants and away from
social ones.[42] Though the judge's remark about a small portion of gays and
lesbians as possibly "curable" is a reminder that the conversion therapy had
not yet been discredited, the testimonies here marked a significant step forward toward bio-fixity.

Buchmeyer was clearly convinced by Baker's evidence and experts. Conversely, he was wholly underwhelmed by the defendants' witnesses. Whereas
the judge struck a sympathetic tone with Marmor and Simon—Buchmeyer
even took time to have Marmor teach the Kinsey scale to the bench—he
was impatient with the defenses' main witness, psychiatrist James Grigson.[43]
An expert in what he called "legal psychiatry," Grigson was better known as
"Dr. Death," a moniker earned through his assistance in the prosecution of
167 capital punishment cases. Grigson was infamous for characterizing the
accused as inherently violent and beyond rehabilitation.[44]

Whereas Grigson preferred biodeterministic narratives of fixity in his
capital punishment work, his testimony in the Baker case stressed malleability. He repeatedly conjured images of at-risk youth whose "normal growth
and behavioral patterns" could be tragically disrupted and spoiled by an encounter with a homosexual adult.[45] In his support for the state, Grigson was
accompanied by fellow psychiatrist Paul Cameron, who would be expelled
from the APA on ethics grounds the following year. Cameron also testified
that homosexuality could not possibly be innate as sexual desire is an "appetite," which by its nature must be acquired.[46] Upon entertaining Grigson's and
Cameron's stale portrayal of homosexuality as psychopathology, Buchmeyer
chided their evidence as "directly contrary to those of the plaintiff's experts—
whose qualifications as experts in the field of homosexuality were outstand-
ing and whose testimony was very credible—and to positions adopted by
various medical and psychiatric associations." He added that Grigson's statements "were flawed, inconsistent, and directly contrary to other credible evidence accepted by this Court."[47]

In his ruling for the court, Buchmeyer applied much of Marmor's testimony to characterize homosexuality as a healthy, mostly fixed disposition
and attempts at curing sexual orientation as futile and harmful. Unswayed
by the state's lingering fears of contagion, Buchmeyer ruled that the constitutional right to privacy as laid out in Roe v. Wade protected Baker and others who might engage in consensual "private homosexual conduct." Contra

those who still saw a rational state interest in preventing the spread of homosexuality, the judge reasoned that there was no longer any rationality left to that approach to governance. In defending this application of privacy case law, Buchmeyer cited evidence that "homosexuality is not a matter of choice. It is fixed at a very early age. Only a small percentage of homosexuals can be changed or 'cured' by psychiatric treatment. The numbers of homosexuals in society are not reduced by criminal laws like § 21.06 [the sodomy ban], nor would they be increased if such laws did not exist."[48]

The odd turns that Baker's case took on appeal demonstrate that at least some opponents of gay rights could sense that the shifting scientific terrain meant that the traditional pathology rationale was no longer reliable. Some conservative state officials would sooner abandon the citadel of sodomy laws than defend them against what was becoming a hostile judiciary. Upon losing at the trial level, District Attorney of Dallas County Henry Wade, District Attorney for the City of Dallas Lee Holt, and State Attorney General Jim Mattox all decided not to appeal to the Fifth Circuit, thereby allowing Buchmeyer's decision striking down the sodomy law to stand.[49]

For those committed to a longer fight, however, the HIV/AIDS crisis afforded some leverage for a right-wing element that had been watching its medical allies fall into disrepute. One interest group, Dallas Doctors Against AIDS, led the local protest against this refusal to appeal.[50] Even more consequentially, District Attorney of Potter County Danny Hill began devising legal maneuvers to force an appeal. After failing in his request that the Texas Supreme Court compel Mattox to appeal, Hill decided that the most straightforward route would be to file on behalf of his own DA office. Relying on a procedural rule that allowed for the introduction of new evidence post-trial, Hill stressed that "AIDS is new evidence," and that the unfolding plague required a reexamination of the pathological thesis.[51]

Hill's appeal centered on an accusation that Marmor and Simon had engaged in fraudulent testimony on behalf of Baker. The district attorney first took on Simon, accusing the sociologist of having erroneously "indicated that there was no evidence that homosexuality was a learned behavior."[52] Hill saved the bulk of his ire for Marmor, whom he attacked for supposedly misrepresenting the psychiatric community as united in the belief that homosexuality was not a psychopathology. To the contrary, Hill cited a 1977 study that held that 69 percent of APA members continued to believe "homosexuality is a pathological adaptation as opposed to a normal variation" despite the official changes made within the APA in 1973.[53] In a prescient accusation, Hill derided Marmor for allegedly implying that gays and lesbians were, in Hill's words, "born that way."[54]

The record of Marmor's testimony and a later affidavit filed in response to this accusation of fraud shows that he never used this language. As usual, Marmor was markedly nuanced in his recounting of the varying etiological hypotheses even as he stressed biological and genetic ones.[55] Though Hill surely distorted Marmor's testimony, his contention that Baker's legal team had intended to depict sexual orientation as biologically immutable was not far from the truth. And while Hill's legal tactics were surely fringe, they would help to move the Supreme Court ever closer to ruling on the constitutionality of sodomy bans.

Baker, Bowers v. Hardwick, and Biology on Appeal

As Baker's case ascended to the Fifth Circuit, where he was represented this time by Lambda Legal, Buchmeyer's decision was overturned by an *en banc* ruling against both his privacy and equal protection claims.[56] At that same moment, the ACLU adopted a similar sodomy ban challenge stemming from the arrest of a gay man in Georgia. There, Michael Hardwick had been arrested by a police officer who had walked into Hardwick's home to serve him a warrant for failing to appear before a court on a previous charge of public drinking. Upon entering the dwelling, the officer witnessed Hardwick engaged in oral sex with a male partner. Unlike Baker, Hardwick lost his case in federal district court but succeeded in convincing the Eleventh Circuit that his constitutional rights to privacy and due process had been violated by Georgia's sodomy statute.[57]

Lambda and the ACLU sensed rightly that the Supreme Court would hear one or both of their cases the following term in order to resolve the circuit split. In an effort to plot the perfect appeal, a coalition of gay rights litigation groups coalesced in 1985 as the Ad-Hoc Task Force to Challenge Sodomy Bans (renamed the Gay Rights Litigators' Roundtable the following year). Led by Lambda Legal director Abby Rubenfeld, the Ad-Hoc Task Force consisted of Lambda, the national ACLU and several state chapters, the NGRA, and several local litigation-oriented groups.[58]

Deliberations over scientific authority featured prominently in the Ad-Hoc Task Force discussions on which case to prioritize and how to present it before the court. One major debate pitted those who wished to emphasize the theme of sexual privacy against those who wanted to center gay *identity* status claims more specifically. There were obvious legal reasons to lean on identity, not least because it allowed litigators to make a robust equal protection clause argument alongside a privacy right one. For that reason, *Baker* was the obvious choice to take to the Supreme Court. Because Georgia's sodomy

law did not textually differentiate between heterosexual and homosexual sodomy the way that Texas's did, Hardwick's case did not feature an equal protection clause argument in addition to its privacy right challenge. A proponent
of going all in on *Baker*, Rubenfeld indicated that Lambda planned to file a
"Homo 101" brief to explain—with citations to expert academic and medical
opinions—the nature and origins of gay and lesbian identities and the special
harm that sodomy bans inflicted.[59]

Some Ad-Hoc Task Force members disagreed on strategic grounds. They
feared that what made *Baker* so attractive also made it twice as risky, as it presented the court with multiple means of foreclosing future legal challenges in
other venues. If the court struck down both the privacy and equal protection
clause arguments in *Baker*, then the task force's alternative route through individual state courts would be imperiled because its appeals to state consti-
tutions' equal protection clauses would be automatically considered as out
of line with federal interpretations. However, even those task force members
who expressed such skepticism noted the advantage of *Baker*'s evidentiary
record, which contained the testimonies of Marmor and Simon. Jim Kellogg,
a representative from the ACLU of Louisiana, remarked that "*Baker* is a his-
toric gold mine. It has all the arguments, facts, issues, etc. about homosexuality and homophobia in the record."[60]

Ultimately, cautious minds prevailed, as the task force placed its bet on the
promise of *Hardwick*'s privacy right challenge. One might suspect that the scientific evidence presented in *Baker* was sidelined along with the rest of that case.
After all, what use was biological evidence if the litigators did not need to meet
the immutability criterion spelled out in *Frontiero*? That the task force's briefs
were replete with this same evidence showcases just how deeply embedded scientific logic and authority were in the minds—and no doubt the Rolodexes—of
the movement's top tacticians and attorneys. Lead litigator Laurence Tribe's arguments before the court were influenced by a recent slew of law reviews citing
the typical array of experts—including Marmor, Money, Weinberg, and Masters
and Johnson—and imploring attorneys to argue that "the Acquisition of Homosexuality is not Subject to Control" and "Sexual Orientation is Immutable."[61]
Drawing from these and related sources, Tribe's brief for Hardwick posited that
homosexuality "may well be a biological condition" and that "in any event [it is]
usually not a matter of choice and rarely subject to modification."[62]

In the amici curiae brief for a coalition headed by Lambda, Rubenfeld along
with Lambda Legal director Evan Wolfson submitted what appears to have
been the aforementioned "Homo 101" document. Here, the attorneys also made
a typical series of references to familiar sources including Bell, Weinberg, and
Smith's influential volume for the Kinsey Institute along with Marmor's 1981

edited volume. Most significantly, the Rubenfeld and Wolfson brief demon-strated how jurists could marry an argument for privacy's protection of *behavior* or conduct to a conception of gay identity that posited *orientation* as existing prior to—and independent of—actual behavior. In mapping the course of contemporary sexology beginning with Kinsey and traversing through the recent work of those like Marmor, they implored the court to understand that "although it is unknown why some people have a same-sex orientation while others do not, the consensus of expert authority is that sexual orientation has already developed by a very early age, independent of isolated sexual experiences."[63] Thus, the privacy right's protection of a person's *choice* to engage in what Georgia defined as criminal sodomy was not adverse to the population's health, safety, and morals. Neither was it a pathology in any sense of the term because it most likely rooted in the first moments of life. By the very nature of gay identity's benign quality and its relatively fixed nature, privacy ought to protect the desire that moves an individual to engage in same-sex consensual intimate relations with another adult. In the simplest terms, *Hardwick's* lack of an equal protection argument did not at all preclude attorneys from underscoring biology.

Privacy's Dusk and the Bioessentialist Horizon

Or so that is what the Ad-Hoc Task Force's leaders and tacticians had in mind for the court's 1986 decision in *Bowers v. Hardwick*. Tragically, the court pumped the brakes on liberal rights expansion just as American gays and lesbians had amassed the resources, allies, and clout that they had presumed would lead to their own sweeping version of *Roe v. Wade*. With the defeat of the privacy right challenge in *Hardwick*, a major constitutional route toward the realization of gay and lesbian rights was closed off, at least at the federal level. The fight for privacy rights would devolve to the states, moving at a slower, albeit steady clip, especially as GOP leaders began to trade in their war on sodomy for one against same-sex marriage.[64]

For the next two decades until the Supreme Court revisited the sodomy question in *Lawrence v. Texas* (2003), the gay rights movement was left with the equal protection clause as its most potent form of federal constitutional redress.[65] As the following chapters demonstrate, advocacy attorneys entered the last decade of the millennium searching more feverishly than ever for a means of declaring gay and lesbian identity immutable, both for the purpose of achieving heightened judicial protections as well as for crafting a new political cultural image of gay and lesbian identity. Advocates would find what they were looking for in that era's expeditions into the human genome and the hunt for the elusive "gay gene."

PART II

Evolutions and Adaptations

5

Rise of the Gay Gene:
Science, Law, Culture, and Hype

The gay gene has loomed large in our social imagination since first coming out nearly three decades ago. In a 1993 issue of *Science*, the cancer researcher-turned-sexologist Dean Hamer employed cutting-edge genomic technologies in an attempt to reveal what it means to be queer.[1] Though novel in its genetic claims, Hamer's study joined a growing cohort of bio-driven theories including work on neuroanatomical causes (i.e., the "gay brain" hypothesis) and similar searches for hormonal ones.[2] Flush with funding from the Human Genome Project's (HGP) boosters, researchers probed strands of DNA in the hopes of elucidating the nature of human identity and social life.[3] Three decades after psychologists first reintroduced biology as one of homosexuality's many "multiple causes," the inner organic truth of sexuality seemed positioned to eclipse all other factors.[4] Just as a range of traits from IQ to alcoholism were being pinned down to discrete genomic markers, so too was sexual orientation deemed a desire encoded within one's biological makeup.

Journalism played no small role in the genomic craze. A captive media quickly became enthralled with "nature versus nurture" debates as science journalists and television news hosts covered even relatively nuanced research in bombastic bioreductive terms.[5] This was true of both conservative and liberal-moderate news sources. "Abortion hope after 'gay genes' finding," reported the right-wing *Daily Mail*.[6] From across the aisle, the *Washington Post* heralded the studies for getting "at the root of the erotic."[7] One chronicler of the pop culture coverage of genomic hype remarked that he could have subtitled his book on the subject "*Reading the New York Times Science News*."[8] Americans could soon hardly open up a popular magazine or flip on the nightly news without being confronted with discussion, debate, and intrigue over the new science of sexuality.

Even more so, LGBTQ+ advocacy groups were responsible for popular-izing and politicizing "nature over nurture" sexual identities. Those like the Human Rights Campaign, PFLAG, and the National Gay and Lesbian Task Force (which had since undergone a more inclusive name change) had spent the past decade and a half promoting the most biodeterministic interpre-tations of sexological studies that they could muster. The gay gene, the gay brain, and the media hype that soon engulfed them were in many ways the culmination of a long series of events that began in the 1950s with the homo-philes' collaborative work with Kinsey Institute researchers. Throughout the late 1980s and 1990s, this evidence would be introduced repeatedly before courts, legislatures, and the voting public, all in the name of equal rights.

The mark of activist collaboration was clear in these new studies as well. Their content and public reception alike were shaped by the modern gay rights movement's liberal version of family values and its dual ethic of domes-ticity and consumption. Hamer's and others' research was conducted in the wake of cultural changes such as the 1980s rise of "the clone"—gay men aping a working-class aesthetic, adorned with plain white T-shirts, blue jeans, and a rugged masculine affect—and the budding straitlaced consumer gay and lesbian demographic.[9] The professional/managerial-class lesbian with a baby in daycare, for instance, was as far removed from the rioters at Stonewall as her straight colleagues were from their sisters' sexual revolution bra-burning days.[10] Though some scientists continued to construe gay men and women as featuring a mismatch of effeminate and butch behavior, many others drew from this changing context in explicitly dismissing the tenet that gender had much to do at all with the nature of sexuality. Sexual orientation had evolved into a distinct natural kind.

The Gay Science (and Scientists)

Simon LeVay's "gay brain" study hit the headlines a full two years before any-one would utter the phrase "the gay gene." In 1991 Harvard medical profes-sor LeVay published a paper in *Science* on the neuroanatomical nature of gay male sexual orientation.[11] By slicing off sections of brain matter from a sam-ple of forty-one cadavers of which sixteen belonged to gay men, LeVay ob-served that the hypothalami of his gay male subjects were, on average, most similar in size to the heterosexual female ones. Armed with these data and an assumption that gay men were essentially female hybrids, LeVay her-alded his findings as evidence that the mystery of gay male desire was no mystery at all.[12] It could be located in the interstitial nucleus of the anterior hypothalamus.

LeVay's message that such data "suggest that sexual orientation has a bio-logical substrate" was, if not a bit stylistically clunky, ready for prime time.[13] Writing in the *New York Times*, science journalist Natalie Angier interviewed a number of gay and lesbian rights advocates for her piece "The Biology of What It Means to Be Gay."[14] A spokesperson for the Lambda Legal Defense Fund linked the matter to civil rights in reasoning that "if, as some have sug-gested, there is a biological basis for homosexuality, it is difficult to fathom on what moral, ethical or religious basis one can reasonably discriminate against homosexuals."[15] In a separate press release, the National Gay and Les-bian Task Force agreed that "if used ethically, the study's conclusions can shed light on human sexuality and prove what we have believed all along—that be-ing gay or lesbian is not necessarily a matter of choice. The only choice we have is to live openly as gay people or live in the silence and shame of the closet." Others like Andrew J. Humm of New York City's Human Rights Com-mission made the matter personal. Admitting that science had affirmed his own subjective experience, Humm was enthusiastic about "the fact that the report talks about homosexual orientation as something innate is good, be-cause that's what most of us experience."[16]

Advocate affirmations of the biological thesis were not themselves any-thing new. The Task Force and other early gay rights nonprofits had been making such pronouncements since their early days in the 1970s when their leaders would swap statistics with Kinsey Institute researchers on the esti-mated "natural" rate of homosexuality or invite sociobiologists to present their biological findings to membership gatherings. What was novel, how-ever, was that Simon LeVay's own identity as a gay man became central to how his evidence was received. In the thrall of the media and activist fanfare that his study incited, LeVay confessed that had he failed to unearth the bio-logical truth of sexual orientation, he would have renounced his scientific ca-reer altogether.[17]

LeVay's statement was indicative of a new trend. Despite having no direct affiliation with the equal rights movement, LeVay's ideological commitment to bioessentialism and his ability to pursue that work as an openly gay scien-tist were built on the previous work of such advocate-scientist alliances. Less than two decades prior, gay and lesbian members of the American Psychiat-ric Association (APA) held clandestine meetings in conference hotel rooms, plotting their plans for reform.[18] At a time when homosexuality was still for-mally classified as a mental pathology, it was no wonder that these research-ers and therapists feared for their careers should they be outed. Following the 1973 reforms at the APA and ensuing developments in other professional associations, the worlds of psychiatry and medicine gradually became more accepting of gay researchers and practitioners. Many professional and academic associations began to form internal committees and caucuses dedicated to studying gay- and lesbian-specific issues and promoting the careers of gay and lesbian researchers (even if those like the notoriously homophobic American Psychoanalytic Association were forced open by an ACLU-backed lawsuit).[19]

Just a few months after LeVay's article appeared in *Science*, another study appeared in the pages of the *Archives of General Psychiatry*. Northwestern psychologist Michael Bailey and Boston University psychiatrist Richard Pillard's paper titled simply "A Genetic Study of Male Sexual Orientation" employed a twins study to make the genomic case for sexual orientation's heritability.[20] Given the influx of National Institutes of Health (NIH) funding for the emergent field of behavioral genetics and the subsequent rise of new academic associations and journals that formed to take advantage of that federal money, it was only a matter of time before the new genomics trained its sights on sexuality.[21] Bailey, for instance, had been mentored by Lee Willerman, a pioneer in behavioral genetics who was renowned for his work on the hereditary nature of personality and intelligence.[22]

Richard Pillard, however, had a far more personal investment in sexology. In the 1970s, Pillard had made the risky move of becoming one of the first openly gay American psychiatrists. At the prodding of National Gay Task Force cofounder Dr. Howard Brown, Pillard had first announced his sexuality to his peers in the 1970s.[23] Shortly after his divorce, Pillard shifted his research focus from drug use, addiction, and anxiety to the hormonal and genetic causes of homosexuality.[24] Throughout the late 1970s and 1980s, Pillard frequently collaborated with sociobiologists like James Weinrich, whose own work was fast becoming a go-to citation among gay and lesbian civil rights leaders.[25]

Indeed, Pillard and Bailey's study found a higher concordance rate among the monozygotic twins than any other pairs—thereby affirming their genomic hypothesis. On the margins, some critics denounced the results as anything but definitive proof of the biological thesis. Writing shortly after the study's publication, biologist Ruth Hubbard and coauthor Elijah Wald noted that in addition to the high concordance rate for identical twin pairs, both brothers in the fraternal pairs were also much more likely to identify as gay than the pairs of non-twin biological brothers, a finding that suggested some determinative social factor rather than a strictly biological one.[26] Furthermore, psychiatrist Miron Baron scorned Pillard and Bailey for neglecting the fact that both men in the adoptive pairs in the same household were more likely to identify as gay than biological brothers who also grew up together, a finding that meant environmental factors could not be ruled out.[27] In riposte to these and other critics who feared that the study might excite would-be social engineers looking to exterminate homosexuality, Pillard and Bailey defended the biological thesis in the *New York Times* as "good news for homosexuals and their advocates." Apparently unaware of the eugenic origins of intelligence testing, Pillard and Bailey argued that "behavioral scientists . . . have long searched for biological underpinnings of traits such as extraversion and intelligence, which no one considers to be negative." Noting also the enthusiasm among their own research subjects, they stressed "the value of discovery, particularly self-discovery."[28]

Aside from a handful of critics, Pillard and Bailey's bio-heavy conclusions were welcomed by an enthusiastic press. The *New York Times* announced that "a new study of twins provides the strongest evidence yet that homosexuality has a genetic basis" while the *Los Angeles Times* concurred that the paper was the "second study in several months to suggest a genetic component to homosexuality."[29] The *Chicago Tribune* similarly reported that the research "provide[d] some of the strongest suggestions to date that sexual orientation is determined in large part by genetics factors."[30]

Likewise, gay and lesbian advocates greeted the study with gusto. Ivy Young, director of the Families Project at the National Gay and Lesbian Task Force, commented that a "study like this, if used ethically, not only sheds light on human sexuality but reinforces what many in the lesbian and gay community have said for years: That homosexuality is not a choice."[31] When Bailey and Pillard published a follow-up study that applied their methods to lesbian pairs, movement leaders once again found the evidence politically attractive.[32] In a statement to the *New York Times*, Lambda Legal's director Paula Ettelbrick remarked that "from a legal perspective, [the study] could make it easier to present the argument that lesbianism isn't a matter of choice, and therefore lesbians should not be discriminated against simply on the basis of sexual orientation."[33] This research was swiftly taken up by those seeking to expand female leadership and representation within advocacy groups.[34]

No study would command nearly the attention and acclaim as did NIH geneticist Dean Hamer's discovery of a genomic marker for homosexuality.[35] Taking advantage of the abundant grant dollars for genomic projects, Hamer and his team assembled forty pairs of gay brothers to test their hypothesis that sexual orientation's genotype was camped out somewhere on the X chromosome. That is exactly what they purported to find. Eighty-two percent of the pairs shared the Xq28 DNA marker on their X chromosomes, which indicated that there was likely a specific gene responsible for male homosexuality somewhere in that genomic vicinity. Hamer's study was immediately heralded as definitive proof of the "nature over nurture" narrative, making him into a media sensation overnight.[36]

The impetus for Hamer's study, the funding streams that made it possible, and its impact could not offer a more convincing case that the new bioessentialism was as much a product of politics as it was routine scientific inquiry. For one, Hamer was clearly inspired by those like LeVay, Pillard, and Bailey who had popularized modern biodeterministic studies of sexuality. Noting that he had grown weary of his own area of specialization (metallothionein-protein-based cancer research), Hamer pounced on the opportunity to try his hand at sexology—a field in which he had no prior professional experience.[37] Eager to join the next generation, Hamer consulted with Pillard and Bailey personally, who advised him on how to recruit twin pairs by placing advertisements in gay and lesbian newspapers.[38] Just as Evelyn Hooker had in the 1950s enlisted her homophile acquaintances in putting together the first modern research program against the pathological model, Hamer initially drew from PFLAG's membership to search for research subjects who had at least one gay male family member before opting for a larger sample of gay brothers solicited through gay community newspapers instead.[39] In both sample populations, Hamer relied on gay men who were curious about the nature of their desire—and perhaps even more so, the potential benefits of being able to explain that desire to others.

In his book *The Science of Desire*, which details this quest for the gay gene, Hamer describes having become an amateur sexologist for political and moral reasons.[40] He recounts having been inspired by tales of reform-minded scientists, who since the late nineteenth century had labored to depathologize and to decriminalize stigmatized sexualities. Hamer thought that his research could offer firepower for those engaged in the trenches of ongoing wars over anti-gay discrimination.[41] He also noted how his evidence would assist attorneys in making equal protection arguments in court. "Many legal experts felt the evidence for a genetic link to homosexuality would strengthen the evidence for immutability," Hamer posited, "and therefore cause tighter scrutiny of laws that permitted discrimination against gays and lesbians in housing, employment, or participation in the political process."[42] It is clear from his own expert testimony before a trial court in Colorado that Hamer believed that he could put some scientific weight behind legal immutability claims.[43]

Hamer did not just work on behalf of equal rights advocates. He also involved them directly in conducting research. As part of a preliminary research proposal, Hamer had assembled an advisory committee to address the "ethical, social, religious, and political issues that might arise as a result of the study."[44] Participants included longtime reformers in the sciences such as

James Weinrich and the Whitman Walker Clinic's medical director Dr. Peter Hawley, as well as movement leaders like the executive director of the Human Rights Campaign Fund Timothy McFeeley and an unnamed representative of PFLAG.[45] In a statement on the group's purpose, Hamer wrote:

> There is continuing conflict between those who regard homosexual orienta- tion as an illness or moral choice and those who view it as one of a spectrum of naturally occurring preferences. Learning about the biology of sexual orien- tation will increase our understanding of this issue and help people with dif- ferent preferences to understand one another. . . . Growing scientific evidence suggests that people don't choose their orientation, whether they are homo- sexual or heterosexual. However, regardless of whether sexual orientation is chosen or not, everyone in America deserves the same basic rights.[46]

When the Human Rights Campaign Fund spokesperson Gregory King wel- comed the study as "very relevant [and] one more piece of evidence that sex- ual orientation is not chosen," he was expressing as much support for the po- litical decision to go looking for the gay gene in the first place as much as he was opining on Hamer's findings.[47]

Taken together, Hamer, Pillard, and Bailey not only provided the gay and lesbian movement its most powerful and persuasive evidence for bioessen- tialism yet.[48] Their studies also affirmed that same-sex attraction and non- normative gender expression were distinct phenomena. Hamer explicitly aimed to dispel the "sissy thesis," which held that gay men are biologically "like women" and lesbians are "like men."[49] Indeed, his 1993 paper showed that the sample pairs with the Xq28 marker did not exhibit heightened rates of gender-atypical presentation or behavior.[50] Contrast this with the 1981 Kin- sey Institute study, which counseled parents against futile efforts to reorient their effeminate sons' and masculine daughters' "homosexual orientations" through forcing boys into competitive sports and buying dolls for girls.[51] In an interview in the *Atlantic* magazine, Pillard likewise distanced his and Bai- ley's research from studies that did little to differentiate gay identity from transsexuality. Pillard posited that transsexuals were often erroneously cast as the "gayest of the gay" when they were likely a different natural kind entirely.[52] To prove this, Pillard and Weinrich urged researchers to look for discrete bio- logical mechanisms for sexual orientation and transsexuality. Two years later, the *New York Times* would begin publishing articles with headlines proclaim- ing "Study Links Brain to Transsexuality."[53]

It would be easy to overemphasize how successful these researchers were in prying gender and sexuality apart from one another. Though Hamer be- lieved that he had struck at the heart of the sissy thesis, he also hypothesized that certain kinds of sexual preference or behavior—such as the likelihood that a gay man takes the bottom role in sex—might be the result of some biological process of feminization.[54] In the same interview in which Pillard invoked biology to wrest transsexuality from homosexuality, he questioned whether gay male identity emerged from an incomplete process of *defeminization* during gestation, a process that he believed might result in a brain organizational pattern he termed "psychosexual androgyny."[55] LeVay's 1991 paper also shared the most commonalities with the previous paradigm in that his supposedly homosexual brains featured hypothalami in between the typical size of heterosexual male and female ones (despite the fact that he devoted the final chapter of his 1993 book *The Sexual Brain* to the notion that transsexuality likely owed itself to a distinct biological process).[56] Despite these scientists' stated intentions to avoid collapsing gender back into sexuality, they continued to inadvertently reify the two with reference to reigning vernacular notions of what it meant to be a man or a woman.[57]

Politicizing the Gay Gene

Gay and lesbian advocacy organizations were quick to embed the new science of sexuality into their press releases, advocacy literature, and campaign field manuals. In the wake of the Pillard and Bailey study, a spokesperson for the Gay and Lesbian Alliance Against Defamation (GLAAD) remarked somewhat exasperatedly "What is surprising to some is that it has taken scientists so long to look carefully at the biological aspects of sexual orientation."[58]

Whereas those like GLAAD latched on to the new science without reserve, others acted with trepidation about unforeseen political risks that might attend the more obvious opportunities that the studies had made available. This blend of enticements and anxieties influenced how and when LGBTQ+ interest groups leaned into the gay gene hype. However, even when spokespersons hedged their endorsements, the movement's rhetoric was *already* saturated with language about a deeply rooted, fixed, and stable sexual essence. As a sign of their ultimate fidelity to science's truth machines, advocates tended to speak in terms of *how much* science had revealed in a given study and what still remained to be discovered. They treated sexuality as an object that had begun to be unearthed, one with roots that were—though not yet entirely visible from the surface—assuredly somewhere deep down in the soil.

The Human Rights Campaign (HRC) was among the least reticent to integrate the findings into its civil rights work. Prior to the genomania of the 1990s, the HRC often publicized new research with an unreservedly biodeterministic interpretation. Its campaign rhetoric was also already soaked in the

bio message. An internal 1989 memo instructed staff to counter right-wing fearmongering by explaining that "it is not possible, however, to 'promote' or 'encourage' [homosexuality] because sexuality is deeply rooted in one's personality and is formed so early in life that it cannot be influenced in any direction by
other people's conscious efforts."[59] Its leaflets from this period often compared
sexual orientation to being left-handed or having blue eyes.[60] Shortly after the
Atlantic published Chandler Burr's front-page article "Homosexuality and Biology" in 1993, HRC members lobbied members of Congress to support antidiscrimination legislation by distributing copies of the essay on Capitol Hill.[61]

    Local groups affiliated with the HRC acted in concert. As Florida-based
gay rights organizers prepared to defend long-standing local ordinances
from a right-wing assault in 1992, they turned to biology to make their case.[62]
The Gainesville Area Human Rights Campaign assembled an informational
packet for its field staff and volunteers, which provided resources and rhetorical advice on how and when to bring up biology. The packet's page on
"Choice and Sexual Orientation" included evidence for "the fixed nature of
homosexual orientation as opposed to homosexuality being a personal, mutable choice."[63] Other regional groups like the Oregon Speaks Out Project distributed training materials, which exhorted field staff to "suggest that sexual
orientation is a genetic or biologically determined orientation and is <u>not</u> a
choice" and to fend off smears that a scientist like Simon LeVay was a mere
"gay militant."[64]

    Throughout the 1990s, PFLAG hosted annual conference workshops with
titles like "Genetics: How Our Jewels Are Set into the Crown" and "Gay Genes:
Homosexuality and Biology."[65] Occasionally though, a PFLAG-sponsored
event offered a chance for members to express incredulity or for critics to
urge a cautious attitude in the face of an inconclusive research agenda. There
was at least as much to lose as to gain, these skeptics warned, if the studies were later discovered to be invalid. As the public was drawn into a volatile national debate over sexual orientation's origin story, PFLAG found itself
reckoning with its long-standing commitment to a bioessentialist theory of
identity and the need to preserve the political authority of sexology—that is,
distinguishing truth from hype—for another day's battle.

    PFLAG walked this tightrope throughout its 1995 publication *"Why Ask
Why?" Addressing the Research on Homosexuality and Biology*, which scru-
pulously examined the new research with one eye on its scientific validity
and another on its political implications.[66] In 1993 PFLAG received a $25,000
matching gift from an anonymous donor with instructions to establish a homosexuality and biology education fund. The bulk of that money would "finance a PFLAG publication . . . that will analyze and disseminate current

research findings on genetic links of homosexuality." The PFLAG leadership undertook the project enthusiastically, noting in their meeting minutes that they were quickly coming to "play an important role in an area in which technology and human rights are becoming increasingly entwined."[67]

The thirty-three-page *"Why Ask Why?"* was the most comprehensive attempt yet to contemplate the new studies and the talking points that they had engendered. Throughout the pamphlet, PFLAG counseled its members on how and when to invoke scientific narratives, how to hedge those narratives so as not to be exposed later as naive or triumphalist, and how to interpret and communicate the findings of each specific study in a manner far more rigorous than they had likely encountered in newspaper coverage or a nightly news broadcast. This was done through a technical parsing of the methodology, conceptual language, and various shortcomings of the Hamer, LeVay, and Bailey and Pillard studies.[68] Careful not to take one side over the other, *"Why Ask Why?"* vacillates between a recognition that such evidence contributes "an important piece in challenging certain forms of homophobia," and the position of critics like Ruth Hubbard who found the studies' conclusions themselves dubious and the notion that societal prejudice might wilt in the light of scientific truth even more absurd.[69]

Such hedging aside, it is clear that the authors of *"Why Ask Why?"* were concerned to more carefully "ask why" rather than to abandon the interrogative completely. One major criticism that they levied against the existing state of the research was that its binaristic assumptions had inadvertently closed off bio explanations for bisexuality and transsexuality. The authors described the paradigm as thus "incomplete," noting that "biological research on homosexuality, for example, does have implications for our understanding of transsexuality," and that researchers "had not addressed these connections because the biological research on homosexuality has, for the most part, specifically excluded those people who identify as transsexual or transgendered."[70] Later in the pamphlet, the authors castigated those studies that relied on the assumption that nonnormative gendered characteristics were an inherent feature of gay and lesbian sexual orientations.[71]

Just as PFLAG published this inward-facing effort to cultivate nuance, its leadership was simultaneously planning an outward-facing campaign based in a mostly uncritical celebration of bioessentialism. In 1994 PFLAG contracted with the consulting firm EDK Associates to develop a nationwide public education and antidiscrimination program titled "Project Open Mind."[72] Upon conducting interviews in Tulsa, Atlanta, and Houston, the firm reported back that "most people believe that homosexuality is innate, and this provides an opening for addressing the issue and setting up the argument for tolerance."[73] This undertaking involved a few steps, the first of which was to lead off an organizing conversation with the bioessentialist narrative. This would assure straight people that providing civil rights and tolerance for gays and lesbians in no way threatened their own sexualities. To this point, the consultants wrote:

> "Explaining" the source of homosexuality allows straight people to reassure themselves that sexuality is a given. . . . If sexuality were a matter of choice, or even contained some degree of choice and ambiguity, people would have to think about a volatile and complex dimension of human experience.[74]

The bioessentialist thesis also furnished a defense against the fear that homosexuality was in any sense contagious.[75] The report advised that advocates avoid the language of "choice" when discussing children especially, as the fear of contamination was so strong that even when respondents initially accepted the biological evidence, they continued to suspect that television coverage of gay rights, for instance, might have an adverse effect on their own child's sexuality.[76] The takeaway from these consultant-conducted interviews was clear: leading off a conversation with evidence for the innate was effective in that it promised to "resolve the public discussion about the nature of sexuality" and to bring about "social peace."[77]

Nevertheless, there were limits to the gay gene's efficacy. Heeding the consultant's warnings, PFLAG advised that while bioessentialism could lay a sturdy foundation for tolerance, such evidence did not automatically cause a person to shed their extant prejudices about the "tragedy" of homosexuality.[78] When EDK interviewers had posed a hypothetical to an intolerant middle-aged male respondent that involved a gay son asking to bring his partner to Thanksgiving dinner, the respondent reconsidered his initial fury upon learning that the son had no control over his attraction.[79] What the bioessentialist argument could not change, though, was the belief that there was still something to pity or despair about this situation. Transcending these biases, analysts argued, would necessitate a pivot from the born this way belief to a message about the joys of queer life and the importance of removing social and legal barriers to flourishing.

Though the National Gay and Lesbian Task Force happily welcomed the news of each new bioessentialist study, its leadership navigated internal tensions over whether to cede truth-telling to science. The Task Force had maintained its close relationships with its Kinsey Institute and related allied researchers since the 1973 battle over pathology at the American Psychiatric Association. It was at the same time, however, home to a diversity of political tendencies, some of which had grown discontent with its liberal assimilationist politics of which the gay gene was emblematic.[80] This stemmed in large part from the fact that the Task Force possessed a dual structural nature. It was at once a national nonprofit interest group and a diffuse network of local and regional activist groups and campaigns. It thus played the insider role and outsider simultaneously by lobbying the halls of Congress while organizing acts of civil disobedience on its doorsteps.[81] So, while the Task Force was home to a fair number of professional civil rights advocates, it was also the refuge of self-styled radicals who were fast becoming enthralled with queer theory conceptions of sexuality and gender as flexible and fluid.

Despite these tensions, the Task Force was in the end a relatively vocal backer of the new studies. In a statement on LeVay's 1991 study, Task Force spokesperson Robert Bray told *USA Today* that the findings "support what we've always believed—being gay is not a choice . . . it may even be determined before birth."[82] In a press release regarding Hamer's 1993 research, Deputy Director of Public Policy Peri Jude Radecic explained that "the NIH Study is an important addition to the growing body of evidence indicating a genetic basis for homosexuality in some people . . . [a]nd it shows that homosexuality is a naturally occurring and common variation among humans—a fact that gay and lesbian people have known all along." Like PFLAG, the Task Force leadership understood that such narratives only contained so much firepower. Task Force spokespersons would frequently follow up their endorsements with a warning that "regardless of the origins of homosexuality, however, discrimination based on sexual orientation is wrong and must end."[83]

There is a myth that the rise of the religious right and the ex-gay community pushed gay rights defenders into making "nature over nurture" arguments. Though these forces surely persuaded many activists and leaders to stick to their guns, right-wing opponents were typically the ones reacting to the nature narrative. James Dobson's Focus on the Family, its policy arm the Family Research Council, and similar conservative outfits began explicitly juxtaposing the gay gene with the rhetoric of "choice" and "lifestyle." Others like the Parents and Friends of Ex-Gays and Gays—an obvious riff on PFLAG's name and mission—positioned itself explicitly against the biological thesis.[84] They too often allied with those like the National Association for Research and Therapy of Homosexuality, which was formed by defectors from more established mental health institutions, the latter of which were cleaning house of any clinician still promoting the pathological thesis.

Some conservative religious groups even accepted the validity of the gay gene while retaining a political opposition to acceptance. In 1998 Focus on the Family broke ground on its Love Won Out ex-gay ministry campaign. Though ex-gay ministries of various types had existed since the early 1970s,

Love Won Out was uniquely dedicated to challenging the normative dimensions of the "by nature" thesis. Love Won Out accepted that sexual orientation was likely formed in part by biological processes, but that spiritual guidance could steer a person away from acting on that sinful disposition.[85] Just as an alcoholic cannot make recourse to his temperament as an excuse, a man who is gay by constitution must learn to live with—and to suppress—his earthly burden.

As the gay and lesbian movement became further entrenched in the world of DC-based interest groups, and the Democratic Party gradually incorporated the fight for gay civil rights into its policy agenda, the tussle over nature and nurture spilled into high politics. The 1992 presidential primary and general election campaigns featured an unprecedented amount of attention on gay and lesbian issues, ranging from military inclusion to national HIV/AIDS funding. Bill Clinton made gains in the Democratic Party primaries by employing the openly gay corporate consultant David Mixner to amass donors from wealthy queer people and support from gay interest groups.[86] While the Democrats courted gays and lesbians, the Republican Party strove to convince its social conservative supporters that it was still their great champion. On the general election campaign trail, Vice President Dan Quayle was deployed to shore up evangelical votes from a base that had become doubtful of Bush's commitment to their cause. In a number of speeches and interviews, Quayle denied the veracity of the new biological studies and denounced same-sex attraction as an immoral "wrong choice."[87] In an interview with the ABC News program *The Week*, the vice president stated plainly that "my viewpoint is that it's more of a choice than a biological situation."[88]

From Preference to Orientation: How Science Made Identity "Stick"

Among the gay gene's accomplishments was its success in changing the very way we speak about sexual identity. This burgeoning bioessentialist sentiment supplied the necessary binding agent to congeal etiologically agnostic terms like "preference" and "desire" into the more resoundingly certain and stable referent "orientation." Not long ago, the orientation language was rarely heard. Throughout the 1970s, activists had lobbied for antidiscrimination municipal ordinances, state laws, and even a national civil rights bill using the language of "affectional or sexual preference."[89] In an early attempt to codify the preference rhetoric, an organization in Minneapolis–St. Paul settled on the term because it evoked the unpredictability of desire—for them, a preference could come and go without undermining the integrity of their personhood.

Though this liberationist ethos flowed downstream from Stonewall, there was a more immediate strategic calculation here too. As one activist put it, the notion of "preference" would protect gays and lesbians "for publicly expressing their affection . . . or even for projecting an image which society does not usually associate with 'masculine' or 'feminine' roles."[90] In lobbying US Representative Bella Abzug to amend Title VII of the Civil Rights Act, which would have prohibited discrimination "on the basis of sex, sexual orientation, or marital status," National Gay Task Force president Bruce Voeller joined the Minnesota-based activists in insisting that the language be changed to "preference." Doing so, Voeller posited, would protect conduct such as holding hands that might not be covered by the orientation language.[91]

Gay rights advocates did occasionally lobby with the term "orientation" throughout the 1970s and 1980s. However, the word itself had yet to be imbued with the logic of bioessentialism. In 1971 the Task Force's progenitor, the New York–based Gay Activists Alliance (GAA), pressed the New York City Council to pass an employment antidiscrimination law that protected persons based on their sexual orientation.[92] Rather than indicating a fixed essence, however, the GAA defined orientation as "the choice of sexual partner according to gender," something that had nothing to do with whether orientation was innate or fixed.[93] Even those groups that endorsed early notions of fixity like the Gay National Rights Lobby (GNRL) warned that "to leave unaddressed the matter of homosexual sexual conduct (or other arguably homosexual conduct) or to protect only the status leaves a gapingly wide loophole which WILL be (ab)used extensively and will render the Gay Rights law a dead letter to all practical intents and purposes."[94] To add additional complexity here, "preference" itself could take on relatively counterintuitive meanings during this moment. For instance, the GAA's close allies at the Kinsey Institute made public statements in the early 1980s on sexual *preference*, which they took to signify "a deep-seated predisposition, probably biological in nature."[95]

As the advocacy movement matured, the savviest among its ranks realized that to become a paragon of pluralist identity politics, they would need a more consistent terminology, one that could conjure the idea of an *essence* at its utterance. Gradually, the term "orientation" came to denote that long-sought-after stability. This reframe would make an early mark in the legislative arena. In 1981 the GNRL began promoting antidiscrimination bills with Judd Marmor's remarks on the relative fixity of orientation.[96] His and others' work were also put to use in a resource guide titled "If Your Constituents Ask . . . ," which counseled sympathetic legislators on how to respond to voters who were dismayed by their representative supporting equal rights for gays and lesbians.[97] The Kinsey Institute's Martin Weinberg even appeared before Congress to testify in support of an early employment protections bill featuring the orientation language.[98]

As the genomania of the 1990s kicked into full gear, "orientation" and its bioessentialist undertones featured heavily in state and federal attempts at passing broad antidiscrimination measures. In the process of drafting the federal Equality Non-Discrimination Act (ENDA) in 1994, the Sexuality Information and Education Council of the United States (SIECUS) advised the ACLU's Gay and Lesbian Rights program's leadership to lobby hard for orientation. They cautioned that the "affectional" terminology that was being tossed around was "politically unworkable," a Trojan horse that would invite all kinds of exemptions and loopholes.[99] When ENDA was introduced in the House of Representatives later that year, the bill's stated intent was "to prohibit employment discrimination on the basis of sexual orientation."[100] Aware of the threat that orientation logic posed, right-wing Christian groups like the Traditional Values Coalition excoriated the "indoctrinating" effects that ENDA would expose to children held "hostage" in classrooms headed by gay and transgender teachers.[101]

Contrary to the claims of political scientists Gary Mucciaroni and Mary Lou Killian, who argued that science did not play a major role in this era's legislative debates, the term "orientation" and attendant discussions of sexual identity as they occurred throughout debates in Congress, state legislatures, and city halls should be understood as featuring bioessentialist notions themselves.[102] Even when gay rights advocates delivered speeches in favor of antidiscrimination laws without specific mentions of scientific evidence—notably, Mucciaroni and Killian find that they actually did invoke scientific rationales at least 17 percent of the time—proponents were *already* speaking the language of fixity, which owed much of its ideological form and its institutional support to biology.[103]

Outside the legislative realm, gay and lesbian press media advocates pressured news outlets to take note of the discursive shift. Throughout the early 1990s, the national media-oriented Gay and Lesbian Alliance Against Defamation endeavored to wipe out terms like "preference," "choice," and "lifestyle" and to replace them with "orientation." In an updated stylebook sent to CNN in 1993, GLAAD recommended the use of "sexual orientation" over "sexual preference," noting that the latter had been crafted into a dog whistle for the right.[104] That same year, GLAAD published a brochure that advised its media allies on how to respond to supporters of Colorado's and Oregon's attempt at constitutionalizing anti-gay discrimination.[105] GLAAD explained that the scientific community had effectively legitimated the equal rights

movement's position on a fixed orientation and had thus rebuffed older theories of pliable preference. Fast-forward to the present: Senate Democrats be-
rated then Supreme Court justice nominee Amy Coney Barrett for invoking
the term "sexual preference" to discuss gay rights doctrine.[106] Nearly thirty
years after the gay gene garnered national attention, the language of orientation still sticks.

Conduct, Status, Immutability: Bioessentialism and the Pursuit of Strict Scrutiny

Prior to the age of genomania, gay rights advocates had already made a practice of peppering their legal briefs with biological content. After a coalition of major civil rights and gay and lesbian organizations lost their case
in *Bowers v. Hardwick* (1986), which temporarily closed off a path through
the substantive due-process-doctrine-based right to privacy, the equal protection clause became *the* most important means of asserting the constitutional rights of queer people. Going forward, legal strategists for the ACLU
and gay rights litigation groups had an especially strong incentive to push
judges and justices to perceive sexual orientation as an immutable category
worthy of heightened judicial protections (per case law requirements). As the
following tour through the era's military inclusion and antidiscrimination legal campaigns shows, attorneys pursued this work deftly, relying on biological
evidence where it appeared beneficial and eschewing it when they discerned
alternative—sometimes less controversial or risky—opportunities for rights
expansions. Far from predetermined itself, the decision to rely on biology was
always a political choice made through negotiation among attorneys, national
gay rights leaders, and local activist groups.

As early as the 1960s, homophile organizations litigated to reverse dishonorable discharges and to reinstate civilians working for the Department
of Defense and related federal agencies.[107] Just as the homophiles had sparred
with the government over whether homosexuality was legal conduct or a status distinction, litigators in the 1980s and 1990s were faced with the argument
that homosexuality could *not* be a protected status condition because its content was defined by the very kind of conduct—that is, same-sex intercourse—
deemed to be without constitutional protection in the *Bowers v. Hardwick*
ruling.[108] In cases like *Woodward v. United States* (1989), the Second Circuit
Court of Appeals ruled that "homosexuality is primarily behavioral in nature," which differentiated it from other protected status categories like race,
religion, and sex.[109]

To combat the idea that sexual identity could not be meaningfully divorced from the act itself, litigators used scientific studies that rendered orientation the product of a predetermined biological element. In *Dahl v. Secretary of the United States Navy* (1993), a federal district court in Florida heard a case involving a plaintiff who—in a clever move to circumvent the *Bowers* status-as-conduct problem—identified as a "stated homosexual" who had abstained from homosexual conduct upon enlisting.[110] To buttress the claim that orientation exists both prior to and in the absence of actual sexual activity, Dahl and his attorneys cited Pillard, Bailey, and LeVay as well as a law review funded by the National Center for Human Genome Research that expounded the legal ramifications of what its authors termed "genetic essentialism."[111] Dahl's attorneys concluded that because "complex combinations of genetic, hormonal, neurological and environmental factors operating prior to birth largely determines what an individual's sexual orientation will be," the soldier should not have been discharged for something that he *was* intrinsically rather than for violating the US Navy's code of conduct—which he claimed that he had not.[112]

Other outed-and-ousted service members rested their legal arguments on the fixed nature of homosexuality as well.[113] In her case for reinstatement in the US Army, Sergeant Miriam Ben-Shalom was assisted by the American Psychological Association, which filed an amicus brief detailing the field's understanding of sexual orientation and its policy position against discrimination.[114] That same year, prominent sexologist Richard Green and psychologist Gregory Herek defended Joseph Steffan's right to reenlist in the navy by arguing that his sexual orientation was "not consciously chosen but rather . . . [is] a basic part of an individual's psyche."[115]

Despite all this, some federal judges and civil rights litigators did not believe that strong bioessentialist evidence was necessarily a requirement for heightened judicial protections. Throughout the 1980s, federal judges had begun to clarify the meaning of immutability, noting how the biological fixity of a trait was just one among many factors that courts could consult in making such determinations. Immigrant status, for instance, is immutable yet not biologically so. Religious belief has also long been regarded as immutable in that coerced renunciations of faith are deemed cruel. In another twist, a 1985 Supreme Court ruling held that although persons with mental disabilities are often immutably so in a biological sense, they do not merit heightened judicial protections.[116] In an oft-cited concurring opinion in *Watkins v. U.S. Army* (1989), Ninth Circuit Court of Appeals Judge William A. Norris delivered the most comprehensive assessment of immutability to date. Norris explained:

At a minimum, then, the Supreme Court is willing to treat a trait as effectively immutable if changing it would involve great difficulty, such as requiring a major physical change or a traumatic change of identity. Reading the case law in a more capacious manner, "immutability" may describe those traits that are so central to a person's identity that it would be abhorrent for government to penalize a person for refusing to change them, regardless of how easy that change might be physically.[117]

According to these criteria, Norris contended that "sexual orientation is immutable for the purposes of equal protection doctrine" because "scientific research indicates that we have little control over our sexual orientation and that, once acquired, our sexual orientation is largely impervious to change."[118] Ergo, forcible attempts to reorient sexuality are inherently cruel.

Though some service members occasionally won individual reinstatements, courts consistently refused to acknowledge a general right to serve. Oftentimes, judges cited the lack of biological evidence as a justification for refusing reenlistments. Despite Norris's support on the Ninth Circuit, that appellate court ultimately closed its own doors to gay service members in the 1990 case *High Tech Gays v. Defense Industrial Security Clearance Office*. There, the court ruled that "homosexuality is not an immutable characteristic; it is behavioral and hence is fundamentally different from traits such as race, gender, or alienage."[119] Dissenting from the *en banc* opinion, Judges William Canby and Norris protested their colleagues' reading of the equal protection clause's scope and mandate. What really needed adjudicating, Canby and Norris argued, was whether an instance of discrimination had resulted from some "unfair branding or resort to prejudice" based on a "class's distinguishing characteristic" rather than whether that characteristic was immutable. Additionally, the judges posited that because homosexuality would be so difficult—if not impossible—to alter, it was by all accounts immutable even if case law did indeed require demonstration of biological immutability. The question that the court should have asked was whether gays and lesbians "choose to be attracted by members of their own sex, rather than by members of the opposite sex? The answer, by the overwhelming weight of respectable authority, is 'no.' . . . Sexual identity is established at a very early age; it is not a matter of conscious or controllable choice."[120]

Despite these losses in the courts, the gay and lesbian movement's investment in Bill Clinton's 1992 presidential campaign offered litigants some much-needed leverage. One of the new president's first agenda items was an overhaul of the military's discriminatory practices. The result was the 1993 Don't Ask, Don't Tell (DADT) reform, which in theory offered expanded protections by actively under-policing conduct in exchange for silence. Still, openly gay service members continued to be considered "an unacceptable risk to the high standards of morale, good order and discipline, and unit cohesion that are the essence of military capability."[121]

For good reason, Don't Ask, Don't Tell was received as a disappointing half-measure. Contra those who read *Bowers v. Hardwick* as tying status and conduct into a knot, DADT wrested them back apart in extending protection to status (e.g., identifying as gay) and denying it to sexual behavior. The reform ironically incentivized conservative service members to infer homosexual conduct from status markers.[122] A service member who made a comment in favor of gay rights, cut their hair in a certain way, or wore a civilian outfit at odds with prevailing gender stereotypes could still be punished on the suspicion of what those markers and utterances revealed. In response to these shortcomings, some litigators began to refashion their approach to status claims by arguing that the act of disclosure itself was protected by the First Amendment.[123] They argued that gay and lesbian identities were defined by much more than sexual behavior; sexual identity congealed a range of emotions, desires, *and* actions—including the speech act of coming out.[124] Despite this subjective-seeming formulation, attorneys continued to feature the familiar references to scientific authority and bio-fixity.[125]

Advocates fought DADT outside the courts in a parallel manner. A 1993 legislative lobbying training manual produced by the Military Freedom Project included a copy of Chandler Burr's "Homosexuality and Biology" article for lobbyists to consult.[126] The National Gay and Lesbian Task Force's Military Freedom Initiative also produced training and educational materials that implored advocates to make comparisons to civil rights reformers who had fought to racially integrate the military in the 1940s. One pamphlet taught activists how to invoke genetic evidence as a rejoinder to assertions that racial integration was about a "non-behavioral characteristic" whereas sexual orientation was a matter of "behavioral choice."[127]

Antidiscrimination cases involving schoolteachers, local and state ordinances, and ballot initiatives were another major site of legal conflict throughout the 1990s. Just like in military inclusion fights, attorneys often challenged discriminatory bans with appeals to immutability. And like in those skirmishes within the armed forces, they occasionally convinced district court judges to overturn discriminatory policies. In a 1991 Kansas-based case involving a male schoolteacher suspected of "homosexual tendencies," a district court judge ruled that the "available scientific evidence . . . strongly supports the view that sexual orientation is not easily mutable."[128] The 1990s were also

a decade of backlash. Right-wing groups during this period frequently lobbied for anti-queer state and local ballot initiatives, labeling antidiscrimination policies as "special rights" to distinguish them from mere civil rights.[129]

In one of the more high-profile skirmishes of the decade, the Equality
Foundation of Greater Cincinnati Inc. and Lambda Legal sought to overturn
an ordinance that had preempted the city from enacting any future antidiscrimination measures on the basis of sexual orientation, conduct, or status.
In the court's words, Lambda's league of expert witnesses had demonstrated
that "sexual orientation is a characteristic which exists separately and indepen-
dently from sexual conduct or behavior" and that it "is not only involuntary,
but is unamenable to change."[130] Although equal rights advocates won in district court, the Sixth Circuit Court of Appeals struck down the lower court's
ruling that gays and lesbians constituted a quasi-suspect class. In its 1995 decision, the Sixth Circuit gestured to other circuit court opinions that had heeded
the Supreme Court's warning in *Bowers* against "tailoring novel fundamental
rights" for gays and lesbians. Strikingly, the court found evidence that sexual
orientation was "an innate and involuntary state of being and set of drives
wholly independent of conduct" to be mostly irrelevant."[131] Homosexual orientation was not an immutable characteristic, the court reasoned, because
gays, lesbians, and bisexuals could conceal their status, especially if they were
not engaging in the kind of sexual behavior that *Bowers* had already placed
outside the bounds of constitutional safeguards. Tragically, Lambda managed
here to win on the terrain of science, but ultimately lost before a court that
could reconcile such evidence with a clampdown on civil rights.

A few years earlier in *Romer v. Evans*, Lambda and the ACLU oversaw a
legal attempt to overturn a Colorado constitutional amendment that had preempted local and state antidiscrimination laws. Throughout the trial court
phase in 1993, lawyers from the national organizations sparred with local activists and attorneys over whether to make immutability a central feature of
their equal protection clause challenge.[132] Having recently lost a slew of military cases in which biology had taken center stage, attorneys for the ACLU
and Lambda planned to combat the discriminatory amendment on other
grounds. They wanted to pivot away from ontology and to argue instead that
gays and lesbians lacked an equal ability to participate in society (another
criterion spelled out plainly in equal protection clause case law).[133] However,
attorneys and activists affiliated with the Colorado Legal Initiatives Project
were intent on making the scientific studies and expert witnesses a key part
of both their trial strategy and constitutional arguments.[134]

Ultimately, lead attorney Jean Dubofsky sided with the local advocates
and brought expert witnesses including Richard Green, Judd Marmor, and

Dean Hamer to testify on the immutable nature of sexual orientation.[135] It is hard to tell which side was more perceptive given that the Supreme Court's landmark ruling in *Romer v. Evans* scored a major victory for equal rights while avoiding the question of immutability altogether, ruling instead that such displays of irrational prejudice or *animus* could not survive the rational basis test, that is, the lowest standard of judicial scrutiny.[136] Either way, the court's refusal to make a definitive call on biology ensured that such internal divisions over when and how to invoke scientific authority would persist.

"The Gay Gene Will Not Protect You"

As liberal gay advocacy groups, decorated in their new biological adornments, took their place in the heavenly chorus of American pluralism, queer dissenters protested at the gates. The gay gene's skeptics within the ranks of the DC-based gay and lesbian nonprofit world were both few in number and tepid in their own wariness. In responding to news of the 1993 Pillard and Bailey study, a spokesperson for the National Center for Lesbian Rights (NCLR) told the *Los Angeles Times* that while the research addressed the fact that "it is awful to be invisible," the organization feared that it undercut the need "to be recognized and protected as a valid associational and lifestyle choice, whether it is genetically based or not."[137] This harkening back to an older tradition of political lesbianism makes sense given that the NCLR formed during the golden age of radical choice rhetoric in the 1970s. However, this rare nod to volition had less to do with that tradition roaring back; more than anything else, it was a last-ditch effort to stitch together a pair of incommensurate perspectives on personhood. Though the NCLR held the contradiction at the advent of the gay gene's popularity, the country's largest advocate for lesbian rights would soon shed this circumspection. Less than two decades later, it would come to pioneer bioessentialist legal arguments for gender identity protections.[138]

Biology's dissidents were at times given opportunities to present their incredulity to national advocacy organizations, though to no great influence. John D'Emilio, historian and founder of the National Gay and Lesbian Task Force's Policy Institute, led that group's board of directors through a discussion titled "Nature or Nurture: Are We Not Queer" in 1993.[139] D'Emilio's liberation-laden caution extended from his own Marxian social constructionist view, which historicized modern gay identity and culture as inventions of the late nineteenth-century transformations in wage labor, urban geographies, and the decline of the agrarian family household.[140] D'Emilio warned against what he termed the "born gay" narrative, noting the thin and contested nature of the scientific research and urging his colleagues to argue "from justice rather than nature."[141]

D'Emilio and others' skepticism, however, was received poorly outside of the academy. Indeed, university humanities departments had become one of the only refuges for such doubters. Organizations like the Gay Academic Union (of which D'Emilio was a founding member) had in the 1970s and 1980s struggled against hostile administrators and department heads to study gay history, which they often did with a historian's attention to contingency. By the 1990s, postmodern and queer theory reworkings of the New Left tradition were thriving in the humanities as high-theory superstars applied Derridean deconstructive and Foucauldian poststructuralist techniques to what they took to be the social fiction of sexuality's stability.[142]

While the gay gene narrative was dissected atop seminar room tables, a new style of queer liberationist worked to deconstruct it in the streets. In the late 1980s and 1990s, direct-action protest groups inspired both by the HIV/AIDS advocacy of ACT UP and the principles of gay liberation formed to oppose their liberal counterparts. Though minuscule in number and influence, those like Queer Nation, the Lesbian Avengers, and Transgender Nation garnered outsize media attention for their confrontational and theatrical tactics.[143] Equipped with queer theory's pronouncements on the unstable, fluid character of desire and the body's inherent resistance to neat sex/gender classifications, these radicals rallied against what they took to be the normalizing project of bioessentialist identity claims.

Looking for ways to beat back these queer theory critics of the gay gene, conservative essayists like then editor of the *New Republic* Andrew Sullivan and the neoconservative writer Bruce Bawer accused the queer apostates of having become de facto collaborators with the homophobic right wing.[144] In summoning strength from natural law theory, Sullivan denounced ACT UP and Queer Nation for having acquiesced to the anti-Enlightenment doctrine of their own religious fundamentalist oppressors.[145] Similarly, Bawer argued in his 1994 book *A Place at the Table* that proof of the innate would allow for gays and lesbian to be fully folded into a classically liberal political order.[146] Not content to join either the liberals in demands for antidiscrimination protections or the radical anarcho demands against state violence, those like Sullivan and Bawer placed their faith in science, changing cultural norms, and the free market to at long last lift gay men and women out from their subordinate condition.[147]

The conservative critics aside, there is some irony in that the most postmodern deconstructionist variants of queer politics adopted a conception of homophobia that essentially mirrored the liberal condemnation of prejudice.

Though the radicals charged liberal advocates with having traded the messy reality of sex for the gay gene's promise of social stability, Queer Nation distributed pieces like "I Hate Straights," a manifesto that reified the straight-gay divide through a critique of homophobia. Contra gay liberation's war cry that it was coming to free the desires locked away in the prison of the heterosexual mind, Queer Nation resentfully decried the "freedom" and "privilege" that straight Americans already enjoyed. Rather than free them of their restrained libidinal energies, Queer Nation promised to "terrorize" and to "frighten" their heterosexual "enemies" into forking over those same privileges to queer people.[148] Though *to be* queer for these activists was not to be a discrete biological kind, their conception of identity certainly did at times crystallize into a solid taxonomic form, one that was then thrown into a presumably zero-sum survival of the fittest struggle with its heterosexual complement.

When radical queer groups did articulate a more expansive notion of shared structural oppression, they did so by drawing historical through lines from early twentieth-century eugenics to present-day biological investigations. In a pamphlet titled *We Will Not Protect You* distributed at the 2005 New York City Gay Pride Parade, ACT UP offered a blend of anti-assimilation queer politics with a panicked plea to evade the slippery scientific slope from genetics to eugenics.[149] In a section titled "The Gay Gene Will Not Protect You," the authors offered a brief tour through the history of race science from the thinkers who inspired Virginia's Racial Integrity Act of 1924 through modern biodeterministic rationales for economic and racial inequality in works like *The Bell Curve*, all before finally arriving at the studies produced by LeVay, Hamer, and Bailey.[150] The message was clear: the gay gene promised liberation but would inevitably lead to a concentration camp.

A sympathetic view would grant the ACT UP activists their Weimer Republic parallel, a regime in which reform-minded sexologists like Magnus Hirschfeld once conducted their work amid a culture of relative sexual libertinism before losing it all to the Third Reich. Hirschfeld himself wound up being derided as the "most dangerous Jew alive" by Adolf Hitler as his research institute (and the legal reforms that he had helped to make possible) burned to the ground. This modern hysteria over the gay gene's eugenic potential, however, mischaracterizes the historical record. It does so in at least one of two ways: by either equating Hirschfeld with his more inegalitarian counterparts like another German sexologist, Richard Freiherr von Krafft-Ebing, who saw aberrant sexualities as indicative of a nervous system disorder—that is, a guilt by shared subject matter—or by making Hirschfeld culpable for the crimes of those who would have happily gone about pathologizing without him. In other words, Hirschfeld's scientific authority lent Weimer-era reformers support for egalitarian changes to the law and social customs whereas Krafft-Ebing's early career description of the homosexual's constitutionally defective physiology rationalized mistreatment.[151] The fact that both men entertained biology broadly construed was incidental to their normative views, legal work, and political intentions. Just as ideas do nothing on their own accord, so, too, are scientific hypotheses themselves inert.

ACT UP's interpretative failings here extend from a surface-level historical comparison, one that collapses various strains of scientific authority across time, space, and political commitment into their most odious form. One could fairly draw connections among those oppressed by the science that legitimated epileptic colonies, sterilization treatments for lower-class southern whites and urban-dwelling immigrants, and racist research enterprises like physiognomy. In these cases, scientific authority *was* deployed for despotic social engineering exercises. But it is much harder to see the same potential for scientific renderings produced and promoted by liberal advocates, either in the past or the present day. Just as Dean Hamer is no Charles Murray, Hirschfeld was no Krafft-Ebing or Hitler, for that matter. ACT UP was on stable ground in arguing that "genes will not save you when someone with power wants to keep you down or to eliminate you"—an ideological cover is, of course, no substitute for political power proper.[152] Yet despite their other political and social limitations, Hamer's study on its own did not swing wide open the back door to eugenics and concentrated state oppression.

Clearly fearful of the future and unsatisfied with the direction of the liberal gay rights movement, some queer dissenters launched mini coups from within national organizations. A small sectarian group called Queer by Choice was formed shortly after its founder, Tom Aqueno, met Mark Gonzales at a national PFLAG conference in 1999, where they attended a panel titled "Homosexuality: Choice or Biology?" Aqueno and Gonzales—both of whom experienced their sexualities as a matter of their own choosing—had been disturbed by the panelists who were described as "wholly on the side of biology, and [who] spoke mockingly of choice, claiming that only a homophobe could believe anyone chose to be gay."[153] They were also alarmed to learn that PFLAG had adopted a statement endorsing the biological thesis in which it derided the choice narrative as right-wing propaganda.[154] In response, the two men formed a small operation that contacted over two hundred PFLAG affiliates and the national leadership with a demand that the members be educated about the scientific and political limitations of the biological frame.

This sparked an internal conversation among the PFLAG board of directors about how to contain what they feared could spiral into crisis. In an email exchange among several national officers, Executive Director Kirsten Kingdon fretted that "this is an issue the right wing would love to use against us. I am more worried about moving too quickly to revise our policy than I am about any negative publicity we might get from the Queer by Choice group."[155] The leadership ultimately decided to solicit a questionnaire to collect members' views on their recent pro-biology statement. The responses sent back to the board reflected a common sentiment: even if bioessentialist studies could not prove definitively that homosexuality was innate, it was best described as something deeply held, stable, and anything but a conscious choice.[156]

Incoming PFLAG president and physician Arnold Drake took the discord as an opportunity to give the most forceful defense of the born this way notion yet. In a draft of his pending inaugural address circulated among the board, Drake declared that "PFLAG believes that this is a biological phenomenon. There is scientific evidence for genetic, anatomic, and environmental (prenatal and postnatal) influences on sexual orientation."[157] This unequivocal endorsement provoked a minor backlash from those who wished to hedge such bold pronouncements, especially given that the studies from which Drake drew were beginning to incur heavy scrutiny by fellow scientists and the national press.[158] Board member Marion Hamer, for instance, was dismayed that the draft drifted far from the tempered approach PFLAG had taken in its *"Why Ask Why?"* pamphlet. Others like Kingdon cautioned that "we know less about lesbians than we do about gays—and we don't know a lot about gays."[159] Notably, Kingdon did not mean that biological evidence would not one day allow for PFLAG to make such statements. She followed up her concern with a hopeful reference to Dean Hamer's recent attempts to recruit lesbians from PFLAG's membership for a new study.

Ultimately, Drake did soften his chest thumping about the biological evidence. In his speech delivered on October 28, 2000, the incoming president explained, "The exact scientific cause of sexual orientation is unknown and is not our major concern. Science has determined that genetics probably plays a part in sexual orientation; how this happens, and to what extent, is unknown." Drake maintained that "choice" was an inappropriate frame through which to comprehend how most gays and lesbians felt about their sexualities, and that "most of our family members feel that they had no conscious choice in their sexual orientation, and we believe them."[160] A post-speech correspondence between Drake and Task Force cofounder Ronald Gold underscores just how committed PFLAG's new president was to the future of the gay gene theory. In that exchange, Drake hammered home his belief in the biological thesis with allusions to various scientific findings and his own faith in the imminence of even more robust evidence. He closed his letter with a reflection on sexual identity as an inner truth, one that could be ignored or suppressed but that was at its core constitutive to one's personhood, writing, "We all DO have choices in what we do with our 'preferences': whether to act on them, whether to suppress them, whether to deny that they exist."[161]

Whither the Gay Gene?

For much of the 1990s, bioessentialism dominated discussions of gay and lesbian identity in venues ranging from nightly broadcast news to the witness stand. The gay gene, the gay brain, and the gay hormonal profile became, for a moment, cultural celebrities. Yet toward the end of the decade, skepticism began to settle in, especially as it became clear that the new gay science's proponents had made epistemic promises that they could not keep. Dean Hamer, for instance, came under fire from fellow geneticists in the years following his press tour touting the gay gene's arrival. In 1999 researchers at the University of Western Ontario famously failed to replicate Hamer's *Science* study, which doused the spark of hubris that Hamer and others had ignited.[162] If researchers could not even agree about the genetic location of where male homosexuality might sit on the X chromosome—let alone find a specific encoding gene for orientation—maybe they would never behold sexuality's truth through mining the human genome.

The gay gene's failure to replicate was only the first of many blows that the born this way thesis would soon incur. From the outset of the Human Genome Project, critics of its booster's most biodeterministic prophecies warned that the search for a single gene for homosexuality or any other complex social phenomenon was doomed, a fraught endeavor that ran more on creative storytelling and promissory notes than it did on any conclusive empirical results.[163] Those cautionary voices wound up sounding quite prescient when the completion of the Human Genome Project undermined these "just-so" evolutionary narratives. The discovery that a mere 20,000 to 25,000 or so genes were directly responsible for the so-called mysteries of human life splashed cold water on the thesis that the genome housed hundreds of thousands of genes that coded for individual proteins—and that those proteins were largely responsible for specific behavioral traits, predispositions, and illnesses.[164] Though the political ideology of biodeterminism would survive this injury, the HGP's completion ruptured the illusion that human nature could be boiled down to individual genes coding for specific traits.

These developments gave pause to some in the LGBTQ+ movement who had hitherto been quite keen on the gay gene. In a response to the Hamer replication paper, a spokesperson for the Human Rights Campaign backtracked on its previous endorsement, clarifying that "we don't believe these studies

should have a significant influence in the public policy debate on whether
to treat gay and lesbian people fairly and equally, whether they conclusively
prove a 'gay gene' or not."[165] And while behind the scenes, the Task Force's
leadership complained about the "bogus science [used] to discredit Hamer,"
in public they came to distance themselves from Hamer's work and future
studies.[166]

The HRC was not alone in tempering its rhetoric. As early as 1993, the
ACLU began to question whether educating the public about sexuality's etiology might actually backfire. In a reflection on the failed fight over Colorado's 1992 anti-gay state constitutional amendment, the ACLU determined
that such campaigns were "not the time to get people to understand and approve of homosexuality."[167] A postmortem report recommended that activists
focus energies on undermining the conservative "family values" frame more
directly by casting such discriminatory policies as motivated by pure vitriol.

On the constitutional front, Justice Anthony Kennedy's opinions in a couple of major gay rights cases would somewhat disincentivize the quest for
suspect class distinction.[168] In *Romer v. Evans*, Kennedy made it clear that
displays of animus like Colorado's constitutional amendment were impermissible because they could not even meet the lowest standard of judicial scrutiny. A law, policy, or state constitutional amendment that explicitly aimed
to undercut the rights of a minority group, Kennedy reasoned, was one that
lacked a legitimate government interest entirely. Later, writing in the Supreme
Court's majority decision in *Lawrence*—which reversed *Bowers* by striking down a Texas sodomy ban—Kennedy evaded the question of status by
grounding the right to same-sex sexual conduct in the principles of liberty
and privacy.[169] These and other doctrinal developments made it unclear if the
court would ever again grant heightened judicial scrutiny to *any* social group,
let alone gays and lesbians.[170]

Lastly, internal expansions and tensions within the movement itself led
to the integration of once-autonomous bisexual and transgender civil rights
groups, many of which disagreed with the biological frame. At a 1998 meeting
of the newly founded National Policy Roundtable, well-established gay and
lesbian nonprofits and litigators met with less-resourced, more marginalized
bisexual and transgender ones to negotiate a united front.[171] There Chai Feldblum, HRC litigator and future commissioner at the Equal Employment Opportunity Commission for the Obama and Trump administrations, fought to
preserve the bioessentialist idea in the face of pressure to do away with scientific taxonomies. Some trans and bisexual organizational leaders opposed
bio-categorizations on the premise that such science was inherently binaristic
and gender-normative. They urged a recommitment to the liberationist-era

sentiment that indicted heterosexism and gender normativity as the foundation of their collective oppression.[172] It would not be long, though, before Pillard's and LeVay's premonitions about a biological explanation for those identity categories would materialize and be put to political use as well.

In all, the 1990s was the decade of gay genomania's triumphant rise and its
fall. While some of the particular claims of geneticists, talking heads, and civil
rights leaders would not survive the decade intact, the broader belief in the
biological heritability of human behaviors and identities would persist long
after the bubble burst. Even as the scientific findings were called into question
and the legal incentives shifted, the LGBTQ+ movement would not—and has
not yet—entirely give up its commitment to bioessentialism.[173] At the dawn
of the twenty-first century, bioessentialism was anything but a fading idea in
queer politics and culture: it was merely preparing for its second act.

6

From Pathology to "Born Perfect":
Marriage Equality and Conversion Therapy Bans

Nearly two decades after the gay gene first entered the cultural lexicon, pop star Lady Gaga enshrined biology on the Top 40 with a booming disco number.[1] Following a year of her campaign work against the US military's discriminatory Don't Ask, Don't Tell policy, Gaga released her 2011 homage to queer culture with a record titled simply *Born This Way*. With lyrics celebrating "gay, straight, or bi/lesbian, or transgender life" punctuated with the anthemic chorus, "baby, I was born this way," the album's title track composed a new slogan for what was, by that point, an idea already in its middle age: that is, the credo that sexual and gender identities are relatively fixed, inborn qualities.

This chapter is about a series of unprecedented civil rights triumphs, and how science, medicine, and mental health made them possible. It is a story about how the Supreme Court came to embrace biology and transformed constitutional interpretation in the process. It is also the story about how organizers of projects like the "Born Perfect" campaign—adorned with a fingerprint logo in which each alternating swirl donned a different color of the rainbow—led the legal charge against conversion therapy (known in the mental health world as "sexual orientation and gender identity change efforts," or SOGICE).[2]

These struggles for civil rights followed immense shifts in how public and mental health experts came to understand sexual desire, gender nonconformity, family life, and the needs of children. In overtaking a previous generation of experts—both within their respective fields and on the witness stand in court—they helped advocates to achieve the privileges of marriage equality and the protections of conversion therapy bans. In both cases, experts flipped the biopolitical script. Whereas such families and children were once deemed social risks—queer adults were cast as the agents of harm and children as the unsuspecting victims—today the reigning consensus cautions quite the opposite. And while the court's marriage decisions have been duly criticized for their concern for the presumably *straight* children of gay parents, the federal judiciary has increasingly recognized the need to protect *gay and trans* children from the harms of conversion therapy. Overall, an emergent orthodoxy holds that, in the absence of social acceptance and legal rights, both adults and youths are at risk of physical and mental harm themselves.

Of course, psychologists, physicians, and social work scholars did not always adopt the caricature of biodeterminism. Many clinicians and researchers who work in affirmative care today avoid discussion of biological referents almost entirely. They tend to hold that sexual and gender identities are fixed and essentially impossible to alter no matter the underlying cause. That nuance, however, has been saved for the realm of scholarly journals and the academic conference circuit. When LGBTQ+-friendly health experts have come to the aid of advocates, they have often been well prepared to sell "born this way" to judges, policymakers, and the public.

It would be difficult to understate either the historical significance of these civil rights victories or the importance of medical experts in realizing them. Marriage equality is the law of the land today. Conversion therapy bans dot the state legislative landscape, covering nearly half of the country.

Yet they are with their limits. First Amendment religious liberty and free speech protections, for instance, offer protection to religious counselors and clergy who spiritually guide church members as long as they are not acting as a licensed clinician.[3] According to a 2019 Williams Institute on Sexual Orientation and Gender Identity Law and Public Policy report, up to fifty-seven thousand youths ages 13–17 will receive conversion therapy from a religious figure before they turn eighteen.[4] More dire, revanchist right-wing forces have enjoyed recent success in at least partially rolling bans back. Though these critics certainly do not levy war in Foucauldian terms, they often criticize conversion bans for molding individuals according to state definitions of health. As the logic goes, these laws compel queer identity to be realized, or at the very least they restrict medicine and the market from providing ways to prevent its realization. Whereas in the past the gay and lesbian argument against such therapies rested in large part on the various coercive influences that led them into the clinician's office, conversion therapy proponents now loudly demand their right to have these options made available.

Maybe most insidiously, queer rights opponents have adopted legal strategies that sidestep the question of ontology altogether and pay lip service to what a properly pluralistic polity demands (that is, a right to discriminate).

Those like the Alliance Defending Freedom, the Becket Fund, the Liberty Counsel, and their corporate libertarian backers like the Kochs and the Bradley Foundation prefer to leverage the First Amendment to combat rights expansions.[5] Given the newly Trumpian shape of the federal judiciary, the free exercise clause and protections for free speech have proven adept at drilling holes into nascent LGBTQ+ citizenship privileges and protections. As the conclusion to this chapter observes, this counter assault not only threatens to curtail queer rights, but instead it takes aim at government's ability to regulate public health and to provide for social welfare more generally. Before delineating these new legal hazards, the following spells out how it is that LGBTQ+ advocates—and their friends in science and mental health—attained these rights and protections in the first place.

Love, Family, and Human Nature

Lest we assume that a coterie of activists and experts managed this all on their own, a little upfront historical perspective is due. On the marriage front, equality advocates benefited from the momentum generated elsewhere as heterosexual marriage has undergone its own modifications.[6] The gendered expectations for that holy covenant have been subsiding gradually for a few reasons. These include the (albeit uneven) incorporation of women into industrial work, second-wave feminism's successes in integrating public life and the professions, the diminishing legal and ideological conflation of marriage and child-rearing, and, certainly not least, macroeconomic changes like the decline in the power of the trade union movement and wage stagnation, which pushed even more women into the workforce—whether they liked it or not.[7] Even before the social upheavals of the 1960s and subsequent arrival of the neoliberal era, the married couple had already been dramatically altered. Despite the federal government's myriad tax breaks incentivizing marriage and its Cold War propaganda touting the strength and stability of the American family, the early twentieth century was marred by marital discord and divorce.[8]

Ironically, the forces that undermined the short-lived nuclear family ideal are the same that gave rise to the modern meaning of heterosexuality; that is, the belief that lifelong coupling between two opposite-sex individuals was neither natural nor guaranteed but instead could easily degenerate into lasciviousness, infidelity, and even homosexuality.[9] Social reformers and sexologists thus reinvented the heterosexual marriage—rechristening the institution as a commitment to sexual satisfaction, romantic love, and relative mutual respect—to preserve it as a normative ideal (in service of a political

economy that still relied heavily upon its gears being greased by such an arrange-
ment, of course).[10] As the sexual revolution and political economic transformations permanently modified the conditions that had fashioned and sustained the industrial age's heterosexual marriage, new ideologies of love, sex,
and family life bloomed.

It is in this context that same-sex marriage and the queer family moved
sequentially through the realms of the impossible, the improbable, and, finally, the *natural*. Until rather recently, the homosexual was charged with
plotting to unravel the fabric of society, tarnish American morals, and—worst
of all—corrupt the nation's children by depriving them of gender-normative
role models. This opposition to queer life was in many ways bipartisan. President Bill Clinton barred federal recognition of same-sex marriages in signing
the 1996 Defense of Marriage Act (DOMA).[11] Soon after, George W. Bush's
adviser Karl Rove made marriage a key wedge issue in the 2004 presidential
election campaign.

As the following lays out, the born this way idea helped to hasten reform
by grounding gay and lesbian personhood in a nonthreatening logic, rendering queer couples as assimilable rather than a menace. To soothe the fretful, the American Civil Liberties Union (ACLU) stressed that heterosexuality was safe because "being gay is not a matter of choice. It is something you
are born with."[12] In the courts, movement attorneys underscored the immutable nature of sexual identity by inviting testimonies from geneticists, social
science scholars, and mental health practitioners. Together, they combated
concerns that gay and lesbian households were inhospitable for rearing children.[13] Most importantly, professional opinion enabled supporters to frame
same-sex marriage as a social imperative. Equality was no threat to the nuclear family, to childhood, or to monogamous romantic love. Rather, it would
fortify those sacred, yet perpetually imperiled, ideals.

The Science of Same-Sex Marriage

In 1990 a group of three same-sex couples walked into a Hawaii state court-
house demanding their right to marry. Although this initial trial would quickly
spawn a series of court cases that would ignite a national conflict over same-
sex marriage, the fight for marriage was far from premeditated.[14] The movement's legal agenda-setters like Lambda Legal and the ACLU were caught off
guard when the queer couples in Hawaii hired private lawyers to wage what
was then a very personal cause.[15] After the Supreme Court of Hawaii's historic
pro-marriage equality ruling in 1993, it became clear that the fight over marriage was a live one.[16]

Throughout that decade, Hawaiian courts, state legislators, and ballot referendum voters sparred over the public health ramifications of sanctioning same-sex marriage. The landmark 1996 state court trial in *Baehr v. Miike* was particularly notable for its lengthy debate among each side's allies in mental health and medicine.[17] In defending its statutory restriction of marriage to heterosexual partners, Hawaii claimed that it had a compelling interest in "protecting health and welfare of children" and in "fostering procreation within a marital setting." The state brought forth Yale University child psychiatrist—and *Good Housekeeping* columnist and Lifetime Television host—Kyle Pruett to make this public health case.[18] Drawing from his work on fatherhood and child development, Pruett reasoned that children thrive in the presence of opposite-sex role models. While Pruett granted that *some* same-sex couples may hurdle over these limitations and make for suitable caregivers, they were far more likely to "provide a more burdened nurturing domain" than opposite-sex ones due to the "overabundance of information about one gender and little information about the other gender." At one point, Pruett even argued that the chromosomal and hormonal linkages between parents and their offspring made biological nuclear families the most preferable of all.

Lambda Legal—which had since leapt into the litigation—and the attorneys for the same-sex couples offered their own public health opinions. The plaintiffs invited two child development psychologists, a pediatric physician, and a sociologist, all of whom marshaled evidence for the scientific soundness of same-sex marriage. Not to be outdone by Pruett's celebrity status, the gay and lesbian couples invited sexologist and *Glamour* magazine's "Sex and Health" columnist Pepper Schwartz to testify on queer parents' capacity to raise children. Lambda Legal's brief built on Schwartz's and the other witnesses' testimony by citing nineteen different studies across the fields of psychology, psychiatry, and sociology.[19] Each of these reports, Lambda Legal asserted, were evidence that same-sex couples did not have an adverse behavioral or psychopathological impact on their children. Instead, the marriage contract incentivized the kinds of durable partnerships and stable household arrangements in which children thrive.

Remarkably, the Hawaiian trial court ruled that the state constitution's equal protection clause did indeed protect same-sex couples. Barring access to marriage, the court argued, was tantamount to impermissible sex discrimination. Not only was this a novel win for gay rights advocates—applying sex discrimination to an instance of sexual *orientation* discrimination was relatively unprecedented—the court also overwhelmingly weighed the plaintiff's evidence as more compelling than the state's own expert advice.[20] In the trial judge's words, the state had "presented insufficient evidence" and "failed to establish a causal link between allowing same-sex marriage and adverse effects upon the optimal development of children." The court even rejected the testimony of one of Hawaii's most virulently anti-marriage experts, psychologist Richard Williams, for what it took to be his fringe position in mainstream mental health research.

Over the next decade, state and federal courts would issue nearly four hundred separate opinions in such cases, many of which centered around protracted disputes over queer advocates' and opponents' expert witnesses and reports.[21] Same-sex couples represented by the Gay & Lesbian Advocates & Defenders (GLAD) won a groundbreaking case before the Massachusetts Supreme Judicial Court in *Goodridge v. Department of Public Health*.[22] Just as Lambda Legal and the plaintiffs had brought child development experts before the court in *Baehr v. Miike*, GLAD assembled resources from the American Academy of Pediatrics positing that there was "no systematic difference between gay and non-gay parents in emotional health, parenting skills, and attitudes toward parenting."[23] GLAD's brief also cited a 1995 American Psychological Association (APA) report showing that "the evidence to date suggests that home environments provided by gay and lesbian parents are as likely as those provided by heterosexual parents to support and enable children's psychosocial growth."[24] GLAD attorneys even rebuked the state's misinterpretation of a study by two prominent sociologists who had actually sought to *undermine* the notion that heterosexual couples exhibited the "gold standard" of parenting.[25]

GLAD's victory before the Massachusetts Supreme Judicial Court wound up resting heavily on its collection of mental health professionals. Not only were same-sex couples fit to parent their children, the court majority wrote, but denying these parents the right to wed would harm the very children that the legislature and Department of Health had purported to protect through its marriage policy.[26] They would deny the children of same-sex couples the psychological benefits of the "immeasurable advantages that flow" from a "secure, protected family unit."[27] For that reason, the high court ruled that such restrictions could not even pass muster with its lowest form of judicial review as there was no rational basis at all to the prohibitions.

In a dissenting opinion, Justice Robert J. Cordy cited psychological and sociological evidence as well, albeit with a far different emphasis than did his colleagues in the majority. While Cordy's dissent has long attracted attention for its spirited defense of the procreative heterosexual married couple, his arguments about the rapidly changing and inconclusive nature of mental health research are even more striking. Cordy contended that although expert opinion no longer pathologized sexual orientation itself or the gay family unit, there were still far too many methodological disputes and conflicts in data interpretation that rendered the question of same-sex marriage inappropriate for the judiciary to decide (the state legislature was conveniently drawing up a bill to deny same-sex marriage rights at this time).[28] Cordy's maneuver exemplified the pivot that social conservatives were forced to make as their own scientific and medical experts were ejected from respectable professional organizations and universities. In the absence of an alternative expert opinion, Cordy chose instead to stir up doubts about the new consensus.

As expert opinion tilted further in favor of gay and lesbian households, emboldened equal rights advocates sought the ultimate legal prize: suspect or quasi-suspect classification protections akin to those afforded to race and sex. This renewed fights over equal protection—and thus over whether gays and lesbian met the criterion of immutability for heightened protections—soon reached state supreme courts in California, New York, New Jersey, Vermont, and Connecticut.[29] By the turn of the millennium, it was perhaps more unclear than ever before just what it took to make a valid immutability argument in court. But while courts had long recognized race as a social and legal category rather than a biological one, judges continued to weigh biological evidence of sexual immutability heavily in their decisions to grant or deny equal rights.

In a case spurred by San Francisco's decision to issue marriage licenses to same-sex couples in 2004, advocates wrangled with conservative opponents over the meaning of immutability.[30] A coalition led by Equality California, Lambda Legal, the ACLU, and the National Center for Lesbian Rights (NCLR) used *In re Marriage Cases* to put their new immutability arguments to the test.[31] Marriage advocates made a dual claim that while they were not legally required to demonstrate a biological inheritance, they could indeed prove that gay and lesbian identities were "fixed."[32] They contended that "the overwhelming weight of current scientific knowledge and mental health practice recognizes that, for the great majority of people—gay and straight alike—sexual orientation is not subject to voluntary change or control." Sexual identity, they argued, was "deeply ingrained" and a "basic component of a person's core identity," and, therefore, merited the greatest form of judicial protection available.[33] In a similar marriage case in Connecticut, the Human Rights Campaign (HRC), NCLR, the National Gay and Lesbian Task Force, and PFLAG cited evidence that "there is broad consensus in the scientific community that, regardless of whether an individual's sexual orientation is caused by genetic makeup, hormonal factors, social environment, or a combination of the three, none of these factors is under an individual's control—and none supports the notion that an individual chooses sexual orientation. Simply put: 'Human beings cannot choose to be either gay or straight.'"[34]

As the marriage cases spread throughout state courts, mental health professionals took the offense on immutability. In the New York case, the American Psychiatric Association and the American Psychological Association filed a joint brief, which would both reinforce advocates' line on immutability while also offering reassurance that children of gay parents were in no danger of developing aberrant gendered behavior or the "wrong" sense of one's gender.[35] Here, the link between the fixed nature of orientation and adjacent biopolitical considerations of marriage, parentage, and children is most apparent. Advocates' expert opinion could be shorn up to assure an anxious polity that same-sex marriage presented no danger to children's mental health, their gender identity, or the nuclear family more generally.

State supreme courts in Connecticut and California heeded these pleas to take the new science of sex and the family seriously. In 2008 the Connecticut Supreme Court ruled that "although we do not doubt that sexual orientation—heterosexual or homosexual—is highly resistant to change, it is not necessary for us to decide whether sexual orientation is immutable in the same way and to the same extent that race, national origin and gender are immutable, because, even if it is not, the plaintiffs nonetheless have established that they fully satisfy this consideration."[36] The court also cited a discussion of immutability in a separate gay rights decision from a 1991 federal district court case, which had concluded that gay and lesbian orientation was a "central defining [trait] of personhood," which was "fixed during early childhood, [and] it is not a matter of conscious or controllable choice."[37] Likewise, the California Supreme Court held that sexual orientation had *already* been proven to be immutable in previous cases where scientific authority was invoked.[38] In this sense, the born this way litigation of the late twentieth century had laid the groundwork for same-sex marriage reform in the twenty-first.

Within months of the California Supreme Court's 2008 ruling that struck down the state's same-sex marriage ban, voters passed Proposition 8, thereby amending the state constitution to proscribe same-sex marriage.[39] This sparked an immediate federal court challenge to Proposition 8 led by the newly formed American Foundation for Equal Rights (AFER), a supergroup composed of Human Rights Campaign leadership, liberal progressive leaders from organizations like the Center for American Progress, a handful of Hollywood icons, and a former Republican National Committee chair.[40] Together, these civil rights advocates arrived to district court linking arms with an impressive array of well-respected and credentialed expert witnesses from the fields of psychology, demography, economics, and history.

During cross-examination, the attorney for Proposition 8 prodded AFER witnesses to undermine the constitutional immutability argument. In one session, social psychologist Gregory Herek was asked to affirm that his field "conceive[d] of sexual orientation as a complex, multi-faceted phenomenon."[41] The Proposition 8 attorney was clever enough to know that while social psychologists generally saw sexual orientation as unresponsive to coerced reorientation, they did not usually make biological claims about its causes. In a stunning reassociation of ideas and authority, Proposition 8 defenders pitted bioessentialism against the theory that sexuality sat on a continuum and was possibly variable across an individual's life span. If homosexuality was not the complement of heterosexuality—if, instead, sexuality slid along a spectrum, an indeterminate desire forever in flux—then gay and lesbian identities were inherently mutable. Further, queer couples were not even a "*discrete* and insular minority" per other equal protection clause criteria due to man's inherent "erotic plasticity."[42] In a bid to salvage immutability, Herek described sexual identity as a cultural gloss that lays atop the "raw material" of sexual desire—a social meaning and language given to a more mysterious and deeper truth impenetrable by one's "choice to redirect it from one sexual object to another."[43] Though Herek admitted that no one knows the specific causes of sexuality, he remained invested in the language of a "core" sexual sense of self.

In his ruling against Proposition 8, district court Judge Vaughn Walker repeatedly referred approvingly to the pro-marriage expert witnesses while denouncing their conservative counterparts as improperly credentialed and on the fringe of professional research and healthcare.[44] Though Walker determined that Proposition 8 did not even meet the low standards of rational basis review—thus making considerations of immutability moot—his decision was clearly informed by a number of biopolitical themes. Walker wrote that sexual orientation was "fundamental to [a] person's identity and is a distinguishing characteristic that defines gays and lesbians as a discrete group," replete with frequent references to Herek's testimony.[45] Citing public health statistics provided by other expert witnesses, the judge also acknowledged that marriage was beneficial for children and was correlated with lower levels of parental drinking, smoking, anxiety, and depression.[46]

Both heartened by the victory against Proposition 8 and undeterred by yet another ruling that eschewed the matter of heightened judicial scrutiny, marriage advocates tried their hand again in a federal challenge to the Defense of Marriage Act.[47] By the time *Windsor v. U.S.* made its way to the Supreme Court in 2013, the Obama administration had taken a staunchly pro-marriage position. As a result, the Justice Department refused to defend DOMA's constitutionality. Incensed by the move, the Republican majority in the House of Representatives used the Bipartisan Legal Advisory Group (BLAG) as a vehicle through which to defend the federal restrictions on same-sex marriage. There, BLAG attorneys clashed with Solicitor General Donald Verrilli Jr. and civil rights litigators over the question of suspect classification—and, as a consequence, biological immutability.[48] For all this conflict over nature, Justice Anthony Kennedy's 2013 majority opinion in *Windsor v. U.S.* punted on the question of immutability and equal protection. Overlooking litigants' arguments for heightened scrutiny under the equal protection clause, Kennedy chose instead to discuss matters of federalism and the state's role in regulating marriage while also expounding his idiosyncratic "human dignity" doctrinal approach.

The Supreme Court's Curious Embrace of Immutability

In the immediate post-*Windsor* aftermath, federal district and appellate courts began to sort through what had become an incredibly complicated and confused case law. Kennedy had left his colleagues on the lower courts with a tangled mess of different tests with which to adjudicate bans on same-sex marriage. In addition to the perplexing dignity standard bequeathed in *Windsor*, Kennedy's previous opinion in *Romer v. Evans* (1996) appeared to hold that most instances of discrimination against gays and lesbians could be struck down with a mere rational basis test. This is oftentimes referred to as "rational basis with a bite" to distinguish it from the usual application of rational basis, which tends to uphold laws rather than strike them down (the logic here being that a heightened standard of judicial scrutiny is not necessary to produce the effects of the stronger intermediate and strict scrutiny standards because most anti-queer discrimination is fundamentally "irrational"). To simplify matters, many federal judges began interpreting both dignity doctrine and the rational basis with a bite test as a mere pitstop en route to a higher standard of judicial protection.[49] This was a signal to advocates that their dream of achieving heightened scrutiny was still on the horizon, and that biological evidence had a role to play.

The Seventh Circuit Court of Appeals decision in *Baskin v. Bogan* stands out for its in-depth consideration of biological immutability.[50] Lawyers for Lambda Legal and the ACLU had good reason to assume that biology would play well in this dual challenge to Indiana's statutory marriage ban and Wisconsin's constitutional ban. Well-known for his prolific public writing, Seventh Circuit Judge Richard Posner was particularly renowned for his essays and books on sociobiology, evolutionary psychology, and the nature of sex and sexuality. In his 1992 book *Sex and Reason*, Posner endorsed neuroscientific studies of sexual orientation as proof that homosexuality could not be "acquired."[51] Reading from Simon LeVay's famous 1991 "gay brain" study in

Science and a slew of related sociobiological studies, Posner found that "the recent evidence of physical differences between the brains of homosexual and heterosexual men will, if confirmed by further research, strongly reinforce the view that homosexual preference is innate rather than cultural."[52]

Between 1992 and the *Baskin* case in 2014, Posner apparently kept up his habit of reading the latest in sexology research. Moreover, new genomic evidence had solidified the judge's belief that such immutable identities merited heightened scrutiny.[53] In his *Baskin* opinion, Posner wrote:

> Our pair of cases is rich in detail but ultimately straight-forward to decide. The challenged laws discriminate against a minority defined by an immutable characteristic, and the only rationale that the states put forth with any conviction—that same-sex couples and their children don't *need* marriage because same-sex couples can't *produce* children, intended or unintended—is so full of holes that it cannot be taken seriously.[54]

Posner dove quickly into the biodeterministic evidence, declaring, "The leading scientific theories of the causes of homosexuality are genetic and neuro-endocrine theories, the latter being theories that sexual orientation is shaped by a fetus's exposure to certain hormones." The judge also drew from sociobiological hypotheses such as the "helper in the nest" theory, which posits male homosexuality as an adaptive trait on the level of the human tribe (effeminate gay men refrained from hunting in order to protect the female and child gatherers).[55] Posner deduced that "there is little doubt that sexual orientation, the ground of the discrimination, is an immutable (and probably an innate, in the sense of in-born) characteristic rather than a choice."[56]

The *Baskin* decision highlights how biology helped to reframe same-sex marriage not as a threat to the family, but its savior. Posner, like many other equal rights advocates, did not disagree with this conception of marriage and the family as important social institutions. He agreed that the marriage contract was chiefly about "enhancing child welfare by encouraging parents to commit to a stable relationship in which they will be raising the child together."[57] In his view, the immutable nature of gays and lesbians led them to desire partners of the same-sex, and it was the state's duty to direct them to wed and to raise happy and health citizens just the same as their opposite-sex counterparts. In this sense, Wisconsin's argument that marriage reform shifted "the public understanding of marriage away from a largely child-centric institution to an adult-centric institution focused on emotion" fell flat.[58] It unduly divorced sexual desire from the drive to couple and to form family units (the latter having somewhat of an evolutionary basis but also apparently in need of state regulatory prodding, e.g., tax incentives).

The year after same-sex marriage proponents won their appeal in *Baskin*, that case and several other challenges to state bans were consolidated by the Supreme Court in *Obergefell v. Hodges* (2015). Once again, litigants presented a mix of immutability claims in pursuit of suspect or quasi-suspect classification. As usual, the majority of the pro-marriage briefs took the position that while case law did not *require* definitive biological proof of immutability, the science showed that gay identity was nonpathological and difficult if not impossible to change. A stronger bioessentialist argument did, however, make its way to the court in a brief submitted by the Leadership Conference on Civil and Human Rights. That coalition comprised a "who's who" in LGBTQ+ and civil rights advocacy, including the Human Rights Campaign, Lambda Legal, the National Gay and Lesbian Task Force, the ACLU, and dozens of similar groups. The Leadership Conference's brief recited the born this way argument—accompanied by numerous citations to scientific journal articles—before quoting Posner's line on orientation as "innate, in the sense of [an] in-born trait."[59]

No shortage of legal commentators have opined on the strange doctrinal moves that Justice Kennedy made in his majority opinion that struck down same-sex marriage bans across the country. A great many of these observations have focused on the legal role that Kennedy's notion of "human dignity" played in *Obergefell*, formulated here as the universal right to marry no matter one's orientation.[60] Others have trained their eye on Kennedy's philosophical ruminations on romantic love, commitment, and the nuclear family— themes that pervaded concurrent campaigns to achieve marriage equality through ballot referenda.[61] Lastly, some scholars have noted Kennedy's concerns for the dignitary harm that children of same-sex couples endure when their parents are denied equality under the law.[62]

While these debates are crucial for comprehending Kennedy's highly unorthodox outlook—only time will tell if Kennedy was on the fringe or the frontier of American constitutional development—they tend to gloss over the ideological nature of *Obergefell*'s lines on immutability. What is especially noteworthy is that the opinion did not turn on a traditional equal protection clause analysis, the only kind that would necessarily trigger a discussion of immutability. Indeed, the court had basically abandoned the prospect of extending suspect classification protections long before the marriage issue ever reached their chambers.[63]

Curiously, Kennedy invoked immutability twice. "Far from seeking to devalue marriage," Kennedy wrote, "the petitioners seek it for themselves because of their respect—and need—for its privileges and responsibilities. And their immutable nature dictates that same-sex marriage is their only real path to this profound commitment." A few pages later, Kennedy included an explicit appeal to scientific authority in explaining that "only in more recent years have psychiatrists and others recognized that sexual orientation is both a normal expression of human sexuality and immutable."[64]

Here, Kennedy flipped the biopolitical script in arguing that not only would same-sex couples not present a threat to the family, but they would buttress it.[65] They would do so precisely because of what he deemed to be their "immutable natures," which led them to seek out lifelong, monogamous, child-rearing family units. At the heart of dignity, therefore, is a deference to scientific expertise. Just as Kennedy's 2007 opinion upholding bans on dilation and extraction (D&X) abortion procedures was premised on "the dignity of human life" and (highly contested) medical ethics and expertise, here, too, Kennedy exalted the role of scientific authority.[66] It is admittedly unclear whether Kennedy was swayed more by the biological evidence proffered by Posner and the Leadership Conference or by the reams of child development research presented to the court. Either way, Kennedy's opinion reveals the ideological appeal of born this way, and how a blend of genomic evidence and child psychology data helped him to see queer couples as suitable biopolitical citizens.

Flipping the Biopolitical Script on Conversion Therapy: Authority, Essence, and Trauma

Just as marriage equality was becoming the law of the land, an explosion of conversion therapy ban campaigns erupted across the country. Debates over the efficacy and soundness of reorientation interventions extend back to the advent of nineteenth-century sexology and social reform. Beginning in the mid-twentieth century, the reigning notion that homosexuality and gender transgression are pathologies was gradually replaced by one that emphasizes sexual and gender identities as both benign and deeply rooted in one's personhood.

By the 1980s, the lines were sharply drawn between two groups. On one side were those researchers allied with the nascent gay and lesbian movement that had formed in the years building up to the 1973 APA reforms to the *DSM*.[67] On the other side of this conflict sat an obstinate old guard. The latter perceived the APA's decision to declassify homosexuality as a mental illness to have been anathema, an unscientific rejection of the field's nearly hundred-year-long tradition of pathologizing non-heterosexual behavior. As the APA and other professional associations were seized by reformers, pro-conversion mental health professionals were increasingly pushed to the edges of scientific inquiry and acceptable therapeutic care.

Conversion therapy practitioners formed an alternative network of institutions that sometimes coordinated with ex-gay religious ones, but which were ultimately committed to the view that their enterprise was a legitimate scientific one.[68] Among the most prominent of these was the National Association for Research and Therapy of Homosexuality (NARTH), formed in 1992 by psychoanalyst Charles Socarides along with clinical psychologist Joseph Nicolosi Sr. and psychiatrist Benjamin Kaufman, all of whom were longtime champions of "reparative" therapy. After hitting its peak in the late 1990s, the ex-gay movement started a downward spiral toward irrelevance in the first decade of the twenty-first century as leaders in both the religious and scientific branches abandoned their efforts. New organizations like Truth Wins Out (itself a reaction to Focus on the Family's Love Won Out ex-gay campaign) formed to collect and augment the voices of the new consensus, often by trumpeting the latest research in genetics, endocrinology, and neuroscience.[69]

As the ex-gay institutional network lay in ruins, almost every mental health or research institution working on matters of sexuality in the United States came to issue statements against conversion therapy practices. In 2009 the American Psychological Association's Task Force on Appropriate Therapeutic Responses to Sexual Orientation released its report declaring that sexual orientation change efforts (SOCE) were intrinsically harmful and wrongfully cast homosexuality as an illness rather than a normal variant of human sexuality.[70] Even though the report made an exception for those practitioners working with patients struggling to reconcile their sexual identities and their moral beliefs under the pretense that such work would promote identity *exploration* rather than the work from the outset toward reorientation, the APA affirmed the notion that sexual orientation was of a mostly fixed and stable quality. As the report's authors wrote, sexual orientation was to be conceived as "tied to physiological drives and biological systems that are beyond conscious choice and involve profound emotional feelings, such as 'falling in love.'"[71] A 2018 statement by the American Psychiatric Association reconfirmed its own stance against conversion therapy for sexual orientation from 1997 and extended it to gender identity.[72] At long last rid of its most recalcitrant conversion therapy sympathizers, the American Psychoanalytic Association also issued a statement in 2012 against efforts to change an individual's gender identity or sexual orientation.[73] Finally, in 2022 the Association for Behavioral and Cognitive Therapies (ABCT) issued a formal apology for its complicity in conversion therapy, which led some members to call for additional measures, including the retraction of decades-old pro-conversion papers by those like past ABCT president David Barlow.[74]

The themes of trauma and suicidality also transformed dramatically during this period.[75] As late as the 1980s, child psychiatrists justified the termination of gay schoolteachers' employment contracts due to the suspected self-harm or suicidality risks that their presence might have for "confused" children.[76] Again, a near complete flip has transpired. Today any and all attempts at reorientation—imposed or volitional—are now characterized as traumatic.[77]

Though the American Psychological Association's report only contains recommendations for clinicians, LGBTQ+ interest groups have used its statement and others like it to limit the legality of a wide array of practices. Currently, among the most active organizations in the fight to end conversion therapy nationwide are the National Center for Lesbian Rights, the Human Rights Campaign, and the Trevor Project, the last of which provides crisis intervention and suicide prevention to LGBTQ+ youths.[78] In their work, these groups have employed a mix of legislation, litigation, bureaucratic complaints, and public education campaigns to put their materials on the harms of conversion therapy into the hands of counselors, teachers, administrators, school nurses, and social workers. Armed with recent statements by the American Psychological Association declaring a "resurgence" of sexual orientation change efforts and studies on the harm, trauma, and incidence of suicide associated with such practices, ban proponents cite these authorities as support for state and federal restrictions.

Since its founding in June 2014, the NCLR's Born Perfect campaign has helped to secure state and municipal legislative bans, particularly those that protect minors. The campaign's advisory committee is made up of a mix of ex-gay survivors, faith leaders, attorneys, and mental health professionals, the last group of which constitutes a majority of the committee. In its own campaigns as well as its collaborative work with both the Trevor Project and the HRC's "Just As They Are" educational campaign, the NCLR has assembled studies, statements, and testimonies by dozens of professional associations including major therapy, counseling, psychiatric, medicine, and social work organizations highlighting the general impossibility of altering one's sexual orientation and the harm that results in attempts to do so. One of the first citations featured on the resources section of Born Perfect's website is to an article published in the *Archives of Sexual Behavior* on conversion therapy that recites the immutability thesis as laid out by famed "gay brain" researcher Simon LeVay.[79] As was the case with marriage reform, ban proponents today advance their legal agenda with a blend of hard-line biodeterminism and psychological research on psychic harm and trauma.

Modern Conversion Therapy Bans and Their Critics

Though conversion therapy's former legion of practitioners has been largely displaced, their mission lives on within some churches, conservative Christian political groups, and on the margins of mental healthcare. Disparate in their philosophical perspectives, these groups share a common belief in the malleability of sexuality and gender identity as well as the therapeutic possibility of controlling aberrant desires. Together, they are presently attempting to shift the balance of power back to conversion-therapy-friendly scientists and practitioners whose authority has steadily shrunk since the late 1970s.

Representatives of various Protestant Evangelical and Baptist sects have recently issued decrees against what they perceive to be the imposition of a secular ideology of bioessentialism that is at odds with their missions. Writing for the Southern Baptist Convention's Ethics & Liberty Commission, Joe Carter characterized bans as a "secular form of religious establishment" wherein the belief that LGBTQ+ identities are immutable is "a matter of orthodoxy" against which one is barred from dissenting.[80] Though it was not taken up for procedural reasons, a resolution introduced before the 2018 meeting of the Southern Baptist Convention called on Baptist leaders to oppose conversion therapy bans on the basis that their doctrines stood in contrast to the inherent "essentialism" that undergird such political interventions.[81] Since its unveiling in September 2017, over twenty-four thousand pastors and religious leaders have signed on to the Council for Biblical Manhood and Womanhood's "Nashville Statement," professing a shared belief that sexuality has a singular purpose within a heterosexual marriage and that one's gender identity must be made congruent with one's biological sex as assigned at birth.[82]

Other theological authorities have argued that the notion of fixity has no bearing on debates over these bans precisely because it is *behavior* that individuals (or parents of individuals) seek to control rather than an orientation they seek to eradicate. The Catechism of the Roman Catholic Church, for example, has no official position on conversion therapy or etiology, but it does state that "homosexual persons are called to chastity."[83] More recent pronouncements by the Vatican have characterized "ideologies of gender" as an affront to the divine creations of man and woman.[84] These teachings have led US Catholic Church associations and their public policy arm to oppose bans that prevent parents and children from accessing professional help with "unwanted urges" and "confusion."[85] Those like Peter Sprigg, a senior fellow for Policy Studies at the Family Research Council, have similarly contended that bans are based in an "opposition to the idea of someone changing their

sexual orientation—even voluntarily, and even when that only means changing external behaviors."[86] The Alliance Defending Freedom has also argued
in court that a "confusion" or dissatisfaction with one's sexual orientation or
gender identity could be best served by mental health practitioners and religious leaders.[87]

Conservative medical organizations operating on the fringe of healthcare advocacy have also organized against bans. Among ban opponents is
the American College of Pediatricians (ACP). This tiny group of 500 physicians broke away from the 67,000-member-strong American Academy of Pediatrics in protest of a measure supporting second-parent adoptions by gay
and lesbian couples.[88] By virtue of its professional-sounding name, the ACP
has garnered outsize influence, especially in the media, where it has broadcast its various stances against LGBTQ+ adoption and same-sex marriage
rights. In a 2018 statement, co-chair of the ACP's Committee on Adolescent
Sexuality André Van Mol defended modern therapeutic techniques, saying
that they were nothing like past coercive and invasive practices. Instead, he
maintained, such practices offer compassionate, lifesaving care to those children and adults experiencing torment over their desires. Van Mol cautioned
that without access to such therapies, some patients would be "unable to heal
[their] wounds, be legislated into a false identity, and be left suicidal and without hope as a result."[89] By inverting the trauma narrative, the ACP has taken
the position that such bans not only violate the freedom of patients to choose
their own care, but they also put those struggling with their identities at risk
of harm or death.

Originally founded in 1943 to oppose a proposed program for national
healthcare, the Association of American Physicians and Surgeons (AAPS)
has also voiced its dissent.[90] The AAPS, which represents several thousand
medical practitioners, has denounced transgender bathroom access policies
as "radical social experiments" based in a "Marxist cultural agenda" and has
accused ban proponents of undermining patients' right of self-determination
with regard to sexuality and gender identity. Like the ACP, the AAPS also as-
serts that bans perpetuate trauma and harm by "requir[ing] physicians to violate their sacred Oath and withhold therapy they believe to be valuable, or
cooperate with treatment they believe to be harmful or immoral."[91]

NARTH, the preeminent ex-gay scientific institution, run by psychologist Joseph Nicolosi Sr. until his death in 2017, has found itself basically alone
in a medical field increasingly accepting of the idea that sexual orientation
is to be embraced rather than reoriented. In an apparent recognition of its
tainted brand, Nicolosi and others reestablished themselves in 2014 as the
Alliance for Therapeutic Choice and Scientific Integrity (ATCSI) Training

Institute.[92] Similar to its predecessor, ATCSI's stated mission is to reclaim the mantle of the truly objective psychological approach. The organization explains its alternative with reference to the Kinsey-inspired theory of a continuum, wherein a person can fall in between exclusively defined orientations and can even move among them. ATCSI also explicitly counterposes the bioessentialism perspective (in its words, that homosexuality is "essentially genetically or biologically determined") with a behaviorist one. Unlike clinical approaches to issues like alcoholism, depression, and grief, ATCSI argues, the mainstream consensus on sexuality has erroneously concluded that any sign of backsliding is evidence that the default orientation is impossible to alter.[93]

The latest Nicolosi venture in reorientation therapy is the Reintegrative Therapy Association (RTA), which has employed cutting-edge research agendas in neuroscience to make new claims for an old purpose. Founded by Nicolosi's son and fellow clinical psychologist Joseph Nicolosi Jr., the RTA purports to promote "a specific combination of established, evidence-based treatment interventions" for those persons unhappy with their same-sex desires.[94] As new research on neuroplasticity—the notion that brain structures are to a certain degree malleable and that changes can occur as a response to environmental conditions—demonstrates, the very brain structures to which those like Simon LeVay and others have attributed the immutability of sexual orientation are, in fact, amenable to alteration.

Nicolosi Jr. and the RTA have based their care regimen in what most in the fields they cite would perceive as misrepresentations of their work. It is one thing to suggest that certain regions in the brain are potentially involved in one's sexual predilections or sense of gender in some nebulous way. It is another to posit that this necessarily entails that a therapist might engage in targeted practices to shape those regions according to a specific plan for how a patient wishes to experience their desire. In fact, this interpretation of neuroplasticity inserts a sort of biodeterminism back into the equation as a handful of neuroanatomical structures are assumed to code for sexual orientation in an "on/off" fashion. Even if these structures are held to be malleable, they are ultimately biological sites hypothesized to be determinative of vast arrays of sexual expression, desire, and identity. Although Nicolosi Jr. acknowledges the complexity that is distorted in simple born this way versus choice formulations of sexual orientation, the RTA's theory and agenda rely upon the same dichotomies that govern the reigning bioessentialist thesis.

In more recent developments, over one hundred psychotherapy researchers and clinicians affiliated with the newly formed Society for Evidence-based Gender Medicine (SEGM) and the international Pediatric and Adolescent Gender Dysphoria Working Group have embroiled themselves in legislative battles over conversion therapy bans and trans hormone access.[95] Their arguments against gender-affirmative treatments such as puberty blockers and similar medical interventions rest on a (largely discredited) 2018 *PLoS One* study on what its author termed "rapid-onset gender dysphoria."[96] In a letter to a leading Endocrine Society journal, SEGM members (along with a pro-conversion-therapy coauthor from the conservative American College of Pediatricians) warned that because "there are no laboratory, imaging, or other objective tests to diagnose a 'true transgender' child," clinicians had carelessly treated scores of "teenage girls" to "rapid onset GD without prior history through social contagion."[97] In 2021 SEGM leadership penned another letter to the *Archives of Sexual Behavior*, noting the "irreversible physical changes" and experience of inhabiting a "gender no-man's land" upon detransitioning.[98] To disseminate their message beyond the insular world of medical journals, gender critical researchers have sat on Heritage Foundation panels and have collaborated with journalists writing for *Quillette* and similar self-styled "free thinking" conservative outlets to denounce such "child abuse and gay eugenics."[99]

Minors, Fraud, and the First Amendment

Over the past decade, conversion therapy ban proponents have enjoyed remarkable success in statehouses. As of May 2021, twenty states, the District of Columbia, Puerto Rico, and no fewer than eighty-three cities and counties have deemed conversion therapy noxious for minors.[100] In addition to bans, some states like Wisconsin have barred taxpayer funds from covering conversion therapy services.[101] LGBTQ+ advocates, too, have fared well in defending these bans in courts, having convinced the Third and Ninth Circuit Courts of Appeals of their bans' constitutionality. State courts in California and New Jersey no longer even recognize conversion therapy practitioners as legitimate scientific experts under general evidentiary standards.[102] However, ban opponents have begun to amass their own victories as well. Social conservative foundations, Christian litigation groups, and their Trump-appointed judicial allies have aggressively fought state bans in court—occasionally, they have won. This penultimate section maps these legal contests over medical truth and authority. It begins with a decade of litigation in California, the birthplace of the modern conversion therapy ban for minors as well as the site of an even more controversial effort to ban therapy for adults. Upon tracing these conflicts as they moved between the California state capitol and federal courts, it concludes with the current circuit court split on bans for minors, a fissure that nearly ensures that the Supreme Court will one day soon hear a case on bans.

In 2012 California proscribed conversion therapy for minors. A coalition led by Lambda Legal, Equality California, the National Center for Lesbian Rights, Mental Health America of Northern California, and Gaylesta (the Psychotherapist Association for Gender and Sexual Diversity) was successful in urging the state to pass the ban.[103] Ted Lieu, state senator and author of the original senate version of the bill, explained that ex-gay therapists should not be permitted to "engage in a practice that the medical community itself has disavowed."[104] Upon signing the ban into law, then governor Jerry Brown similarly stated that "this bill bans non-scientific 'therapies' that have driven young people to depression and suicide. These practices have no basis in science or medicine and they will now be relegated to the dustbin of quackery."[105]

For the first five years of the ban's existence, ex-gay proponents including Christian conservative legal organizations, leaders in NARTH, and individual practitioners fought the law in federal court. Their various challenges rested on the free speech rights of mental health practitioners, the right of parents to dictate care for their children, and religious liberty rights. In the first of two federal district-level challenges to the law, Judge William B. Shubb of the Eastern District of California ruled against the ban on free speech grounds. Shubb also questioned evidence of conversion therapy's harms, noting that the state's claims were "based on questionable and scientifically incomplete studies that may not have included minors."[106] The following day, Judge Kimberly J. Mueller of the Eastern District of California upheld the ban in a related challenge, citing the state's power to regulate medical care.

In October 2013, the Ninth Circuit Court of Appeals resolved the conflict in favor of the state.[107] In the introduction to her majority opinion, Judge Susan P. Graber narrated the history of homosexuality's trajectory from pathology to the current scientific consensus. Accordingly, Graber ruled that the law was based in the "well-documented, prevailing opinion of the medical and psychological community that SOCE has not been shown to be effective and that it creates a potential risk of serious harm to those have experienced it."[108] In response to the freedom of speech challenge, Graber argued that not every instance of speech—especially professional speech—is immune to the state's police power to ensure the public's health, safety, and welfare. Similarly, Graber noted that while parents did retain some constitutionally mandated rights over their children, those rights did not extend to a "fundamental right to choose a mental health professional with specific training," especially not one offering services deemed harmful and out of the mainstream.[109] In a second federal case, ban opponents—some of whom were spiritual counselors practicing mental healthcare with state-issued licenses—complained that their First Amendment establishment and free exercise rights had been denied. Graber again ruled against the challengers, explaining that California had not stepped into the realm of spiritual counseling and guidance when it prevented licensed mental health professionals from engaging in conversion efforts.[110]

Emboldened by the federal judiciary's refusal to overturn California's ban, lawmakers and dozens of advocacy groups and professional mental health organizations pursued even stronger legislation. Styled as a measure against fraudulent business practices, California Senator Evan Low introduced AB 2943: "Unlawful Business Practices: Sexual Orientation Change Efforts" in February 2018.[111] This bill came on the heels of similar bills in Connecticut and the New York City Council, related anti-fraud complaints made by the NCLR and the HRC to the Federal Trade Commission in 2016, and early fraud-based litigation efforts. AB 2943 would have made it unlawful under the state's Consumer Legal Remedies Act to advertise or to sell SOCE-based services to adults on the basis that such treatments are deceptive in nature.[112]

This attempt at an expanded ban courted controversy immediately from social conservatives claiming that such an expansion presented a direct threat to religious liberty.[113] At the helm of this opposition was the California Family Council, a state affiliate of the Family Research Council, which assembled a coalition of local, state, and national organizations against AB 2943.[114] In a 2018 legal memorandum, the conservative Alliance Defending Freedom (ADF) spelled out the plan to challenge the law's constitutionality. AB 2943, ADF attorneys argued, would impermissibly censor speech because the sale of religious books or the ticketing of events where reorientation was discussed could potentially be regulated.[115] The ADF also argued that the ban would limit an individual's right to access "the spectrum of available knowledge" within the context of the counselor-client relationship. Finally, the ADF asserted that the free exercise of religion was also at peril as religious instruction concerning the sinfulness of homosexuality and gender nonconformity could fall under the ban. Here, the ADF cited an instance in which state lawmakers called upon Michigan's attorney general to investigate whether a ministry had violated the state consumer protection act in conducting SOCE workshops.

Throughout the legislative debate over AB 2943, Senator Low defended the bill as providing a balance between queer equality and First Amendment concerns, noting that only relationships involving the exchange of money for services would fall under state regulation.[116] Others in the chamber disagreed vehemently. Self-described ex-gay pastor Jim Domen gestured to a portrait of his wife and children while complaining that AB 2943 considered his family a "fraud." In a sentiment couched in pluralist logic, Domen explained that "there is nothing wrong with me [and] there is nothing wrong with members of the LGBT community."[117] According to this formulation, the bill struck no such balance of rights and equality; rather, it denied the autonomy of one group (and targeted those assisting the realization of its autonomy) by favoring another's (the organized LGBTQ+ political community and the reigning scientific consensus).

Shockingly, Low shelved the measure after winning the vote handily on the senate floor. He did so shortly after embarking on a statewide listening tour to hear out the religious opposition in an attempt to understand why he had failed to mollify their anger and fear. Expressing his relief with Low's decision, Jonathan Keller, president of the California Family Council, celebrated the tabling of a bill that he believed would have "tragically limited our ability to offer compassionate support related to sexual orientation and gender identity, and even to preach Jesus' message of unconditional love and life transformation."[118] In a more recent statement, however, Low cautioned against the expectation that a new version of the expanded ban would contain anything akin to a religious exemption. In an allusion to cases like *Masterpiece Cakeshop*—the 2018 case in which Christian traditionalist and baker Jack Phillips asserted a First Amendment right to deny same-sex couples the right to purchase a custom wedding cake—Low stated that lawmakers would "not provide a religious license to discriminate . . . [j]ust like there should not be a religious exemption to deny me from being served in a restaurant, we will not provide a blanket guide to discriminate."[119]

Conflicts over fraud have since expanded beyond the California context. The US Senate may soon consider similar legislation. In 2015 and then again in 2019, US House Representative Ted Lieu (CA-D) introduced the Therapeutic Fraud Prevention Act, which would grant the Federal Trade Commission the authority to prohibit conversion therapy services as consumer fraud.[120] While leaders at the Trevor Project framed the proposal as a measure protecting youth, the language of the bill indicates a much broader scope. As drafted, the law would "prohibit, as an unfair or deceptive act or practice, commercial sexual orientation conversion therapy, and for other purposes," that is, any consumer service that works against the realization of one's presumably true sexual or gender identity.[121] Given these persistent efforts, another round of legislative conflict over fraud is likely imminent.

Even closer on the horizon, however, may be a Supreme Court challenge to conversion therapy bans for minors. Since Graber's two opinions for the Ninth Circuit and a similar ruling for the Third Circuit, the federal judiciary has become more averse to regulations of healthcare provider speech.[122] In 2018 the Trump-shaped Supreme Court ruled against a California reproductive rights law and took a swipe at conversion therapy bans along the way. Writing for the 5–4 conservative majority in *NIFLA v. Becerra* (2018), Justice Clarence Thomas compared the bans to laws that compel religiously affiliated pro-life pregnancy centers to provide information about state-funded reproductive healthcare options. Both regulations of speech, Thomas argued, were suspect because they discriminated on the basis of the speech's content and viewpoint (i.e., against providers' pro-life and pro-conversion-therapy sentiments).[123] Despite California's insistence that it was within its constitutional authority to regulate healthcare, the Supreme Court ruled that the "professional speech" of crisis center providers did not—except in very rare circumstances—merit fewer protections than other forms of expressive speech.[124]

Two years later, an Eleventh Circuit Court of Appeals panel headed up by two Trump-appointed judges applied the *NIFLA* precedent in a conversion therapy ban case. In *Otto v. City of Boca Raton* (2020), the Eleventh Circuit struck down two municipal ordinances in Florida that—just as in the case of that California reproductive healthcare case—allegedly targeted the content and viewpoint of practitioners' speech. Noting the inherently speech-oriented nature of "talk therapy," the judges ruled that conversion therapists who brought the suit (along with the legal aid of the Liberty Counsel) had been unjustly silenced for their unpopular viewpoint. The therapists had spurned the ordinances' viewpoint that "sexual orientation is immutable, but gender is not," and feared that they would soon lose their private practices as a result.[125]

The Eleventh Circuit opinion also rebuffed claims that children's mental and physical health presented a compelling interest to override First Amendment protections. Upon evaluating the usual slew of expert reports and peer-reviewed studies demonstrating the harm and trauma associated with conversion therapy, the Trump-appointed judges wrote that the local governments "offer assertions rather than evidence."[126] Although ban proponents offered a "mountain of rigorous evidence" purporting to demonstrate harm, the judges observed that there was little work done on "nonaversive" therapy—that is, techniques which do not involve "reprimand, punishment, or shame."[127] This is despite the fact the APA has suggested that this conversion therapy "light" approach also causes harm and that further research on *any* change effort would be unethical.[128] To further underscore the idea that conversion therapy is a matter of unsettled science, the court gestured to early editions of the *DSM* that had classified homosexuality as a psychopathology and disorder. The judges cautioned here that "it is not uncommon for professional organizations to do an about-face in response to new evidence for new attitudes";

therefore, such "broad prophylactic rules" on conversion talk therapy for minors could not be justified with references to today's purportedly incomplete and volatile scientific consensus.[129] Thus, the Eleventh Circuit ruled that the potential threat to a child's well-being was not enough to override the professional speech of the therapists who wished to "cure" them.

The Pluralist Threat and the Limits of Biopolitical Citizenship

After a streak of wins last decade, conversion ban and same-sex marriage advocates find themselves once again on the defense. The nature of the conservative assault is markedly different this time around. Today equal rights opponents frequently avoid going for the jugular on questions of ontology, a pivot that reveals some cognizance of their losing record on this front. Instead, they invert pluralist principles and the broader liberal rights paradigm to their benefit.

In recent years, social conservatives in the GOP and conservative religious interest groups use the language of "competing rights" to render Christian traditionalists as the victims of oppressive tolerance. This was the strategy in *Masterpiece Cakeshop* as well as the 2022 redux of that case in *303 Creative LLC v. Elenis*, both of which were litigated by the Alliance Defending Freedom.[130] As the argument goes, Christian wedding cake bakers (just like spiritual counselors practicing mental healthcare) just want to be left alone. They ask simply that they be allowed to exercise their constitutional free speech and religious liberty rights in peace.[131] None of this is born of animus nor of misrecognition, their attorneys declaim. Traditionalists seek not to discriminate against their queer neighbors, but rather wish only the freedom to deny service to gay and lesbian shoppers and to offer therapeutics solutions to patients' (purportedly) unwanted—note, not *unnatural*—desires.

There is unfortunately little room here to refute the myriad of hypocrisies, sleight of hand, and slippery slopes that characterize these constitutional appeals.[132] The recent involvement of corporate libertarian-funded outfits like Americans for Prosperity in *Fulton v. City of Philadelphia*—a case concerning taxpayer-supported religious social service contractors that refuse to place children with gay foster and adoptive parents—shows that this recent torrent of anti-queer litigation targets not just LGBTQ+ rights and personhood but the very egalitarian underpinnings of the American social welfare state.[133]

The day after Justice Thomas and his conservative brethren handed down the *NIFLA* decision, the Supreme Court issued its opinion in *Janus v. AFSCME*.[134] In a one-two punch, the court both limited the state's power to regulate access to reproductive care—and potentially the health of LGBTQ+

minors—and decimated public-sector unionism. As Gordon Lafer has shown, the right-wing attack on the labor movement has been inextricably intertwined with its broader project of eroding the state's welfare programs and regulatory authority.[135] Given the success of President Trump and Senator Mitch McConnell's judicial entrenchment scheme, these concurrent raids on queer rights, labor law, and state power show no sign of abating soon.[136]

What does this all spell for the future of born this way politics? Given the conservative wing's current 6–3 majority on the Supreme Court and the incipient barrage of First Amendment carve-outs to nascent LGBTQ+ rights victories, the bioessentialist approach to identity and citizenship may prove impotent against the social conservative opposition's mutated form. Recall the ex-gay pastor who could neatly square the existence of LGBTQ+ people in the abstract with his own insistence that the law strike a pluralistic balance between the rights of traditionalists like himself and those of sexual and gender minorities. In other instances, such as the Eleventh Circuit's ruling against conversion therapy bans for minors, the fight remains on the terrain of medical knowledge, although the strategy there has been to undermine what it is that professionals can confidently be said to know about harm, trauma, and coercion rather than to protest the mere existence of the queer or trans child in total. In fact, this tactic owes its origins to the immediate post-1973 moment when the mental illness model of homosexuality first lost its dominion in the APA.

It remains true, as the following chapter and conclusion observe, that conflicts over trans rights are still replete with robust narratives of ontology and a scientific record to match. Neither party in that conflict appears willing to cede much ground on the question of essence just yet. In general, though, the nature of LGBTQ+ personhood is far less likely to be challenged outright today than ever before. The project of equal rights and full citizenship is instead far more likely to be undercut through these newly crafted—still ever nefarious—means. Therein lies the limits of scientific authority.

The Scientific Gaze in Transgender
and Bisexual Politics

For all of the born this way idea's shortcomings, a failure to adapt is not one of them.[1] Dubbed the "The Transgender Tipping Point" by *TIME* magazine, the past decade has witnessed an unprecedented expansion of transgender visibility and legal rights reforms.[2] As gender norms were disrupted and rapidly reconfigured, biological storytellers stepped in to explain—to rationalize—why these social changes have occurred. In her coming-out interview with *ABC News*, former Olympian Caitlyn Jenner reintroduced herself as a trans woman who had been beset, since early childhood, by feelings that she was "stuck in the middle," unable to live her true gender nor reconcile herself to life as a *Wheaties*-branded paragon of masculinity.[3] Responding to interviewer Diane Sawyer's question "Are you a woman?" Jenner answered, "My brain is much more female than it is male."[4] A few months earlier, teenage television personality Jazz Jennings repeated the biological mantra in a children's book based on her own transition experience. Jennings wrote, "I have a girl brain and a boy body."[5]

This was not the first time that American media became transfixed on such transgressions. Programs like *The Jerry Springer Show*, which remained on the air through 2018, and other lurid daytime television shows frequently scandalized audiences with "gender reveals" that devolved into brawls between allegedly deceptive trans women and their duped lovers. Other segments brought together transitioning parents and their aghast children, the latter of whom frequently joined bands with the host to ridicule their fallen guardian.[6] These televised spectacles were themselves only the most recent gawking at gender by mass media. Decades before the first chair was ever thrown angrily across Springer's set, the public was exposed to the transition tale of Christine Jorgensen, WWII soldier turned transsexual tabloid star.

Despite the at times indelicate questions posed by interviewers like Saw-yer, the second decade of the new millennium was strikingly unique: news anchors and journalists approached their subjects with an unparalleled com-passion and a seemingly genuine curiosity about why someone might chart a gendered path beyond what was stamped on their birth certificate. Politi-cal leaders and legal advocates soon joined these celebrations of nature's gen-der diversity. Tony Vera, the former chief legal counsel for the Human Rights Campaign, reasoned that just as the gay and lesbian movement had "achieved marriage equality and other legal protections by insisting that our same-sex attraction was not something we could readily change, [the] same argument can benefit the cause of justice and fairness for transgender Americans."[7] Brandishing fistfuls of medical journal studies in a debate with Fox News host Tucker Carlson, Jillian Weiss of the Transgender Legal Defense & Education Fund similarly made a bio-themed legal case against the Trump administra-tion's trans military ban.[8] Since then, trans identity has increasingly become a cultural boogeyman for social conservatives who rev their electoral base by clamping down on the trans right to pee, change clothes in a locker room, serve in the military, access transition-related healthcare, and play sports. For those seeking to calm renewed fears of social contagion and to secure basic civil rights protections, reaching for the "born trans" narrative has become second nature.

Though it has enjoyed less cultural fanfare, bisexual identity has also been proffered a fresh biological sheen as of late. In 2005 Michael Bailey of '90s gay gene fame first clashed with movement advocates over who ought to have the most authoritative voice in defining bisexuality. At the center of this contro-versy was the American Institute of Bisexuality (AIB), a small activist outfit with deep pockets and a propensity to subject sexual identity to inspection. After a study of sexual arousal patterns led Bailey and the media to ponder aloud whether bisexuality even "exists," the AIB stepped in to fund new re-search that might reverse those conclusions. Musing animatedly about what medical technologies applied properly might disclose, AIB president John Sylla speculated: "Can we see differences in the brains of bisexual people us-ing fMRI technology? How many bisexual people are there—regardless of how they identify?"[9]

The answer to the first question—at least according to new AIB-backed research by Bailey and subsequent *New York Times* coverage—was a resound-ing "yes." Other recent studies praised by Dean Hamer, father of the gay gene thesis, and gay brain researcher Simon LeVay tell an evolutionary story us-ing brain scans and measures of blood flows to genitals. Bisexual men might be insatiable "hyper-heterosexuals" with libidos kicked into overdrive, some surmise, while women may be simply predisposed to sexual fluidity.[10] What unites these and related origins stories is an overarching interpretation: bisexual orientation is real, and we have the science to back it up.

These developments in trans and bi identity politics run contrary to past prognostications about the exclusionary world that born this way advocates were making. Academics and activists alike warned that the gay and lesbian movement's bioessentialist investments would have an adverse impact on bisexual and transgender civil rights struggles.[11] Presumably, bisexuality's skirting of the hetero-homo divide and its implicit acknowledgment of "choice" combined with transgender identity's ambiguous relation to commonsense notions of biological sex would keep all but the most heteronormative gays and lesbians forever locked outside the bounds of this scientific logic. Bioessentialism has instead proven surprisingly adaptive to these ends. To extend the evolutionary metaphor, the "B" and "T" of LGBT have morphed to better "fit" the established environmental terrain.

The brand of queer pessimism that counseled otherwise was always remarkably shortsighted given a longer historical view of sexology. Since the nineteenth-century advent of the modern study of sex, clinicians and researchers have bundled together various forms of gender nonconformity and same-sex desire. Policymakers, too, have rarely bothered to differentiate between "exclusive" homosexuals and one-off affairs nor have they neatly distinguished cross-gendered mannerisms and dress from decisions regarding sex object choice. Only in the mid-twentieth century did reformers find cause to siphon off gay and lesbian identities from the fount of desire's other deviancies.

Despite recent adjustments to how we discuss these disparate identities on the surface, that act of splitting off has always been uneven and incomplete—perhaps by its very nature. As cultural anthropologist Roger Lancaster has observed, the scientific study of sexuality has always been beholden to vernacular cultural assumptions about what it means to be a "real" or "natural" man or woman.[12] Is it the gay or bisexual man who appears suspiciously female—or perhaps a hormonal hybridization of man and woman—when subject to a battery of biological tests? Or are transsexuals the true in-betweeners, defined by a neuroanatomy and endocrine profiles that defy their assigned sex and divulge a deeper truth? The social always slips back in, leading even the most taxonomy-happy researchers to code sexual and gendered subjects according to criteria that suture back together a barely severed connective tissue. So, while a cis-hetero bias has surely pervaded scientific study as it does elsewhere in contemporary society, it does not function to simply impede the creation of novel born this way narratives for once-marginalized minorities. Scientific storytelling has been far less inhibited and far more inventive than that.

To that end, this chapter illustrates how "LGBT" has always been a fundamentally biopolitical construction. In Linnaean terms, it is a genus comprised of what are taken now to be four separate species, all of which share a not-so-distant common ancestry. The following begins in the mid-nineteenth century, prior to when science, social movements, and the state wrest gay and lesbian identities apart from other forms of sexual and gender nonconformity. It goes on to sketch twentieth-century developments in medical techniques, healthcare institutions, and advocacy groups, all of which kept "LG" apart from "BT." It turns then to the ironic process through which scientific narratives and medical authorities assisted the integration of transgender and bisexual identity politics into mainstream interest groups and civil rights legal advocacy.

The second half of the chapter maps developments that have occurred mainly at the end of the twentieth century through present day. The first two sections trace how transgender identity became legally legible throughout conflicts over employment discrimination, prisoner rights, bathroom access, and participation in sex-segregated sports leagues, and how conservatives have leaned on "competing rights" and medical "uncertainties" in their opposition. The penultimate section then recounts how a team of sexologists, the *New York Times*, and the American Institute of Bisexuality afforded bisexual identity its very own bio-essence. The chapter ends with a consideration of the adaptive landscape of American LGBTQ+ politics and its comparably adaptive right-wing opposition.

Conjoined at Birth: Science, Sex, and Gender since the Nineteenth Century

Throughout the late nineteenth century, researchers, clinicians, and policymakers tended not to make sharp distinctions between homosexual desire and gender nonconformity. The German sexologist Karl Heinrich Ulrichs, for instance, coined the term "urning" to describe a third sex, one that combined the body of a man and the psyche or soul of a woman.[13] Writing a few decades later, another German, the psychiatrist Richard von Krafft-Ebing, crafted his own classificatory system for those he deemed sexual "inverts," plagued by deformed nervous systems and atypically gendered physiognomic features and physical mannerisms. Similarly, British sexologist Havelock Ellis also concluded that an embryonic defect might account for both exclusive homosexuality and its non-exclusive variant (i.e., bisexuality), both of which existed on a continuum as different degrees of the same kind. Most complicatedly, Freud was frustrated by his inability to generate a coherent schema that could explain three related yet conflicting constructs: binary biological sex, seemingly innate bisexual capacities, and a great variety of means of speaking and enacting desire.[14] Altogether, these sociomedical categories often crowded together the effeminate man, the brutish woman, the uncanny transsexual, and those whose tastes placed them between and among these and other so-called deviants.

Some nineteenth-century reformers came to specialize in matters of gender nonconformity. In 1897 Berlin-based sexologist Magnus Hirschfeld founded his social policy-oriented Scientific-Humanitarian Committee, and in 1919 he brought his research and advocacy under the roof of the Institute for Sexual Science in Berlin.[15] Like his predecessors, Hirschfeld trained his eye on a wide range of "sexual intermediaries," persons who exhibited eclectic mixes of sex characteristics, erotic inclinations, and gendered habits and physiologies.[16] He developed a theory of *transvestitism*, which included both those who donned cross-gendered dress and those who sought to physically transform their bodies. Inspired by advances in hormonal research and surgical techniques, Hirschfeld brought together a wide array of physicians and researchers at the institute and, in 1928, he assembled his colleagues in the World League for Sexual Reform, which expanded legislative attempts to curb police violence and other social strictures on free gender expression.[17] Tragically, Hirschfeld's work was cut short by the rise of Nazism. Shortly after the Nazis burned down the Institute for Sexual Science and its treasure trove of papers, Hirschfeld fled Germany and—after a world tour promoting his blend of egalitarian scientific study and social reform—died in exile in 1935.[18]

Though the institute lay incinerated, Hirschfeld's collaborators spread his influence far beyond Germany. One such physician named Harry Benjamin had emigrated to the United States much earlier in 1913. By the end of WWII, Benjamin became a leading authority in transsexual research and healthcare. In his adopted home, he joined the ranks of American reformers like the sexologist Alfred Kinsey, who had himself just revealed the eroticism of everyday American life in his two volumes on male and female sexual habits.[19] The immediate postwar moment was a paradoxical one for gender and sexual freedom; the war had both led to abundant queer experiences among soldiers who carried their desires back into civilian life as well as a proliferation of new institutions for studying, tracking, and quashing those desires.[20] When Christine Jorgensen made headlines upon returning home from her Danish surgeons' operating theater, public health officials and policymakers sought to stomp out such procedures stateside.[21]

As for social movement politics, gender nonconformity and fluid sexuality were largely kept out from the burgeoning gay and lesbian interest-group apparatus. Homophile and lesbian leaders expended much effort throughout the 1950s and 1960s to cultivate an ethnic minority model status for gay identity. Accordingly, the rallying cry "Gay Is Good" (itself copped from Black civil rights advocates) and its accompanying logic of a fixed, natural, and non-communicable sexuality required a strict border between homo and hetero. The homophiles also held tightly on to gender conformity, fearing that anything other than a respectable (what we might term today as "heteronormative") gender presentation might scare off a potentially persuadable public.[22] Indeed, homophile leaders criticized even the most sympathetic sexologists whenever they conflated femininity and male homosexuality in their observations and especially when such researchers dared to associate gays and lesbians with transvestites, transsexuals, and cross-dressers.[23] A survey in the homophile journal *ONE* showed that a majority of members believed transsexuals to be pathologically neurotic; likewise, the homophiles feared that Christine Jorgensen's popularity threatened to add "male castration" to the list of curative interventions for homosexuality.[24] Given that California had recently funded prominent gender researchers like Karl Bowman to search for such "causes and cures"—Bowman's experiments included hormonal and surgical castrations for imprisoned male sex offenders—their worries were not unfounded.[25] Further, the fear of guilt by association could often run both ways. Virginia Prince, founder of several cross-dressing social and advocacy groups that were all explicitly heterosexual, deliberately distanced her groups' work from gay advocacy as a means of avoiding the vice patrol.[26]

In the post-Stonewall moment of 1969, the New Left social movements similarly made little space for bisexual and trans identifiers. The era's gay liberationists along with the left-wing of the women's rights movement and its lesbian separatist offshoots shared in a suspicion of these forms of transgression. This last group—the lesbian separatists who populated outfits like the Radicalesbians among others—condemned bisexual women's fraternizing with the male enemy, imploring all women to adopt *political* lesbianism for its presumed catalytic potential for liberation.[27] Given this, adopting a bisexual identity proper was akin to treason. And though they occasionally paid lip service to a shared struggle, New Left liberationists were just as likely to express outright hostility toward the transsexuals and transvestites among their ranks. Famed New Left "anti-psychiatrist" psychiatrist Thomas Szasz, for instance, supported homosexuality's removal from the *DSM* while bemoaning trans surgical care as an antifeminist abomination of modernity, a "male-supremacist obscenity."[28]

Lesbian separatists in particular also kept the anti-transsexual torch lit through and beyond the social revolutions of the 1960s and 1970s.[29] Whether through exclusionary policies at cultural events like the Michigan Womyn's Music Festival or their frequent citations to Janice Raymond's infamous *The Transsexual Empire*, a book that accused transgender women of "raping" the female form, the era's organized lesbian groups kept trans persons at a distance.[30] Radical lesbian feminism became increasingly unmoored from its (already loose) left-wing heritage, as evinced by the 1980s coalitions that brought together feminists and social conservative anti-pornography crusaders, both of whom were revolted by these and other allegedly misogynistic representations and appropriations of womanhood. To this day, transexclusionary radical feminists continue to link arm in arm with Christian conservative forces in their cross-ideological efforts to contain and to squash trans life and identity.[31]

As a consequence, bisexual and trans-based political communities have historically developed at some distance from gay and lesbian ones.[32] While the HIV/AIDS crisis sometimes united disparate queer groups, the crisis also stirred suspicion toward bisexuals, who were cast as perilously promiscuous and, accordingly, especially hazardous vectors of infection.[33] Studies from the era indicate that bisexual men oftentimes incurred similar prejudicial treatment from gays and lesbians as they did from straight Americans.[34] Bisexuality was thus rendered pathological, yet another contagion threatening the health of the body politic.

Though the media today celebrates those like Sylvia Rivera and Marsha P. Johnson, as the face of an earlier, more subterranean transgender moment, contemporary trans politics traces more directly back to medical pioneers and the patient-centric advocacy groups that sprung up around them. Harry Benjamin's 1966 book, *The Transsexual Phenomenon*, was a watershed moment in trans advocacy and healthcare.[35] Its publication inspired activists—and, notably, the wealthy trans businessman and philanthropist Reed Erickson—to demand increased medical research and regimens of surgical care and hormone therapies.[36] The medical interventions themselves became more available as treatments that were long available in Europe were imported and new ones emerged from innovations in endocrinology.[37]

To make sense of these ruptures in what a term like "sex" ultimately signified, a new cohort of physicians and psychiatrists began to theorize—and popularize—the term *gender*. Those like John Money, Robert Stoller, Joan and John Hampson, and Richard Green turned their attention to a wide variety of gender-nonconforming individuals ranging from intersexed patients to those we think of today as "classically" transsexual (that is, those who articulated the "born in the wrong body" narrative).[38] From their early work in the 1950s through their establishment of the first gender identity clinics at universities like UCLA and Johns Hopkins beginning in the late 1960s, these researchers began to see gender nonconformity in children of a very young age.[39] In making sense of their clinical experiences, Money and Stoller in particular employed terms like "gender role" and "identity," respectively, each stressing the significance of child developmental processes and behaviorally learned social roles—that is, the different moments a person's gender experience took root and why so-called mismatches occurred between biology and sense of self.[40]

Mirroring research into homosexuality's nature and origins during this time, these clinicians moved the origins of gender identity development back to the age of two years old; somewhat differently, however, was the insistence that both intersexed and gender "confused" children could be guided toward the "correct" gender identity before a deleterious one was entrenched.[41] In fact, just as homosexuality was removed from the *DSM*, the diagnosis "Gender Identity Disorder in Children" was written into the third edition in order to help meet the demands of that imperative.[42] There were notable disagreements over the exact role that environment and biology played within this early cohort of clinicians. While Stoller launched an early effort to wed this behaviorist model of learned gender with an understanding that biological substrates common to *all* human beings might play a role, he emphatically rejected the hypothesis that transsexuals possessed a distinct biological makeup that set them apart from the norm.[43] At the same time, Money was moving away from the behaviorist model to one that entertained genetic and hormonal causes.[44]

Though all of these clinicians would persist in conflating deep feelings of one's gender with aspects of sexual preference, the psychological study and treatment of gender nonconformity increasingly differentiated trans personhood from gay and lesbian identity. Indeed, as new clinical theories were expounded and medical techniques standardized, a great institutional chasm soon separated sexuality from gender identity. As gay and lesbian advocates made headway in reforming the American Psychiatric Association (APA) in 1973 and other mental health institutions soon thereafter, disorder-based diagnoses for transsexuality and transvestitism remained encased in the amber of the *Diagnostic Statistical Manual of Mental Disorders*, which was updated only slightly in 1980 to include "gender identity disorder."[45] The substitution of the "disorder language" for a depathologized "gender dysphoria" classification would not occur until 2013.[46] As a result of the APA's intransigence, standards for trans healthcare were developed and disseminated through other institutional means. Building on his career-long commitment to trans health-care, Benjamin and his acolytes founded the Harry Benjamin International Gender Dysphoria Association (which goes today by the name of the World Professional Association for Transgender Health, or WPATH) in 1979 to do that work.

Not every new institution, however, was made in the mold of WPATH, an organization that was at the time almost entirely professionally driven and near singularly focused on crafting and implementing standards of trans healthcare. Rather, the term "transgender" came into use throughout the late 1980s and early 1990s to encompass all sorts of gender variance ranging from intersex persons to transsexuals to genderqueer.[47] Advocate-led organizations includ-ing the American Educational Gender Information Service and the Interna-tional Foundation for Gender Education were founded to serve those in the crosshairs of rigid state and medically imposed sex classifications.[48] Activists in these and similar organizations occasionally adopted an anti-medical out-look while a new crop of queer gender theorists in and outside of academia underscored the human body's malleability as they called for visions of gen-der as performative *genre*.[49] The original umbrella conception of transgender was ultimately short-lived as evinced by repeat controversies over the place of disability in gender rights advocacy and the development of an independent patient-and-parents-centric intersex rights movement.[50] The biosocial char-acter of the institutions that developed among doctors, clinicians, lawyers, ad-vocates, and the identifiers themselves essentially guaranteed that the gender-expansive conception of transgender would lose out to a biomedical one.

Perhaps most consequential for the biomedical model's triumph over competing trans epistemologies was the mainstream gay and lesbian advo-cacy movement's receptivity to science-backed identity categories. As late as the early 2000s, gay and lesbian interest groups were hesitant to integrate transgender rights into their missions, fearing that a conservative backlash might sink all ships.[51] These fears were not unfounded; though groups like the Human Rights Campaign had become known entities within the DC donor universe and the Democratic Party alike, they were also reckoning with what was fomenting into a national assault on the same-sex marriage issue. Behind the scenes, however, the HRC and dozens of organizational representatives and activists were building an LGBT alliance through a series of semi-annual meetings.[52] The meeting minutes from these gatherings along with internal memos, pamphlets, published research reports, and litigation strategies dem-onstrate how the "T" was integrated largely according to the born this way logic that had already come to define gay and lesbian identities.

PFLAG was an early adopter of trans rights rhetoric. One of the group's campaign pamphlets from 1995 directly linked the question of biology to civil rights reform. There, PFLAG leaders explained that trans persons may possess "a genetic predisposition that would cause the person to want to be a member of the other sex."[53] The pamphlet went on to gesture toward a number of possible origins stories in a manner that reflected PFLAG's long-standing approach to a scientific literature that stressed multiple causes and the organization's own desire to forefront the biological ones.[54] In its 1998 mission statement, PFLAG amended its usual script on sexual orientation's biological origins to include transsexuality.[55] In its emphasis on etiology, the statement read: "transsexuality . . . may be caused by the bathing of a fetus by opposite birth sex hormones while *in utero*, or perhaps by some spontaneous genetic mutation, which is also one of the theories of the origin of homosexuality."[56]

The Human Rights Campaign was considerably more tepid in its support. Having invested heavily in a gender-conforming image of gay identity, its leadership was wary about implicitly collapsing sexual orientation and gender identity into one another. As HRC leaders wrestled with *how* to blend trans rights into its agenda, they fretted particularly over the budding transgender movement's own internal fissures regarding medical and psychiatric classifications and what an unresolved debate over etiology might risk. After all, how could the HRC—already at this time the premier interest-group advocate for gay and lesbian rights—integrate a population that might buck the born this way trend? Just a few years later in 2001, the HRC found a way to join those like PFLAG and the National Gay and Lesbian Task Force in affirming trans rights. The following year, the HRC published its ongoing public opinion research that affords some insight into how its fretful leadership reconciled their worries.[57] In its polling, the HRC had asked respondents whether they saw being transgender as a choice over which people retained some degree of agency or a condition into which a one is born. Armed with data demonstrating the congruence between a "by nature" account of orientation and of gender identity, the HRC began to endorse trans rights more publicly than ever before.

Tensions over the biological narrative have persisted especially within the realm of bisexual activism. Although bisexual groups were assimilated into the gay and lesbian advocacy movement alongside trans ones, bisexual identity has often been sidelined or given mere lip service. Even as bisexual nonprofit leaders successfully got their name on the bill for the March on Washington for Lesbian, Gay, and Bi Equal Rights and Liberation, the title for the march was self-consciously crafted to avoid the term "Bisexual" in an attempt to direct attention away from sexual practices, particular the promiscuity and non-monogamy that were commonly associated with bisexuality.[58]

There is certainly much truth to the sentiment that these marginalized identities have been incompletely integrated. But even more so, the history of trans and bisexual assimilation into the gay and lesbian movement reflects again just how tightly bound sexuality and gender truly are. Though various disparate social epistemologies and medical institutions have differentiated sexuality and gender in innumerable ways since the nineteenth century—many of which endure today—the two are never so distinct that their orbits do not intersect. Indeed, their gravitational pulls perpetually threaten to collapse one back into the other.

Legally Trans: The Contested Meanings of Sex, Gender, and Gender Identity

Since the days of Magnus Hirschfeld's reform work in Germany and Harry Benjamin's parallel efforts in the United States, biomedical and psychological evidence have been central to trans legal advocacy (which, in the tradition of legal pluralism's preference for undifferentiated monoliths, is frequently meant to mean *transsexual*). Throughout the mid- to late twentieth century, reformers successfully shifted the state prerogative away from policing gender transgression as criminally fraudulent to a concern that medical professionals certify trans identity's permanence, generally through documentation of surgical procedures (today laws governing identity documents tend to substitute psychiatric and personal attestations for surgical requirements).[59] What has changed in recent years is that the law has become fixated on a different kind of permanence. Biological theories concerning gender identity's essence have become more legally relevant than ever.

This transformation has been in no small part thanks to the gay and lesbian movement's successes with the born this way logic. Gay and lesbian advocates primed judges to look out for expert-endorsed, biologically backed assertions of identity and immutability. In the 1995 case *Brown v. Zavaras*, the Tenth Circuit drew a thread between the scientific studies and expert witnesses in its previous gay rights cases and recent trans rights ones.[60] Citing military exclusion and antidiscrimination law cases that involved arguments about sexual orientation's immutability, the court contemplated that transsexuality also might owe its origins to genetics or other biological factors.[61] In cases involving prisoners' rights, asylum seekers, and civil rights law protections, trans rights were gradually won on these terms. In the process, reform litigation displaced narrowly construed notions of biological "sex" in the law with novel biological theories of gender identity as *sex itself*.

In the early 2000s, prisoners' rights litigators began arguing that the denial of hormonal and surgical care to trans inmates violates the Eighth Amendment's prohibition on "cruel and unusual punishment." To do so, attorneys drew on *Estelle v. Gamble* (1976), a case in which the Supreme Court held that the corrections officials must not exhibit "deliberate indifference" to prisoners' medical needs.[62] Much like in the conversion therapy ban cases in the following decade, litigators relied on mental health and medical experts who warned that withholding healthcare would result in psychological injury and heightened risks of self-harm and suicide due to the nature of gender identity.

Recent trans inmate healthcare cases have largely turned on the question of whether professional medical opinion is unified in its support for hormonal therapies or if the field is fragmented, in flux, or ultimately uncertain whether such care is medically, and therefore constitutionally, necessary.[63] In a victory against Wisconsin's Inmate Sex Change Prevention Act, the American Civil Liberties Union (ACLU) and Lambda Legal successfully beat back the legislature's broad denial of healthcare in a landmark Seventh Circuit case.[64] Alongside the plaintiffs' own expert witnesses, the American Medical Association filed its own brief to make clear there was indeed a medical consensus: hormonal therapies are paramount for patient health, and psychotherapeutic care alone (Wisconsin's alternative treatment program) is inadequate.[65] Although attorneys focused their attention on medical care proper here, Lambda litigators apparently felt the weight of the bioessentialist evidence in their pocket. Tucked into its initial complaint was the assertion that "gender dysphoria may not be a psychiatric condition but might, in fact, be caused by biological or physiological factors."[66]

Implicitly acknowledging that medical opinion had turned against an older therapeutic model that typically promoted gender "reorientation" over "affirmation," the Wisconsin GOP sought instead to cast doubt on just how settled the new consensus opinion truly was. In another harbinger of what was to come in conversion therapy ban cases, the state relied on anti-choice reproductive rights doctrine to make their case here. Citing *Gonzales v. Carhart* (2007), a decision that upheld the Partial-Birth Abortion Ban Act of 2003, Wisconsin posited that state and federal legislatures are afforded broad deference in matters of unsettled medical opinion. Ultimately, the Seventh Circuit rejected the state's argument that "[gender identity disorder] is a condition about which there is limited knowledge and vast uncertainty," siding instead with plaintiff's expert witnesses and allies.[67] The following year, a federal district judge appointed by none other than President Ronald Reagan deliv-ered a similar verdict.[68] In a ruling that echoed judges in the early homophile-era cases who grew impatient with public health officials' legal chicanery and shaky medical evidence of sexual psychopathologies, Judge Mark Wolf found that Massachusetts had cherry-picked unrepresentative medical experts to defend its own withholding of trans healthcare treatments.

Advocates have been continually beset by circuit court splits on the ques-tion of hormonal treatments and surgeries. In 2014 the First Circuit over-turned Wolf's verdict.[69] Several years later, trans rights litigators scored a his-toric victory in 2019 when the Ninth Circuit held that trans inmates merit access to gender confirmation surgery as well as hormonal treatments.[70] A sympathetic Ninth Circuit panel fended off claims that the WPATH Stan-dards of Care do not constitute a medical consensus by citing the National Center for Lesbian Rights' expert witness—none other than Dr. Randi Ettner, one of the authors of the WPATH standards' latest edition.[71] The following year, trans prisoner rights were dealt a serious blow in 2020 when the Elev-enth Circuit denied transition care using the testimony of an outlier psy-chiatrist (along with fearmongering about the costs of state-provided med-ical assistance).[72] Lastly, in the realm of the Federal Bureau of Prisons, the US District Court for the Southern District of Illinois issued an order to the bureau in April 2022 demanding that a trans prisoner be afforded gender-affirmative surgical care.[73] Transgender asylum seekers have also been lever-aging medical expertise to assist their political status as an imperiled minor-ity group. At the turn of the millennium, trans asylum petitioners benefited enormously from their association with gays and lesbians, a group that had begun to enjoy some protections as the United States became increasingly—albeit unevenly—unwilling to send sexual minorities to countries where be-ing "out" might be the difference between life and death.[74] This was the case for Geovanni Hernandez-Montiel, a self-proclaimed "gay man with a female sexual identity."[75] In its 2000 ruling in favor of Hernandez-Montiel, the Ninth Circuit acknowledged that such effeminate men were a distinct social minor-ity group in Mexico and, therefore, deserved protections on par with simi-lar sexual minorities. More recently, immigration and Article III courts have more finely discerned differences between gender identity and sexual orien-tation by invoking categories like gender identity disorder and gender dys-phoria.[76] As asylum law scholar Stefan Vogler has observed, the methods de-ployed to make determinations about who requires asylum are eclectic: they range from personal narratives to medical experts to journal citations. How-ever, they also involve a sort of biological backstop as evinced by the number of successful trans asylum seekers who describe the need for hormonal and

SCIENTIFIC GAZE IN TRANSGENDER AND BISEXUAL POLITICS   173

surgical interventions and who espouse a belief that they were born into the wrong body.[77]

Just as trans identity was being uncoupled from sexual orientation in asylum law, gender identity was becoming reassociated with the notion of "sex" in statutory and constitutional civil rights law. Throughout the late twentieth century, courts were the main vehicle by which trans advocates ought to expand statutory Title VII employment protections against sex discrimination and constitutional equal protection for trans persons as a suspect class akin to sex. These typically took the form of long-shot attempts to expand the juridical category of "sex" to include transsexuals and other gender nonconformists.[78] Until very recently, trans advocates were neglected by even the paltry number of city and state ordinances protecting sexual minorities; today, still fewer than half of states expressly prohibit employers from discriminating against employers on the basis of gender identity.[79] And while the Equality Act (passed by the House of Representatives but now stuck in partisan limbo in the Senate) would provide federal statutory protections for gender identity, the HRC and others have a bad track record on trans rights at the national level. Nearly two decades ago, these groups accepted that striking trans rights protections from the Equality Act's forebearer, the Employment Non-Discrimination Act, was an acceptable price to pay for gay and lesbian protections.[80]

This is the context in which Ramona Holloway, a trans woman who had undergone hormonal and surgical transition procedures while employed at an accounting firm, sued upon being terminated for those very acts of medical transition.[81] Holloway contested her employers' argument that Title VII prohibition on sex discrimination in the workplace did not apply to her, arguing to the contrary that her "sex transformation" afforded her such protections. Moreover, Holloway argued that if Title VII had indeed been expressly written to exclude transsexuals, then the equal protection clause required that the judiciary expand the meaning of "sex," given that transsexuals constituted a minority group defined in large part by the immutability of their experience of sex. In *Holloway v. Arthur Andersen Company* (1977), the Ninth Circuit dismissed both claims, observing that the immutability criterion for suspect classification as delineated in *Frontiero v. Richardson* (1973) had not been met, and that transsexuality ought not be considered biologically immutable in the same sense as (cis) womanhood.[82] Well into the twenty-first century, circuit court cases continued to slam the door shut in these cases.[83] In an exemplary opinion from 1984, the Seventh Circuit stated emphatically that a trans woman "is entitled to any personal belief about her sexual identity she desires . . . [b]ut even if one believes that a woman can be so easily created from what remains of a man, that does not decide this case."[84]

In 1989 a landmark Title VII case before the Supreme Court made the "sex" in "sex discrimination" more capacious than ever, thereby inciting new endeavors to squeeze gender identity into its confines. The case was spurred by the accounting firm Price Waterhouse's stubbornly sexist refusal to promote Anne Hopkins. Despite her impeccable record of securing lucrative business contracts and satisfying clients, Hopkins was repeatedly passed over for partnership due to what her superiors perceived as overtly masculine behavior and mannerisms, her aggressiveness and brusqueness, and, overall, her failure to conform to "ladylike" standards. Hopkins argued that "but for" the imposition of these gendered tropes, she would have been promoted. The court agreed with Hopkins that at the heart of Title VII was the principle that such gender nonconformists—that is, cis women who did not stick to society's gender scripts—were protected against such sex stereotypes.[85] If sex could be interpreted so broadly, trans advocates started to muse, maybe it could fit any number of gender benders—notably, not just the transsexuals who were taken to have "crossed the divide" into a new stable sex category— who had suffered under sex-stereotyping bosses and coworkers.[86]

Trans plaintiffs did fair far better in sex discrimination cases in the wake of *Price Waterhouse*; however, most did so by leveraging psychiatric evidence, diagnostic criteria and treatment standards, and an innatist logic that framed gender transgression as the very core of a medically legible identity.[87] The Sixth Circuit, for instance, ruled in 2004 that the Title VII sex-stereotyping principle protected a transgender firefighter during her transition precisely because her new feminine appearance was "in accordance with both international medical protocols for treating GID" and the American Psychiatric Association's guidelines.[88] The following year, the ACLU successfully sued the Library of Congress for rescinding a job offer upon learning that the candidate, Diane Schroer, was transgender. The DC district court was taken with the ACLU's medical and social work experts on gender identity, noting that Schroer had "develop[ed] a medically appropriate plan for transitioning from male to female" and was subsequently discriminated against when the employer learned that she "intended to become, legally, culturally, and physically, a woman."[89]

In contrast to those making unequivocal statements about their fixed identities backed up by medical expertise, ostensibly cisgender employees who protest gendered grooming standards have been regularly denied Title VII protections despite the sex stereotyping that clearly underlies them.[90] The Ninth Circuit infamously upheld such gendered dress codes in a 2006 ruling against a female bartender who had refused to wear facial makeup on the job.[91] That may all change now that the Supreme Court has interpreted Title VII broadly in *Bostock v. Clayton County* (2020) to encompass both "sexual ori-entation" and "gender identity."[92] The ACLU, for one, believes that the tide has turned against these standards. In June 2021, its attorneys sent a letter to Alaska Airlines arguing that *Bostock*'s logic goes far beyond previous circuit court cases and actually prohibits these kinds of employer-mandated dress codes, which they claim harm nonbinary and gender-nonconforming indi-viduals.[93] It remains to be seen whether gender nonconformists of all stripes might finally find a spot in the law or whether the high court has simply af-firmed the implicit innatist undergirding of previous cases.

Born Trans: Bathroom Bills, School Board Policies, and the Rights of Trans Youth

Over the past decade, trans rights reformers have been met with hostile bath-room bills, sports restrictions, and bans on gender-affirming healthcare for trans youth. Faced with such aggressive attempts to regulate trans life, advo-cates have asserted the reality and permanency of trans personhood by once more anchoring gender identity to sex. This legal strategy functions by trans-forming gender identity into "sex" as it appears in statutory civil rights law like Title VII and IX as well as the Fourteenth Amendment's equal protection clause. Trans litigators have leveraged neuroanatomical and other forms of biological evidence that suggests that gender identity is not only one deter-minant of sex, but instead is *the* major causal factor at play. Importantly, gen-der is not cultural, but instead it is biological and resides in the brain. Gen-der *expression* may be a malleable matter of choice, but gender *identity* is far from volitional; in fact, this concept of gender identity provides a biological anchoring to explain why an individual may choose to alter their gender ex-pression, to bring it into alignment with their deeply rooted identity.

Outside of the courts, civil rights groups have settled on a media strategy that centers trans children as the victims of these rights restrictions, a conve-nient foil against narratives of sexual predators who shape-shift their gender presentations to access the vulnerable. This emphasis undoubtedly reflects the very real and dire threats that gender-nonconforming youths face today as students are kicked off sports teams and gender-affirmative parents are ac-cused of child abuse.[94] But as was the case for gay and lesbian advocates de-cades ago, the innocent figure of the child has also offered advocates an ex-ceptionally amenable site for inscribing theories of immutability and to drum up sympathy for those who are, by accident of their birth, "born that way."[95]

The social conservatives camped out in governors' mansions, state legisla-tures, family values groups, corporate-backed foundations—and, from 2017 to

2021, President Trump's executive branch—have resisted this redefinition of sex. In riposte, they have made appeals to a mix of science and "common sense" that sex—usually defined with reference to a person's genitals, chromosomes, and that fleeting moment when a physician announces their meaning at the time of birth—establishes important natural differences between men and women that necessitate sex-segregated facilities.[96] This is the most straightforward, and most often discussed, dimension to the right wing's position in these battles over reform. What has gone mostly unnoticed though is the fact that social conservatives have for years now made recourse to the traditional feminist theory distinction between sex as biology and gender as cultural as a means of keeping gender identity far apart from the former.[97] In their defense of traditional sex-segregated facilities and gendered social norms, conservatives have somewhat strangely acquiesced to the idea that gender and sex are perhaps not so congruent, that there can be some degree of "mismatch" between cultural expectations and what they take to be the biological "facts of life."

Twenty sixteen was the year of the trans bathroom panic. While the fight that erupted over North Carolina's infamous House Bill (HB) 2 was novel in its national scope, opponents of trans rights had been restricting trans bathroom access at least as far back as 2008.[98] That year in Gainesville, Florida, a conservative group called Citizens for Good Public Policy ran a campaign branding a pro-trans-rights ordinance as an invitation for wig-wearing predatory men to prowl the city's public restrooms.[99] In the years in between the Gainesville fight and the one in the Raleigh state capitol, the Obama administration gradually incorporated gender identity into its interpretations of federal civil rights law including Title VII and Title IX. Various Equal Employment Opportunity Commission and the US Departments of Justice and Education rulings and directives expanded the notion of sex to include, among other things, the right of trans persons to use the restroom at work and in public places of accommodation that best suits them.[100] Far from being sui generis, HB 2 catalyzed growing conservative discontent. It sparked a national debate over trans rights, which then vice president Joe Biden had just four years prior prophesized would be the "civil rights issue of our time."[101]

Following an especially contentious special legislative session on March 23, 2016, North Carolina's Republican Governor Pat McCrory signed HB 2 into law, thereby nullifying a recently passed Charlotte ordinance that would have protected gay and transgender persons from various forms of discrimination. HB 2 quickly became a matter of national political controversy as Attorney General Loretta Lynch announced in May 2016 that the federal government was suing North Carolina for its "state-sponsored discrimination" that imposed hardship on persons for "something they cannot control."[102] Beyond Lynch's statement, the DOJ lawsuit waded directly into the biological debate in observing that "an individual's 'sex' consists of multiple factors, which may not always be in alignment. Among those factors are hormones, external genitalia, internal reproductive organs, chromosomes, and gender identity, which is an individual's internal sense of being male or female." The DOJ further stated that "although there is not yet one definitive explanation for what determines gender identity, biological factors, most notably sexual differentiation in the brain, have a role in gender identity development."[103]

In its own suit against HB 2, the ACLU advanced an even more biodeterministic argument than the DOJ in its statement that "gender identity is the primary determinant of sex [and] is fixed at an early age and highly resistant to change through intervention."[104] The National Center for Lesbian Rights (NCLR) went further still in its own brief. In a bid for equal protection clause protections akin to those for sex, the NCLR and coalition of trans groups posited the biological immutability of gender identity.[105] To buttress its claim, the NCLR cited an article titled "Evidence Supporting the Biological Nature of Gender Identity" coauthored by Joshua Safer, the founding medical director of the Center for Transgender Medicine and Surgery at Boston Medical Center and inaugural president of the United States Professional Association for Transgender Health. In that meta study, Safer and his colleagues concluded that brain studies offered the most convincing evidence for the "organic basis of transgender identity."[106]

Barraged by a flurry of lawsuits, the McCrory administration filed both its own countersuit and hopped aboard two separate lawsuits that coalesced nearly two dozen GOP-controlled states rallying against the Obama administration's expansive interpretation of sex discrimination.[107] Across these suits, the states continually distinguished sex—deemed a biological category determined by one's anatomy and genes—from gender identity—a malleable psychological quality outside the scope of civil rights law. Not to be outdone by the opposition, Governor McCrory enlisted biostatistician Lawrence Mayer to testify on behalf of HB 2.[108] At the time, Mayer was collaborating on research with his former Johns Hopkins University colleague Paul McHugh, a psychiatrist who had been instrumental in shuttering the university's pioneering gender identity clinic in 1979.[109] In a sprawling review covering decades of sexological and gender science research for the journal *New Atlantis*, Mayer and McHugh concluded that biological sex is innate and gender identity is a culturally determined social construct.[110] Taking aim at research on sexual orientation as well, they posited that the born this way hypothesis likely did not hold either for gays and lesbians or transgender persons, and was little more than a liberal fantasy.[111]

Though a corporate-led boycott and subsequent electoral backlash induced North Carolina lawmakers to repeal HB 2, school board administrators across the country found themselves in federal court defending their trans bathroom policies.[112] The majority of these cases have pitted trans advocates against big money-backed conservative outfits like the Alliance Defending Freedom (ADF) and small groups of "concerned" anti-reform parents, students, and school administrators.[113] The most well-known of these is *Gloucester County School Board v. G. G.*, a case brought by the ACLU on behalf of Gavin Grimm, a transgender student who was denied the use of the men's room at his Virginia high school.[114] Grimm's case garnered national attention in 2016 when the US Supreme Court agreed to hear the school board's appeal after the Fourth Circuit Court of Appeals ruled in favor of Grimm's rights under Title IX. In the Fourth Circuit's ruling, the question of gender identity was slightly eclipsed by an administrative law dispute over the Department of Education's procedural means of reinterpreting "sex" under Title IX, which made Grimm's case a proxy fight by anti-regulatory conservatives against the entire federal bureaucracy's constitutional authority.[115]

This scuffling over administrative law aside, the ACLU made biology the centerpiece of its media campaign and litigation. In an address to the school board that was subsequently publicized by the ACLU and LGBTQ+ media outlets, Grimm demanded that his rights be respected because his transgender identity is a "scientific fact." Just as oncology patients did "not choose to have cancer," Grimm reasoned, he did not "choose to be born transgender."[116] In court, the ACLU framed its equal protection clause argument with the Safer study on the biological basis of gender identity. Challenging the school board's contention that sex is static and gender identity is merely subjective, the ACLU argued that "'gender identity' is an established medical concept, referring to one's sense of oneself as belonging to a particular gender. It is an innate and immutable aspect of personality, with biological roots."[117]

ACLU attorneys also assured the court that "Gavin has never argued that the Board should accept his 'mere assertion' that he is transgender. He has provided ample corroboration from his doctors, his parents, and his state identification documents. He is following a treatment protocol from his healthcare providers in accordance with widely accepted standards of care for treating gender dysphoria." According to this argument, it is not enough to ask Grimm whether he is transgender; rather, his identity is always subject to scrutiny, as evinced in the ACLU's guarantee that "if school administrators have legitimate concerns that a person is pretending to be transgender, a letter from the student's doctor or parent can easily provide corroboration."[118] Based on this biopolitical form of citizenship and rights guarantees, trans students would be constantly at risk of being commanded to "show one's papers" in quite a literal sense.

Confronted by the school board's own medical experts, it is understandable that the ACLU and others so often fought fire with fire. In a brief submitted with the pediatric endocrinologist Paul Hruz, Mayer and McHugh defended the school board's distinction between the biological-fixed nature of sex and gender's socially constructed and culturally determined form.[119] They even cited Judith Butler's *Gender Trouble* to posit that "gender is a fluid concept with no truly objective meaning" and is, therefore, something entirely distinct from the "innate and immutable" quality of sex.[120] While this comically misrepresents Butler's theory of performativity, the distinction is part of a conservative strategy that casts gender identity as "fuzzy and mercurial" and without stable meaning.[121]

As Grimm's case has bounced back and forth between the Supreme Court and the Fourth Circuit, similar cases brought by trans students who—along with litigators for organizations like Lambda Legal, the NCLR, and the Transgender Law Center—have recruited expert witnesses from gender identity clinics. Though recent ethnographies reveal that such clinicians do not uniformly subscribe to strictly biomedical theories of gender identity—no doubt some clinicians do, but many others approach etiology with nuance and favor open-ended, patient-driven explorations of gender—attorneys are adept at squeezing out their expert witnesses' most deterministic sentiments.[122] Diane Ehrensaft, director of Mental Health at the University of San Francisco Child and Adolescent Gender Center, has frequently served in this expert witness role. In testimonies for Lambda Legal and the NCLR, Ehrensaft has testified that gender identity ought to be legally protected due to its biologically immutable nature and the futility of reparative therapeutic attempts to alter it.[123] Propounding her theory of trans etiology before a district court in western Pennsylvania, Ehrensaft explained, "There is a medical consensus that gender identity is innate and that efforts to change a person's gender identity are unethical and harmful to a person's health and well-being. Biological factors, most notably sexual differentiation in the brain, have a role in gender identity development. Gender identity is the most important and determinative factor in establishing a person's sex."[124] Ergo, gender identity *is* sex.

Whereas Ehrensaft served as science ambassador for the NCLR and Lambda, the Transgender Law Center has relied on Dr. R. Nicholas Gorton, a physician who has served on the research committee of WPATH, the medical advisory board of the University of California, San Francisco Center of Excellence for Transgender Health, and the American Medical Association's LGBT Advisory Committee. In his testimony for a 2016 Wisconsin case,

Gorton echoed Ehrensaft's remarks on biological immutability and condemned the school board's insistence that sex chromosomes alone determined biological sex.[125] Gorton explained that his task was to "assist the person in transitioning to living in accordance with their true sex" by nurturing the seed of a gender identity.[126] Thus far, federal district and appellate courts appear to be quite receptive to the revered status of the gender clinician and the validity of the biomedical theory of gender identity. Seemingly convinced by Ehrensaft's testimony, a Pennsylvania district court judge accepted that "being transgender is not a 'preference,' that being transgender has a medically recognized biological basis, and that it is an innate and non-alterable status."[127] In a 2017 ruling in favor of trans student Ash Whitaker, a unanimous court observed, "This is not a case where a student has merely announced that he is a different gender. Rather, Ash has a medically diagnosed and documented condition."[128]

In recent years, anti-trans state legislators and social conservative foundations have opened up new theaters of conflict over trans youth healthcare access and sex-segregated sports programs.[129] These right-wing new attacks—which snowballed from 41 bills in 2018 to 238 bills in 2022—once again turn on questions of biological sex and who among the medical establishment has the authority to declare its contours.[130] Immediately following West Virginia's passage of one of the nation's first anti-trans sports bans, the ACLU sued on behalf of B.J.P., an eleven-year old girl who was suddenly barred from her middle-school sports teams.[131] The ACLU condemned HB 3293 for promoting "unfounded stereotypes" about trans girls and testosterone as well as "false scientific claims" concerning biological sex.[132] In what reads like a copy-and-paste from its bathroom bill case briefs, attorneys referenced the "medical consensus that there is a significant biologic component underlying gender identity," which itself is a "fundamental component of [trans] identity that is durable and deeply rooted."[133]

In an upgrade from its HB 2 days, the ACLU invited Joshua Safer as an expert witness to topple the shaky science upon which the HB 3293 was based.[134] Speaking in part as a coauthor of the Endocrine Society's trans healthcare protocols, Safer concurred that "considerable scientific evidence has emerged demonstrating a durable biological element underlying gender identity"; while "the detailed mechanisms are unknown," Safer hedged, "there is a medical consensus that there is a significant biologic component underlying gender identity."[135] As such, gender identity has very little to do with how we generally think of gender as "socially contingent behaviors, attitudes, or personality traits that a society designates as masculine or feminine."[136] Registering this strong assertion from biology, Arkansas retorted with a culturalist critique. "Transgender status thus is not rooted in biology, but in 'what is normative' in a particular 'culture and historical period,'" state's attorneys asserted, and a gender identity that "is culturally determined, can remain 'fluid,' and can even rapidly toggle between different identities. . . . This is the opposite of an immutable characteristic."[137]

Although the fate of anti-trans youth sports and healthcare access legislation remains uncertain, the post-*Bostock* legal climate has proven congenial to bathroom-focused fights. In cases involving trans high school students, the Eleventh and Fourth Circuits reasoned that the expansive interpretation of sex in Title VII prompted a corresponding change in Title IX's parameters.[138] And despite Justices Samuel Alito and Clarence Thomas's laments, the Supreme Court has refused to take up a subsequent appeal in Grimm's case.[139] If the inegalitarians are to have their way on the bathroom rights issue, they will likely need to sidestep matters of biology and ontology to achieve their ends.

For this reason, social conservatives have not nearly invested all of their armaments in the war over biological sex. The Alliance Defending Freedom has led a clever two-front strategy: while lawmakers and right-wing lobbies deny the basic reality of a psychologically healthy transgender identity within state legislatures, others have pursued national legislation and concurrent federal litigation that shrewdly concedes the existence of the trans population while calling for "accommodation" and "balancing" acts. The ADF has for several years now asked the Supreme Court to rule on the statutory and constitutional right to privacy that cis women allegedly have that would prohibit trans women from accessing women's restrooms, locker rooms, homeless shelters, prisons facilities, and more.[140] As the argument goes, trans persons deserve basic accommodations—for example, designated single-stall restrooms—but cannot, for the sake of (cis) women's hard-won equal rights, be allowed into sex-segregated ones that clash with their assigned-at-birth sex status. Although the court has yet to take up one of these privacy-based challenges and the legislative equivalent in the GOP's Fairness for All Act (an alternative to the more robust pro-LGBTQ+ Equality Act that uses religious freedom to poke holes in civil rights law) remains stalled, the ADF-led conservative coalition remains resolute in its opposition to reform.

In addition to the faux-pluralist stance, GOP state legislators and governors have passed anti-trans youth healthcare laws. Those like the Heritage Foundation have buttressed these efforts through its in-house research on the purported link between suicidality and gender-affirming medical care.[141] As of March 2022, fifteen states have passed laws that restrict healthcare to transgender youth, and many more have proposed such legislation.[142] Some of these even criminalize pediatricians and parents who assist procuring and delivering such care for transgender youth. The intent here is obvious: the legislations' chilling effect would compel many medical professionals to close shop on youth gender identity healthcare.[143] Preempting the provision of trans healthcare mirrors GOP ongoing attempts to regulate abortion out of existence. In 2021 the Texas GOP managed to pass SB 8, a law that authorizes individual members of the public to sue and collect (at least) $10,000 from any person who aids and abets an abortion performed six weeks after pregnancy.[144] Immediately upon the law going into effect, abortion providers shuttered clinics and refused to perform abortions for any pregnant person past that six-week deadline. The abortion parallel is instructive in another sense too. Pro-life advocates gradually ramped up the opposition until they could finally pass and defend one of these so-called "heartbeat bills" in court.[145] While queer advocates and their allies in corporate America initially prevented a few of these anti-trans bills from becoming law, Republican governors have become increasingly willing to buck those they decry as "woke capitalists" and to sign these rights restrictions into law.[146] So, while a handful of Republican governors found cause to veto these particular transgender healthcare laws in their first iteration, we have probably witnessed just the first shots fired in what will likely become a recurrent conflict.[147]

The New Biopolitics of Bisexuality

Bisexuality may buck the binary in some important respects, but it is not immune to biopolitics. As far back as the 1980s, the sexologists who spent their days studying homosexuality speculated that there may be individual biological processes that attend to each degree of sexuality on the Kinsey scale, meaning that there may be *multiple* biological forms of bisexuality. Of course, when these scientists presented at PFLAG's national conferences or had their studies summarized for readers of HRC press releases and National Gay Task Force newsletters, the focal point was "exclusive" homosexuality and its hypothesized origins—the rest was merely footnotes.

While there has clearly been room for such bio explanations and representations of bisexual identity for some time now, the crucial mixture of sexology, political enthusiasm, and legal incentives that had coagulated into gay, lesbian, and transgender biopolitics was mostly lacking. Those bisexual groups that did exist—these included public health and HIV/AIDS-focused nonprofits and community centers along with relatively small-time bisexual street activists and lobbying groups—were far less enthralled with the language and logic of fixity. They were oftentimes much more willing to speak about sexual desire and romantic attachment in terms of agency and contingency.[148] Despite this tradition of skepticism, the iterative and compounding developments in scientific research, media attention, and advocacy that had manufactured gay, lesbian, and trans biopolitical identities would come to bear on bisexual ones. The end of the assembly line eventually did produce a bisexual variant of born this way, but it did not do so on the terms of those activists in existing bisexual political groups or even the mainstream gay and lesbian movement.

This modern story of how bisexuality was biologized begins with a very old piece of medical equipment—the phallometric device. In the 1950s, Czech psychiatrist Kurt Freund developed the first sexological device to leverage plethysmography (a voluminal measurement of blood flow).[149] Far from egalitarian in its origins, Freund's instrument was primarily used by the Czech military to assess the validity of conscripted soldiers' requests for reprieve from combat. In other words, whether they were *really* gay or simply cowards. Later in the 1960s, psychologists and psychiatrists would use the device to assess their conversion therapy techniques. Since then, it has been put to a wide variety of uses ranging from pedophilia detection to pharmaceutical trials for drugs that treat impotence.[150]

To contemporary ears, phallometric devices likely sound like a fairly vulgar, even barbaric, means of assessing the truth of sexual subjectivity. The total denial that a speech act could accurately convey desire or identity runs against colloquial language about voicing one's authentic truth. However, gay rights advocates have long accepted that these biometric measurements, no matter how coarse or uncouth, furnish considerable strength to their identity claims. Throughout the 1960s and early 1970s fights over the pathological thesis, the homophiles found allies among sympathetic behavioral psychologists like Gerald Davison, who had abandoned conversion therapy practices and renounced diagnoses that labeled gays and lesbians as mentally ill.[151] Unlike their intra-disciplinary adversaries in psychoanalysis who promised to wrest homosexual desire free from the unconscious, some behavioralists were conducting phallometric experiments that disconfirmed conversion therapy's efficacy. While coercive techniques could *quell* homosexual arousal, some reform-minded psychologists granted, therapeutic interventions could not meaningfully *prompt* heterosexual ones.[152]

Gay rights proponents discovered that these phallometric findings reinforced their political message that to be gay was to possess a fixed, potentially biological essence. In the late 1990s, Wayne Besen and his colleagues at the Human Rights Campaign encouraged the use of phallometric testing when their prominent APA ally Robert Spitzer went rogue and decided to once more test ex-gay narratives and conversion therapy's promise.[153]

Besen and his singularly focused anti-conversion-therapy organization, Truth Wins Out, continued to pitch the penile plethysmograph, "no-lie MRI" brain scans, and the lie-detecting polygraph as essential defenses against ex-gay empiricism.[154]

Half a century after self-declared homosexual men were first subjected to Freund's invasive examinations, Northwestern University psychologist and gay twins study coauthor Michael Bailey and his lab put the technology to use in a study of bisexuality that sparked a movement-wide debate.[155] For their 2005 article, Bailey and his colleagues used a penile plethysmograph to measure arousal patterns in self-identified homosexual, heterosexual, and bisexual men as they viewed pornographic stimuli, some showcasing only men and others involving only women.[156] Upon examining the research subjects' blood flows and variations in erection circumference, they observed that the bisexual men did not actually demonstrate a "bisexual pattern" of arousal. The majority of these subjects were only aroused by images of same-sex activity in the stimuli, and a small minority were aroused only by heterosexual stimuli. Bailey and his coauthors determined that bisexuality must be less a hardwired sexual predisposition than it is a means of interpreting desire.[157] Accordingly, they wrote that "when self-report is suspect, genital arousal may provide a more valid measure." Just as "genital arousal to stimuli depicting children is an effective method of assessing pedophilia, even among men who deny attraction to children," phallometric measurements tell a truth much deeper than any one individual's self-classification can reveal.[158]

Denouncements from all corners of the LGBTQ+ universe registered immediately. The day after the *New York Times* published its coverage—which ran under the title "Gay, Straight, or Lying?"—the National Gay and Lesbian Task Force began coordinating a large group including the movement's media arm, Gay and Lesbian Alliance Against Defamation (GLAAD), as well as Bi-Net USA, the National Bisexual Network, and the Bisexual Resource Center of Boston to issue a counterstatement.[159] In its three-page rebuttal, the coalition took Bailey to task on both empirical and ethical grounds.[160] In a reversal of the movement's long-standing, if not tepid at times, embrace of phallometric instruments, the authors criticized such testing as methodologically controversial and ill-equipped to capture the complex blend of physiological *and* cognitive factors that constitute sexual identity.[161] Speaking on behalf of the Bisexual Resource Center, Sheeri Kirtzer stated plainly that "bisexuality exists and identity doesn't need science to back it up."[162]

Not everyone was so dissatisfied with Bailey et al.'s venture into bisexuality. Whereas most LGBTQ+ advocacy group leaders perceived the study and media coverage as an existential threat, the leadership of the American Institute of Bisexuality (AIB) saw an opportunity to steer Bailey in their preferred direction. Unlike most bisexual advocacy groups, the AIB was founded with a scientific mission. Its founder, the psychiatrist Fritz Klein, gained notoriety within early bisexual activist circles upon publishing his 1978 study, *The Bisexual Option*, which added variables like "emotional preference" to the traditional Kinsey scale.[163] Two decades after the volume's publication, Klein founded the AIB with an expansive mission to assist research in all aspects of bisexual life including health disparities and the special psychological challenges of navigating bisexuality in a binaristic world.[164]

Whereas the Task Force denounced Bailey, AIB's president John Sylla sought instead to court him with dinners and research funds in the hope that he could convince the scientist to take another look at bisexuality. In a subsequent *New York Times* article, Sylla recounts telling Bailey that he had simply not "found" any truly bisexual men yet (despite the fact that self-identified bisexual men had made up a third of the original study's participant population). One board member noted that the quality of the pornographic stimuli was so poor that it likely lacked external validity. The women in the videos, he observed, appeared to be "cracked out" and that no man who truly loved women could have felt arousal upon viewing such depraved and sympathy-inducing content.[165] Along with their research design comments, the AIB leadership doled out funds from its $17 million endowment to support an additional study with the rather explicit understanding that Bailey would try his best to deliver a positive verdict on bisexuality's existence.

In 2011 Bailey and Allen Rosenthal published the AIB-funded follow-up study "Sexual Arousal Patterns in Bisexual Men Revisited."[166] The results were straightforward: subjects who self-reported a bisexual predisposition were found to have corresponding genital sexual arousal patterns. This time around, the pool of research subjects was chosen with more exacting criteria. Rather than recruiting through advertisements in major LGBTQ+ publications like they had in the past, Bailey and Rosenthal targeted online bisexual forums. Each subject was also required to have had sexual experiences with a man and a woman in addition to a romantic relationship with both a man and a woman that had lasted the duration of at least three months. In a report promoting this new research, the AIB criticized the Task Force for its previous attacks on phallometric testing. The AIB also described how it had funded forthcoming work that employed other biometric instruments including fMRI brain scans and pupil dilators to probe bisexual identity.[167]

In keeping with its role as credulous media mouthpiece, the *New York Times* documented the reversal with a headline reading: "No Surprise for Bisexual Men: Report Indicates They Exist."[168] BiNet USA publicly congratulated both the AIB for achieving their goals as well as the "brave folks" who opted to participate.[169] Truth Wins Out declared that "the latest scientific research is explicitly clear that bisexuality is a very real sexual orientation that can be tested and measured."[170] The AIB leadership were also invited to *Bi Talk*, a podcast hosted by Adrienne Williams, who had just been publicly recognized by the Obama White House for having founded the Bi Social Network.[171] Though Williams pressed the AIB representatives on her own measurement and ethics concerns, she ultimately conceded that scientific inquiry is a net positive for political advocacy and that future arousal studies ought to incorporate bisexual women.[172]

Those who had rejected Bailey's first premises remained unsurprisingly unconvinced. Robyn Ochs, a leader active in groups including BiNet USA, and Ellyn Ruthstrom, president of the Bisexual Resource Center of Boston, both reiterated that bisexuality's mosaic is far too complex and varied to be reduced to a static snapshot in a lab.[173] Granting that the revamped study may help some readers struggling with their bisexual desires, Jim Larsen of the Bisexual Organizing Project rebuffed the notion that self-report was an invalid measure.[174] Some bisexual advocates were less upset with the substance of the study but instead regretted that the AIB had wastefully channeled so much funding into arousal studies. When a *New York Times* journalist interviewed activists in the wake of the AIB-funded Bailey study, he found that "many bisexuals would prefer that money go to studies that will help solve health disparities that bisexual people face, rather than another study looking at arousal in a lab setting."[175] The Bisexual Resource Center had indeed just launched its Bisexual Health Awareness Month project (a project that has since been adopted by the Human Rights Campaign), which sought to highlight poor rates of physical health, depression and suicide, and poverty in bisexual youth especially.[176]

These disparity-themed healthcare campaigns are themselves an indication of how powerful the biopolitical perspective on identity has become.[177] Ironically, the left-of-center queer critics of the AIB reify bisexual identity as a discrete and homogeneous category much the same as bio-essentialists like Bailey do. Rather than employing biometric devices, however, they collapse a vast range of socioeconomic factors and experiences into relatively crude statistical aggregations. The same crowd that claims that bisexual personhood cannot be placed in a box has promoted a population-level measurement that produces a similar effect—they use a scientific classification and measurement of identity (in this case, population demographics and public health data) to describe the supposedly shared condition of everyone swept up into that category and then compare that category to other reifications (e.g., heterosexual cisgender men and women, trans persons, etc.).

This all has interpretative and political consequences. The oft-slung term "biphobia" undoubtedly captures the social stigma that many bisexual persons encounter and even some of its social ramifications for mental health and overall well-being; however, it does very little to illuminate how extant health and economic inequalities often produce, texture, and compound the deleterious effects of stigma and harm that can be traced directly back to bisexual experience (meaning that the "experience" itself is highly variegated).[178] Notably, basic interpretive errors abound in this disparity research, some of which have sparked debate between trans and bisexual advocates. The Williams Institute's LGBT Poverty Study, for instance, made headlines after its 2019 report found that bisexual cisgender men and women were found to experience rates of poverty akin to those for transgender individuals.[179] Upon disaggregating by age, however, what the data actually show is that the disproportionate rate of bisexual poverty is mainly due to the fact that "youth" is a confounder: that is, cis women who identify as bisexual tend to be skew young, which inflates the rate of poverty in the age-aggregated statistic.[180]

Faulty findings aside, this process of reification is well-suited for nonprofits seeking grant money for further disparity studies and for small-scale, identity-targeted interventions. Those like Jessica Haggett Silverman, president of the Bisexual Resource Center, come by this orientation honestly. In a 2021 *New York Times* report on bisexuality's "double closet," Silverman recited a statistic that has become a staple of bisexual advocacy: less than 1 percent of grant funding to LGBTQ+ groups winds up in the coffers of bisexual-specific groups.[181] And based on the suspicious absence of any mention of universal healthcare reform in the annual Bisexual Health Awareness Month campaign platform, this approach also directs attention and momentum away from the single-payer solution, Medicare for All, which would tackle many of the basic causes of these health disparities. The latter would at the very least disproportionately benefit those bisexual-identified persons who tend to be located toward the lower end of the class hierarchy. It is striking that nearly every side in this saga relied on some form of biopolitical legitimation to advance its perspective on bisexuality.

Just as the scientific and political forces that produce these biopolitical taxonomies are remarkably iterative and adaptive, so too has Bailey's bisexuality research program endured and evolved. In 2017 with more funding from the AIB, the Bailey lab conducted fMRI research and found their bisexual male subjects had a distinct brain activity pattern that separated their responses to pornographic stimuli from their exclusively heterosexual and homosexual counterparts.[182] And in 2020, the lab struck again with the largest bisexual arousal study to date (this time featuring the AIB's John Sylla as a

coauthor).[183] Showing little repentance for the strong premises that had provoked ire a decade and a half ago, Bailey doubled down on his first premises
in an interview, stating, "If a man produces a clear arousal pattern in our procedure, I trust that result more than I trust what that man says about his feelings [because] that for men, the best understanding of sexual orientation is a
sexual arousal pattern."[184]

Now that the team's biometric data and beliefs about orientation's physiological essence appear to be firmly positioned on the side of bisexuality's
reality, intra-movement opposition has gone silent. The queer press outlets
that did cover the latest research published pieces amounting to a collective
"duh."[185] With the existential threat vanquished, it became safe once more for
advocates to concede that sexology done correctly tells no lies. The *Advocate*'s
coverage put it succinctly: "A new study makes clear what we already knew to
be an absolute truth: Male bisexuality exists."[186]

The Adaptive Landscape

Though we might forgive those pessimists who surmised otherwise, the born
this way ideology has clearly proven capacious enough to absorb transgender
and bisexual identities. As the foregoing account and this book's final chapter
spell out, even the queerest of Americans may soon find their blood flows and
brains subjected to the same taxonomies that long ago transformed gays and
lesbians from predators and pedophiles into upstanding citizens in a liberal
pluralist political order. It appears that gender transgression and sexual inde-
terminacy have no intrinsic critical "edge" or permanent position outside of
the bounds of liberal assimilation.

Or so this is the most positive story that one can tell. The darker side to
this tale is that the scientific authority that once won gays and lesbians their
civil rights is potentially ill-equipped to protect many LGBTQ+ Americans
from equally adaptive right-wing forces. The GOP and its social conservative
allies have found means of attacking civil rights that do not rely on winning
over the medical establishment or returning inegalitarian scientific experts
from the fringe. The conservative right to privacy, "competing rights" claims
by Christian traditionalists, and the criminalization of trans youth healthcare
are likely to be only the first efforts to weaken nascent LGBTQ+ civil rights.

Pathology may even roar back as well. Florida Governor Ron DeSantis has
exemplified how the right wing might navigate the etiological impasse. In his
defense of the state's anti-trans athlete law, DeSantis declared, "We're going to
go based off biology, not based off etiology [the cause of a disease or abnormal condition] when we're doing sports."[187] Gender inegalitarians have thus

found a means of undermining etiology's significance that still invokes biology. The GOP may avoid denying trans identity's existence by positing that sex and gender are simply different kinds, the former being biological and "real," and the latter being the domain of uncertain medical interventions and cultural aberrations—or perhaps even pathological psychological and physiological conditions. Whatever the future may hold, we would do well to update our understandings of how adaptive these scientific ideologies truly are.

Beyond Born This Way:
Fluid Desires, Fixed Identities,
and Entrenched Inequalities

Amid the corporate feeding frenzy of Pride Month 2021, Nabisco's Oreo brand partnered with PFLAG to offer the most diversity a dollar bill could buy. "To help you celebrate however you identify," the Oreo Cookie Twitter account announced, "we're giving away 3,000 limited-edition OREOiD" packages and selling many more.[1] Each order offered several customizable creme colors representing a range of options from the old-school rainbow hue to the newly minted Pansexual Flag.[2]

There is, of course, nothing terribly new about a business's willingness to market an old product with the sheen of social justice (the Pride-themed Oreo cookies are notably no different in flavor from their dichromatic counterparts). There is something quite novel, however, in PFLAG's embrace of pansexuality. Formed in reaction to the nascent religious right's family values campaigns, PFLAG has been notorious for its cautious conservatism.[3] The group was an early adopter of the biological thesis precisely because it allowed them to impose an impasse between hetero and homo, thereby warding off contagion anxieties. PFLAG's politics was the paragon of what queer theorists have long lamented as "homonormativity"—a desexualized, gender-normative, pro-family, citizen-consumer ideology wagering that gays and lesbians were capable of integrating into American social life without spoiling its morals and habits.[4] Today PFLAG applauds the very norm busters that it implicitly wrote out of its founding principles. It is not alone, either. Both the Human Rights Campaign and PFLAG now celebrate identities that elude familiar binary thinking.[5] The National LGBTQ Task Force even modified its official name (several times in fact) to reflect the expansive and flexible ways that gender and sexuality can be experienced.

The conservative Supreme Court's stunning 2020 decision in *Bostock v. Clayton County* (2020) also turned legal doctrine in an unexpectedly queer direction. In his majority opinion, the Trump-appointed Justice Neil Gorsuch strayed from his former mentor Justice Anthony Kennedy's routine references to science and gay identity. Instead, Gorsuch expanded the meaning of "sex" in Title VII employment protections to broadly encompass sexual orientation *and* gender identity. Wielding a textualist interpretive style—an approach to judicial decision-making regarded by most as inherently conservative— Gorsuch reasoned that civil rights law prohibited an employer from firing "an individual merely for being gay or transgender" because such an action is, at its core, motivated by sex.[6] If a boss fires a lesbian worker for marrying someone of the "wrong" sex or a trans or nonbinary person for expressing themselves with the gendered garb of the presumed "opposite" sex, then that employer has engaged in impermissible sex discrimination. In opting for this capacious definition of sex, the court seemingly fulfilled the gay liberation dream of an antidiscrimination law that protects a person not on the basis of who she might *be* but rather because sexual and gender stereotyping standards are deemed themselves to be oppressive constraints. As the philosophy goes, the harm of discrimination imperils all those who, for whatever reason, sit outside conformist assumptions about the nature of men and women, the norms of masculinity and femininity, and the essence of heterosexuality and homosexuality.

In law, culture, and social movement politics, the issue of etiology now appears surprisingly beside the point. Fluidity and flexibility are in; fixity and conventional binaries are out. Yet in each of these domains, we can also find a paradoxically persistent reach for narratives of permanence and stability. And looming behind those stories and logics, we often find a scientific apparatus able and willing to back them up.

Ten days after Caitlyn Jenner graced the cover of *Vanity Fair* in the summer of 2015, NAACP activist Rachel Dolezal was outed as "transracial" by a vindictive police chief.[7] A predictable fight broke out: conservative commentators sought to undermine Jenner's gender transition by stressing the perceived lunacy of Dolezal's self-identification as Black.[8] Trans advocates responded in turn by underscoring the hardwired biological reality of gender identity. The pattern perseveres. More recently, Senate Democrats excoriated then Supreme Court nominee Amy Coney Barrett for her use of the term "sexual preference," denouncing it as a dog whistle for right-wing canards about "choice" and the possibility of conversion.[9] Finally, it is not actually clear whether the court's decision in *Bostock* will apply equally to every act of discrimination against gender and sexual nonconformists. After all, litigants in lower courts are still far more likely to win their cases when they produce some scientifically backed narrative of gender identity than are those gender benders without such a forensic alibi.[10]

How is it that we have found ourselves with what at least appear on the surface to be competing—possibly incommensurate—commitments to fluidity and fixity? In the words of sociologist Rogers Brubaker, what can explain this puzzling tension "between idioms of choice, autonomy, subjectivity, and self-fashioning on the one hand and idioms of givenness, essence, objectivity, and nature on the other?"[11] And what are we to make of those instances where biology abates and a queer cultural essentialism steps up to the plate to do much of the same mystifying ideological work as did its biological ancestors? To sum up this line of inquiry, what truth *and* absurdity is there in the claim that we have found ourselves at the edge of born this way?

State of Flux

First, take a recent episode from our present moment of flux. In August 2019, an international team of scientists accompanied by researchers from the ancestry home-testing firm 23andMe published the largest study to date on the biological determinants of sexual orientation. When its findings invited a slew of headlines declaring "There Is No 'Gay Gene,'" LGBTQ+ advocates were forced to reconcile their half-century-long project with this reinterpretation of the human genome.[12] Perhaps unexpectedly, many found cause to agree.[13]

Drawing from a sample of nearly 500,000 individuals, culled from data from the UK Biobank and 23andMe's records, geneticist Andrea Ganna and his coauthors put to the test an updated perspective on sexuality's nature and origins. By using a genome-wide association study (known in the field as a "GWAS"), the scientists were not looking for a direct gene-to-trait relationship. Modern post-genomic research—meaning those studies conducted following the completion of the Human Genome Project—typically reject blunt assertions of "nature over nurture." They also eschew the search for a singular gene that codes for a complex human trait.[14] Instead of charting the kind of causal pathway that runs from a chromosomal location to a characteristic like height or hair color, Ganna and his team examined how many different bits of genetic material might contribute to sexual behavior. In the technical parlance, they observed how a multitude of single nucleotide polymorphisms (SNPs, for short) give some direction to desire.

Upon accounting for all of the SNPs that could be traced back to same-sex behavior, Ganna and his team concluded that the genetic contribution was at most between 8 and 25 percent. More notably, the researchers discerned the actual location of only five individual SNPs accounting for this variance—together, those SNPs could explain less than 1 percent of the variation in sexual behavior. Despite the entrepreneurial efforts of the short-lived "How Gay Are You?" app's developers, the data provided essentially no predictive power to genetically assess any one individual's orientation.[15]

What this deep dive into the human genome may have uncovered is that social and cultural factors might play the greatest role in shaping human sexuality. In contrast to a previous generation's work on the human genome, post-genomic era inquiries are frequently lauded for their alleged nuance. For an example of their own care in reporting results, Ganna and the other investigators were upfront about the limitations of measuring sexuality's incalculable complexities. According to their own hedging, the study's dichotomous variable for sexual behavior "collapses rich and multifaceted diversity among nonheterosexual individuals."[16] Additionally, rather than taking identity as a "thing" in itself, they distinguished attraction, behavior, and identity as correlated yet distinct. In light of evidence suggesting that heterosexual and homosexual attraction are not inversely related but instead come in a wide variety of mixes and matches, they even recommended overhauling the Kinsey scale.[17] The constraints of traditionally operationalized categories surely neglected—in their own words—"the intricacies of the social and cultural influences on sexuality."[18]

The Ganna study's positive reception among LGBTQ+ advocates marks a shift from bold pronouncements on *the* biological origins of sexual orientation to a more nuanced, more sociocultural, story. The fact that social movement spokespersons could bear to embrace these findings says much more about changes in the broader social world than it does about the malleability of queer advocates' own attitudes. But what had changed?

Since the early rights activists and their allies in mental health and sexology first sanitized gay identity with a nonthreatening genetic origins story, the nuclear family and its sexual norms have transformed dramatically. The strict policing of sexuality and gender expression throughout most of the twentieth century was an extension of the way that work, consumption, and the family were organized. Due to reigning beliefs about the aberrant, potentially contagious nature of "deviant" sexualities, the early homophile and lesbian political associations of the 1950s and '60s often positioned themselves as a naturally occurring and benign minority group. If, as the sociobiologist

E. O. Wilson mused, homosexuality was an adaptive trait that reserved a handful of effeminate men to watch over female gatherers and to rear children, then there was no threat to the straight majority.[19]

Gradually, the male breadwinner and the patriarchal family have been replaced by a less-gendered division of work and greater freedom to choose how one associates, couples, or sleeps around. Notably, the economic necessity of having multiple wage earners in a family is an important part of that story. Of course, none of this could have been achieved without the struggle of activists, gay employee groups, nonprofit advocacy organizations, and law firms. Nevertheless, the world has been steadily transforming beyond the apparent need for such rigid categories of gender expression and sexual experience.

At first, some queer activists and intellectuals saw lingering troubles in this new normal, characterized by the respectability culture of gay and lesbian life and its own strict tenets regarding marriage, monogamy, and heteronormativity.[20] However, that moment when the stark line between gay and straight was made benign, yet untraversable, lasted for only about the past three decades. Today many people are abstaining from standard social scripts and living fluid and abundantly diverse sexual and gendered lives. Gallup data from 2020 showed a marked increase in queer identification for Generation Z, over 15 percent of whom self-identify as LGBT.[21] A study conducted by GLAAD found a comparable rate of 20 percent among eighteen- to thirty-four-year-old Americans.[22] In one of the most robust self-report studies done to date, nearly 10 percent of surveyed high school students identified as gender diverse (operationalized as any gender identity incongruent with their assigned sex/gender at birth).[23] To put that into perspective, four short years ago the number was presumed to be less than 2 percent.

So, while the Ganna GWAS keeps the born this way idea alive for those inspired by the promissory note that so often accompanies sociogenomic research—"if not today's genetic research, then tomorrow's will surely reveal the greater truth of human nature"—it also reflects a reality in which equal rights advocates no longer fear that the loss of a strict "by nature" narrative would be an existential one. We would be justified then in wondering if biology has begun to lose its allure.

State of Stability

There is, however, another way to tell that same story. At least as much as it left room for today's diverse and pliable expressions of gender and sexuality, the Ganna study was a sign of the biological perspective's tenacity. The broader cultural discussion of the Ganna GWAS quickly devolved into a parsing of "how" and "how much" genetics and hormones might explain the findings. Although media outlets like the *New York Times* and the *Washington Post* got the message that the search for a *singular* gay gene was over, they hyped the discovery of these new genetic determinants, making scant reference to just how small a role those variants might ultimately play.[24] As stalwart defenders of the biological thesis were quick to note, the GWAS did not slam the door on old-school biodeterminism. Indeed, on the study's second-year anniversary, the authors of a similarly designed undertaking trumpeted a solution to the "Darwinian paradox" of same-sex behavior.[25] Even Ganna noted that future research may find additional genetic and hormonal determinants. Maybe what we have inherited is a composite picture of essentialism—a capacious, less rigidly biodeterministic one—but a bioessentialism all the same.

Just as yesteryear's genomania did not run purely on the press's exaggerations and maverick researchers alone, there are also deeper, more fundamental explanations for our incessant appetite for genomic truths. The first is the most vulgarly materialist: biotechnologies remain an important sector in the American economy. When measured as an industry, biotech is on par with chemical production, utilities, mining, and the computing and electronics industries.[26] Additionally, biotechnologies are at the heart of the modern US university system, where much research into human behavior and identity has been historically conducted. In the decades since Reaganite deregulators loosened restrictions on federally funded research and private enterprise, genomic-based start-ups have increasingly blurred the line between academic research and capital accumulation.[27] One need not adopt a technologically reductive outlook to see that if what we have is a burgeoning biotech industry, then all sorts of questions begin to appear like biological problems.

Many of these ventures are biomedical in nature and amass vast quantities of data on human health and behavior. In July 2019, for example, the pharmaceutical company BioNTech broke investor fundraising goals in Europe for its personalized immune treatments based in mRNA; the following year, it worked alongside Pfizer to create a COVID-19 vaccine (notably while using German funds to create and US funding to produce).[28] Stores of genomic data like the UK Biobank's colossal collection of half a million Britons' biomedical information demonstrate how government funding and charitable donations have created repositories that—while constructed primarily for medical research—function as low-lift data mines for those seeking to test hypotheses about human difference.[29]

The personal genomics industry—which is parasitic on these larger-scale endeavors—has played an outsize role in keeping biological narratives alive. At their core, DNA home-testing firms like 23andMe are motivated by an economic imperative to assemble data and market drugs to a consumer base taken by the epistemic promise of bioreductivism. In the case of the Ganna GWAS, 23andMe provided both personnel and data on the genetic profiles of over 100,000 individuals' data. When interviewed about the Ganna GWAS, 23andMe senior scientist Fah Sathirapongsasuti explained that "the study is in part a response to gay, lesbian, and bisexual people's curiosity about themselves . . . research and information about sex and sexuality is among the categories most requested by 23andMe's customers."[30] Just as the fraudulent race-targeted heart medication BiDil was infamously marketed to African American patients a decade ago, so too have some firms been able to make a buck off those eager to learn their genomic personhood.[31] In other words, post-genomic research into sexual orientation's nature is a by-product of the late neoliberal-era nexus where investment-driven state policies, the private biomedical industry, and consumer demand converge.

This is, of course, not the rosy egalitarian future that some DNA-testing advocates foretold, one in which evidence of humanity's genetic mixture and the myth of "pure" racial types would lead to bioessentialism's withering away.[32] Harvard population geneticist David Reich made headlines in 2018 when he claimed that new techniques in DNA extraction might reveal both the falsity of our inherited racial tropes *and* evidence for regional genetic differences that map suspiciously back on to traditional racial distinctions.[33] Reich drew ire from his colleagues across medicine and the social sciences for repeatedly conflating the terms "population" and "race" while reviving the long-standing misbelief that sickle cell anemia is exclusive to Western and Central African ancestry.[34]

As a whole, the post-genomic age has been disappointingly reductive. After the Human Genome Project revealed far too few coding genes to directly account for complex traits like homosexuality and addiction, propagandists in the vanguard like *New York Times* journalist (and race science aficionado) Nicholas Wade made a quick pivot, identifying new genetic mechanisms for old reductive ideas.[35] Among those undeterred by the setback was famed behavioral psychologist Robert Plomin, who has since updated his own characteristic reductivism for the GWAS paradigm.[36] In his 2018 book *Blueprint: How DNA Makes Us Who We Are*, Plomin forecasted a world in which we technocratically sort persons by innate competency and skill into various educational and employment opportunities.[37] A younger cohort led by behavior geneticist Kathryn Paige Harden has given a new liberal spin to bioreductivism. Harden has predicted that fresh research into the genetic heritability of crime, promiscuity, and intelligence will transcend its eugenics origins and undermine the "myth of meritocracy."[38]

Though bioessentialism thrives under the light of the TED Talk stage and in the pages of pop psychology best sellers, its influence is even more widespread than it first appears. So ubiquitous is the mentality today that modern critics will sometimes deride one reductive study while leveraging *another* equally reductive outlook as the very premise of their objection. Ironically, some of the Ganna GWAS's most vocal critics repurposed strong biodeterministic assumptions for their opprobrium. Whereas Ganna was emphatic that no statistical measure could predict an individual's orientation, researchers affiliated with the Broad Institute condemned the *Science* study for unwittingly inviting future discrimination in the form of gene editing or embryo selection.[39] In the timbre of their rebuke, one can hear an earlier generation of critics' fearful cries about the gay gene's neo-eugenic potential.

The Ganna GWAS has also faced criticism that its data was racially skewed from the outset.[40] Such critics point to the fact that the data drawn from the Biobank and 23andMe trace back to subjects with European ancestry. Postgenomics in general has been confronted by this particular race-based criticism as of late.[41] We ought to ponder the implicit suggestions of this brand of critique (that is, beyond the fact that race and ancestry are nowhere near equivalents). What do we gain from such complaints about the lack of a sample's diversity other than the upper hand in an argument that ends with everyone surmising that maybe the genetic origin of homosexuality varies according to ancestry? Take it a step further. Maybe a queer man of African descent has a genotypically different sexuality from his European-descended partner. Is this really the road that skeptics of reductivism wish to travel?

That ostensibly well-intentioned criticisms can rest on a logic that extends back to Madison Grant and like-minded nineteenth-century race scientists should be a cause for some concern. This trend, for instance, has severe implications for public health. In the midst of the COVID-19 pandemic, the *New York Times* reported on a study indicating that there were, in fact, no genetic differences between Black and white Americans that might contribute to COVID-19 mortality differences.[42] The hypothesis itself—that an increased genetic susceptibility to the coronavirus might be the province of all Americans classified as Black versus all those classified as white—is rooted firmly in race-scientific premises.[43] To be fair to the researchers, they had found that social and environmental determinants like occupation, income, and housing were the main culprits of the early COVID racial disparities (they discovered that the race gap is actually a class gap, which subsequent research has confirmed).[44] But even prestigious academic publications like the *New England Journal of Medicine* have begun publishing papers on "Embracing Genetic Diversity to Improve Black Health," replete with approving citations to work on the genetic variation among "the three major races of man, Caucasoids, Negroids, and Mongoloids."[45] This reinvestment in race's bio-essence should give pause to those critics who save all their breath for condemning studies that lack diversity. The real travesty to truth and equality alike is this resurgent taxonomic impulse.

State of Anxiety

We might still ask what particular political inducements have led LGBTQ+ advocates to shore up science once again. The first answer is the simplest one: the grim threat of discrimination and injury persist. The past several decades have undoubtedly been a period of unprecedented gender and sexual egalitarianism. But it has also invited counter trends such as a revanchist right-wing backlash to newfound civil rights. In 2022, 238 anti-LGBTQ+ bills were introduced in state legislatures, an alarming number of which have been signed into law since.[46] Though there are new freedoms to be exercised in our new world of sexual and gender diversity, there is also a palpable anxiety about how fresh they are.

The rekindled right-wing threat has come equipped with novel medical narratives about contagion and mental illness. The theme of pathology pervaded a 2021 campaign called "The Promise of America's Children" launched by titans of conservativism including the Heritage Foundation, the Alliance Defending Freedom, and the Family Policy Alliance. Placing trans youths' access to healthcare and sports participation in its sights, the right-wing coalition promises to help parents and legislators "to make the healthiest decisions for treatment of gender dysphoria" and to oppose "government initiatives [that] promote destructive ideas about gender identity" and expose children to "gender ideology."[47] The Heritage Foundation along with prominent GOP Senator Chuck Grassley have also made heavy use of *Wall Street Journal* writer Abigail Shrier's 2020 book, *Irreversible Damage: The Transgender Craze Seducing Our Daughters*, in their opposition to the Equality Act.[48] In her book, Shrier popularized the notion of "trans trending," a so-called modern "pandemic" wherein young biological girls transition as a hopeless means of reckoning with mental health issues, social pressures, and gender inequality.[49] Adding LGBTQ+ protections to federal civil rights law, conservative leaders and Shrier argue, would further endanger young women and jeopardize the entire legal project of women's equality.[50]

There are many parallels here with early twentieth-century fears of sexual contagion.[51] Notably, Shrier and the researchers whom she cites repeatedly acknowledge the reality of *truly* transgender adults. They also admit that there may yet be a means of diagnostically detecting "true" trans youth from those who have been contaminated. The rest, however, are the sad victims of a sick society. They are the damage done by undue medical experimentations and modernity's degraded gender norms.

Keeping with historical parallels, where there is fear of social contagion, the queer mental illness trope is not far away. Once banished from the *DSM* and regarded as taboo among respectable psychologists, the mental illness model of homosexuality has enjoyed renewed attention. None other than the infamous sexologist Michael J. Bailey has resuscitated the pathogenic concept. Recall that Bailey was the coauthor of a famous gay gene study as well as a paper that denied bisexuality's existence based on a lack of biological data (he recanted the latter position upon finding affirmative biological data). In keeping with the bioessentialist tradition, Bailey wrote a book in 2003 contending that many trans women are actually *autogynephilic* perverts who transition out of an erotic desire to possess a feminine body.[52]

In a 2020 paper, Bailey again reintroduced concerns over queer mental illness in his proposal that researchers reconsider the validity of the minority stress model. That theory—which has become an orthodoxy in recent decades—holds that queer people register far higher rates of mental illness because they are more likely to be plagued by social stigma and legal discrimination.[53] However, recent genomic work like the Ganna GWAS has found correlates between same-sex sexual orientation and mental illnesses including neuroticism and depression. Bailey's contention is that these genetic clues indicate a reverse causality at play: mental illness conditions a person to believe that they are the victim of far more prejudice and persecution than they actually incur.[54] Ergo, a genetically determined neurotic worldview generates the *experience* of stigma and stress (termed "rejection sensitivity"), which then manifests as disparate rates of self-reported mental health outcomes.

It is a sick irony that one of the LGBTQ+ movement's go-to sources for "yes, Virginia, there *is* a gay gene" has revived one of sexology's most odious myths. Bailey's conclusion is reminiscent of the very research that psychologist Evelyn Hooker helped the early Mattachine Society homophiles to discredit.[55] The bio paradigm that has housed Bailey throughout his professional career has proven itself capacious enough for both his own and others' emancipatory *and* noxious premises.[56] Though the new peddlers of pathology often frame themselves as brave truth tellers in an age of ideological conformity—apparently born without a sense of shame, Bailey recently squeezed "biodeterminists" into Martin Niemöller's famous "First they came . . ."—there remain serious risks to the health, safety, and legal rights of LGBTQ+ Americans.[57]

It is the pangs of a justifiable anxiety that habitually lead advocates back to biology once again, whether to articulate an authentic self or to dispel the fear of disease. As the reworked advocacy narrative goes, we *know* that queer identity is both multifaceted and anything but inert; however, we also understand that identity to *be* somewhat stable and discernible, maybe even under a microscope. In the last instance, subjectivity continues to be cast as emergent of some objective quality (this is often put in biodeterministic terms, but as we have seen, it could very well come in the form of a cultural or biosocial essentialism as well). Complexity, contingency, and new social prerogatives aside, this ought not be mistaken as some wish fulfillment of queer theory; rather, the dream of bioessentialism is still alive in a post-genomic era.

State of Inequality

The ongoing right-wing blitz on LGBTQ+ civil rights and democracy paired with rising rates of inequality that touch the labor and lives of all working Americans—queer, straight, or in between—ought to prompt reflection on how we came to this condition and how we might emerge intact from it.[58] Lest one think that this is a story of American exceptionalism, backlash has brewed against multicultural neoliberalism across Europe as well.[59] For example, the National Rally in France has called for the repeal of marriage equality for gays and lesbians while the AfD in Germany, Fidesz in Hungary, and the Right Wing of the Republic in Poland foment rage and electoral support by denouncing EU-sanctioned "gender studies" programs and similar university-based egalitarian reforms.[60] At the 2022 Conservative Political Action Committee meeting in Budapest, Viktor Orbán claimed the mantle of biology for reactionary ends. "What is the difference between far-right denial of science and the LGBTQ movement's denial of biology?" the Hungarian prime minister asked rhetorically.[61]

This presents that perennial question that stalks egalitarians of all stripes: What is to be done? The usual response—be it pitched as reform or revolution—presumes that an LGBTQ+-led advocacy coalition must be at the helm and that its proposals be narrowly tailored for the particularities of queer life. Social movement scholars, queer theorists, and activists alike stick to a script of "resistance" and "disruption" that often neglects both the reality of civil rights progress as well as the real rot of neoliberalism that exacerbates all other social inequities.[62] Yet half a century of upward wealth redistribution and the decimation of the labor movement that had won the (since collapsed) comforts of the New Deal order necessitate an approach qualitatively different from either mainstream interest groups or anarcho-activist sects can muster. Indeed, digging up inequality at its roots might very well eradicate or at least undermine the potency of queer scapegoating efforts. An unapologetically robust program of social spending and ideological defense of public goods (e.g., single-payer healthcare with trans healthcare coverage and public housing with built-in antidiscrimination principles) more generally might at last loosen the grip that donor-dependent nonprofits, civil rights litigation groups, and well-intentioned self-styled radicals have held for decades over what constitutes a truly egalitarian politics.

Until we take that social democratic turn, our political order's legitimation crisis is ripe for the kind of sex panics and scapegoating that previous crises have produced. However, it is not clear yet if rising rates of economic immiseration and social inequalities will come to haunt the LGBTQ+ movement and its decision to "come out" as biological beings. It is plausible that the past few decades' installation of legal safeguards and egalitarian attitudinal shifts are well entrenched, or at least enough so that queer people will not be so easily blamed this time around.[63] But if history is at all a reliable guide, someone will be.

We would do well then not to oversell the notion that our political culture has turned meaningfully away from biological reductivism not least because its various political acolytes continue to find it useful. Like the leading scientific paradigms of previous epochs, contemporary scientific studies of human difference tend to rationalize—not merely reflect—the present status quo of society as the natural order of things. Today's cutting-edge post-genomic research, for instance, purports to show how markers such as IQ, education, income, and wealth at retirement can be rendered heritable. It does so in ways that treat the relationships among these variables as natural, thereby rationalizing today's socioeconomic inequalities.[64]

One such study—notably led by a coauthor on both the 2019 and 2021 same-sex behavior GWAS papers—mapped geographic clustering of genetic variants associated with traits like education.[65] Its authors observed how those who fled dying coal towns also took their genetic predispositions for educational attainment out of the countryside's genomic pool and into the cities. This study on education and migration lends support to those who would perceive the poor of the postindustrial English north and the affluent of the urbanized south as the product of natural sorting mechanisms, rather than the consequence of political decisions such as the assault on miners' unions and the welfare state.

Just like the Ganna GWAS, this research indexes changes in the social world and depicts their effects as more or less natural. It is, of course, hard to deny that measures of intelligence and levels of formal education correlate

with some heritable cognitive element, particularly one that might assist individuals in the steep climb up present-day social hierarchies. And although
the researchers did observe that a stronger social safety net would benefit the
ravaged towns, their foundational commitment to a tight, naturalistic relationship between education and prosperity shifts the sources of inequality
away from the very structural conditions that made educational talent and resources a precondition for a middle-class livelihood. Translated for an American audience, this narrative about uplift, education and ability could have
easily been spun by the Appalachian exile J. D. Vance of *Hillbilly Elegy* fame.

Again, there is a cross-ideological quality to this sort of reductivism that
is at present rewriting the racialized underclass narrative to include poor
and working-class whites (although those like Charles Murray of *The Bell
Curve* infamy have always cast the underclass as multiracial).[66] For instance,
many social scientists posit the "white working class" as an actually existing social formation in the world rather than a sloppy statistical aggregation.
Political scientists often attribute fuzzy abstractions like "status anxiety" and
"out-group racial resentment" to explain the Trump vote and public opinion spikes in authoritarian attitudes, as if racial resentment were an intrinsic
quality of a white working-class monolith rather than an ideology conjured
by right-wing operators seeking a scapegoat.[67] *Deaths of Despair* authors
Anne Case and Angus Deaton exemplified this approach in their work on low
rates of education, substance abuse habits, and adverse health and mortality outcomes.[68] These various traits and behaviors are used to tautologically
taxonomize low-income white workers and the unemployed as a subspecies
apart. As has been the case at least since the days of Oscar Lewis's midcentury sociological examinations of the so-called culture of poverty and Daniel
Patrick Moynihan's underclass-themed poverty analyses, this perspective has
been able to account both for the supposed biologically based cognitive limits
of a given population and its degenerative cultural temperament.[69] In that
sense, nature and nurture have never been as incommensurate as they have
been made out to be.

Post-genomics and related reductive paradigms today are thus playing out
the rationalizing functions that scientific inquiries into historically contingent identities and behavioral patterns always perform. Accordingly, they can
generate some relatively valid postulates—it is likely that our sexualities and
genders are textured by a mix of social experience, the firing off of neurons,
hormonal swirls, and the transcription of DNA. But such science also allows
defenders of the status quo—in all its libidinally liberated, economically dev-
astated glory—to cast the world as it appears as the way that the world was

meant to be. It also appears to be opening up a back door to scientific rationales for class-based inequalities (which have historically morphed quite easily into ascriptive ideologies of racial and ethnic difference) that were once thought to have been eradicated from legitimate scientific inquiry.[70] For all the high-powered machinery, impressive statistical methods, and massive data sets that go into this knowledge production, we have inherited once again a collection of "just-so stories"—that is, accounts of human nature depicted through a diverse confluence of causes rather than strictly genetic factors—now updated for our post-genomic age.

Agency, Uncertainty, and the Desire to Know

It is fortunate that achieving meaningful equality does not depend much at all on "knowing" the true nature of desire or identity. This is not to say that professional researchers and clinicians do not and should not retain a privileged position in combating malevolent myths about the hazards of "trans trending" and coerced reorientation remedies. To the contrary, it is not clear that anyone would be better off if medical experts were to make a forced exodus from LGBTQ+ advocacy. Utopic fantasies about radical autonomy and self-definition are just that. They ring out with the anarcho echoes of a naively anti-institutional liberation politics that has misunderstood both the promises and problems of scientific authority. But while thwarting political foes oftentimes does call for evidence of what sexual orientation and gender identity are *not*—that is, injurious or infectious—we need not pin down their elusive origins and ontology to be politically or personally liberated.

What would be far more salubrious is a political economy that permits sexual and gender exploration, equivocation, and fulfillment (however one defines this mixture of aim and object). Just as a politics centered around public goods would fend off inequality's scapegoating tendencies, so, too, could it furnish the agency to live as one wishes. There are, for instance, complex reasons that one might seek conversion therapy, including the threat of economic or social ruin. Even organizations like the Human Rights Campaign—which is so prone to using identity as an analytic to comprehend inequality's causes and solutions—recently admitted in a policy paper that economic factors are largely responsible for the epidemic of violence and death among POC trans women.[71] Reforms to healthcare, housing, and wages, the report noted, are suitable policy targets to ameliorate these disproportionate rates of harm and immiseration. Altogether, these are at least as much the symptoms of a highly unequal political economic order as they are an indictment of a homophobic and transphobic society. Accordingly, these social ills might be best addressed through a politics of redistribution, social welfare policies, and a systemic shift of power away from capital.[72]

The materialist-minded pragmatist is faced with a tricky game of doing two potentially contradictory things at once. On the one hand, advocates need to remain vigilant and well-armed to deflect accusations of pathology and contagion whenever and wherever they gain traction. On the other hand, one must do this while avoiding the temptation to nail identity back down with simple yet hopelessly flawed bioessentialist narratives—these remain the dominion of nonprofit-based social movement forces that are structurally inept at pursuing a broader policy agenda against inequality.

That may be an arduous task, though not at all a futile one. LGBTQ+ history is rife with moments when trade union movements and fights for gender and sexual equality converged upon a set of shared interests. The first fights waged by queer workers were led by the militant Marine Cooks and Stewards Union back in the 1930s.[73] Later battles for the rights of gay and lesbian public schoolteachers brought together sexual minorities and their allies in the American Federation of Teachers in California as well as the UAW, the United Steelworkers, the Teamsters, Culinary Workers, and Postal Workers. Each constituent group in the Workers Conference to Defeat the Briggs Initiative recognized that a right-wing attack on the rights of one group of workers could quickly escalate into an injury to all.[74] How prescient they were in light of today's billionaire-led barrage on the rights of queer couples and laborers alike.

This denouement may provoke a pang of disappointment for some. For those who hold out for a purer process of scientific discovery or who place their faith in a more refined set of measurement techniques, this may sound unduly Luddite-ish. For the reader who has grown attached to what has become standard issue in the coming-out tool kit, there is likely something dissatisfying or even disturbing about the redirect. After all, who does not want a glimpse into profound truths about oneself? And for anyone who has ever felt such a yearning, how implausible is it that any call to go "beyond identity" could scratch that itch? How could a story about the ultimate futility of such sense-making stories make up for all the personal anguish, familial grief, frustration, indignity, and cruelty that continue to be meted out in this country and elsewhere? Most of all, who am I to tell you—or anyone else—to stop searching?

At least for the charges of harboring Luddite sentiments, I have a defense. Students of modernity from Marx and Engels to Marshall Berman and many others still have been captivated with the malleability of sexuality and gender.[75] Rather than searching for static truths, historians and anthropologists have meticulously documented all the myriad ways that behaviors and status markers are codified into law, how blood and anatomy is classified by science, and how ordinary human beings make and remake their routines, communal practices, and meta-accounts of themselves. Science and medicine have played a constitutive role in those processes and will continue to do so, maybe indefinitely. Try as we might to tie down the complexities of a timeless human nature, however, the social tide will roll back in to wash it away. Mercifully, living as freer selves is not conditional on such heavy-handed pronouncements.

We ought then to be cognizant about how the desire "to know" is textured by our circumstances. The sociopolitical configurations of public and private life, the economic organization of work, the scientific innovations, the funding to use them, and the subcultures and social movements that spring up around the deeper structures of society: these all generate a tension between what is that we *might* be able to know that we once did not and, conversely, what we often *think* that we already know or what we *can* know or what is politically advantageous or even existential *to know*. One could only believe that biology—all by its lonesome—might bestow on us our basic truths if they were to ignore the investments and influences that have always motivated these pursuits. So, just as struggles, victories, and setbacks for civil rights are likely to endure, so too will debates over nature and identity rage on.

Acknowledgments

My household takes as its motto a quote from the psychoanalyst Donald Moss: "The surface always claims to be total." That adage sums up my suspicion toward pat biological narratives of human desire and identity. It also dismisses as fiction that a book is ever really written by the author whose name appears on the cover. This is my effort to excavate and account for the brilliant advice, gracious encouragement, and loving care that could not fit on the title page.

This project has been germinating since my earliest years in higher education. Georgia Wralstad Ulmschneider, Michael Wolf, Jeffrey Malanson, James Toole, David Schuster, and the late James Lutz nurtured my interest in all things law and civil rights. Among the many things they have imparted to me, the one that I hold most dear is the belief that public institutions of higher education are invaluable to democratic societies. We have much to win back—and hopefully to gain even more—on this front.

At the University of Pennsylvania, I was fortunate to have mentors who modeled how one might combine rigorous empirical research with dead-serious normative commitments. No other scholar could match Adolph Reed Jr. in this regard. This book's most primitive ancestor dates back to a seminar paper that I wrote for Adolph's course on race and American political thought. Rogers M. Smith guided that paper's development into a dissertation as he did my own growth as a scholar. Our disagreements on some matters are no secret (in fact, they are in print!), yet I could not have asked for a more generous, brilliant, or principled adviser. Anne Norton taught me not only how to merge the artificially separated worlds of political theory and American politics, but also to have the courage of one's convictions in the face of critics who would rather hear the melody of hegemony rehearsed once more. My outside dissertation reader, mentor, and friend Roger Lancaster has indelibly shaped my thinking about what it actually means to study gender and sexuality as a materialist. In addition to advising my work from Virginia and Mexico, he has also shared his own book chapter drafts with me; whatever title might be given to his forthcoming monograph on gay identity in Mexico, I consider this book and his own to be relatives, born of the same desire to expose the class character of identitarianism.

At Penn, I was lucky to learn from and alongside Osman Balkan, Andrew Barnard, Aaron Bartels-Swindells, David Bateman, Matthew Berkman, Guazman Castro, Sarah Cate, Merlin Chowkwanyun, Anthony Grasso, Danielle Hanley, Archana Kaku, Juman Kim, Gregory Koutnik, Daniel Moak, James Morone, Katherine Rader, Gabriel Raeburn, Emily Regier, Carly Regina, Javier Revelo-Rebolledo, Gabe Salgado, Nathaniel Shils, Emma Teitelman, Elspeth Wilson, Robinson Woodward-Burns, and Tali Ziv. The first draft of many of these pages was written as I scurried between meetings of the Graduate Employees Together at the University of Pennsylvania (GET-UP) and the intimidating halls of offices and labs where I sought out coworkers who might become fellow unionists.

My appointment in the Princeton University Society of Fellows gave me the precious gifts of time, money, and supportive colleagues and friends. Dara Strolovitch was an ideal postdoctoral mentor; my only regret is that our overlap at Princeton was so short. My thanks is reserved for all those at Princeton who read and encouraged my work on this book, especially Dara, Josh Freedman, Tiffany C. Fryer, Michael Gordon, Maya Kronfeld, Amanda Lanzillo, Ayah Nuriddin, Natalie Prizel, Andrew Reynolds, Melissa Reynolds, Sahar Sadjadi, Aniruddhan Vasudevan, and Beate Witzler. Princeton opened the doors to so many more readers and friends including Patrick Grzanka, Katrina Karkazis, and Greta LaFleur. An extraordinary set of reader comments by Todd Cronan, Stephen Engel, Marie-Amélie George, Roger Lancaster, Anna Lvovsky, and Sahar Sadjadi was made possible by a Society of Fellows–sponsored book manuscript conference. My incredible undergraduate research assistant Alice McGuinness gave me a few bouts of necessary respite from this book as we broke ground together on a second.

I have benefited from invitations to present this work at Columbia University's Precision Medicine and Society program (in conjunction with Harvard University's GenderSci Lab); UCLA's Institute for Society and Genetics; the Law and Humanities Junior Scholars Workshop (special thanks to David Cruz, Andrew Lakoff, and Naomi Mezey); Princeton University's Program in Gender and Sexuality Studies; Princeton University's Bodies of Knowledge Working Group; Princeton University's Queer Politics Workshop; the

University of Massachusetts Amherst's Center for Justice, Law, and Societies; the University of Pennsylvania's Andrea Mitchell Center for the Study of Democracy and its Gender, Sexuality, and Women's Studies Graduate Colloquium; Swarthmore College; Lehigh University; Queens College, City University of New York; Mount Holyoke College; and the University of Florida. I enjoyed wonderfully helpful chairs, discussants, and audiences at the annual gatherings of the American Political Science Association, the Law & Society Association, the Society for Social Studies of Science, the Western Political Science Association, and the Northeastern Political Science Association.

I also benefited from generous funding provided by the National Endowment for the Humanities, the Social Science Research Council, the American Association of University Women, a Council on Science and Technology Summer Grant from Princeton University, and a host of other smaller grant awards from Princeton and the University of Pennsylvania. Any views, findings, conclusions, or recommendations expressed in this publication do not necessarily reflect those of the National Endowment for the Humanities.

Several chapters in this book were derived from previously published articles in *Perspectives on Politics*, *Politics & Gender*, *GLQ: A Journal of Lesbian and Gay Studies*, and *nonsite*. Other venues including the *Nation*, *Boston Review*, *Psyche*, and the *Philadelphia Inquirer* published essays that feature some of the book's ideas in their most inchoate forms. My thanks to Don Guttenplan, Matt Lord, Adam McGee, Sam Haselby, and Elena Gooray for breaking me of bad academic writing habits and polishing my arguments. A summary essay on this book's arguments appears in an edited volume titled the *Code of Life: Who We Are and Could Become*, which has been produced by the German Hygiene Museum in Dresden to accompany a special exhibit.

Like all those who do historical research, I am extremely indebted to the archivists who work behind the scenes to make the past intelligible to us. I am grateful to all those whose labor makes possible the Human Sexuality Collection at Cornell University; the ONE National Gay & Lesbian Archives at the University of Southern California; the Seeley G. Mudd Manuscript Library at Princeton University; the Kinsey Institute for Research in Sex, Gender, and Reproduction at Indiana University; the New York LGBT Community Center National History Archive; and the New York Public Library Archives & Manuscripts.

I write these words during the first week of my position as assistant professor of public law in the Mount Holyoke College Department of Politics. In an era of retrenchment, I feel like I have won the lottery simply by having this job (this is, in fact, not merely a "feeling" but instead the conclusion that anyone equipped with the appropriate descriptive statistics would come to find). It is an embarrassment of riches that I have joined this particular group of scholars.

My parents taught me early on that education can be a virtue, but not without some aim beyond mere self-edification or aggrandizement. It is my hope that this book and my other writings reflect a commitment to a greater good—a more egalitarian world than the one that I have inherited. Special thanks are owed to my father, who read every word (sometimes twice) in these pages and then so many others scattered across emails that barely qualify as prose. And to my mother, who like so many other educators works too hard and for too little as she keeps the promise of public education alive.

My deepest gratitude is for Briana Last, who reminds me daily that "all flowers in time bend towards the sun" while gently guiding every word that I have written toward that end. More profoundly, she has imparted to me that love is a mysteriously powerful, awe-inspiring force, one which is irreducible to whatever organic elements may be involved. The true nature of desire continually eludes me, yet I know that all of mine is for you.

Notes

Introduction

1. National Oceanic and Atmospheric Administration, "U.S. Climate Summary for June 2021: Hottest June on Record," July 9, 2021, https://www.climate.gov/news-features/understanding -climate/us-climate-summary-june-2021-hottest-june-record.

2. Owen Meyers, "Review of Lady Gaga, *Born This Way the Tenth Anniversary*," June 2, 2021, https://pitchfork.com/reviews/albums/lady-gaga-born-this-way-the-tenth-anniversary/.

3. Don't Ask, Don't Tell Repeal Act of 2010 (H.R. 2965, S. 4023).

4. Department of Justice, "Statement of the Attorney General on Litigation Involving the Defense of Marriage Act," February 23, 2011, https://www.justice.gov/opa/pr/statement-attorney -general-litigation-involving-defense-marriage-act; *United States v. Windsor*, 570 U.S. 744 (2013).

5. National Center for Lesbian Rights, "Born Perfect: The Campaign to End Conversion Therapy," 2019, http://www.nclrights.org/our-work/bornperfect/.

6. *Obergefell v. Hodges*, 576 U.S. 644 (2015), 8, 4.

7. Abigail Shrier, *Irreversible Damage: The Transgender Craze Seducing Our Daughters* (Washington, DC: Regnery, 2020).

8. For classic science and technology studies work on this and related themes, see Bruno Latour, *We Have Never Been Modern*, trans. Catherine Porter (Cambridge, MA: Harvard University Press, 1993); Paul Rabinow, *Essays on the Anthropology of Reason* (Princeton, NJ: Princeton University Press, 1996); Ian Hacking, *The Social Construction of What?* rev. ed. (Cambridge, MA: Harvard University Press, 2000); Sheila Jasanoff, ed., *States of Knowledge: The Co-Production of Science and the Social Order* (London: Routledge, 2004), 2–3, 13.

9. Vera Whisman, *Queer by Choice: Lesbian, Gay Men, and the Politics of Identity* (New York: Routledge, 1996); J. S. Morandini et al., "Essentialist Beliefs, Sexual Identity Uncertainty, Internalized Homonegativity and Psychological Wellbeing in Gay Men," *Journal of Counseling Psychology* 62, no. 3 (2015): 413–24.

10. Jonathan Marks, *Tales of the Ex-Apes: How We Think about Human Evolution* (Oakland: University of California Press, 2015), 157–59.

11. Jonathan Marks, *Why I Am Not a Scientist: Anthropology and Modern Knowledge* (Berkeley: University of California Press, 2009), 141–60; Michael Gordin, *On the Fringe: Where Science Meets Pseudoscience* (New York: Oxford University Press, 2021).

12. R. C. Lewontin, Steven Rose, and Leon J. Kamin, *Not in Our Genes: Biology, Ideology, and Human Nature*, 2nd ed. (Chicago: Haymarket Books, 2017).

13. Steven Epstein, "Gay Politics, Ethnic Identity: The Limits of Social Construction," *Socialist Review* 17 (May–August 1987): 9–54; Rogers M. Smith, "The Politics of Identity and the Task of Political Science," in *Problems and Methods in the Study of Politics*, ed. Ian Shapiro, Rogers M. Smith, and Tarek E. Masoud (New York: Cambridge University Press, 2004), 42–66; Rogers M. Smith, *Stories of Peoplehood: The Politics and Morals of Political Membership* (New York: Cambridge University Press, 2006), 101, 121; Rogers M. Smith, *Political Peoplehood: The Roles of Values, Ideas, and Identities* (Chicago: University of Chicago Press, 2015).

14. Stephen Engel, *Fragmented Citizenship: The Changing Landscape of Gay and Lesbian Lives* (New York: New York University Press, 2016); Paisley Currah, *Sex Is as Sex Does: Governing Transgender Identity* (New York: New York University Press, 2022). As such, it corrects the record of more pessimistic accounts: John D. Skrentny, *The Minority Rights Revolution* (Cambridge, MA: Harvard University Press, 2022), 263–327.

15. Adriana Petryna, *Life Exposed: Biological Citizens after Chernobyl* (Princeton, NJ: Princeton University Press, 2002); Nikolas Rose, *The Politics of Life Itself: Biomedicine, Power, and Subjectivity in the Twenty-First Century* (Princeton, NJ: Princeton University Press, 2006); Steven Epstein, *Inclusion: The Politics of Difference in Medical Research* (Chicago: University of Chicago Press, 2007); Kelly E. Happe, Jenell Johnson, and Marina Levina, *Biocitizenship: The Politics of Bodies, Governance, and Power* (New York: New York University Press, 2018).

16. Michel Foucault, *The History of Sexuality*, vol. 1, trans. Robert Hurley (New York: Vintage, 1990).

17. Petryna, *Life Exposed*; Epstein, *Inclusion*.

18. Margot Canaday, *The Straight State: Sexuality and Citizenship in Twentieth-Century America* (Princeton, NJ: Princeton University Press, 2009); Richard Valelly, "LGBT Politics and American Political Development," *Annual Review of Political Science* 15 (2012): 313–32.

19. Elazar Barkan, *The Retreat of Scientific Racism: Changing Concepts of Race in Britain and the United States between the World Wars* (New York: Cambridge University Press, 1992); Rogers M. Smith, *Civic Ideals: Conflicting Visions of Citizenship in U.S. History* (New Haven, CT: Yale University Press, 1999); Stephen Skowronek, Stephen Engel, and Bruce Ackerman, eds., *The Progressives' Century: Political Reform, Constitutional Government, and the Modern American State* (New Haven, CT: Yale University Press, 2016). Though scientific governance has its antecedents in the eighteenth and early nineteenth centuries, the Progressive Era witnessed far vaster and more enduring changes to administrative power and legal institutions; see Theodore M. Porter, *Genetics in the Madhouse: The Unknown History of Human Heredity* (Princeton, NJ: Princeton University Press, 2020).

20. Michel Foucault, *Security, Territory, Population: Lectures at the Collège de France, 1977–1978*, ed. Michel Senellart (New York: Picador, 2009); Andrew Jewett, *Science, Democracy, and the American University: From the Civil War to the Cold War* (New York: Cambridge University Press, 2012).

21. Sheila Jasanoff, "A Century of Reason: Experts and Citizens in the Administrative State," in *The Progressives' Century*, ed. Skowronek, Engel, and Ackerman, 383. See also Sheila Jasanoff, *The Fifth Branch: Science Advisers as Policymakers* (Cambridge, MA: Harvard University Press, 1990); Daniel P. Carpenter, *The Forging of Bureaucratic Autonomy: Reputations, Networks, and Policy Innovation in Executive Agencies, 1862–1928* (Princeton, NJ: Princeton University Press, 2001); Philip Kitcher, *Science in a Democratic Society* (Buffalo, NY: Prometheus Books, 2011).

22. Daniel J. Kevles, *In the Name of Eugenics: Genetics and the Uses of Human Heredity* (Cambridge, MA: Harvard University Press, 1995), 55.

23. *Frye v. U.S.*, 293 F. 1013 (D.C. Cir. 1923); Sheila Jasanoff, *Science at the Bar: Law, Science, and Technology in America* (Cambridge, MA: Harvard University Press, 1995).

24. Alfred C. Kinsey et al., *Sexual Behavior in the Human Male* (Philadelphia: W. B. Saunders, 1948); Alfred C. Kinsey et al., *Sexual Behavior in the Human Female* (Philadelphia: W. B. Saunders, 1953).

25. Estelle B. Freedman, "'Uncontrollable Desires': The Response to the Sexual Psychopath, 1920–1960," *Journal of American History* 74 (June 1987): 90.

26. Ronald Bayer, *Homosexuality and American Psychiatry: The Politics of Diagnosis* (New York: Basic Books, 1981).

27. Peter Dobkin Hall, *Inventing the Nonprofit Sector and Other Essays on Philanthropy, Voluntarism, and Nonprofit Organizations* (Baltimore: Johns Hopkins University Press, 1992); Judith Sealander, *Private Wealth and Public Life: Foundation Philanthropy and the Reshaping of American Social Policy from the Progressive Era to the New Deal* (Baltimore: Johns Hopkins University Press, 1997); Joan Roelofs, *Foundations and Public Policy: The Mask of Pluralism* (Albany: SUNY Press, 2003), 121–56; Jane Mayer, *Dark Money: The Hidden History of the Billionaires Behind the Rise of the Radical Right* (New York: Anchor, 2017).

28. E. E. Schattschneider, *The Semi-Sovereign People: A Realist's View of Democracy in America* (New York: Holt, Rinehart and Winston, 1960), 20–46; Alice O'Connor, *Poverty Knowledge: Social Science, Social Policy and the Poor in Twentieth-Century U.S. History* (Princeton, NJ: Princeton University Press, 2001); Theda Skocpol, *Diminished Democracy: From Membership to Management in American Civic Life* (Norman: University of Oklahoma Press, 2003); Dara Strolovitch, *Affirmative Advocacy: Race, Class, and Gender in Interest Group Politics* (Chicago: University of Chicago Press, 2007); Jacob S. Hacker and Paul Pierson, *Winner-Take-All Politics: How Washington Made the Rich Richer—and Turned Its Back on the Middle Class* (New York: Simon & Schuster, 2010); Judith Stein, *Pivotal Decade: How the United States Traded Factories for Finance in the Seventies* (New Haven, CT: Yale University Press, 2010); Nina Eliasoph, *Making Volunteers: Civic Life after Welfare's End* (Princeton, NJ: Princeton University Press, 2011), 116; Matthew Dean Hindman, *Political Advocacy and Its Interested Citizens: Neoliberalism, Postpluralism, and LGBT Organizations* (Philadelphia: University of Pennsylvania Press, 2018), 82.

29. Rogers Brubaker, *Ethnicity without Groups* (Cambridge, MA: Harvard University Press, 2004).

30. This is the same logic by which one might take up the popular transhistorical position that the Greeks were "gay," in that the category here transcends the historically situated group (no matter how little sense it makes to transpose a cultural identity from the industrial capitalist era on to sexual relations in antiquity). David M. Halperin, *How to Do the History of Homosexuality* (Chicago: University of Chicago Press, 2002).

31. Jacob S. Hacker et al., *The American Political Economy: Politics, Markets, and Power* (New York: Cambridge University Press, 2021).

32. Sheldon Krimsky, *Biotechnics and Society: The Rise of Industrial Genetics* (Westport, CT: Greenwood Press, 1991), 61–68; Toby A. Appel, *Shaping Biology: The National Science Foundation and American Biological Research, 1945–1975* (Baltimore: Johns Hopkins University Press, 2000), 7; Kaushik Sunder Rajan, *Biocapital: The Constitution of Postgenomic Life* (Durham, NC: Duke University Press, 2006); Melinda Cooper, *Life as Surplus: Biotechnology and Capitalism in the Neoliberal Era* (Seattle: University of Washington Press, 2008).

33. Theodosius Dobzhansky, *Mankind Evolving: The Evolution of the Human Species* (New Haven, CT: Yale University Press, 1962), 23.

34. National Gay Task Force, "Expert Testimony in Child Custody Cases," 1979, collection 7301, box 153, folder 17, National Gay and Lesbian Task Force Records, 1973–2000, Division of Rare and Manuscript Collections, Cornell University Library, Ithaca, NY; Marie-Amélie George, "The Custody Crucible: The Development of Scientific Authority about Gay and Lesbian Parents," *Law and History Review* 34, no. 2 (May 2016); Marie-Amélie George, *Becoming Equal: American Law and the Rise of the Gay Family* (New York: Cambridge University Press, forthcoming).

35. Ruth Hubbard, "Genomania and Health," *American Scientist* 83, no. 1 (1995): 8–10; Rodney Loeppky, *Encoding Capital: The Political Economy of the Human Genome Project* (London: Routledge, 2004); Jenny Reardon, *Race to the Finish: Identity and Governance in an Age of Genomics* (Princeton, NJ: Princeton University Press, 2004); Nathaniel Comfort, *The Science of Human Perfection: How Genes Became the Heart of American Medicine* (New Haven, CT: Yale University Press, 2012); Katie Jennings, "How Human Genome Sequencing Went from $1 Billion a Pop to under $1,000," *Forbes*, October 28, 2020, https://www.forbes.com/sites/katiejennings/2020/10/28/how-human-genome-sequencing-went-from-1-billion-a-pop-to-under-1000/?sh=3167bcd8cea9.

36. Aaron Panofsky, *Misbehaving Science: Controversy and the Development of Behavior Genetics* (Chicago: University of Chicago Press, 2014), 169.

37. Dean H. Hamer et al., "A Linkage between DNA Markers on the X Chromosome and Male Sexual Orientation," *Science* 261, no. 5119 (July 16, 1993): 321–27; Simon LeVay, "A Difference in Hypothalamic Structure between Heterosexual and Homosexual Men," *Science* 253, no. 5023 (August 30, 1991): 1034–37.

38. Nicholas Goldberg, "How 2.8 Million California Voters Nearly Banned Gay Teachers from Public Schools," *Los Angeles Times*, August 4, 2021, https://www.latimes.com/opinion/story/2021-08-04/gearhart-briggs-initiative-ban-gay-teachers-proposition-6.

39. Roger N. Lancaster, *Sex Panic and the Punitive State* (Berkeley: University of California Press 2011), 42–43.

40. Maayan Sudai et al., "Law, Policy, Biology, and Sex: Critical Issues for Researchers," *Science* 376, no. 6595 (May 19, 2022): 802–4.

41. These scientific and medical institutions augmented the power and authority of LGBTQ+ legal support structures. Charles R. Epp, *The Rights Revolution: Lawyers, Activists, and Supreme Courts in Comparative Perspective* (Chicago: University of Chicago Press, 1998); Ellen Andersen, *Out of the Closets and into the Courts: Legal Opportunity Structure and Gay Rights Litigation* (Ann Arbor: University of Michigan Press, 2005).

42. Tom Waidzunas, *The Straight Line: How the Fringe Science of Ex-Gay Therapy Reoriented Sexuality* (Minneapolis: University of Minnesota Press, 2015).

43. Mark Joseph Stern, "Trump Judges Block Laws Banning LGBTQ 'Conversion Therapy' for Minors," *Slate*, November 20, 2020, https://slate.com/news-and-politics/2020/11/trump-judges-conversion-therapy-lgbtq.html.

44. Janet Halley, "Sexual Orientation and the Politics of Biology: A Critique of the Argument from Immutability," *Stanford Law Review* 46, no. 3 (February 1994): 511–12; Kenji Yoshino, "The Epistemic Contract of Bisexual Erasure," *Stanford Law Review* 52 (January 2000): 405; Shane Phelan, *Sexual Strangers: Gays, Lesbians, and Dilemmas of Citizenship* (Philadelphia: Temple University Press, 2001), 78; Nancy J. Knauer, "Science, Identity, and the Construction of the Gay Political Narrative," *Law & Sexuality* 12 (2003): 1–87; Emily R. Gill, "Beyond Immutability: Sexuality and Constitutive Choice," *Review of Politics* 76, no. 1 (Winter 2014): 93–117.

45. Jo Wuest, "The Scientific Gaze in American Transgender Politics: Contesting the Meanings of Sex, Gender, and Gender Identity in the Bathroom Rights Cases," *Politics & Gender* 15, no. 2 (June 2019): 336–60.

46. Benjamin G. Bishin, Justin Freebourn, and Paul Teten, "The Power of Equality? Polarization and Collective Mis-Representation on Gay Rights in Congress, 1989–2019," *Political Research Quarterly* (2020), https://doi.org/10.1177%2F1065912920953498.

47. Gayle Rubin, "The Traffic in Women: Notes on the 'Political Economy' of Sex," in *Toward an Anthropology of Women*, ed. Rayna Reiter (New York: Monthly Review Press, 1975), 157–210; Gayle Rubin, "Thinking Sex: Notes for a Radical Theory of the Politics of Sexuality," in *Pleasure and Danger: Exploring Female Sexuality*, ed. Carole Vance (Boston: Routledge & Kegan Paul, 1984), 267–319.

48. Brief for Dr. Paul R. McHugh, MD, Dr. Paul Hruz, MD, PhD, and Dr. Lawrence S. Mayer, PhD, as Amici Curiae Supporting Petitioner, *G. G. v. Gloucester County School Board*, No. 16-273, January 10, 2017, 3–4, 9; Judith Butler, *Gender Trouble: Feminism and the Subversion of Identity* (New York: Routledge, 2016).

49. Anne Fausto-Sterling, *Sexing the Body: Gender Politics and the Construction of Sexuality* (New York: Basic Books, 2000); Rebecca Jordan-Young, *Brain Storm: The Flaws in the Science of Sex Differences* (Cambridge, MA: Harvard University Press, 2011); Cordelia Fine, *Testosterone Rex: Myths of Sex, Science, and Society* (New York: W. W. Norton, 2017); Sudai et al., "Law, Policy, Biology, and Sex," 802–4.

50. Nina Hagel, "Alternative Authenticities: Thinking Transgender without Essence," *Theory & Event* 20, no. 3 (2017): 600; see also Sahar Sadjadi, "Deep in the Brain: Identity and Authenticity in Pediatric Gender Transition," *Cultural Anthropology* 34, no. 1 (2019): 103–29.

51. Tey Meadow, *Trans Kids: Being Gendered in the Twenty-First Century* (Oakland: University of California Press, 2018); Joshua Franklin, "Following the Child's Lead: Care and Transformation in a Pediatric Gender Clinic" (PhD diss., University of Pennsylvania, 2020). For a history of the gender clinic, see Sandra Eder, *How the Clinic Made Gender: The Medical History of a Transformative Idea* (Chicago: University of Chicago Press, 2022).

52. Edward Stein, *The Mismeasure of Desire: The Science, Theory, and Ethics of Sexual Orientation* (Oxford: Oxford University Press, 1999), 71–92; Suzanna Walters, *The Tolerance Trap: How God, Genes, and Good Intentions Are Sabotaging Gay Equality* (New York: New York University Press, 2014).

53. Kacie M. Kidd et al., "Prevalence of Gender-Diverse Youth in an Urban School District," *Pediatrics* 147, no. 6 (2021), https://doi.org/10.1542/peds.2020-049823; Jeffrey M. Jones, "LGBT Identification in U.S. Ticks Up to 7.1%," *Gallup*, February 11, 2022, https://news.gallup.com/poll/389792/lgbt-identification-ticks-up.aspx.

54. John D'Emilio, "Capitalism and Gay Identity from Powers of Desire," in *Powers of Desire: The Politics of Sexuality*, ed. Ann Snitow, Christine Stansell, and Sharon Thompson (New York: Monthly Review Press, 1983), 100–113.

55. Lillian Faderman, *Odd Girls and Twilight Lovers: A History of Lesbian Life in Twentieth-Century America* (New York: Columbia University Press, 1991); George Chauncey, *Gay New York: Gender, Urban Culture, and the Making of the Gay Male World, 1890–1940* (New York: Basic Books, 1994).

56. Britni De La Cretaz, "More High Schoolers Are Gender-Diverse than We Thought," *them*, May 20, 2021, https://www.them.us/story/high-schooler-gender-diversity-study.

57. Human Rights Campaign and the National Center for Lesbian Rights, "Just as They Are," HRC.org, 2017, https://www.hrc.org/resources/just-as-they-are.

58. Lisa Diamond, "Sexual Fluidity and the City," *Harvard University Press Blog*, February 2, 2012, http://harvardpress.typepad.com/hup_publicity/2012/02/sexual-fluidity-and-the-city.html; Sian Ferguson, "What Does It Mean to Be Both Aromantic and Asexual?" *Healthline*, November 19, 2019, https://www.healthline.com/health/aromantic-asexual; Joshua Barajas, "Why a First-of-Its-Kind Count of Nonbinary Adults Is Crucial to Our Understanding of LGBTQ Communities," *PBS*, June 2, 2021, https://www.pbs.org/newshour/nation/why-a-first-of-its-kind -count-of-nonbinary-adults-is-crucial-to-our-understanding-of-lgbtq-communities.

59. Richard C. Lewontin, *Biology as Ideology: The Doctrine of DNA* (New York: HarperCollins, 1993).

60. Walter Benn Michaels, *Our America: Nativism, Modernism, and Pluralism* (Durham, NC: Duke University Press, 1995), 16.

61. Daniel T. Rodgers, *Age of Fracture* (Cambridge, MA: Harvard University Press, 2011); Rogers Brubaker, "The Dolezal Affair: Race, Gender, and the Micropolitics of Identity," *Ethnic and Racial Studies* 39, no. 3 (2016): 414–48.

62. Wendy Brown famously dubbed these concessions to a narrow legal model of antidiscrimination as "wounded attachments." The recursive act of claiming a stable, delimited, and legally legible identity, Brown posited, becomes the primary defense against discrimination. Wendy Brown, *States of Injury: Power and Freedom in Late Modernity* (Princeton, NJ: Princeton University Press, 1995); Wendy Brown, "Theorizing Powers: Response to Critics," *Polity* 54, no. 3 (2022).

63. Brown's later work on tolerance notably took sexual identity's intractability to be an obstacle to things like marriage reform, which had already scored its first state-level victory three years prior to the book's publication date. Wendy Brown, *Regulating Aversion: Tolerance in the Age of Identity and Empire* (Princeton, NJ: Princeton University Press, 2008), 90, 99–100.

64. Michael C. Dawson, *Behind the Mule: Race and Class in African-American Politics* (Princeton, NJ: Princeton University Press, 1995). For a cogent critique of Dawson's "linked fate" notion and the "black utility heuristic" concept, see Adolph Reed Jr., *Stirrings in the Jug: Black Politics in the Post-Segregation Era* (Minneapolis: University of Minnesota Press, 1999), 46.

65. Jeff Donn, "Fingers of Gays, Lesbians Said to Reveal One Cause of Homosexuality," *Associated Press*, March 29, 2000; Engel, *Fragmented Citizenship*, 192.

66. Alphonso David and Katie Keith, "Every LGBTQ+ Person Needs Health Insurance," *Advocate*, June 15, 2021, https://www.advocate.com/commentary/2021/6/15/every-lgbtq-person -needs-health-insurance.

67. Cedric Johnson, *Revolutionaries to Race Leaders: Black Power and the Making of African American Politics* (Minneapolis: University of Minnesota Press, 2007); Preston H. Smith II, *Racial Democracy and the Black Metropolis: Housing Policy in Postwar Chicago* (Minneapolis: University of Minnesota Press, 2012); Adam Hilton, *True Blues: The Contentious Transformation of the Democratic Party* (Philadelphia: University of Pennsylvania, 2021).

68. Ally Mutnik, "LGBTQ Advocates Target a New Way to Grow Political Power: Redistricting," *Politico*, August 11, 2021, https://www.politico.com/amp/news/2021/08/11/lgbtq-grow -political-power-redistricting-503549.

69. Christina Hanhardt, *Safe Space: Gay Neighborhood History and the Politics of Violence* (Durham, NC: Duke University Press, 2013); Amin Ghaziani, *There Goes the Gayborhood* (Princeton, NJ: Princeton University Press, 2014).

70. Sylvia Ann Hewlett, Melinda Marshall, and Laura Sherbin, "How Diversity Can Drive Innovation," *Harvard Business Review*, December 2013, https://hbr.org/2013/12/how-diversity -can-drive-innovation.

71. Heidi Peiper, "Starbucks and Lady Gaga Create Cups of Kindness Collection," 2017, https://stories.starbucks.com/stories/2017/starbucks-and-lady-gaga-create-cups-of-kindness -collection/.

72. Freedom for All Americans, "Legislative Tracker," 2020, https://www.freedomforall americans.org/2020-legislative-tracker/2020-student-athletics/.

73. Epstein, *Inclusion*; Adolph Reed Jr. and Merlin Chowkwanyun, "Race, Class, Crisis: The Discourse of Racial Disparity and Its Analytical Discontents," *Socialist Register* 48 (2012), https:// socialistregister.com/index.php/srv/article/view/15650; Myrl Beam, *Gay, Inc.: The Nonprofitiza- tion of Queer Politics* (Minneapolis: Minnesota University Press, 2018).

74. Joanna Wuest, "The Racial Disparity Politics of Biomedical Research: Disaggregat- ing Categories into New Essentialisms," *nonsite*, Winter 2020, https://nonsite.org/the-racial -disparity-politics-of-biomedical-research-disaggregating-categories-into-new-essentialisms/.

75. Amy Guckman and Betsy Reed, *Homo Economics: Capitalism, Community, and Lesbian and Gay Life* (London: Routledge, 1997); Alexandra Chasin, *Selling Out: The Gay and Lesbian Movement Goes to Market* (New York: Palgrave Macmillan, 2000); Joanna Wuest, "Beyond Inter- sectionality," *The Nation*, February 24, 2020, https://www.thenation.com/article/politics/sanders -intersectionality-working-class/.

76. Amit Paley, "Addressing the Flaws in Our Mental Healthcare System Could Save Young LGBTQ Lives," *Time*, July 23, 2021, https://time.com/6082824/mental-health-save-young-lgbtq-lives/.

77. Trevor Project, "Corporate Partners," 2021, https://www.thetrevorproject.org/about/cor porate-partners/.

78. Thomas Piketty, *Capital in the Twenty-First Century* (Cambridge, MA: Harvard Uni- versity Press, 2014); Gordon Lafer, *The One Percent Solution: How Corporations Are Remaking America One State at a Time* (Ithaca, NY: Cornell University Press, 2017).

79. Joanna Wuest, "After Liberation: Sex, Social Movements, and Capital since the New Left," *Polity* 54, no. 3 (2022): 478–502.

80. Sigmund Freud, *Three Essays on the Theory of Sexuality: The 1905 Edition* (London, Verso, 2017); Shulamith Firestone, *The Dialectic of Sex: The Case for Feminist Revolution* (Lon- don: Verso, 2015); Herbert Marcuse, *Eros and Civilization: A Philosophical Inquiry into Freud*, 2nd ed. (Boston: Beacon Press, 1966); Dennis Altman, *Homosexual: Oppression and Liberation*, 2nd ed. (New York: New York University Press, 1993).

81. Cathy J. Cohen, "Punks, Bulldaggers, and Welfare Queens: The Radical Potential of Queer Politics?" *GLQ* 3, no. 4 (1997): 437–65; Michael Warner, *The Trouble with Normal: Sex, Politics, and the Ethics of Queer Life* (Cambridge, MA: Harvard University Press, 1999); Lisa Dug- gan, *The Twilight of Equality? Neoliberalism, Cultural Politics, and the Attack on Democracy* (Bos- ton: Beacon Press, 2003); Lee Edelman, *No Future: Queer Theory and the Death Drive* (Durham, NC: Duke University Press, 2004); José Esteban Muñoz, *Cruising Utopia: The Then and There of Queer Futurity* (New York: New York University Press, 2009); Craig A. Rimmerman, *The Lesbian and Gay Movements: Assimilation or Liberation?*, 2nd ed. (New York: Routledge, 2014); Dean Spade, *Normal Life: Administrative Violence, Critical Trans Politics and the Limits of Law*, rev. ed. (Durham, NC: Duke University Press, 2015); Jeffrey Escoffier, *American Homo: Com- munity and Perversity* (London: Verso Books, 2018); Martin Duberman, *Has the Gay Movement Failed?* (Berkeley: University of California Press, 2019).

82. Admittedly, one latter-day liberationist variant in the Foucauldian tradition commences with the white flag of defeat, an admission that acts of resistance sans revolution are all that is left after the death of both grand theory and the demise of total ideologies.

83. Erwin Chemerinsky and Howard Gillman, *The Religion Clauses: The Case for Separating Church and State* (New York: Oxford University Press, 2020).

84. *Masterpiece Cakeshop v. Colorado Civil Rights Commission*, 584 U.S. ___ (2018); *303 Creative LLC v. Elenis*, No. 21-476.

85. Joanna Wuest, "A Conservative Right to Privacy: Legal, Ideological, and Coalitional Transformations in U.S. Social Conservatism," *Law & Social Inquiry* 46, no. 4 (2021): 964–92; Joanna Wuest, "Assuaging the Anxious Matriarch: Social Conservatives, Radical Feminists, and Dark Money against Trans Rights," in *Feminism Against Cisness*, ed. Emma Heaney (Durham, NC: Duke University Press, 2023).

86. Regrettably, some prominent liberal legal scholars have taken the bait. Andrew Koppelman and Robin Fretwell Wilson in particular have urged accommodation for the "little guy" no matter that well-funded firms and conservative nonprofits like the Alliance Defending Freedom and the Heritage Foundation have hand-selected folksy, sympathetic victims for their political theater. Andrew Koppelman, *Gay Rights vs. Religious Liberty? The Unnecessary Conflict* (New York: Oxford University Press, 2020); Fairness for All Initiative, "Foster Care and Adoption," n.d., https://www.fairnessforallinitiative.com/foster-adoption.

87. Naomi Oreskes and Erik M. Conway, *Merchants of Doubt: How a Handful of Scientists Obscured the Truth on Issues from Tobacco Smoke to Climate Change* (New York: Bloomsbury, 2011).

88. Michael D. Gordin, "Weird Science," *Los Angeles Review of Books*, March 14, 2022, https://lareviewofbooks.org/article/weird-science/; Mario Biagioli and Alain Pottage, "Dark Transparency: Hyper-Ethics at Trump's EPA," *Los Angeles Review of Books*, March 19, 2022, https://lareviewofbooks.org/article/dark-transparency-hyper-ethics-at-trumps-epa/.

89. Mary Ziegler, *Abortion and the Law in America: Roe v. Wade to the Present* (New York: Cambridge University Press, 2020); Sahar Sadjadi, "The Vulnerable Child Protection Act and Transgender Children's Health," *Transgender Studies Quarterly* 7, no. 3 (2020): 508–16; Annie Lowrey, "The Most Important Study in the Abortion Debate," *Atlantic Monthly*, June 11, 2022, https://www.theatlantic.com/ideas/archive/2022/06/abortion-turnaway-study-roe-supreme-court/661246/.

90. Liz Scott Lamagdeleine, "What Is Gender-Affirming Medical Care for Transgender Children? Here's What You Need to Know," *Texas Tribune*, August 4, 2021, https://www.texastribune.org/2021/08/04/gender-affirming-care-transgender-texas/.

91. *Daubert v. Merrell Dow Pharmaceuticals, Inc.*, 509 U.S. 579 (1993); Memorandum in Support of Defendant-Intervenor and the State of West Virginia's Motion to Exclude Expert Testimony of Dr. Deanna Adkins, *B.P.J. v. West Virginia State Board of Education*, S.D. WV, No. 2:21-cv-00316, May 12, 2022, https://www.aclu.org/sites/default/files/field_document/308_memo_iso_state_of_west_virginia_and_lainey_armistead_daubert_motion_for_adkins.pdf.

92. GLAAD, "GLAAD Responds to 'Real Time with Bill Maher' Segment 'Along for the Pride,'" GLAAD.org, May 21, 2022, https://www.glaad.org/blog/glaad-responds-%E2%80%98real-time-bill-maher%E2%80%99-segment-along-pride-1.

93. Eric Kauffmann, "Born This Way? The Rise of LGBT as a Social and Political Identity," Center for the Study of Partisanship and Ideology, May 30, 2022, https://cspicenter.org/reports/born-this-way-the-rise-of-lgbt-as-a-social-and-political-identity/.

94. Azeen Ghorayshi, "Report Reveals Sharp Rise in Transgender Young People in the U.S.," *New York Times*, June 10, 2022, https://www.nytimes.com/2022/06/10/science/transgender-teenagers-national-survey.html.

95. Emily Bazelon, "The Battle over Gender Therapy," *New York Times Magazine*, June 15, 2022, https://www.nytimes.com/2022/06/15/magazine/gender-therapy.html.

96. Shrier, *Irreversible Damage*; Abigail Shrier, "Top Trans Doctors Blow the Whistle on 'Sloppy' Care," *Common Sense*, October 4, 2022, https://www.commonsense.news/p/top-trans -doctors-blow-the-whistle; Zachary Evans, "New York Times Passed on Trans Doctor's Op-Ed Warning against Reckless Treatment of Gender Dysphoric Children," *Yahoo News*, October 5, 2021, https://www.yahoo.com/video/york-times-passed-trans-doctor-183152130.html.

97. Joanna Wuest and Briana Last, "With Gay Adoption Decision, Will the Supreme Court Erode the Regulatory State?," *Boston Review*, April 15, 2021, http://bostonreview.net/law-justice /joanna-wuest-briana-last-fulton-v-philadelphia-supreme-court-gay-adoption; Joanna Wuest, "The Dead End of Corporate Activism," *Boston Review*, May 18, 2022, https://bostonreview .net/articles/the-dead-end-of-corporate-activism/; Joanna Wuest and Briana S. Last, "Church against State: How Industry Groups Lead the Religious Liberty Assault on Civil Rights, Social Welfare, and the Administrative State" (forthcoming in the *Journal of Law, Medicine & Ethics*, Spring 2024). See also Benjamin George Bishin et al., *Elite-Led Mobilization and Gay Rights: Dispelling the Myth of Mass Opinion Backlash* (Ann Arbor: University of Michigan Press, 2021).

98. Amanda Hollis-Brusky, *Ideas with Consequences: The Federalist Society and the Conservative Counterrevolution* (New York: Oxford University Press, 2015); Kevin M. Kruse, *One Nation under God: How Corporate America Invented Christian America* (New York: Basic Books 2015); Lafer, *The One Percent Solution*; Alexander Hertel-Fernandez, *State Capture: How Conservative Activists, Big Businesses, and Wealthy Donors Reshaped the American States—and the Nation* (New York: Oxford University Press, 2019); Jane Mayer, "The Big Money Behind the Big Lie," *New Yorker*, August 9, 2021, https://www.newyorker.com/magazine/2021/08/09/the-big -money-behind-the-big-lie; Walker Bragman and Alex Kotch, "How the Koch Network Hijacked the War on COVID," *Daily Poster*, December 22, 2021, https://www.dailyposter.com/how -the-koch-network-hijacked-the-war-on-covid/.

99. Elizabeth Sepper, "Free Exercise Lochnerism," *Columbia Law Review* 115, no. 6 (2015): 1452–520; *Burwell v. Hobby Lobby Stores, Inc.*, 573 U.S. 682 (2014); *Fulton v. City of Philadelphia*, 593 U.S. ___ (2021).

100. Ellena Erskine, "We Read All the *Amicus* Briefs in *Dobbs* So You Don't Have To," *SCOTUSblog*, November 30, 2021, https://www.scotusblog.com/2021/11/we-read-all-the-amicus -briefs-in-dobbs-so-you-dont-have-to/; *Dobbs v. Jackson Women's Health Organization*, No. 19-1392, 597 U.S. ___ (2022).

101. Colin Crouch, *Post-Democracy after the Crises* (Cambridge: Polity, 2020); Adolph Reed Jr., "The Whole Country Is the *Reichstag*," *nonsite* (2021), https://nonsite.org/the-whole -country-is-the-reichstag. For more on neoliberal authoritarianism, see also Ian Bruff and Cemal Burak Tansel, eds., *Authoritarian Neoliberalism: Philosophies, Practices, Contestations* (London: Routledge, 2020).

102. Joanna Wuest and Briana Last, "Dark Money, the Supreme Court, and the Fate of LGBTQ+ Rights," *The Nation*, June 21, 2021, https://www.thenation.com/article/politics/dark -money-lgbtq-rights/.

103. *Americans for Prosperity Foundation v. Bonta*, 594 U.S. ___ (2021).

104. Terri Jennings Peretti, *Partisan Supremacy: How the G.O.P. Enlisted Courts to Rig America's Election Rules* (Lawrence: University Press of Kansas, 2020).

105. Paul Liem and Eric Montague, eds., "Toward a Marxist Theory of Racism: Two Essays by Harry Chang," *Review of Radical Political Economics* 17, no. 3 (1985); Adolph Reed Jr.,

"Unraveling the Relation of Race and Class in American Politics," *Political Power and Social Theory* 15 (2002): 265–74; Karen E. Fields and Barbara J. Fields, "Slave, Race, and Ideology in the United States of America," in *Racecraft: The Soul of Inequality in American Life* (London: Verso, 2012), 111–48; Lewontin, Rose, and Kamin, *Not in Our Genes*; Jonathan Marks, *Is Science Racist?* (Cambridge: Polity, 2017), 28.

106. David Valentine, *Imagining Transgender: An Ethnography of a Category* (Durham, NC: Duke University Press, 2007).

107. Schattschneider, *The Semi-Sovereign People*, 20–46.

108. Adolph Reed Jr., *The South: Jim Crow and Its Afterlives* (New York: Verso, 2022).

109. Jessica Blatt, *Race and the Making of American Political Science* (Philadelphia: University of Pennsylvania Press, 2018); Catherine Bliss, *Social by Nature: The Promise and Peril of Sociogenomics* (Stanford, CA: Stanford University Press, 2018); Angela Saini, *Superior: The Return of Race Science* (Boston: Beacon Press, 2019); Adolph Reed Jr. and Merlin Chowkwanyun, "Racial Health Disparities and Covid-19—Caution and Context," *New England Journal of Medicine* 383 (2020): 201–3.

110. Scott H., "23andMe Studies the Genetics of Sexual Orientation," *23andMe Blog*, November 7, 2012, https://blog.23andme.com/23andme-research/23andme-studies-the-genetics -of-sexual-orientation/.

111. Michael Yudell et al., "Taking Race Out of Human Genetics," *Science* 351, no. 6273 (February 5, 2016): 564–65.

112. Yulin Wang and Michal Kosinski, "Deep Neural Networks Are More Accurate than Humans at Detecting Sexual Orientation from Facial Images," *Journal of Personality and Social Psychology* 114, no. 2 (2018): 246–57; Katyanna Quach, "The Infamous AI Gaydar Study Was Repeated—And, No, Code Can't Tell If You're Straight or Not Just from Your Face," *The Register* (March 5, 2019), https://www.theregister.com/2019/03/05/ai_gaydar/.

113. Paul Lewis, "'I Was Shocked It Was So Easy': Meet the Professor Who Says Facial Recognition Can Tell If You're Gay," *The Guardian*, July 7, 2018, https://www.theguardian.com/technol ogy/2018/jul/07/artificial-intelligence-can-tell-your-sexuality-politics-surveillance-paul-lewis.

114. GLAAD, "GLAAD and HRC Call on Stanford University and Responsible Media to Debunk Dangerous and Flawed Report Claiming to Identify LGBTQ People through Facial Recognition Technology," GLAAD.org, 2018, https://www.glaad.org/blog/glaad-and-hrc-call-stan ford-university-responsible-media-debunk-dangerous-flawed-report.

115. Curtis M. Wong, "Queer Groups Condemn Study Claiming Computers Can Tell If You're Gay from Photos," *HuffPost*, September 8, 2017, https://www.huffpost.com/entry /stanford-study-sexuality_n_59b2b8e1e4b0dfaafcf7b4a5.

116. Jürgen Habermas, *Legitimation Crisis* (Boston: Beacon Press, 1975); Roger Lancaster, "Welcome to the New Legitimation Crisis," *Common Dreams*, March 7, 2020, https://www.common dreams.org/views/2020/03/07/welcome-new-legitimation-crisis-bernie-sanders-vs-plutocrats.

117. Stephen Jay Gould, *The Mismeasure of Man*, rev. and exp. ed. (New York: W. W. Norton, 1999), 28.

118. Arlene Stein, *The Stranger Next Door: The Story of a Small Community's Battle over Sex, Faith, and Civil Rights* (Boston: Beacon Press, 2002).

119. JoAnn Wypijewski, *What We Don't Talk About: Sex and the Mess of Life* (New York: Verso, 2021); Melissa Gira Grant, "QAnon and the Cultification of the American Right," *New Republic*, February 1, 2021, https://newrepublic.com/article/161103/qanon-cultification-american -right.

120. Sewell Chan and Eric Neugeboren, "Texas Republican Convention Calls Biden Win Illegitimate and Rebukes Cornyn over Gun Talks," *Texas Tribune*, June 18, 2022, https://www.texastribune.org/2022/06/18/republican-party-texas-convention-cornyn/.

121. David M. Halperin and Trevor Hoppe, eds., *The War on Sex* (Durham, NC: Duke University Press, 2017).

122. Adam Tooze, *Crashed: How a Decade of Financial Crises Changed the World* (New York: Viking, 2018).

123. Yasmin Nair, "The Gay Gene Will Not Protect You," *Bilerico Report on LGBTQ Nation*, March 13, 2011, http://bilerico.lgbtqnation.com/2011/03/the_gay_gene_will_not_protect_you_1.php.

124. Adolph Reed Jr., "Intellectual Brown Shirts," *The Progressive* 58, no. 12 (1994): 15–17.

125. Marshall D. Sahlins, *The Use and Abuse of Biology: An Anthropological Critique of Sociobiology* (Ann Arbor: University of Michigan Press, 1976); Roger Lancaster, *The Trouble with Nature: Sex in Science and Pop Culture* (Berkeley: University of California Press, 2003); Susan McKinnon, *Neo-Liberal Genetics: The Myths and Moral Tales of Evolutionary Psychology* (Chicago: Prickly Paradigm Press, 2005).

126. Fields and Fields, *Racecraft*. Indeed, Charles Murray and Richard J. Herrnstein's ur-text of modern race science, *The Bell Curve: Intelligence and Class Structure in American Life* (New York: Simon & Schuster, 1996), celebrated the inherent intelligence of the rich while denigrating the allegedly natural lower rates of cognitive functioning among the poor, both Black and white.

127. Richard C. Lewontin, "The Inferiority Complex," *New York Review of Books*, October 22, 1981.

128. Lancaster, *The Trouble with Nature*, 345.

Chapter One

1. Franklin E. Kameny, "Does Research into Homosexuality Matter?" *The Ladder* 10, no. 1 (May 1965): 14–20; Florence Conrad, "Research Is Here to Stay," *The Ladder* 8, nos. 10 & 11 (July/August 1965): 15–21; Franklin E. Kameny, "Emphasis on Research Has Had Its Day," *The Ladder* 10, no. 1 (October 1965): 23–26; Kristin G. Esterberg, "From Illness to Action: Conceptions of Homosexuality in *The Ladder*, 1956–1965," *Journal of Sex Research* 27, no. 1 (1990): 65–80.

2. David F. Greenberg, *The Construction of Homosexuality* (Chicago: University of Chicago Press, 1988); Jennifer Terry, *An American Obsession: Science, Medicine, and Homosexuality in Modern Science* (Chicago: University of Chicago Press, 1999), 43.

3. Michel Foucault, *The History of Sexuality*, vol. 1, trans. Robert Hurley (New York: Vintage, 1990).

4. Terry, *An American Obsession*, 90; Laurie Marhoefer, *Sex and the Weimar Republic: German Homosexual Emancipation and the Rise of the Nazis* (Toronto: University of Toronto Press, 2015).

5. George W. Stocking Jr., *Race, Culture, and Evolution: Essays in the History of Anthropology* (Chicago: University of Chicago Press, 1968).

6. Harry Oosterhuis, *Stepchildren of Nature: Krafft-Ebing, Psychiatry, and the Making of Sexual Identity* (Chicago: University of Chicago Press, 2000); Alison M. Downham Moore, "The Historicity of Sexuality: Knowledge of the Past in the Emergence of Modern Sexual Science," *Modern Intellectual History* 18, no. 2 (2021): 403–26.

7. Jack Drescher, "A History of Homosexuality and Organized Psychoanalysis," *Journal of the American Academy of Psychoanalysis and Dynamic Psychiatry* 36, no. 3 (2008): 443–60.

8. Elazar Barkan, *The Retreat of Scientific Racism: Changing Concepts of Race in Britain and the United States between the World Wars* (New York: Cambridge University Press, 1992); Siobhan Somerville, "Scientific Racism and the Invention of the Homosexual Body," in *The Gender/Sexuality Reader: Culture, History, and Political Economy*, ed. Micaela di Leonardo and Roger Lancaster (London: Routledge, 1997), 37–52; Margot Canaday, *The Straight State: Sexuality and Citizenship in Twentieth-Century America* (Princeton, NJ: Princeton University Press, 2009); Adam Cohen, *Imbeciles: The Supreme Court, American Eugenics, and the Sterilization of Carrie Buck* (New York: Penguin Books, 2017).

9. Foucault, *The History of Sexuality*, 1:68–69.

10. Terry, *An American Obsession*, 178–266.

11. Robert Beachy, *Gay Berlin: Birthplace of a Modern Identity* (New York: Viking, 2015); Anna Lvovsky, *Vice Patrol: Cops, Courts, and the Struggle over Urban Gay Life before Stonewall* (Chicago: University of Chicago Press, 2021).

12. John D'Emilio, *Sexual Politics, Sexual Communities: The Making of a Homosexual Minority in the United States, 1940–1970*, 2nd ed. (Chicago: University of Chicago Press, 1998), 22–25; Martin Meeker, *Contacts Desired: Gay and Lesbian Communications and Community, 1940s–1970s* (Chicago: University of Chicago Press, 2006).

13. Allan Bérubé, *Coming Out under Fire: The History of Gay Men and Women in World War II* (New York: Simon & Schuster, 1990); David K. Johnson, *The Lavender Scare: The Cold War Persecution of Gays and Lesbians in the Federal Government* (Chicago: University of Chicago Press, 2004).

14. Stephen Engel, *Fragmented Citizenship: The Changing Landscape of Gay and Lesbian Lives* (New York: New York University Press, 2016), 84–97.

15. D'Emilio, *Sexual Politics*, 60–63.

16. Jonathan Ned Katz, *Gay American History: Lesbians and Gay Men in the U.S.A.* (New York: T. Y. Crowell, 1976), 91–92.

17. There were, however, a handful of notable exceptions. H. L. Small, "Socialism and Sex," reprinted in Christopher Phelps, "A Neglected Document on Socialism and Sex," *Journal of the History of Sexuality* 16, no. 1 (January 2007): 1–13.

18. D'Emilio, *Sexual Politics*, 64–66; Stephen M. Engel, *The Unfinished Revolution: Social Movement Theory and the Gay and Lesbian Movement* (New York: Cambridge University Press, 2001), 31; Mattachine Society, "Statement of Purpose of the Mattachine Society," in *We Are Everywhere: A Historical Sourcebook of Gay and Lesbian Politics*, ed. Mark Blasius and Shane Phelan (New York: Routledge, 1997), 283–84.

19. Daniel Hurewitz, *Bohemian Los Angeles and the Making of Modern Politics* (Berkeley: University of California Press, 2007).

20. Friedrich Engels, *The Origin of the Family, Private Property and the State* (New York: Penguin, 2010).

21. Alfred C. Kinsey et al., *Sexual Behavior in the Human Male* (Bloomington: Indiana University Press, 1998); Alfred C. Kinsey et al., *Sexual Behavior in the Human Female* (Bloomington: Indiana University Press, 1998).

22. Jim Becker, "Was Stonewall Possible without Dr. Alfred Kinsey?" *Baltimore Out Loud*, October 25, 2019, https://baltimoreoutloud.com/wp/was-stonewall-possible-without-dr-alfred -kinsey/.

23. D'Emilio, *Sexual Politics*, 83; Terry, *An American Obsession*, 304, 323, 349.

24. D'Emilio, *Sexual Politics*, 42.

25. D'Emilio, 70–74.

26. Engel, *The Unfinished Revolution*, 32.

27. D'Emilio, *Sexual Politics*, 78–80.

28. Martin Meeker, "Behind the Mask of Respectability: Reconsidering the Mattachine Society and Male Homophile Practice, 1950s and 1960s," *Journal of the History of Sexuality* 10, no. 1 (January 2001): 78–116; Whitney Strub, "The Homophile Is a Sexual Being: Wallace de Ortega Maxey's Pulp Theology and Gay Activism," *Journal of the History of Sexuality* 25, no. 2 (May 2016): 323–53.

29. Meeker, "Behind the Mask of Respectability," 79.

30. Sigmund Freud, *Three Essays on the Theory of Sexuality: The 1905 Edition* (London: Verso, 2017).

31. Tom Waidzunas, *The Straight Line: How the Fringe Science of Ex-Gay Therapy Reoriented Sexuality* (Minneapolis: University of Minnesota Press, 2015), 36; D'Emilio, *Sexual Politics*, 42; Eli Zaretsky, *Political Freud: A History* (New York: Columbia University Press, 2015).

32. Dagmar Herzog, *Cold War Freud: Psychoanalysis in an Age of Catastrophes* (New York: Cambridge University Press, 2016), 58–67.

33. American Psychiatric Association, *Diagnostic and Statistical Manual of Mental Disorders*, 1st ed. (Washington, DC: American Psychiatric Association, 1952).

34. David K. Johnson, *Buying Gay: How Physique Entrepreneurs Sparked a Movement* (New York: Columbia University Press, 2019), 58–70.

35. Donald Webster Cory, *The Homosexual in America: A Subjective Approach* (New York: Greenberg, 1951); Albert Ellis, "Rumors about My Anti-Homosexual Views: A Reply to Kristin Gay Esterberg," *Journal of Sex Research* 27, no. 4 (November 1990): 645–46; John D'Emilio, *Making Trouble: Essays on Gay History, Politics, and the University* (London: Routledge, 1992); Waidzunas, *The Straight Line*, 54. Ellis adhered to a belief in "innate bisexuality" but was firmly opposed to the "exclusive homosexual" as a natural sexual variant.

36. Cory, *The Homosexual*, xi, 5.

37. Ronald Bayer, *Homosexuality and American Psychiatry: The Politics of Diagnosis* (New York: Basic Books, 1981), 76.

38. Curtis Dewees letter to Wardell Pomeroy, September 2, 1963, Gebhard Era Correspondence, 1960–1969, part 1: A–Z, file cabinet 4, drawer 5, Mattachine Society 1960s, Kinsey Institute for Research in Sex, Gender, and Reproduction, Bloomington, IN.

39. D'Emilio, *Sexual Politics*, 88.

40. D'Emilio, 94.

41. Bayer, *Homosexuality and American Psychiatry*, 79–80.

42. Daughters of Bilitis, "Statement of Purpose (1955)," in *We Are Everywhere*, ed. Blasius and Phelan, 328; Marcia M. Gallo, *Different Daughters: A History of the Daughters of Bilitis and the Rise of the Lesbian Rights Movement* (New York: Carroll & Graf, 2006).

43. Daughters of Bilitis, "What about the DOB? (1959)," in *We Are Everywhere*, ed. Blasius and Phelan, 328–30.

44. Esterberg, "From Illness to Action," 70–71.

45. Esterberg, 67–69.

46. Esterberg, 72.

47. Daughters of Bilitis, "What about the DOB? (1959)," 330.

48. Franklin Kameny, "Gay Is Good," in *We Are Everywhere*, ed. Blasius and Phelan, 366–76.

49. David K. Johnson, "Franklin E. Kameny," in *Before Stonewall: Activists for Gay and Lesbian Rights in Historical Context*, ed. Vern Bullough (Binghamton, NY: Harrington Park Press, 2002), 209–18.

50. Eric Cervini, *The Deviant's War: The Homosexual vs. the United States of America* (New York: Farrar, Straus and Giroux, 2020), 73.

51. Barry D. Adam, *The Rise of a Gay and Lesbian Movement* (New York: Twayne, 1995), 76.

52. D'Emilio, *Sexual Politics*, 213.

53. David Carter, *Stonewall: The Riots That Sparked the Gay Revolution* (New York: St. Martin's Press, 2010), 39–40.

54. Adam, *The Rise of a Gay and Lesbian Movement*, 77.

55. Marc Stein, *City of Sisterly and Brotherly Loves: Lesbian and Gay Philadelphia, 1945–1972*, 2nd ed. (Philadelphia: Temple University Press, 2004), 232; Marc Stein, *Rethinking the Gay and Lesbian Movement* (New York: Routledge, 2012), 71.

56. Mattachine Society of Washington, "Committee on Picketing and Other Lawful Demonstrations: Regulations for Picketing," n.d., Frank Kameny Papers, Library of Congress, available at http://www.kamenypapers.org/images/KamenyPicketInstructions.jpg.

57. Gallo, *Different Daughters*, 155–57.

58. North American Conference of Homophile Organizations, Minutes from Fourth Meeting (August 1968), Gerber/Hart Library and Archives, http://www.gerberhart.org/wp-content/uploads/2016/03/North-American-Conference-of-Homophile-Orgs-Minutes-August-1968.pdf.

59. Henry Abelove, "How Stonewall Obscures the Real History of Gay Liberation," *Chronicle of Higher Education Review*, June 26, 2015, http://www.chronicle.com/article/How-Stonewall-Obscures-the-231099/.

60. Society for Individual Rights, "Homosexuals Call for Completion of American Revolution," 1968, collection 2011.075, box 1, folder 1, Society for Individual Rights (SIR) Records, ONE National Gay & Lesbian Archives, Los Angeles, CA.

61. D'Emilio, *Sexual Politics*, 73–74.

62. Waidzunas, *The Straight Line*, 54.

63. Evelyn Hooker, "A Preliminary Analysis of Group Behavior of Homosexuals," *Journal of Psychology* 42 (1956): 219; Evelyn Hooker, "The Adjustment of the Male Overt Homosexual," *Journal of Projective Techniques* 21 (1957): 18–31.

64. Waidzunas, *The Straight Line*, 55.

65. Thomas Szasz, *The Myth of Mental Illness: Foundations of a Theory of Personal Conduct* (New York: Harper & Row, 1961); Thomas Szasz, "What Psychiatry Can and Cannot Do," *Harper's Magazine* 228 (February 1964): 50–53.

66. Michel Foucault, *The Birth of the Clinic: An Archaeology of Medical Perception* (New York: Vintage, 1994).

67. Thomas Szasz, "Legal and Moral Aspects of Homosexuality," in *Sexual Inversion: The Multiple Roots of Homosexuality*, ed. Judd Marmor (New York: Basic Books, 1965), 124–39.

68. Martin Hoffman, *The Gay World: Male Homosexuality and the Social Creation of Evil* (New York: Basic Books, 1968).

69. Hendrik Ruitenbeek, *The Problem of Homosexuality in Modern Society* (Boston: Dutton, 1963).

70. C. A. Tripp, "Psychiatric Moralists in Unison," January 1966, collection 2007-009, box 4, folder 8, Judd Marmor Papers, ONE National Gay & Lesbian Archives, Los Angeles, CA.

71. Irving Bieber et al., *Homosexuality: A Psychoanalytic Study of Male Homosexuals* (New York: Basic Books, 1962); Judd Marmor, ed., *Sexual Inversion: The Multiple Roots of Homosexuality* (New York: Basic Books, 1965).

72. Franklin Kameny to Paul Gebhard, May 10, 1969, Gebhard Era Correspondence, 1960–1969, part 1: A–Z, file cabinet 4, drawer 5, Franklin Kameny, Kinsey Institute for Research in Sex, Gender, and Reproduction, Bloomington, IN.

73. Richard Inman to Paul Gebhard, August 30, 1965, Gebhard Era Correspondence, 1960–1969, part 1: A–Z, file cabinet 4, drawer 5, Mattachine Society 1960s, Kinsey Institute for Research in Sex, Gender, and Reproduction, Bloomington, IN.

74. Richard Inman to Walter Alvarez, cc: Harry Benjamin, Wardell Pomeroy, and Paul Gebhard, May 5, 1966, Gebhard Era Correspondence, 1960–1969, part 1: A–Z, file cabinet 4, drawer 5, Mattachine Society 1960s, Kinsey Institute for Research in Sex, Gender, and Reproduction, Bloomington, IN.

75. Paul Gebhard to Richard Inman, January 5, 1966, Gebhard Era Correspondence, 1960–1969, part 1: A–Z, file cabinet 4, drawer 5, Mattachine Society 1960s, Kinsey Institute for Research in Sex, Gender, and Reproduction, Bloomington, IN.

76. Terry, *An American Obsession*, 43.

77. Gerald N. Grobe, *From Asylum to Community: Mental Health Policy in Modern America* (Princeton, NJ: Princeton University Press, 1991), 273–301.

78. *One, Incorporated v. Olesen*, 355 U.S. 371 (1958); *Griswold v. Connecticut*, 381 U.S. 479 (1965); William B. Lockhart and Robert C. McClure, "Obscenity Censorship: The Core Constitutional Issue—What Is Obscene?" *Utah Law Review* 7, no. 3 (1961): 289–303; Henry L. Minton, *Departing from Deviance: A History of Homosexual Rights and Emancipatory Science in America* (Chicago: University of Chicago Press, 2002), 240; Craig J. Konnoth, "Created in Its Image: The Race Analogy, Gay Identity, and Gay Litigation in the 1950s–1970s," *Yale Law Journal* 119, no. 2 (2009): 316–72; David Minto, "Perversion by Penumbras: Wolfenden, *Griswold*, and the Transatlantic Trajectory of Sexual Privacy," *American Historical Review* 123, no. 4 (2018): 1093–121; Mary Ziegler, *Beyond Abortion: Roe v. Wade and the Battle for Privacy* (Cambridge, MA: Harvard University Press, 2018); *Roth v. United States*, 354 U.S. 476 (1957).

79. *One, Incorporated v. Olesen*, 241 F.2d 772 (9th Cir. 1957), 77.

80. Lvovsky, *Vice Patrol*. As Lvovsky documents, the pathological account was occasionally used by bar owners as well as those busted for cruising as a defense; bar owners could argue that homosexuality was largely invisible and thus impossible to police, whereas those who were arrested could plea for leniency.

81. *Stoumen v. Reilly*, 37 Cal.2d 713 (1951).

82. Patricia A. Cain, "Litigating for Lesbian and Gay Rights: A Legal History," *Virginia Law Review* 79, no. 7 (October 1993): 1551–642.

83. *Talley v. California*, 390 U.S. 1031 (1968); Joyce Murdoch and Deb Prince, *Courting Justice: Gay Men and Lesbians v. the Supreme Court* (New York: Basic Books, 2001), 144–46.

84. *Vallerga v. Dept. Alcoholic Bev. Control*, 53 Cal. 2d 313, 347 P.2d 909, 1 Cal. Rptr. 494 (p. 315).

85. [Cited from *Vallerga*] *Re Kaczka and Trobiano*, 333 A.B.C. Bulletin 1063, Item 1 (April 21, 1955).

86. *One Eleven Wines & Liquors, Inc. v. Div. Alcoholic Bev. Control*, 235 A.2d 12 (N.J. 1967).

87. *Inman v. City of Miami*, 197 So.2d 50, 51 (1967), cert. denied, 201 So.2d 895 (Fla. 1967), and cert. denied, 389 U.S. 1048 (1968).

88. Executive Order 10450, 18 FR 2489, 3 CFR, 1949–1953 Comp., p. 936 (April 27, 1953).

89. David K. Johnson, "Homosexual Citizens: Washington's Gay Community Confronts the Civil Service," *Washington History* 6 (Fall/Winter 1994–95): 44–63; *Cole v. Young*, 351 U.S. 536 (1956).

90. Cervini, *The Deviant's War*, 37–43.

91. *Kameny v. Brucker*, 282 F.2d 823 (D.C. Cir. 1960) (upholding the dismissal), cert. denied, 365 U.S. 843 (1961); William N. Eskridge Jr., "Some Effects of Identity-Based Social Movements on Constitutional Law in the Twentieth Century," *Michigan Law Review* 100, no. 8 (August 2002): 2169.

92. *Scott v. Macy*, 349 F.2d 182 (D.C. Cir. 1965); *Scott v. Macy*, 402 F.2d 644, 648 (D.C. Cir. 1968).

93. *Durham v. U.S.*, 214 F.2d 862 (D.C. Cir. 1954); Bernard Wolfman, "Introduction," *University of Pennsylvania Law Review* 123, no. 2 (December 1974): 243–46.

94. *Norton v. Macy*, 417 F.2d 1161, 1167 (D.C. Cir. 1969).

95. *Norton v. Macy* (1969), fn. 5. The test was later codified into law in the Civil Service Reform Act of 1978. Pub. L. No. 95-454, §907, 92 Stat. 1111, 1227.

96. *Scott v. Macy* (1965), 184 fn. 12; Clara Thompson, "Changing Concepts of Homosexuality in Psychoanalysis," *Psychiatry: Journal of the Biology and Pathology of Interpersonal Relations* 10, no. 183 (1947).

97. Thompson, "Changing Concepts of Homosexuality," 187; *Norton v. Macy* (1969), fn. 28.

98. National Institute of Mental Health, "Final Report of the Task Force on Homosexuality," 1969, collection 7301, box 154, folder 34, National Gay and Lesbian Task Force Records, 1973–2017, Division of Rare and Manuscript Collections, Cornell University Library, Ithaca, NY. Only three of the fifteen final members of the Task Force signed on to a dissent.

99. ONE Inc., "February 1971 Newsletter," *ONE Inc.*, collection 2014.109, box 1, folder 21, Stanley R. Brossette Papers, ONE National Gay & Lesbian Archives, Los Angeles, CA.

100. Margot Canaday, "'Who Is a Homosexual?': The Consolidation of Sexual Identities in Mid-Twentieth-Century American Immigration Law," *Law & Social Inquiry* 28, no. 2 (April 2003): 351–86; Marc Stein, "*Boutilier* and the U.S. Supreme Court's Sexual Revolution," *Law and History Review* 23, no. 3 (Fall 2005): 491–536.

101. American Law Institute, "Model Penal Code: Official Draft and Explanatory Notes: Complete Text of Model Penal Code as Adopted at the 1962 Annual Meeting of the American Law Institute at Washington, D.C." (Philadelphia: American Law Institute, May 24, 1962); Canaday, *The Straight State*, 218–19.

102. The Immigration and Nationality Act of 1952 (Pub. L. 82-414, 66 Stat. 163, enacted June 27, 1952).

103. Canaday, *The Straight State*, 214–20.

104. Murdoch and Prince, *Courting Justice*, 91.

105. *Rosenberg v. Fleuti*, 374 U.S. 449 (1963).

106. Eskridge, "Some Effects of Identity-Based Social Movements," 2166–67.

107. Stein, "*Boutilier*," 497–98, 530.

108. Canaday, *The Straight State*, 242–43.

109. *Boutilier v. INS*, 363 F.2d 488, 496 (2d Cir. 1966), 496.

110. *Boutilier*, 494.

111. This parallels the INS's approach to a similar question about scientific taxonomies and folk notions of natural human kinds in *United States v. Bhagat Singh Thind*, 261 U.S. 204 (1923).

112. *Boutilier*, 497.

113. Stein, "*Boutilier*," 531–32.

114. Canaday, *The Straight State*, 243.

115. Stein, "*Boutilier*," 531–32.

116. *Boutilier v. INS*, 387 U.S. 118 (1967), 125–35.

117. Engel, *Fragmented Citizenship*, 120–23.

118. Canaday, "'Who Is a Homosexual?,'" 383.

Chapter Two

1. Jennifer Terry, *An American Obsession: Science, Medicine, and Homosexuality in Modern Society* (Chicago: University of Chicago Press, 1999), 373.

2. For a more tempered and holistic account of the cultural and political significance of gay liberation, see Jim Downs, *Stand by Me: The Forgotten History of Gay Liberation* (New York: Basic Books, 2016).

3. Ronald Bayer, *Homosexuality and American Psychiatry: The Politics of Diagnosis* (New York: Basic Books, 1981).

4. Geeti Das, "Mostly Normal: American Psychiatric Taxonomy, Sexuality, and Neoliberal Mechanisms of Exclusion," *Sexuality Research and Social Policy* 13, no. 4 (2016): 390–401; Abram J. Lewis, "'We Are Certain of Our Own Insanity': Antipsychiatry and the Gay Liberation Movement, 1968–1980," *Journal of the History of Sexuality* 25, no. 1 (January 2016): 83–113; Regina Kunzel, "The Rise of Gay Rights and the Disavowal of Disability," in *The Oxford Handbook on Disability History*, ed. Catherine Kudlick, Kim Nielsen, and Michael A. Rembis (New York: Oxford University Press, 2018), 459–76.

5. Jeffrey Escoffier, "Left-Wing Homosexuality: Emancipation, Sexual Liberation, and Identity Politics," *New Politics* 12, no. 45 (2008), http://newpol.org/content/left-wing-homosexuality-emancipation-sexual-liberation-and-identity-politics.

6. Juliet Mitchell, "Women: The Longest Revolution," *New Left Review* 1, no. 40 (1966): 11–37; Kate Millett, *Sexual Politics* (New York: Avon Books, 1969); Shulamith Firestone, *The Dialectic of Sex: The Case for Feminist Revolution* (London: Verso, 2015).

7. Herbert Marcuse, *An Essay on Liberation* (Boston: Beacon Press, 1971); Herbert Marcuse, "Liberation from the Affluent Society," in *The Dialectics of Liberation*, ed. David Cooper (London: Verso, 2015).

8. Herbert Marcuse, *Eros and Civilization: A Philosophical Inquiry into Freud*, 2nd ed. (Boston: Beacon Press, 1966); Herbert Marcuse, *One-Dimensional Man*, 2nd ed. (Boston: Beacon Press, 1991); Russell Jacoby, *Social Amnesia: A Critique of Conformist Psychology from Adler to Laing* (Boston: Beacon Press, 1975).

9. Firestone, *The Dialectic of Sex*, 11, 53–5, 174, 215.

10. Marcuse, *Eros and Civilization*, xv, 50; Jacoby, *Social Amnesia*.

11. Dennis Altman, *Homosexual: Oppression and Liberation*, 2nd ed. (New York: New York University Press, 1993), 82, 88–89.

12. Like Freud, Altman conceived of heterosexual genital love as essentially utilitarian and a mode of social organization that led to the "strong repression of all sexual urges other than those that are genital and heterosexual." Altman, *Homosexual*, 82. Where Altman deviated from Freud, however, was in his subsequent claim—one which he ascribes to Marcuse—that "the homosexual represents a constant reminder of the repressed part of human sexuality, only in his

or her interest in their own sex, but also in the variety of nonconventional sexual behaviour that homosexuality implies" (88). He also contemplated that "anatomy has forced the homosexual to explore the realities of polymorphous eroticism" (88). Though homosexuality is surely distinguishable from purely reproductive-oriented heterosexual behavior, Altman's description of sexual practices between or among individuals of the same gender clearly are not polymorphously perverse in the way that Freud depicted the childhood experience of nongenital tactile pleasures. Indeed, Altman strayed quite far from Freud and Marcuse alike in imputing such practices with the radical potential to overthrow the surplus repression that late capitalist society had deployed to channel unruly desires into "productive" genital-based sexual relations.

13. Marcuse, *One-Dimensional Man*, 72–75.

14. Martha Shelley, "Gay Is Good," in *Out of the Closets: Voices of Gay Liberation*, Twentieth Anniversary ed., ed. Karla Kay and Allen Young (New York: New York University Press, 1992), 31–33.

15. Shelley, 34.

16. Jeffrey Weeks, "Ideas of Gay Liberation," *Gay News* 6 (September 1, 1972): 6.

17. Third World Gay Revolution, "The Oppressed Shall Not Become the Oppressor," in *We Are Everywhere: A Historical Sourcebook of Gay and Lesbian Politics*, ed. Mark Blasius and Shane Phelan (New York: Routledge, 1997), 400–401.

18. Weeks, "Ideas of Gay Liberation," 6.

19. Firestone, *The Dialectic of Sex*, 97; Craig Hanson, "LA-GLF vs. Dorothy Healey," February 18, 1971, collection 2012.031, box 1, folder 19, Gay Liberation Front LA, ONE National Gay & Lesbian Archives, Los Angeles, CA; "The Combahee River Collective Statement," April 1977, History Is a Weapon, http://historyisaweapon.com/defcon1/combrivercoll.html.

20. Jim Fouratt, "Homosexual," in *Come Out!: Selections from the Radical Gay Liberation Newspaper* (New York: Times Change Press, 1970), 16, collection 2012.031, box 1, folder 6, Gay Liberation Front LA, ONE National Gay & Lesbian Archives, Los Angeles, CA.

21. David, "Gay Relationship," *Gay Community* 1, no. 1, n.d., collection 127, box 1, folder 40, Michael O'Grady Papers, New York LGBT Community Center National History Archive, New York, NY.

22. Altman, *Homosexual*, 115.

23. Carl Wittman, "Refugees from Amerika: A Gay Manifesto," in *Out of the Closets*, ed. Kay and Young, 331.

24. Sigmund Freud, *Three Essays on the Theory of Sexuality: The 1905 Edition* (London: Verso, 2017); Red Butterfly, "Comments on Carl Wittman's 'A Gay Manifesto'" (Provincetown, MA: Pagan Press, 1970), https://paganpressbooks.com/jpl/TRB-WITT.HTM.

25. Wittman, "Refuges from Amerika," 331.

26. Ronald J. Carrier, "Hartford Connecticut Gay Liberation Front Letter to Stanley Brossette Questionnaire," February 6, 1971, collection 2014.109, box 1, folder 4, Stanley R. Brossette Papers, ONE National Gay & Lesbian Archives, Los Angeles, CA.

27. Gay Liberation Front, Los Angeles, "Statement of Purpose," c. 1969–70, collection 2012.031, box 1, folder 23, Gay Liberation Front LA, ONE National Gay & Lesbian Archives, Los Angeles, CA.

28. Martin Duberman, *Has the Gay Movement Failed?* (Berkeley: University of California Press, 2019), 10.

29. Gay Liberation Front, Los Angeles, "Homosexuality Is Not a Sickness," n.d., collection 2012.031, box 1, folder 19, Gay Liberation Front LA, ONE National Gay & Lesbian Archives, Los

Angeles, CA. Though pitched in a far different register, the liberationist attitude here resembles Evelyn Hooker's hypothesis for why homosexual patients might seek psychiatric care. Contemporary social scientists might also see similarities between the liberationist view and their minority stress theory.

30. Gay Liberation Front, Los Angeles, "A Statement on Gay Liberation," October 24, 1970, collection 2012.031, box 1, folder 19, Gay Liberation Front LA, ONE National Gay & Lesbian Archives, Los Angeles, CA.

31. Red Butterfly, "An Anthropological Perspective," in *Out of the Closets*, ed. Kay and Young, 160.

32. Craig Hanson, "LA-GLF vs. Dorothy Healey," February 18, 1971, collection 2012.031, box 1, folder 19, Gay Liberation Front LA, ONE National Gay & Lesbian Archives, Los Angeles, CA.

33. Gay Liberation Front, St. Louis, "Letter to Stanley Brossette Questionnaire," 1971, collection 2014.109, box 1, folder 4, Stanley R. Brossette Papers, ONE National Gay & Lesbian Archives, Los Angeles, CA.

34. "FREE: Gay Liberation of Minnesota Brochure," n.d., collection 2014.109, box 1, folder 6, Stanley R. Brossette Papers, ONE National Gay & Lesbian Archives, Los Angeles, CA.

35. "Come Out! Editorial Collective of the GLF-NY Letter to Stanley Brossette Questionnaire," 1971, Collection 2014.109, box 1, folder 4, Stanley R. Brossette Papers, ONE National Gay & Lesbian Archives, Los Angeles, CA.

36. Radicalesbians, "The Woman-Identified Woman," in *Out of the Closets*, ed. Kay and Young, 172–77. See also Rita Mae Brown, "Hanoi to Hoboken: A Round Trip Ticket," in *Out of the Closets*, ed. Kay and Young, 195–201; Gay Revolutionary Party Women's Caucus, "Realesbians and Politicalesbians," in *Out of the Closets*, ed. Kay and Young, 177–81.

37. Rebecca Jennings, "'The Most Uninhibited Party They'd Ever Been To': The Postwar Encounter between Psychiatry and the British Lesbian, 1945–1971," *Journal of British Studies* 47 (October 2008): 883–904; Emily K. Hobson, *Lavender and Red: Liberation and Solidarity in the Gay and Lesbian Left* (Oakland: University of California Press, 2016), 58–61.

38. Stephen Donaldson, "The Bisexual Movement's Beginnings in the 70s: A Personal Retrospective," in *Bisexual Politics: Theories, Queries, and Visions*, ed. Naomi Tucker (Binghamton, NY: Haworth Press, 1995), 31–45.

39. Gay Revolutionary Party Women's Caucus, "Realesbians and Politicalesbians," 178. See also Paula C. Rust, *Bisexuality and the Challenge to Lesbian Politics: Sex, Loyalty, and Revolution* (New York: New York University Press, 1995).

40. Wittman, "Refugees from Amerika," 331.

41. Gay Liberation Front, Los Angeles, "Gay Liberation Demands," n.d., collection 2012.031, box 1, folder 19, and Gay Liberation Front, Los Angeles, "Peace and Freedom Party Platform Section," n.d., collection 2012.031, box 1, folder 22, Gay Liberation Front LA, ONE National Gay & Lesbian Archives, Los Angeles, CA.

42. Altman, *Homosexual*, 159.

43. "Transsexual Conference in Miami," *Drag Queens: A Magazine about the Transvestite* 1, no. 1 (1971): 8.

44. "Viewpoint: Drag Queen vs. Transvestite," *Drag Queens: A Magazine about the Transvestite* 1, no. 1 (1971): 11.

45. Anne Harrington, *Mind Fixers: Psychiatry's Troubled Search for the Biology of Mental Illness* (New York: W. W. Norton, 2020).

46. Sigmund Freud, "A Letter from Freud," *American Journal of Psychiatry* 107 (1951): 786–87, https://doi.org/10.1176/ajp.107.10.786.

47. Marcuse, *Eros and Civilization*, 248–49, 254–55; Bayer, *Homosexuality and American Psychiatry*, 28–29; Jack Drescher, "A History of Homosexuality and Organized Psychoanalysis," *Journal of the American Academy of Psychoanalysis and Dynamic Psychiatry* 36, no. 3 (2008): 443–60; Freud, *Three Essays on the Theory of Sexuality*.

48. Tom Waidzunas, *The Straight Line: How the Fringe Science of Ex-Gay Therapy Reoriented Sexuality* (Minneapolis: University of Minnesota Press, 2015), 43–45.

49. Of course, the designation of "heterosexual" itself here is a slippery one that through the early twentieth century encompassed acts deemed pathological—such as opposite-sex promiscuity—as well as normative reproductive sex within a monogamous couple. Jonathan Ned Katz, *The Invention of Heterosexuality* (Chicago: University of Chicago Press, 2007).

50. Richard Krafft-Ebing, *Psychopathia Sexualis, with Especial Reference to the Antipathic Sexual Instinct: A Medico-Forensic Study*, trans. Franklin S. Klaf (New York: Arcade, 1965).

51. American Psychiatric Association, *Diagnostic and Statistical Manual of Mental Disorders*, 1st ed. (Washington, DC: American Psychiatric Association, 1952), 38–39.

52. Dagmar Herzog, *Cold War Freud: Psychoanalysis in an Age of Catastrophes* (New York: Cambridge University Press, 2016), 65–67.

53. Kenneth Lewes, *The Psychoanalytic Theory of Male Homosexuality* (New York: Simon & Schuster, 1988), 323; Kate Davison, "Cold War Pavlov: Homosexual Aversion Therapy in the 1960s," *History of the Human Sciences* 34, no. 1 (2020): 89–119.

54. Waidzunas, *The Straight Line*, 51. A true exemplar of science's egalitarian contradictions, Eysenck was notoriously enthralled with IQ-based race science. Andrew M. Colman, "Race Differences in IQ: Hans Eysenck's Contribution to the Debate in the Light of Subsequent Research," *Personality and Individual Differences* 103 (2016): 182–89.

55. Waidzunas, *The Straight Line*, 59–61.

56. Rachael I. Rosner, "Aaron T. Beck's Drawings and the Psychoanalytic Origin Story of Cognitive Therapy," *History of Psychology* 15, no. 1 (2012): 1–18. Just prior to his renunciation of psychoanalysis, Beck coauthored a paper on the causes of homosexuality and means of weakening its drive; Leon J. Paul and Aaron Beck, "Psychodynamics of Male Homosexuality," *International Journal of Psycho-Analysis* (1961): 43–48.

57. Michelle G. Craske, *Theories of Psychotherapy: Cognitive-Behavioral Therapy* (Washington, DC: American Psychological Association, 2010).

58. Tom Waidzunas and Steven Epstein, "'For Men Arousal Is Orientation': Bodily Truthing, Technosexual Scripts, and the Materialization of Sexualities through the Phallometric Test," *Social Studies of Science* 45, no. 2 (April 2015): 187–213.

59. M. P. Feldman and M. J. MacCulloch, *Homosexual Behaviour: Therapy and Assessment* (Oxford: Pergamon, 1971); Waidzunas, *The Straight Line*, 64–65.

60. RadioLab, "UnErased: Dr. Davison and the Gay Cure," November 21, 2018, https://www.wnycstudios.org/podcasts/radiolab/articles/unerased-davidson-gay-cure.

61. Irving Bieber et al., *Homosexuality: A Psychoanalytic Study of Male Homosexuals* (New York: Basic Books, 1962), 303.

62. Franz J. Kallmann, "Twin and Sibship Study of Overt Male Homosexuality," *American Journal of Human Genetics* 4, no. 2 (1952): 136–46.

63. Terry, *An American Obsession*, 365.

64. Charles Socarides, *The Overt Homosexual* (New York: Grune & Stratton, 1968).

65. Bayer, *Homosexuality and American Psychiatry*, 34–37.

66. American Psychiatric Association, *Diagnostic and Statistical Manual of Mental Disorders*, 2nd ed. (Washington, DC: American Psychiatric Press, 1968), 79; Waidzunas, *The Straight Line*, 59.

67. Evelyn Hooker, "A Preliminary Analysis of Group Behavior of Homosexuals," *Journal of Psychology* 42 (1956): 219; Evelyn Hooker, "The Adjustment of the Male Overt Homosexual," *Journal of Projective Techniques* 21 (1957): 18–31.

68. Shadia Kawa and James Giordano, "A Brief Historicity of the *Diagnostic and Statistical Manual of Mental Disorders*: Issues and Implications for the Future of Psychiatric Canon and Practice," *Philosophy, Ethics, and Humanities in Medicine* 7, no. 2 (2012): https://doi.org /10.1186/1747-5341-7-2.

69. Thomas S. Kuhn, *The Structure of Scientific Revolutions* (Chicago: University of Chicago Press, 1962).

70. Society for Individual Rights, "Annual Report," February 1966, collection 2011.075, box 1, folder 1, Society for Individual Rights (SIR) Records, ONE National Gay & Lesbian Archives, Los Angeles, CA.

71. Bayer, *Homosexuality and American Psychiatry*, 42.

72. National Association for Mental Health, "Statement on Homosexuality," 1970, collection 3465, John E. Fryer Papers, Historical Society of Pennsylvania, Philadelphia, PA.

73. Gay Liberation Front, Los Angeles, "To the National Association for Mental Health Re: Position Statement on Homosexuality and Mental Illness," n.d., collection 2012.031, box 1, folder 22, Gay Liberation Front LA, ONE National Gay & Lesbian Archives, Los Angeles, CA.

74. Chicago Gay Liberation Front, "A Leaflet for the American Medical Association," in *Out of the Closets*, ed. Kay and Young, 145–47.

75. Bayer, *Homosexuality and American Psychiatry*, 99; Tony DeRosa, "Off Dr. Feldman! (On Reconstituting as Psychologist's Convention with Gay:Power)," n.d., collection 2012.031, box 1, folder 19, Gay Liberation Front LA, ONE National Gay & Lesbian Archives, Los Angeles, CA.

76. Gary Alinder, "Gay Liberation Meets the Shrinks," in *Out of the Closets*, ed. Kay and Young, 141–45.

77. Alix Spiegel, "81 Words," *This American Life*, January 18, 2002, https://www.thisamerican life.org/radio-archives/episode/204/81-words.

78. Spiegel.

79. Bayer, *Homosexuality and American Psychiatry*, 40; Briana Last, "Is Racism a Disease?" *nonsite* 33 (2020), https://nonsite.org/is-racism-a-disease/.

80. Jack Drescher and Joseph P. Merlino, *American Psychiatry and Homosexuality: An Oral History* (Abingdon, UK: Taylor & Francis, 2012), xvii.

81. Drescher and Merlino, 104–9.

82. LGBT Issues Committee of the Group for the Advancement of Psychiatry, "The Declassification of Homosexuality by the American Psychiatric Association," Association of LGBTQ Psychiatrists, http://www.aglp.org/gap/1_history/#declassification.

83. Drescher and Merlino, *American Psychiatry and Homosexuality*, xvii.

84. Robert Stoller et al., "A Symposium: Should Homosexuality Be in the APA Nomenclature?" *American Journal of Psychiatry* 130, no. 11 (1973): 1207–16, https://doi.org/10.1176 /ajp.130.11.1207.

85. Ken Hausman, "Trailblazing Psychiatrist Leaves Legacy of Social Caring," *Psychiatric News*, June 3, 2011, https://psychnews.psychiatryonline.org/doi/10.1176/pn.46.11.psychnews_46 _11_3_2.

86. Stoller, "A Symposium."

87. Dorothy M. Bernstein, "The Broken Brain: The Biological Revolution in Psychiatry," *JAMA Psychiatry* 253, no. 12 (1985): 1798; Robert Spitzer, "The Story of Robert L. Spitzer's Paper, 'An Examination of Wilhelm Reich's Demonstrations of Orgone Energy,'" *Scientific Review of Mental Health Practice* 4, no. 1 (2005), https://www.srmhp.org/0401/spitzer.html.

88. Kawa and Giordano, "A Brief Historicity of the *Diagnostic and Statistical Manual of Mental Disorders*."

89. Geoff Watts, "Alfred Mordecai Freedman," *The Lancet*, May 28, 2011, https://www.thelancet.com/journals/lancet/article/PIIS0140-6736(11)60773-3/fulltext.

90. Jack Drescher, "Out of DSM: Depathologizing Homosexuality, *Behavioral Sciences* 5 (2015): 565–75, https://doi.org/10.3390/bs5040565.

91. Drescher, "Out of DSM."

92. Radiolab, "UnErased."

93. One would do well to avoid the allure of present hagiographic accounts of the AABT and declassification, which mostly absolve behaviorists of their complicity (and pin the blame wholly on psychoanalysis). Gregory Caruso, dir., *Conversion* (Bristol Pictures, 2022).

94. Caruso.

95. Marie-Amélie George, "Expressive Ends: Understanding Conversion Therapy Bans," *Alabama Law Review* 68, no. 3 (2017): 803.

96. David H. Barlow, Gene G. Abel, and Edward B. Blanchard, "Gender Identity Change in Transsexuals: Follow-Up and Replications," *Archives of General Psychiatry* 36, no. 9 (1979): 1001–7; Colleen Flaherty, "Beliefs Change," *Inside Higher Ed*, June 14, 2022, https://www.insidehighered .com/news/2022/06/14/conversion-therapy-apology-statement-raises-questions.

97. Herzog, *Cold War Freud*, 76.

98. Bayer, *Homosexuality and American Psychiatry*, 155.

99. Mary Bernstein, "Are the Courts the Way to Queer Rights?," *Boston Review*, May 9, 2022, https://bostonreview.net/articles/are-the-courts-the-way-to-queer-rights/.

100. Stoller, "A Symposium," 1207. Similarly, Davison noted how little evidence existed at the time that homosexuality might be hormonally or genetically determined; G. Terence Wilson and Gerald D. Davison, "Behavior Therapy and Homosexuality: A Critical Perspective," *Behavior Therapy* 5 (1974): 16–28.

Chapter Three

1. Theda Skocpol, *Diminished Democracy: From Membership to Management in American Civic Life* (Norman: University of Oklahoma Press, 2003); Dara Strolovitch, *Affirmative Advocacy: Race, Class, and Gender in Interest Group Politics* (Chicago: University of Chicago Press, 2007); Jacob S. Hacker and Paul Pierson, *Winner-Take-All Politics: How Washington Made the Rich Richer—and Turned Its Back on the Middle Class* (New York: Simon & Schuster, 2010); Lillian Faderman, *The Gay Revolution: The Story of the Struggle* (New York: Simon & Schuster, 2015), 252.

2. Kim Phillips-Fein, *Invisible Hands: The Businessmen's Crusade against the New Deal* (New York: Basic Books, 2010), 219; Daniel K. Williams, *God's Own Party: The Making of the Religious Right* (New York: Oxford University Press, 20211), 170–76; Daniel Schlozman, *When Movements Anchor Parties: Electoral Alignments in American History* (Princeton, NJ: Princeton University Press, 2015), 202–12.

3. Clifford J. Rosky, "Fear of the Queer Child," *Buffalo Law Review* 61, no. 3 (2013); Judith Levine, "Father Knows Best," *Boston Review*, April 5, 2022, https://bostonreview.net/articles /dont-say-gay-laws-dont-care-about-kids/; Marie-Amélie George, *American Law and the Rise of the Gay Family* (New York: Cambridge University Press, forthcoming).

4. Theodosius Dobzhansky, *Mankind Evolving: The Evolution of the Human Species* (New Haven, CT: Yale University Press, 1962), 23.

5. John D'Emilio, "Organizational Tales: Interpreting the NGLTF Story," in *The World Turned: Essays on Gay History, Politics, and Culture* (Durham, NC: Duke University Press, 2002), 99–199.

6. Dennis Altman, *Homosexual: Oppression and Liberation*, 2nd ed. (New York: New York University Press, 1993); Democratic Party, "1980 Democratic Party Platform," August 11, 1980, The American Presidency Project, https://www.presidency.ucsb.edu/documents/1980-democratic -party-platform.

7. "Dr. Howard J. Brown, 50, Dies: First City Health Services Chief," *New York Times*, February 3, 1975, http://www.nytimes.com/1975/02/03/archives/dr-howard-j-brown-50-dies-first -city-health-services-chief-lindsay.html.

8. Ronald Gold, "Speech at the Third Anniversary Celebration of the Gay Activist Alliance of New Jersey," September 27, 1974, Gebhard Era Correspondence, 1970–1979, part 2: A–Z, file cabinet 5, drawer 1, National Gay Task Force (Bruce Voeller, Executive Director), Kinsey Institute for Research in Sex, Gender, and Reproduction, Bloomington, IN.

9. Gold, "Speech at the Third Anniversary Celebration of the Gay Activist Alliance of New Jersey."

10. Bruce Voeller, "NGTF: Our Past and Future," *It's Time: Newsletter of the National Gay Task Force Special Bonus Issue*, n.d., collection MC#001, box 1127, folder 31, subgroup 2, Legal Case Files Series, American Civil Liberties Union Records, Seeley G. Mudd Manuscript Library at Princeton University, Princeton, NJ.

11. Paul Gebhard letter to Ronald Gold, February 21, 1977, Gebhard Era Correspondence, 1970–1979, part 2: A–Z, file cabinet 5, drawer 1, National Gay Task Force (Bruce Voeller, Executive Director), Kinsey Institute for Research in Sex, Gender, and Reproduction, Bloomington, IN; Paul Gebhard letter to the National Gay Task Force, "Memorandum on the Incidence of Homosexuality in the United States," March 18, 1977, and Paul Gebhard letter to National Gay Task Force, June 29, 1977, collection 7301, box 166, folder 39, National Gay and Lesbian Task Force Records, 1973–2917, Division of Rare and Manuscript Collections, Cornell University Library, Ithaca, NY.

12. Scott de Orio, "The Creation of the Modern Sex Offender," in *The War on Sex*, ed. David M. Halperin and Trevor Hoppe (Durham, NC: Duke University Press, 2017), 247–67.

13. Paul Gebhard letter to Bruce Voeller, October 27, 1977, Gebhard Era Correspondence, 1970–1979, part 2: A–Z, file cabinet 5, drawer 1, National Gay Task Force (Bruce Voeller, Executive Director), Kinsey Institute for Research in Sex, Gender, and Reproduction, Bloomington, IN. For recent and classic statements on queer theory and the figure of the child, see Lee Edelman, *No Future: Queer Theory and the Death Drive* (Durham, NC: Duke University Press, 2004); Steven Angelides, *The Fear of Child Sexuality: Young People, Sex, and Agency* (Chicago: University of Chicago Press, 2019).

14. Gebhard to Voeller, October 27, 1977.

15. Parents of Gays, Newsletter, November 8, 1976, collection 1857, box 1, folder 2, Jeanne Manford Papers, 1972–1995, New York Public Library Archives & Manuscripts, New York, NY.

16. PFLAG, "Our Story," https://www.pflag.org/our-story.

17. Didi Herman, *The Antigay Agenda: Orthodox Vision and the Christian Right* (Chicago: University of Chicago Press, 1997); Tina Fetner, *How the Religious Right Shaped Lesbian and Gay Activism* (Minneapolis: University of Minnesota Press, 2008).

18. Heather Murray, *Not in This Family: Gays and the Meaning of Kinship in Postwar North America* (Philadelphia: University of Pennsylvania Press, 2010), 114.

19. Lauren Berlant, *The Queen of America Goes to Washington City: Essays on Sex and Citizenship* (Durham, NC: Duke University Press, 1997); Judith Stein, *Running Steel, Running America: Race, Economic Policy and the Decline of Liberalism* (Durham: University of North Carolina Press, 1998), 87; Judith Stein, *Pivotal Decade: How the United States Traded Factories for Finance in the Seventies* (New Haven, CT: Yale University Press, 2010).

20. Melinda Cooper, *Family Values: Between Neoliberalism and the New Social Conservatism* (New York: Zone Books, 2017).

21. Roger Lancaster, *The Trouble with Nature: Sex in Science and Pop Culture* (Berkeley: University of California Press, 2003), 338.

22. Rosemary Hennessy, *Profit and Pleasure: Sexual Identities in Late Capitalism*, 2nd ed. (New York: Routledge, 2017).

23. Those accounts that depict the concurrent rise of neoliberalism and the nuclear family's renaissance often run the risk of telling such tales in too neatly functionalist of terms (after all, from today's vantage it is not clear at all that neoliberalism *needs* traditional gender and social roles despite the late-twentieth-century disquiet). Nevertheless, this moment undoubtedly witnessed a shift in responsibility away from the social and—to paraphrase Margaret Thatcher—onto the backs of individuals and their families. Douglas Keay, "Interview with Margaret Thatcher," *Woman's Own*, September 23, 1987, available at https://www.margaretthatcher.org/document/106689.

24. Parents of Gays, "Parents of Gays Speak Out," March 13, 1975, collection 1857, box 1, folder 1, Jeanne Manford Papers, 1972–1995, New York Public Library Archives & Manuscripts, New York, NY.

25. Jean Smith letter to *Newsweek*, June 1, 1977, collection 1857, box 1, folder 3, Jeanne Manford Papers, 1972–1995, New York Public Library Archives & Manuscripts, New York, NY. There are parallels here with feminist demands for reproductive rights that might ameliorate the societal costs of a high birth rate: Jenny Brown, *Birth Strike: The Hidden Fight over Women's Work* (Oakland, CA: PM Press, 2019).

26. Barbara Ehrenreich, *Fear of Falling: The Inner Life of the Middle Class* (New York: Pantheon, 1989).

27. Martin Meeker, "Behind the Mask of Respectability: Reconsidering the Mattachine Society and Male Homophile Practice, 1950s and 1960s," *Journal of the History of Sexuality* 10, no. 1 (January 2001): 78–116.

28. John D'Emilio, *Sexual Politics, Sexual Communities: The Making of a Homosexual Minority in the United States, 1940–1970*, 2nd ed. (Chicago: University of Chicago Press, 1998).

29. Society for Individual Rights, "Annual Report," February 1966, collection 2011.075, box 1, folder 1, Society for Individual Rights (SIR) Records, ONE National Gay & Lesbian Archives, Los Angeles, CA.

30. Elizabeth A. Armstrong, *Forging Gay Identities: Organizing Sexuality in San Francisco, 1950–1994* (Berkeley: University of California Press, 2002), 114.

31. California Voters Pamphlet, General Election, November 7, 1978, https://web.archive .org/web/20060818145437/http://library.uchastings.edu/ballot_pdf/1978g.pdf.

32. National Gay Task Force, *Answers to a Parent's Questions about Homosexuality*, est. 1979, collection 1857, box 1, folder 4, Jeanne Manford Papers, 1972–1995, New York Public Library Archives & Manuscripts, New York, NY.

33. Jean Smith letter to Dan Rather, May 17, 1977, collection 1857, box 1, folder 3, Jeanne Manford Papers, 1972–1995, New York Public Library Archives & Manuscripts, New York, NY.

34. Roger N. Lancaster, *Sex Panic and the Punitive State* (Berkeley: University of California Press 2011), 42–43.

35. Carl Wittman, "Refugees from Amerika: A Gay Manifesto," in *Out of the Closets: Voices of Gay Liberation*, Twentieth Anniversary ed., ed. Karla Kay and Allen Young (New York: New York University Press, 1992), 338.

36. Donn Teal, *The Gay Militants: How Gay Liberation Began in America, 1969–1971* (New York: St. Martin's Press, 1995), 281–82.

37. David Thorstad, "Man/Boy Love and the American Gay Movement," *Journal of Homosexuality* 20, nos. 1–2 (1991): 251–74.

38. Thorstad, 251–52.

39. Duddly Clendinen, "Group Promoting Man-Boy Love Is the Focus of Police Inquiry," *New York Times*, January 1, 1983, http://www.nytimes.com/1983/01/01/us/group-promoting-man -boy-love-is-the-focus-of-police-inquiry.html; Thorstad, "Man/Boy Love," 252.

40. Thorstad, "Man/Boy Love," 253–54.

41. Elazar Barkan, *The Retreat of Scientific Racism: Changing Concepts of Race in Britain and the United States between the World Wars* (New York: Cambridge University Press, 1992); Daniel J. Kevles, *In the Name of Eugenics: Genetics and the Uses of Human Heredity* (Cambridge, MA: Harvard University Press, 1995); Jay Hatheway, *Gilded Age Construction of Homophobia* (New York: Palgrave Macmillan, 2003), 122.

42. Kenneth S. Kendler, "From Many to One to Many: The Search for Causes of Psychiatric Illness," *Journal of the American Medical Association Psychiatry*, June 19, 2019, https://doi .org/10.1001/jamapsychiatry.2019.1200.

43. Sarah S. Richardson, *Sex Itself: The Search for Male and Female in the Human Genome* (Chicago: University of Chicago Press, 2013).

44. Soraya de Chadarevian, *Designs for Life: Molecular Biology after World War II* (New York: Cambridge University Press, 2002), 132, 256.

45. Raymond LePage and Caroline Albert, "Fifty Years of Development in the Endocrinology Laboratory," *Clinical Biochemistry* 39, no. 5 (May 2006): 542–57; Kaushik Sunder Rajan, *Biocapital: The Constitution of Postgenomic Life* (Durham, NC: Duke University Press, 2006); Melinda Cooper, *Life as Surplus: Biotechnology and Capitalism in the Neoliberal Era* (Seattle: University of Washington Press, 2008).

46. Sheldon Krimsky, *Biotechnics and Society: The Rise of Industrial Genetics* (Westport, CT: Greenwood Press, 1991), 61–68; Toby A. Appel, *Shaping Biology: The National Science Foundation and American Biological Research, 1945–1975* (Baltimore: Johns Hopkins University Press, 2000), 7; Rajan, *Biocapital*, 5–6.

47. *Diamond v. Chakrabarty*, 447 U.S. 303 (1980); Chadarevian, *Designs for Life*, 353.

48. Vernon A. Rosario, "An Interview with Judd Marmor, MD," *Journal of Gay & Lesbian Psychotherapy* 7, no. 4 (2003): 23–34.

49. Judd Marmor, ed., *Sexual Inversion: The Multiple Roots of Homosexuality* (New York: Basic Books, 1965).

50. Marmor, 5.

51. Jessica Resnick, "Franz Josef Kallmann (1897–1965)," *The Embryo Project Encyclopedia*, April 6, 2017, https://embryo.asu.edu/pages/franz-josef-kallmann-1897-1965 (Accessed May 12, 2020).

52. Marmor, *Sexual Inversion*, 6; Franz J. Kallmann, "Twin and Sibship Study of Overt Male Homosexuality," *American Journal of Human Genetics* 4, no. 2 (1952): 136–46.

53. Kallman, "Twin and Sibship Study," 145.

54. Marmor, *Sexual Inversion*, 7–9; Dobzhansky, *Mankind Evolving*, 122–23.

55. Judd Marmor, ed., *Homosexual Behavior: A Modern Reappraisal* (New York: Basic Books, 1980), xi, 8.

56. Rosario, "An Interview with Judd Marmor," 28.

57. Judd Marmor, "Homosexuality: Nature or Nurture," *Harvard Medical School Mental Health Letter*, October 1985, 5–6, collection 2007.009, box 1, folder 5, Judd Marmor Papers, ONE National Gay & Lesbian Archives, Los Angeles, CA.

58. Marmor, 5–6.

59. Richard C. Friedman, *Male Homosexuality: A Contemporary Psychoanalytic Perspective* (New Haven, CT: Yale University Press, 1988), 11–12, 27.

60. Richard A. Isay, *Being Homosexual: Gay Men and Their Development*, rev. ed. (New York: Vintage, 2009), 14–15.

61. Charles Socarides, *Homosexuality* (Lanham, MD: J. Aronson, 1978).

62. Alan P. Bell, Martin S. Weinberg, and Sue K. Hammersmith, *Sexual Preference: Its Development in Men and Women* (Bloomington: Indiana University Press, 1981).

63. Indiana University Press, "Conclusions from Kinsey Study on Sexual Preference," *Indiana University Press Book News*, October 12, 1981, 2, collection 7301, box 166, folder 62, National Gay and Lesbian Task Force Records, 1973–2017, Division of Rare and Manuscript Collections, Cornell University Library, Ithaca, NY.

64. Indiana University Press, "New Kinsey Study Challenges Myths about Sexual Orientation," *Indiana University Press Book News*, October 12, 1981, 2, collection 7301, box 166, folder 62, National Gay and Lesbian Task Force Records, 1973–2017, Division of Rare and Manuscript Collections, Cornell University Library, Ithaca, NY.

65. Anne Fausto-Sterling, "Gender/Sex, Sexual Orientation, and Identity Are in the Body: How Did They Get There?" *Journal of Sex Research* 56, nos. 4–5 (2019): 547.

66. "Report to Psychologists: Panel Says Gays Still Face Bias," *San Francisco Chronicle*, August 25, 1981, collection 7301, box 153, folder 21, National Gay and Lesbian Task Force Records, 1973–2017, Division of Rare and Manuscript Collections, Cornell University Library, Ithaca, NY.

67. C. A. Tripp, "Review of *Sexual Preference: Its Development in Men and Women*," *Journal of Sex Research* 18, no. 2 (1982): 183–86.

68. Carmel McCoubrey, "Alan P. Bell, 70, Researcher of Influences on Homosexuality," *New York Times*, May 24, 2002, https://www.nytimes.com/2002/05/24/us/alan-p-bell-70-researcher-of-influences-on-homosexuality.html.

69. Richardson, *Sex Itself*.

70. Jennifer Terry, *An American Obsession: Science, Medicine, and Homosexuality in Modern Science* (Chicago: University of Chicago Press, 1999), 159; Bernice L. Hausman, *Changing Sex: Transsexualism, Technology, and the Idea of Gender* (Durham, NC: Duke University Press, 1995), 27–29.

71. Günter Dörner, *Hormones and Brain Differentiation* (Amsterdam: Elsevier Scientific Publishing, 1976); Günter Dörner, "Letter to the Editor," *Archives of Sexual Behavior* 12, no. 6

(1983). Dörner's studies were shaped by the politics of gay liberation in his home country of East Germany. There, Dörner was embroiled in controversy over whether he had intended to categorize homosexuality as a disability that might be prevented via in utero intervention. While chastised by the German Society for Sex Research for the allegedly inegalitarian implications of his research, Dörner assisted a number of Federal Republic of Germany lawyers who requested biological evidence to help exonerate their clients who had been charged with sodomy prior to the 1968 reforms that struck such prohibitions from the books. Thus, in East Germany as well as the United States, the science of sexology was influenced and textured by political and legal developments and incentives. For more on East Germany and gay liberation, see Samuel Clowes Huneke, *States of Liberation: Gay Men between Dictatorship and Democracy in Cold War Germany* (Toronto: University of Toronto Press, 2022).

72. Bell, Weinberg, and Hammersmith, *Sexual Preference*, 230.

73. Brian Gladue, Richard Green, and Ronald Hellman, "Neuroendocrine Response to Estrogen and Sexual Orientation," *Science* 225, no. 4669 (1984): 1496–99.

74. Virginia M. Apuzzo, "Statement on SUNY Study on Hormones," 1984, collection 7301, box 188, folder 63, National Gay and Lesbian Task Force Records, 1973–2017, Division of Rare and Manuscript Collections, Cornell University Library, Ithaca, NY.

75. Gladue, Green, and Hellman, "Neuroendocrine Response to Estrogen and Sexual Orientation."

76. See also N. McConaghy and A. Blaszczynski, "A Pair of Monozygotic Twins Discordant or Homosexuality: Sex-Dimorphic Behavior and Penile Volume Responses," *Archives of Sexual Behavior* 9, no. 123 (1980): 129–30.

77. Marshall D. Sahlins, *The Use and Abuse of Biology: An Anthropological Critique of Sociobiology* (Ann Arbor: University of Michigan Press, 1976).

78. E. O. Wilson, *Sociobiology: The New Synthesis* (Cambridge, MA: Harvard University Press, 1975).

79. Richard C. Lewontin, *Biology as Ideology: The Doctrine of DNA* (New York: HarperCollins, 1993), 88–90; Lancaster, *The Trouble with Nature*, 92.

80. Wilson, *Sociobiology*, 22. Donna Haraway penned the definitive takedown of Wilson's and others' uncritical adoption of these primate studies, which themselves were conducted and theorized from an unduly anthropomorphic vantage point. Donna Haraway, *Primate Visions: Gender, Race, and Nature in the World of Modern Science* (New York: Routledge, 1989).

81. Wilson, *Sociobiology*, 22.

82. Lucy Cooke, *The Truth about Animals: Stoned Sloths, Lovelorn Hippos, and Other Tales from the Wild Side of Wildlife* (New York: Basic Books, 2018).

83. E. O. Wilson, *On Human Nature, with a New Preface* (Cambridge, MA: Harvard University Press, 2004), 144. Though Wilson wrote of a "potential for bisexuality in the brain," his ultimate concerns were the twin phenomena of "full homosexuality" and "full heterosexuality."

84. Wilson, 145. Wilson associated homosexuality with the evolutionary character of altruism in human societies: "There is, I wish to suggest, a strong possibility that homosexuality is normal in a biological sense, that it is a distinctive beneficent behavior that evolved as an important element of early human social organization. Homosexuals may be the genetic carriers of some of mankind's rare altruistic impulses" (143).

85. Aaron Panofsky, *Misbehaving Science: Controversy and the Development of Behavior Genetics* (Chicago: University of Chicago, 2014), 139–41.

86. Wilson, *On Human Nature*, 145; Panofsky, *Misbehaving Science*, 147.

87. Richard C. Pillard and James D. Weinrich, "Evidence of Familial Nature of Male Homosexuality," *Archives of General Psychiatry* 4, no. 8 (1986): 808–12, https://doi.org/10.1001/archpsyc.1986.01800080094012.

88. Pillard and Weinrich, 808.

89. Marie-Amélie George, "The Custody Crucible: The Development of Scientific Authority about Gay and Lesbian Parents," *Law and History Review* 34, no. 2 (May 2016): 487–529; Gay Rights National Lobby, "If Your Constituents Ask . . ." (1980), collection 7712, box 30, folder 46, Human Rights Campaign Records, 1975–2015, Division of Rare and Manuscript Collections, Cornell University Library, Ithaca, NY.

90. National Gay Task Force, *Answers to a Parent's Questions about Homosexuality*, est. 1979, collection 1857, box 2, folder 10, Jeanne Manford Papers, 1972–1995, New York Public Library Archives & Manuscripts, New York, NY.

91. National Gay Task Force, *Answers to a Parent's Questions*.

92. National Gay Task Force, *Twenty Questions about Homosexuality*, est. 1979, 2, collection 1857, box 2, folder 12, Jeanne Manford Papers, 1972–1995, New York Public Library Archives & Manuscripts, New York, NY.

93. George, "The Custody Crucible."

94. Barbara Gittings to Susan Wallace, RN, March 31, 1977, collection 6397, box 73, folder 13, Barbara Gittings and Kay Tobin Lahusen Gay History Papers and Photographs, 1855–2009, New York Public Library Archives & Manuscripts, New York, NY.

95. Murray, *Not in This Family*, 118–19.

96. Adele Starr letter to Henry Gammill, April 27, 1977, collection 1857, box 1, folder 3, Jeanne Manford Papers, 1972–1995, New York Public Library Archives & Manuscripts, New York, NY.

97. Starr to Gammill, April 27, 1977.

98. Lawrence Starr letter to Jack Kilpatrick, June 6, 1977, collection 1857, box 1, folder 3, Jeanne Manford Papers, 1972–1995, New York Public Library Archives & Manuscripts, New York, NY.

99. Jean Smith letter to Ann Landers, September 8, 1977, collection 1857, box 1, folder 3, Jeanne Manford Papers, 1972–1995, New York Public Library Archives & Manuscripts, New York, NY.

100. PFLAG, "Our Story."

101. Murray, *Not in This Family*, 119.

102. Evelyn Hooker, "Facts and Misconceptions about Homosexuality," 1984, collection 7616, box 8, folder 84-LBI, Parents, Families and Friends of Lesbians and Gays (PFLAG) Records, Division of Rare and Manuscript Collections, Cornell University Library, Ithaca, NY.

103. Martin Weinberg, "Development of Sexual Orientation," 1986, collection 7616, box 9, folder 86-S, Parents, Families and Friends of Lesbians and Gays (PFLAG) Records, Division of Rare and Manuscript Collections, Cornell University Library, Ithaca, NY.

104. June Reinisch, "Biological Factors in Psychosexual Development," 1987, collection 7616, box 9, folder 87-27, Parents, Families and Friends of Lesbians and Gays (PFLAG) Records, Division of Rare and Manuscript Collections, Cornell University Library, Ithaca, NY; Giovanni Breu, "As Did Kinsey, June Reinisch Takes the Plain Brown Wrapper Off the Study of Sex," *People*, December 3, 1984, http://people.com/archive/as-did-kinsey-june-reinisch-takes-the-plain-brown-wrapper-off-the-study-of-sex-vol-22-no-23/.

105. June Reinisch et al., "Sex Differences Emerge during the First Year of Life," in *Women, Men, and Gender: Ongoing Debates*, ed. Mary Roth Walsh (New Haven, CT: Yale University

Press, 1997), 37–43; Linda L. Carli, "No, Biology Does Not Create Gender Differences in Personality," in *Women, Men, and Gender,* ed. Walsh, 44–54.

106. Breu, "As Did Kinsey."

107. PFLAG, *Why Is My Child Gay?* (1988), 1, collection 7616, box 17, folder 28, Parents, Families and Friends of Lesbians and Gays (PFLAG) Records, Division of Rare and Manuscript Collections, Cornell University Library, Ithaca, NY.

108. Gilbert Herdt, *The Sambia: Ritual and Gender in New Guinea* (San Diego, CA: Harcourt Brace Jovanovich, 1987).

109. PFLAG, *Why Is My Child Gay?*

110. PFLAG, 6; The other two questions posed to the researchers had more to do with reparative therapy than etiology specifically.

111. PFLAG, 9. Weinberg's full response to the question was simply: "My guess: Biological factors for homosexuality and heterosexuality; conditioning for various degrees of bisexuality."

112. PFLAG, 6.

113. PFLAG, 1.

114. Lewontin, *Biology as Ideology*, 15.

115. Lewontin, 93.

116. Herbert Marcuse, *An Essay on Liberation* (Boston: Beacon Press, 1971); Dennis Altman, *The Homosexualization of America: The Americanization of the Homosexual* (New York: St. Martin's Press, 1982); Steven Epstein, "Gay Politics, Ethnic Identity: The Limits of Social Construction," *Social Review* 93–94 (May–August 1987): 9–54.

117. Richard Lewontin, *It Ain't Necessarily So: The Dream of the Human Genome and Other Illusions,* 2nd ed. (New York: New York Review Books, 2001); Susan McKinnon, *Neo-Liberal Genetics: The Myths and Moral Tales of Evolutionary Psychology* (Chicago: Prickly Paradigm Press, 2005).

Chapter Four

1. *Frontiero v. Richardson*, 411 U.S. 677 (1973); *Reed v. Reed*, 404 U.S. 71 (1971).

2. *Frontiero v. Richardson*, 686.

3. Paisley Currah, "Searching for Immutability: Homosexuality, Race and Rights Discourse," in *A Simple Matter of Justice?: Theorizing Lesbian and Gay Politics*, ed. Angelia R. Wilson (London: Cassell, 1995), 51–90; Jennifer Terry, *An American Obsession: Science, Medicine, and Homosexuality in Modern Society* (Chicago: University of Chicago Press, 1999), 393–94; Edward Stein, "Immutability and Innateness Arguments about Lesbian, Gay, and Bisexual Rights," *Chicago Kent Law Review* 89, no. 597 (2014): 597–640; Lisa M. Diamond and Clifford J. Rosky, "Scrutinizing Immutability: Research on Sexual Orientation and U.S. Legal Advocacy for Sexual Minorities," *Journal of Sex Research* 53, nos. 4–5 (2016): 363–91; Mary Ziegler, "Perceiving Orientation: Defining Sexuality after Obergefell," *Duke Journal of Gender Law and Policy* 23, no. 2 (2016): 233.

4. Society of Individual Rights of Ohio Inc., "Amicus Brief for SIR of Ohio Inc. in *Jones and Knight v. James Hallahan*," 1970, collection 2011.075, box 1, folder 7, Society for Individual Rights (SIR) Records, ONE National Gay & Lesbian Archives, Los Angeles, CA.

5. Carlos A. Ball, *Same-Sex Marriage and Children: A Tale of History, Social Science, and Law* (New York: Oxford University Press, 2014); Marie-Amélie George, *American Law and the Rise of the Gay Family* (New York: Cambridge University Press, forthcoming).

6. National Gay Task Force, "Expert Testimony in Child Custody Cases," 1979, collection 7301, box 153, folder 17, National Gay and Lesbian Task Force Records, 1973–2000, Division of Rare and Manuscript Collections, Cornell University Library, Ithaca, NY.

7. Marie-Amélie George, "The Custody Crucible: The Development of Scientific Authority about Gay and Lesbian Parents," *Law and History Review* 34, no. 2 (May 2016): 487–529.

8. *Joseph Acanfora v. Board of Education of Montgomery County* No. 72-1136-Y (D. Md.), 359 F. Supp. 843 (1973). Similar cases like one pursued by the ACLU also featured experts in child psychiatry. In these early years, psychiatrists themselves were often still indebted to a paradigm that emphasized homosexuality as an aberration and something that could be correctly oriented toward heterosexuality. See, for example, the statement of one expert witness in the *Gaylord* case who explained that "homosexuality is acquired, not inherited, and that, while a student's sexual orientation was probably fixed by the time he got to high school, he still had a choice as to his behavior." *Gaylord v. Tacoma School District* 85 Wn.2d 348 (1975) 535 P.2d 80.

9. Jackie Blount, *Fit to Teach: Same-Sex Desire, Gender, and School Work in the Twentieth Century* (Albany: State University of New York Press. 2004), 117. The National Education Association also provided Acanfora with legal funding. Additionally, the Washington GAA worked outside the courts in successfully pushing the District of Columbia Board of Education to ban discrimination against employees for their sexual orientations.

10. "Testimony of Doctor Felix P. Heald," *Acanfora v. Board of Education*, The Case of Joe Acanfora, April 13, 1973, http://www.joeacanfora.com/subpages/legalcases/testimony_heald.html.

11. "Testimony of Doctor Reginald Spencer Lourie," *Acanfora v. Board of Education*, The Case of Joe Acanfora, April 13, 1973, http://www.joeacanfora.com/subpages/legalcases/testimony_lourie.html.

12. *Joseph Acanfora v. Board of Education of Montgomery County.*

13. John Money, "Hermaphroditism, Gender, and Precocity in Hyperadrenocorticism: Psychologic Findings," *Bulletin of the Johns Hopkins Hospital* 96, no. 3 (1955): 253–63; John Money, J. G. Hampson, and J. L. Hampson, "An Examination of Some Basic Sexual Concepts: The Evidence of Human Hermaphroditism," *Bulletin of the Johns Hopkins Hospital* 97, no. 4 (1955): 301–19.

14. "Testimony of Doctor John William Money," *Acanfora v. Board of Education*, The Case of Joe Acanfora, April 16, 1973, http://www.joeacanfora.com/subpages/legalcases/testimony_money .html; John Money and Anke Ehrhardt, *Man & Woman, Boy & Girl: The Differentiation and Dimorphism of Gender Identity from Conception to Maturity* (Baltimore: Johns Hopkins University Press, 1972).

15. Bernice L. Hausman, *Changing Sex: Transsexualism, Technology, and the Idea of Gender* (Durham, NC: Duke University Press, 1995), 79, 94–98; Suzanne Kessler, "The Medical Construction of Gender: Case Management of Intersexed Infants," *Signs* 16, no. 1 (1990): 3–26.

16. Money also thought that an effeminate young boy could be reoriented with therapy to present as less feminine; however, this did not necessarily alter his inner sense of being, which could manifest in transsexuality or homosexuality.

17. "Testimony of Doctor John William Money."

18. "Testimony of Doctor William Stayton," *Acanfora v. Board of Education*, The Case of Joe Acanfora (April 14, 1973), http://www.joeacanfora.com/subpages/legalcases/testimony_stayton .html.

19. "Testimony of John William Money."

20. *Joseph Acanfora v. Board of Education of Montgomery County.*

NOTES TO PAGES 96–100

21. *Joseph Acanfora v. Board of Education of Montgomery County* (quoting from *Frontiero* 4612).

22. *Joseph Acanfora v. Board of Education of Montgomery County* (applying *Reed v. Reed*); *Romer v. Evans*, 517 U.S. 620 (1996).

23. *Rowland v. Mad River Local School District*, 730 F.2d 444 (6th Cir. 1984), cert. denied, 470 U.S. 1009 (1985).

24. Ellen Andersen, *Out of the Closets and into the Courts: Legal Opportunity Structure and Gay Rights Litigation* (Ann Arbor: University of Michigan Press, 2005), 66–70. The ACLU would come to reverse its position that sodomy bans were constitutionally permissible in 1967.

25. Marie-Amélie George, "The Harmless Psychopath: Legal Debates Promoting the Decriminalization of Sodomy in the United States," *Journal of the History of Sexuality* 24, no. 2 (2015): 225–61.

26. Jon J. Gallo et al., "The Consenting Homosexual and the Law: An Empirical Study of Enforcement and Administration in Los Angeles County," *UCLA Law Review* 13, no. 3 (March 1966): 644–832.

27. Ziegler, "Perceiving Orientation," 324.

28. *Doe v. Commonwealth's Attorney of Richmond*, 425 U.S. 901 (1976).

29. *Enslin v. North Carolina*, 425 U.S. 903 (1976), denying cert. to 25 N.C. App. 662, 214 S.E.2d 318 (1975).

30. *Enslin* Brief for Appellant before the Fourth Circuit (May 6, 1977), 4–5.

31. W. Cecil Jones, "*Doe v. Commonwealth's Attorney*: Closing the Door to a Fundamental Right of Sexual Privacy," *Denver Law Journal* 53 (1976): 553–76. Dr. Frank Kameny of the Task Force served as the only expert witness in *Doe*. Order issued by Dupree in response to petitioner's habeas petition, No. 76-0149-HC *Eugene Enslin v. Darryl Wallford, etc.* (January 3, 1977).

32. *Enslin* Brief for Appellant before the Fourth Circuit (May 6, 1977), 6–8.

33. *Enslin* Brief, 6–8.

34. *Enslin* Brief, 64.

35. *Enslin* Brief, 64.

36. *Enslin* Brief, 52, 54.

37. *Baker v. Wade*, 553 F. Supp. 1121 (N.D. Tx. 1982).

38. *Baker v. Wade* (1982).

39. James C. Barber, letter to Judd Marmor, October 6, 1980, collection 2007.009, box 2, folder 1, Judd Marmor Papers, ONE National Gay & Lesbian Archives, Los Angeles, CA.

40. *Baker v. Wade* (1982). The plaintiffs also brought two other expert witnesses before the court. The first of these was theologian Victor Furnish, who argued that Christianity does not clearly condemn consensual same-sex conduct. The second was psychologist and Dallas school board member Dr. Harryette Ehrhardt.

41. *Baker v. Wade* (1982).

42. Judd Marmor, ed., *Homosexual Behavior: A Modern Reappraisal* (New York: Basic Books, 1980), xi.

43. Testimony of Judd Marmor in *Baker v. Wade*, June 15, 1981, collection 2007.009, box 2, folder 1, Judd Marmor Papers, ONE National Gay & Lesbian Archives, Los Angeles, CA.

44. Mike Anglin, "The 'Baker vs. Wade' Litigation," The Dallas Way, November 23, 2017, http://www.thedallasway.org/stories/written/2017/11/23/baker-vs-wade.

45. *Baker v. Wade* (1982), 1132.

46. Testimony of Paul Cameron in *Baker v. Wade*, November 1982, collection 2007.009, box 2, folder 3, Judd Marmor Papers, ONE National Gay & Lesbian Archives, Los Angeles, CA.

47. *Baker v. Wade* (1982), 1132.

48. *Baker v. Wade* (1982), 1140, 1143.

49. Chronology of *Baker v. Wade*, n.d., Donald F. Baker Collection (The Dallas Way), University of North Texas Libraries Special Collections, UNT Digital Library, https://digital.library.unt.edu/ark:/67531/metadc947630/m1/1/.

50. Lillian Faderman, *Gay Revolution: The Story of the Struggle* (New York: Simon & Schuster, 2015), 542.

51. Brief in Support of Motion to Set Aside Final Judgment and Reopen the Evidence, No. CA-3-79-1434-R filed by defendant Danny Hill in *Baker v. Wade* (April 25, 1983), collection 2007.009, box 2, folder 4, Judd Marmor Papers, ONE National Gay & Lesbian Archives, Los Angeles, CA.

52. Brief in Support of Motion to Set Aside Final Judgment and Reopen the Evidence, 12.

53. Brief in Support of Motion to Set Aside Final Judgment and Reopen the Evidence, 13–14; Harold Lief, "Sexual Survey #4: Current Thinking on Homosexuality," *Medical Aspects of Human Sexuality* 11 (1977): 1171–81.

54. Defendant's Reply to the Plaintiff's Brief in Opposition to Motion to Set Aside Final Judgment and Reopen the Evidence, and Brief in Support Thereof, No. CA-3-79-1434-R filed by defendant Danny Hill in *Baker v. Wade*, June 10, 1983, collection 2007.009, box 2, folder 7, Judd Marmor Papers, ONE National Gay & Lesbian Archives, Los Angeles, CA.

55. Judd Marmor Affidavit, July 5, 1983, collection 2007.009, box 2, folder 8, Judd Marmor Papers, ONE National Gay & Lesbian Archives, Los Angeles, CA.

56. *Baker v. Wade*, 743 F.2d 236 (5th Cir. 1984).

57. *Bowers v. Hardwick*, 760 F.2d 1202 (11th Cir. 1985).

58. William N. Eskridge Jr., *Dishonorable Passions: Sodomy Laws in America, 1861–2003* (New York: Viking, 2008).

59. Minutes of Lambda Legal Defense and Education Fund meeting, November 16, 1985, Donald F. Baker Collection (The Dallas Way), University of North Texas Special Collections, https://digital.library.unt.edu/ark:/67531/metadc947507/.

60. Minutes of Lambda Legal Defense and Education Fund meeting, December 13, 1985, Donald F. Baker Collection (The Dallas Way) (AR0843), University of North Texas Libraries Special Collections, UNT Digital Library, https://texashistory.unt.edu/ark:/67531/metadc947237/m1/.

61. Harris M. Miller II, "An Argument for the Application of Equal Protection Heightened Scrutiny to Classifications Based on Homosexuality," *Southern California Law Review* 57, no. 797 (1984): 797–836; Note, "The Constitutional Status of Sexual Orientation: Homosexuality as a Suspect -Classification," *Harvard Law Review* 98, no. 1303 (1985): 1285–309; Brief for *Baker*'s Writ for Certiorari to SCOTUS Laurence Tribe, Kathleen Sullivan, Brian Koukoutchos, and James C. Barber (1985), University of Pennsylvania Law Microfiche.

62. Currah, "Searching for Immutability," 57.

63. Brief of *Amici Curiae* Abby R. Rubenfeld, Legal Director, Evan Wolfson, Cooperating Attorney, Lambda Legal Defense and Education Fund, Inc., Gay and Lesbian Advocates and Defenders (GLAD), the Bar Association for Human Rights of Greater New York, the Massachusetts Lesbian and Gay Bar Association, and the Gay & Lesbian Alliance Against Defamation, Inc., No. 85-140 in *Bowers v. Hardwick* (January 31, 1986) (Westlaw).

64. Eskridge, *Dishonorable Passions*, 269, 276–77.

65. *Lawrence v. Texas*, 539 U.S. 558 (2003).

Chapter Five

1. Dean H. Hamer et al., "A Linkage between DNA Markers on the X Chromosome and Male Sexual Orientation," *Science* 261, no. 5119 (July 16, 1993): 321–27.

2. Simon LeVay, "A Difference in Hypothalamic Structure between Heterosexual and Homosexual Men," *Science* 253, no. 5023 (August 30, 1991): 1034–37.

3. Richard Lewontin, *It Ain't Necessarily So: The Dream of the Human Genome and Other Illusions*, 2nd ed. (New York: New York Review of Books, 2001).

4. Judd Marmor, ed., *Sexual Inversion: The Multiple Roots of Homosexuality* (New York: Basic Books, 1965).

5. Peter Conrad and Susan Markens, "Constructing the 'Gay Gene' in the News: Skepticism in the US and British Press," *Health* 5, no. 3 (2001): 373–400; Sarah A. Wilcox, "Cultural Context and the Conventions of Science Journalism: Drama and Contradiction in Media Coverage of Biological Ideas about Sexuality," *Critical Studies in Media Communication* 20, no. 3 (September 2003): 225–47.

6. Alex Andreou, "Can We Please Stop Obsessing about Male Homosexuality?" *The Guardian*, February 14, 2014, https://www.theguardian.com/commentisfree/2014/feb/14/obsessing-about -male-homosexuality.

7. Deborah Franklin, "At the Root of the Erotic," *Washington Post*, January 1, 1995, https:// www.washingtonpost.com/archive/entertainment/books/1995/01/01/at-the-root-of-the-erotic /96cb7a6c-689a-4e39-85fb-859bef690fdb/.

8. Roger Lancaster, *The Trouble with Nature: Sex in Science and Pop Culture* (Berkeley: University of California Press, 2003), xi.

9. Dennis Altman, *The Homosexualization of America: The Americanization of the Homosexual* (New York: St. Martin's Press, 1982); Jeffrey Escoffier, *American Homo: Community and Perversity* (Berkeley: University of California Press, 1998); Lisa Duggan, "The New Homonormativity: The Sexual Politics of Neoliberalism," in *Materializing Democracy: Toward a Revitalized Cultural Politics*, ed. Russ Castronovo and Dana D. Nelson (Durham, NC: Duke University Press, 2002), 179.

10. While this representation was rooted in reality—there was indeed an emergent gay and lesbian demographic of this character—it was far from generalizable. A disproportionate number of gays and lesbians lived then, as they do now, in poverty. Williams Institute, "LGBT Poverty in the United States," October 2019, UCLA School of Law, https://williamsinstitute.law.ucla .edu/publications/lgbt-poverty-us/.

11. LeVay, "A Difference in Hypothalamic Structure between Heterosexual and Homosexual Men."

12. Anne Fausto-Sterling, "Review: The Brain and Sexual Behavior," *BioScience* 44, no. 2 (1994): 102–4; Lancaster, *The Trouble with Nature*, 242. As Roger Lancaster has observed, LeVay's research design was fundamentally flawed given that he had obtained his data from cadavers of men who had died from AIDS, a disease for which medical treatment can significantly impact brain structures. Anne Fausto-Sterling also criticized LeVay for selectively neglecting the similarities in cell clusters between the gay and straight male subjects.

13. LeVay, "A Difference in Hypothalamic Structure between Heterosexual and Homosexual Men," 1034.

14. Natalie Angier, "The Biology of What It Means to Be Gay: Will a New Scientific Study Further Homosexual Rights or Homophobia?" *New York Times*, September 1, 1991, E1.

15. Angier, E1.

16. National Gay and Lesbian Task Force, "Statement on Salk Institute Study on 'Biological Basis for Sexual Orientation,'" August 29, 1991, collection 7301, box 207, National Gay and Lesbian Task Force, 1973–2017, Division of Rare and Manuscript Collections, Cornell University Library, Ithaca, NY.

17. Lancaster, *The Trouble with Nature*, 242.

18. Ronald Bayer, *Homosexuality and American Psychiatry: The Politics of Diagnosis* (New York: Basic Books, 1981).

19. Erica Goode, "On Gay Issue, Psychoanalysis Treats Itself," *New York Times*, December 12, 1998, B7, https://www.nytimes.com/1998/12/12/arts/on-gay-issue-psychoanalysis-treats-itself .html.

20. Michael Bailey and Richard Pillard, "A Genetic Study of Male Sexual Orientation," *Archives of General Psychiatry* 48, no. 12 (December 1991): 1089–96.

21. Aaron Panofsky, *Misbehaving Science: Controversy and the Development of Behavior Genetics* (Chicago: University of Chicago, 2014), 167–71.

22. Karen Freeman, "Lee Willerman, 57, Authority on Genes' Role in Intelligence," *New York Times*, January 31, 1997, https://www.nytimes.com/1997/01/31/us/lee-willerman-57-authority -on-genes-role-in-intelligence.html.

23. Paul E. Lynch, "An Interview with Richard C. Pillard, MD," in *American Psychiatry and Homosexuality: An Oral History*, ed. Jack Drescher and Joseph P. Merlino (Binghamton, NY: Harrington Park Press, 2007), 240.

24. Richard Pillard and Sherwood Rose, "Plasma Testosterone Levels in Homosexual Men," *Archives Sexual of Behavior* 3 no. 5 (1974): 453–58.

25. Richard C. Pillard and James D. Weinrich, "Evidence of Familial Nature of Male Homosexuality," *Archives of General Psychiatry* 4, no. 8 (1986): 808–12, https://doi.org/10.1001/arch psyc.1986.01800080094012.

26. Elijah Hubbard and Ruth Wald, *Exploding the Gene Myth* (Boston: Beacon Press, 1993), 97.

27. Miron Baron, "Genetic Linkage and Male Sexual Orientation," *British Medical Journal* 307, no. 6900 (August 7, 1993): 337–38.

28. Michael Bailey and Richard Pillard, "Are Some People Born Gay?," *New York Times*, December 17, 1991, available at https://www.cs.cmu.edu/afs/cs.cmu.edu/user/scotts/bulgarians /nature-nurture/bailey-pillard.html.

29. Associated Press, "Gay Men in Twin Study," *New York Times*, December 17, 1991, https:// www.nytimes.com/1991/12/17/science/gay-men-in-twin-study.html; Thomas H. Maugh II, "Science/Genetics and Homosexuality: Survey of Identical Twins Links Biological Factors with Being Gay," *Los Angeles Times*, December 15, 1991, https://www.latimes.com/archives/la-xpm -1991-12-15-mn-1023-story.html.

30. Jean Latz Griffin, "Twin Study Suggests Sex Preference Genetic," *Chicago Tribune*, December 16, 1991, http://www.chicagotribune.com/news/ct-xpm-1991-12-16-9104230051-story.html.

31. Griffin.

32. J. Michael Bailey et al., "Heritable Factors Influence Sexual Orientation in Women," *Archives of General Psychiatry* 50, no. 3 (1993): 217–23.

33. Natalie Angier, "Study Suggests Genes Sway Lesbians' Sexual Orientation," *New York Times*, March 12, 1993, A11.

34. Associated Press, "Link to Lesbianism Found," *New York Times*, March 3, 1998, https:// www.nytimes.com/1998/03/03/science/link-to-lesbianism-found.html.

35. Hamer et al., "A Linkage between DNA Markers on the X Chromosome and Male Sexual Orientation."

36. Edward Stein, *The Mismeasure of Desire: The Science, Theory, and Ethics of Sexual Orientation* (Oxford: Oxford University Press, 2001).

37. Dean Hamer and Peter Copeland, *The Science of Desire: The Search for the Gay Gene and the Biology of Behavior* (New York: Simon & Schuster, 1994), 19–20.

38. Hamer and Copeland, 27–31.

39. Hamer and Copeland, 48–49.

40. Hamer and Copeland, 48–49.

41. Hamer and Copeland, 19–20.

42. Hamer and Copeland, 22.

43. Hamer and Copeland, 210.

44. Dean Hamer, "Research Proposal: Biological Determinants of Sexual Orientation," May 28, 1991, collection 7301, box 127, folder 48, National Gay and Lesbian Task Force, 1973–2017, Division of Rare and Manuscript Collections, Cornell University Library, Ithaca, NY.

45. The other committee members were Reverend Jeanne Mackenzie of the Westminster Presbyterian Church and Judge Pauline Newman of the Court of Appeals of the Federal Circuit, the latter of whom was most likely asked to serve as an expert in patent law and biotechnologies.

46. Hamer, "Research Proposal."

47. Hamer and Copeland, *The Science of Desire*, 210.

48. Simon LeVay and Dean Hamer, "Evidence for a Biological Influence in Male Homosexuality," *Scientific American* 270, no. 5 (1994): 44–49.

49. Hamer and Copeland, *The Science of Desire*, 150–51.

50. Hamer and Copeland, 166–68.

51. "New Kinsey Study Challenges Myths about Sexual Orientation," *Indiana University Press Book News*, October 12, 1981, 2, collection 7301, box 166, folder 62, National Gay and Lesbian Task Force Records, 1973–2017, Division of Rare and Manuscript Collections, Cornell University Library, Ithaca, NY.

52. Chandler Burr, "Homosexuality and Biology," *Atlantic Monthly*, March 1993, 60.

53. Natalie Angier, "Study Links Brain to Transsexuality," *New York Times*, November 2, 1995, https://www.nytimes.com/1995/11/02/us/study-links-brain-to-transexuality.html.

54. Hamer and Copeland, *The Science of Desire*, 168–69.

55. Burr, "Homosexuality and Biology," 60, 62.

56. Lancaster, *The Trouble with Nature*, 240–42; Simon LeVay, *The Sexual Brain* (Cambridge, MA: MIT Press, 1993), 131–35.

57. Lancaster, *The Trouble with Nature*, 19.

58. Maugh, "Science/Genetics and Homosexuality."

59. Human Rights Campaign Fund, "Promoting Homosexuality," 1989, collection 7712, box 154, folder 46, Human Rights Campaign Records, 1975–2015, Division of Rare and Manuscript Collections, Cornell University Library, Ithaca, NY.

60. Human Rights Campaign Fund, "National Coming Out Day: Resource Guide to Coming Out," 1998, and Human Rights Campaign Fund, "Equality: A Winning Message," 2000, collection 7712, box 30, folder 32, Human Rights Campaign Records, 1975–2015, Division of Rare and Manuscript Collections, Cornell University Library, Ithaca, NY.

61. Burr, "Homosexuality and Biology"; Lancaster, *The Trouble with Nature*, 275.

62. Mireya Navarro, "Gay Rights Battle Flares in Florida," *New York Times*, December 12, 1994, https://www.nytimes.com/1994/12/12/us/gay-rights-battle-flares-in-florida.html.

63. Gainesville Area Human Rights Campaign, "Information Packet on Sexual Orientation and Human Rights," 1992, collection 7712, box 9, folder 1, Human Rights Campaign Records, 1975–2015, Division of Rare and Manuscript Collections, Cornell University Library, Ithaca, NY.

64. Oregon Speaks Out Project, "Questions and Answers on Gay and Lesbian Issues," August 25, 1994, collection 2008.063, box 1, folder 29, William E. Weinberger Collection on the Law and Gay and Lesbian Rights, ONE National Gay & Lesbian Archives, Los Angeles, CA.

65. Ruth Abramson, "Genetics: How Our Jewels Are Set into the Crown," 1991, collection 7616, box 11, folder 91-24, and PFLAG, "Gay Genes: Homosexuality and Biology," 1995, collection 7616, box 15, folder 95-P32, Parents, Families and Friends of Lesbians and Gays (PFLAG) Records, Division of Rare and Manuscript Collections, Cornell University Library, Ithaca, NY.

66. PFLAG, "'Why Ask Why?': Addressing the Research on Homosexuality and Biology," 1995, collection 7616, box 43, folder 50, Parents, Families and Friends of Lesbians and Gays (PFLAG) Records, Division of Rare and Manuscript Collections, Cornell University Library, Ithaca, NY.

67. PFLAG, "Celebrating Real Family Values: 1993 Annual Report, October 1, 1992, to September 30, 1993," 1994, 12, collection 7616, box 49, folder 2, Parents, Families and Friends of Lesbians and Gays (PFLAG) Records, Division of Rare and Manuscript Collections, Cornell University Library, Ithaca, NY.

68. PFLAG, "'Why Ask Why?,'" 12–18.

69. PFLAG, 7–8.

70. PFLAG, 7–8.

71. PFLAG, 21–22.

72. PFLAG, "Project Open Mind: Messages for a Public Education Campaign Report," 1995, collection 7616, box 19, folder 16, and PFLAG, "Project Open Mind Campaign Manual: Telling the Truth about Lesbians and Gays," 1995, collection 7616, box 19, folder 1, Parents, Families and Friends of Lesbians and Gays (PFLAG) Records, Division of Rare and Manuscript Collections, Cornell University Library, Ithaca, NY.

73. PFLAG, "Project Open Mind: Messages for a Public Education Campaign Report," 9.

74. PFLAG, "Project Open Mind: Messages for a Public Education Campaign Report," 22.

75. PFLAG, "Project Open Mind Campaign Manual," 24.

76. PFLAG, "Project Open Mind Campaign Manual," 27–28.

77. PFLAG, "Project Open Mind Campaign Manual," 30.

78. PFLAG, "Project Open Mind Campaign Manual."

79. PFLAG, "Project Open Mind Campaign Manual," 47.

80. Lancaster, *The Trouble with Nature*, 21–22.

81. John D'Emilio, *The World Turned: Essays on Gay History, Politics, and Culture* (Durham, NC: Duke University Press, 2002), 100–102.

82. Marilyn Elias, "Difference Seen in Brains of Gay Men," *USA Today*, August 3, 1992, 8D.

83. National Gay and Lesbian Task Force, "Press Release: NGLTF Statement on NIH Genetics Study," July 15, 1993, collection 7301, box 208, National Gay and Lesbian Task Force Records, 1973–2017, Division of Rare and Manuscript Collections, Cornell University Library, Ithaca, NY.

84. Parents and Friends of Ex-Gays and Gays, "Setting the Record Straight on the Science," PFOX blog, March 22, 2015, http://pfox-exgays.blogspot.com/2015/03/setting-record-straight-on-science.html.

85. Love Won Out, "Frequently Asked Questions," n.d., https://web.archive.org/web/200 81217080150/http://www.lovewonout.com/questions/.

86. John Gallagher and Chris Bull, *Perfect Enemies: The Battle between the Religious Right and the Gay Movement*, updated ed. (Lanham, MD: Madison Books, 2001), 73–78; Jeffrey Schmalz, "The 1992 Elections: The States—the Gay Issues; Gay Areas Are Jubilant over Clinton," November 5, 1992, *New York Times*, https://www.nytimes.com/1992/11/05/nyregion/the-1992-elections -the-states-the-gay-issues-gay-areas-are-jubilant-over-clinton.html.

87. Wilcox, "Cultural Context and the Conventions of Science Journalism," 233.

88. Karen De Witt, "The 1992 Campaign: The Vice President; Quayle Contends Homosexuality Is a Matter of Choice, Not Biology," *New York Times*, September 14, 1992, https://www .nytimes.com/1992/09/14/us/1992-campaign-vice-president-quayle-contends-homosexuality -matter-choice-not.html.

89. "Legislation," *Sexual Law Reporter* 1 (January 1976): 5–6, Unmarriedamerica.org, http:// www.unmarriedamerica.org/Archives/1974–1979-Sexual-Law-Reporter/1975-Sexual-Law -Reporter.pdf.

90. Mary Ziegler, "Perceiving Orientation: Defining Sexuality after Obergefell," *Duke Journal of Gender Law and Policy* 23, no. 2 (2016): 228–29.

91. Ziegler, 228, 233.

92. Gay Rights Activists, "The Fight for a Gay Civil Rights Law in New York City," 1975, collection 2010.002, box 1, folder 8, Gay Activists Alliance New York, ONE National Gay & Lesbian Archives, Los Angeles, CA; Gay Rights Activists, "Legislative History of the Homosexual Bill," January 22, 1986, collection 061, box 1, folder 43, Coalition for Lesbian and Gay Rights Records, LGBT Community Center National History Archive, New York City, NY.

93. Ziegler, "Perceiving Orientation," 227.

94. Ziegler, 3.

95. "Report to Psychologists: Panel Says Gays Still Face Bias," *San Francisco Chronicle*, August 25, 1981, collection 7301, box 153, folder 21, National Gay and Lesbian Task Force Records, 1973–2017, Division of Rare and Manuscript Collections, Cornell University Library, Ithaca, NY.

96. Gay Rights National Lobby, "Congressional Hearings: Gay Civil Rights Legislation," 1981, collection 2011.053, box 1, folder 2, Gay Rights National Lobby, ONE National Gay & Lesbian Archives, Los Angeles, CA.

97. Gay Rights National Lobby, "If Your Constituents Ask . . . ," 1980, collection 2011.053, box 1, folder 2, Gay Rights National Lobby, ONE National Gay & Lesbian Archives, Los Angeles, CA.

98. Gay Civil Rights Hearing before House Employment Opportunities Subcommittee on H.R. 1454, January 27, 1982, collection 2011.053, box 1, folder 2, Gay Rights National Lobby, ONE National Gay & Lesbian Archives, Los Angeles, CA.

99. Alan E. Gambrell (of SIECUS) to Alexander Robinson (ACLU), Re: L/G Civil Rights Bill (December 21, 1992), collection Subseries 5C Washington D.C. Office on Legislation, box 4383, American Civil Liberties Union Records, Seeley G. Mudd Manuscript Library at Princeton University, Princeton, NJ.

100. US Congress, House, *Employment Non-Discrimination Act of 1994*, HR 4636, 103rd Cong., 2d session., introduced in House on June 23, 1994, https://www.congress.gov/bill/103rd-cong ress/house-bill/4636/text.

101. Marie-Amélie George, "Expressive Ends: Understanding Conversion Therapy Bans," *Alabama Law Review* 68, no. 3 (2017): 839.

102. Gary Mucciaroni and Mary Lou Killian, "Immutability, Science and Legislative Debate over Gay, Lesbian and Bisexual Rights," *Journal of Homosexuality* 47, no. 1 (2004): 53–77.

103. Mucciaroni and Killian, 61.

104. John McLendon and Barry Bryant, "Letter to Alyssa Levy about CNN and GLAAD Stylebook," May 26, 1993, collection 7669, box 15, GLAAD Records, 1985–2001, Division of Rare and Manuscript Collections, Cornell University Library, Ithaca, NY.

105. GLAAD, "Civil /Rights, Democracy, & Amendment 2," 1993, collection 7669, box 15, GLAAD Records, 1985–2001, Division of Rare and Manuscript Collections, Cornell University Library, Ithaca, NY.

106. Patrick R. Grzanka, "Amy Coney Barrett Was Criticized for Using the Term 'Sexual Preference.' Should We Care?," *Washington Post*, October 20, 2020, https://www.washington post.com/nation/2020/10/20/amy-coney-barrett-was-criticized-using-term-sexual-preference -should-we-care/.

107. Allan Bérubé, *Coming Out under Fire: The History of Gay Men and Women in World War II*, Twentieth Anniversary ed. (Chapel Hill: University of North Carolina Press, 2010), 57, 84.

108. Patricia A. Cain, "Litigating for Lesbian and Gay Rights: A Legal History," *Virginia Law Review* 79, no. 7 (October 1993): 1551–642; Janet Halley, "Sexual Orientation and the Politics of Biology: A Critique of the Argument from Immutability," *Stanford Law Review* 46, no. 3 (February 1994): 511–12; Emily R. Gill, "Beyond Immutability: Sexuality and Constitutive Choice," *Review of Politics* 76, no. 1 (Winter 2014): 93–117.

109. *Woodward v. United States*, 871 F.2d 1068 (Fed. Cir. 1989), 1076.

110. *Dahl v. Secretary of the United States Navy*, 830 F. Supp. 1319 (M.D. Fla. 1993).

111. *Dahl v. Secretary of the United States Navy*; Rochelle Cooper Dreyfuss and Dorothy Nelkin, "The Jurisprudence of Genetics," *Vanderbilt Law Review* 45, no. 2 (March 1992): 313–48.

112. *Dahl v. Secretary of the United States Navy*, 1324.

113. Halley, "Sexual Orientation and the Politics of Biology"; citing *Steffan v. Aspin*, 8 F.3d 57, 64–68 (D.C. Cir. 1993), 62 U.S.L.W. 2309 (D.C. Cir. Jan 7, 1994).

114. American Psychological Association, "Brief for Amicus Curiae," *Ben-Shalom v. Secretary of the U.S. Army* (7th Cir.) (April 1989), https://www.apa.org/about/offices/ogc/amicus/benshalom.pdf.

115. Joseph Steffan, "Memorandum of Law in Support of Plaintiff's Cross-Motion for Summary Judgement and in Opposition to Defendants' Motion for Summary Judgment," *Steffan v. Cheney* (District Court for the District of Columbia), 1989, collection 2008.063, box 1, folder 25, William E. Weinberger Collection on the Law and Gay and Lesbian Rights, ONE National Gay & Lesbian Archives, Los Angeles, CA.

116. *City of Cleburne v. Cleburne Living Center, Inc.*, 473 U.S. 432 (1985). See also *Lyng v. Castillo*, 477 U.S. 635 (1986); *Bowen v. Gilliard*, 483 U.S. 587 (1987).

117. *Watkins v. U.S. Army*, 875 F.2d 69 (9th Circ., 1989).

118. *Watkins v. U.S. Army*, citing from Harris M. Miller II, "An Argument for the Application of Equal Protection Heightened Scrutiny to Classifications Based on Homosexuality," *Southern California Law Review* 57, no. 797 (1984): 797–836.

119. *High Tech Gays v. Defense Indus. Sec. Clearance Office*, 895 F.2d 563 (9th Cir. 1990), 573.

120. *High Tech Gays v. Defense Indus. Sec. Clearance Office*, 573.

121. Don't Ask, Don't Tell, Don't Pursue, Pub. L. 103-160, div. A, title V, § 571(a)(1), Nov. 30, 1993, 107 Stat. 1670.

122. Janet Halley, *Don't: A Reader's Guide to the Military's Anti-Gay Policy* (Durham, NC: Duke University Press, 1999), 5–7.

123. Chai R. Feldblum, "Sexual Orientation, Morality, and the Law: Devlin Revisited," *University of Pittsburgh Law Review* 57, no. 237 (1995–96): 237–336; *Able v. United States*, 44 F.3d 128 (2d Cir. 1995); *Philips v. Hunger* (No. 95-35293) (9th Cir. 1995).

124. Feldblum, "Sexual Orientation, Morality, and the Law," 297–98.

125. Human Rights Campaign Fund and the National Organization for Women, "Amici Curiae Brief of the Human Right Campaign Fund et al., in Support of Appellees," *Able v. United States* (No. 95-6111) (2d Cir. 1995).

126. Military Freedom Project, "Training Manual," 1993, collection 7616, box 29, folder 57, Parents, Families and Friends of Lesbians and Gays (PFLAG) Records, Division of Rare and Manuscript Collections, Cornell University Library, Ithaca, NY.

127. National Gay and Lesbian Task Force Military Freedom Initiative, "Countering Military Arguments against Gay and Lesbian Service Members: Questions and Answers," February 1993, collection 7301, box 208, National Gay and Lesbian Task Force, 1973–2017, Division of Rare and Manuscript Collections, Cornell University Library, Ithaca, NY.

128. *Jantz v. Muci*, 759 F. Supp. 1543, 1548 (D. Kan. 1991).

129. Amy L. Stone, *Gay Rights at the Ballot Box* (Minneapolis: University of Minnesota Press, 2012).

130. *Equality Foundation of Greater Cincinnati, Inc. v. City of Cincinnati*, 860 F. Supp. 417 (S.D. Ohio 1994), 426.

131. *Equality Foundation of Greater Cincinnati, Inc. v. City of Cincinnati*, 54 F.3d 261 (6th Cir. 1995), 266, 267.

132. *Evans v. Romer*, 854 P.2d 1270 (Colo. 1993).

133. Lisa Keen and Suzanne B. Goldberg, *Strangers to the Law: Gay People on Trial* (Ann Arbor: University of Michigan Press, 2000), 37–38; American Civil Liberties Union, "Sexual Orientation Discrimination 1994 in Subseries 5C: Washington D.C. Office of Legislation," 1994, call no. MC001.03.05_c09326, box 4383, American Civil Liberties Union Records, Seeley G. Mudd Manuscript Library at Princeton University, Princeton, NJ.

134. Keen and Goldberg, *Strangers to the Law*, 38.

135. Keen and Goldberg, 43–73.

136. *Romer v. Evans*, 517 U.S. 620 (1996).

137. Thomas H. Maugh II, "Genetic Component Found in Lesbianism, Study Says: Science: Research on Twins Shows That Environment Also Plays a Role, Although Unclear, in Sexual Orientation," *Los Angeles Times*, March 12, 1993, http://articles.latimes.com/1993-03-12/news/mn-10187_1_female-sexual-orientation.

138. Jo Wuest, "The Scientific Gaze in American Transgender Politics: Contesting the Meanings of Sex, Gender, and Gender Identity in the Bathroom Rights Cases," *Politics & Gender* 15, no. 2 (2019): 336–60.

139. John D'Emilio, Task Force, "Minutes of the Meeting of the Board of Directors National Gay and Lesbian Task Force Policy Institute National Gay and Lesbian Task Force," January 22–24, 1993, collection 7301, box 3, folder 40, National Gay and Lesbian Task Force Records, 1973–2017, Division of Rare and Manuscript Collections, Cornell University Library, Ithaca, NY; John D'Emilio, "Born Gay?," in *The World Turned*, 154–64. Though the archived meeting minutes only indicate that a "John D." gave this presentation, the first footnote in D'Emilio's "Born Gay?" essay notes that he delivered an earlier version of this essay to the Task Force's board of directors.

140. John D'Emilio, "Capitalism and Gay Identity from Powers of Desire," in *Powers of Desire: The Politics of Sexuality*, ed. Ann Snitow, Christine Stansell, and Sharon Thompson (New York: Monthly Review Press, 1983): 100–113.

141. D'Emilio, "Born Gay?," 163.

142. David M. Halperin, *How to Do the History of Homosexuality* (Chicago: University of Chicago Press, 2002); Michael Warner, *The Trouble with Normal: Sex, Politics, and the Ethics of Queer Life* (Cambridge, MA: Harvard University Press, 1999). For an account of how these scholars often unwittingly welcomed essentialism in through the back door, see Walter Benn Michaels, *The Shape of the Signifier: 1967 to the End of History* (Princeton, NJ: Princeton University Press, 2006).

143. Craig A. Rimmerman, *The Lesbian and Gay Movements: Assimilation or Liberation?*, 2nd ed. (New York: Routledge, 2014), 58–59.

144. Paul Robinson, *Queer Wars: The New Gay Right and Its Critics* (Chicago: University of Chicago Press, 2005).

145. Andrew Sullivan, "The Politics of Homosexuality," *New Republic*, May 10, 1993, https://newrepublic.com/article/122044/gay-politics-collide-personal-life.

146. Bruce Bawer, *A Place at the Table: The Gay Individual in American Society* (Delran, NJ: Simon & Schuster, 1994).

147. Andrew Sullivan, *Virtually Normal: An Argument about Homosexuality* (London: Picador, 1996), 171; Milton Friedman, *Capitalism and Freedom,* Fortieth Anniversary ed. (Chicago: University of Chicago Press, 2002).

148. Sherry Wolf, *Sexuality and Socialism: History, Politics, and Theory of LGBT Liberation* (Chicago: Haymarket Books, 2009).

149. ACT UP New York, *We Will Not Protect You*, actupny.org, 2005.

150. Richard Herrnstein and Charles Murray, *The Bell Curve: Intelligence and Class Structure in American Life* (New York: Simon & Schuster, 1996).

151. Jennifer Terry, *An American Obsession: Science, Medicine, and Homosexuality in Modern Science* (Chicago: University of Chicago Press, 1999), 43–53; Alison M. Downham Moore, "The Historicity of Sexuality: Knowledge of the Past in the Emergence of Modern Sexual Science," *Modern Intellectual History* 18, no. 2 (2021): 403–26. On Ulrichs's urging, Krafft-Ebing later joined decriminalization efforts.

152. ACT UP New York, *We Will Not Protect You.*

153. Queer by Choice, "Timeline of Our PFLAG Protest," February 7, 2001, collection 7616, box 43, folder 22, Parents, Families and Friends of Lesbians and Gays (PFLAG) Records, Division of Rare and Manuscript Collections, Cornell University Library, Ithaca, NY.

154. PFLAG, "Queer by Choice Questionnaire," August 22, 2000, collection 7616, box 43, folder 22, Parents, Families and Friends of Lesbians and Gays (PFLAG) Records, Division of Rare and Manuscript Collections, Cornell University Library, Ithaca, NY.

155. Kirsten Kingdon, "Email to bmckew, cyn, Michael Anderson, Jay Heavner, Heather Wright," May 24, 2000, collection 7616, box 43, folder 22, Parents, Families and Friends of Lesbians and Gays (PFLAG) Records, Division of Rare and Manuscript Collections, Cornell University Library, Ithaca, NY.

156. PFLAG, "Queer by Choice Questionnaire."

157. Dora B. Goldstein, "Email Subject: Gay by choice draft," June 15, 2000, collection 7616, box 43, folder 22, Parents, Families and Friends of Lesbians and Gays (PFLAG) Records, Division of Rare and Manuscript Collections, Cornell University Library, Ithaca, NY.

158. Cynthia Newcomer, "Email Subject: RE: Statement on Choice," June 16, 2000, collection 7616, box 43, folder 22, Parents, Families and Friends of Lesbians and Gays (PFLAG) Records, Division of Rare and Manuscript Collections, Cornell University Library, Ithaca, NY.

159. Kingdon, "Email to bmckew, cyn, Michael Anderson, Jay Heavner, Heather Wright."

160. PFLAG, "Diversity—Rescinded 10/20/00," October 28, 2000, PFLAG.org, http://web.archive.org/web/20011218052616/http://www.pflag.org/about/diversity.html.

161. President Arnold M. Drake, MD, "Email to Ronald Gold," December 27, 2000, collection 7616, box 43, folder 22, Parents, Families and Friends of Lesbians and Gays (PFLAG) Records, Division of Rare and Manuscript Collections, Cornell University Library, Ithaca, NY.

162. George Rice et al., "Male Homosexuality: Absence of Linkage to Microsatellite Markers at Xq28," *Science* 284, no. 5414 (April 23, 1999): 665–67.

163. Roger N. Lancaster, "Sex, Science, and Pseudoscience in the Public Sphere," *Identities: Global Studies in Culture and Power* 13, no. 1 (2006): 101–38.

164. Roger N. Lancaster, "Sex and Race in the Long Shadow of the Human Genome Project," *Social Science Research Council Race and Genomics Forum*, June 7, 2006, http://raceandgenomics.ssrc.org/Lancaster/index.html.

165. Erica Goode, "Study Questions Gene Influence on Male Homosexuality," *New York Times*, April 23, 1999, https://www.nytimes.com/1999/04/23/us/study-questions-gene-influence-on-male-homosexuality.html.

166. National Gay and Lesbian Task Force, "Email FW: Hamer Hammered by New Scientific Study, FRC Says," March 22, 1999, collection 7301, box 266, National Gay and Lesbian Task Force, 1973–2017, Division of Rare and Manuscript Collections, Cornell University Library, Ithaca, NY.

167. American Civil Liberties Union, "Anti-Gay Ballot Initiatives: An Analysis of Colorado's Amendment 2—Strategies to Defeat Other Initiatives," 1993, collection 2007.013, box 19, folder 2, American Civil Liberties Union of Southern California, ONE National Gay & Lesbian Archives, Los Angeles, CA.

168. *Romer v. Evans*.

169. *Lawrence v. Texas*, 539 U.S. 558 (2003).

170. Halley, "Sexual Orientation and the Politics of Biology," 503–68; Evan Gerstmann, *The Constitutional Underclass: Gays, Lesbians, and the Failure of Class-Based Equal Protection* (Chicago: University of Chicago, 1999).

171. Zein Murib, "Trumpism, Citizenship, and the Future of the LGBTQ Movement," *Politics & Gender* 14, no. 4 (2018): 649–72.

172. Murib, 665.

173. Patricia McBroom, "Press Release: UC Berkeley Psychologist Finds Evidence That Male Hormones in the Womb Affect Sexual Orientation," *University of California, Berkeley Campus News*, March 29, 2000, https://www.berkeley.edu/news/media/releases/2000/03/03-29-2000a.html; Dani Doughton, "Born Gay? How Biology May Drive Orientation," *Seattle Times*, June 15, 2005, https://www.seattletimes.com/seattle-news/born-gay-how-biology-may-drive-orientation/; Ed Yong, "Brains of Gay People Resemble Those of Straight People of Opposite Sex," *National Geographic*, June 20, 2008, https://www.nationalgeographic.com/science/article/brains-of-gay-people-resemble-those-of-straight-people-of-opposite-sex.

Chapter Six

1. Katie Zezima, "Lady Gaga Goes Political in Maine," *New York Times*, September 20, 2010, https://www.nytimes.com/2010/09/21/us/politics/21gaga.html.

2. National Center for Lesbian Rights, "Born Perfect: The Campaign to End Conversion Therapy," 2019, https://www.nclrights.org/our-work/born-perfect/ ; Joanna Wuest, "From Pathology

to 'Born Perfect': Science, Law, and Citizenship in American LGBTQ+ Advocacy," *Perspectives on Politics* 19, no. 3 (2021): 838–53.

3. Marie-Amélie George, "Expressive Ends: Understanding Conversion Therapy Bans," *Alabama Law Review* 68, no. 3 (2017): 793–853.

4. Williams Institute, "Conversion Therapy and LGBT Youth," UCLA School of Law, June 2019, https://williamsinstitute.law.ucla.edu/publications/conversion-therapy-and-lgbt-youth/.

5. *Hosanna-Tabor Evangelical Lutheran Church and School v. Equal Employment Opportunity Commission*, 565 U.S. 171 (2012); *Burwell v. Hobby Lobby Stores, Inc.*, 573 U.S. (2014); *Masterpiece Cakeshop v. Colorado Civil Rights Commission*, 584 U.S. ___ (2018); *Our Lady of Guadalupe School v. Morrissey-Berru*, 591 U.S. ___ (2020); *Fulton v. City of Philadelphia*, 593 U.S. ___ (2021).

6. Joe Rollins, *Legally Straight: Sexuality, Childhood, and the Cultural Value of Marriage* (New York: New York University Press, 2018), 1–8.

7. Nancy Cott, *Public Vows: A History of Marriage and the Nation* (Cambridge, MA: Harvard University Press, 2000), 150, 159, 166–67, 182, 185, 191–93, 204–5; Stephanie Coontz, *Marriage, a History: How Love Conquered Marriage* (New York: Penguin Book, 2005), 247–80; Priscilla Yamin, *American Marriage: A Political Institution* (Philadelphia: University of Pennsylvania Press, 2012).

8. Roger Lancaster, *The Trouble with Nature: Sex in Science and Pop Culture* (Berkeley: University of California Press, 2003), 309–11; Valerie Schweizer, "Divorce: More than a Century of Change, 1900–2018," National Center for Family & Marriage Research at Bowling Green State University, 2020, https://www.bgsu.edu/content/dam/BGSU/college-of-arts-and-sciences/NCFMR/documents/FP/schweizer-divorce-century-change-1900-2018-fp-20-22.pdf.

9. Jonathan Ned Katz, *The Invention of Heterosexuality* (Chicago: University of Chicago Press, 2007); Heather R. White, *Reforming Sodom: Protestants and the Rise of Gay Rights* (Chapel Hill: University of North Carolina Press, 2015).

10. Stanley Cavell, *Pursuits of Happiness: The Hollywood Comedy of Remarriage* (Cambridge, MA: Harvard University Press, 1984).

11. The Defense of Marriage Act (DOMA) Pub. L. 104-199, 110 Stat. 2419, enacted September 21, 1996, 1 U.S.C. § 7 and 28 U.S.C. § 1738C.

12. American Civil Liberties Union, "ACLU Message Points for Same-Sex Couples and the Federal Marriage Amendment," (2003) (copy available from the author).

13. Carlos A. Ball, *Same-Sex Marriage and Children: A Tale of History, Social Science, and Law* (New York: Oxford University Press, 2014). Notably, cases involving parental adoption rights enjoyed some early successes precisely because of their low visibility when same-sex marriage was under the national spotlight. Alison Gash, *Below the Radar: How Silence Can Save Civil Rights* (New York: Oxford University Press, 2015), 8.

14. Stephen Engel, *Fragmented Citizenship: The Changing Landscape of Gay and Lesbian Lives* (New York: New York University Press, 2016), 194–95.

15. Although a handful of gay rights activists and attorneys had brought marriage to court in the 1970s, these had been largely lost causes from the outset. *Baker v. Nelson*, 191 N.W.2d 185 (Minn. 1971), af1d, 409 U.S. 810 (1972); John Singer and Paul Barwick, *A Legal Brief on the Legitimacy of Gay Marriage: Singer & Barwick vs. Hara* (Seattle: n.p., 1972); *Jones v. Hallahan*, 501 S.W.2d 588 (Ky. 1973); *Singer v. Hara*, 522 P.2d 1187 (Wash. Ct. App. 1974), appeal denied, 84 Wash. 2d 1008 (1974); Jack Baker, "Defining 'Gayness' under the Law," *Minneapolis Star*, March 19, 1974, 8A, Gebhard Era Correspondence, 1970–1979, part 2: A–Z, file cabinet 4, drawer 3, Kinsey Institute for Research in Sex, Gender, and Reproduction, Bloomington, IN.

16. *Baehr v. Lewin*, 852 P.2d 44 (Hawaii 1993).

17. *Baehr v. Miike*, 910 P.2d 112 (1996).

18. Beth Kleid, "Dr. Kyle Pruett: Lifetime's New Parental Guide," *Los Angeles Times*, July 11, 1993, https://www.latimes.com/archives/la-xpm-1993-07-11-tv-11980-story.html.

19. Lambda Legal, "Brief of *Amici Curiae* & Certificate of Service," *Baehr v. Miike*, Civil No. 91-1394-05 (October 10, 1996), https://www.lambdalegal.org/sites/default/files/baehr_hi_199 61011_amici-marriage-scholars.pdf.

20. Hawaiian voters would later nullify this victory through a referendum on the state constitution.

21. Rollins, *Legally Straight*, 41.

22. *Goodridge v. Department of Public Health*, 798 N.E.2d 941 (Mass. 2003).

23. Gay & Lesbian Advocates & Defenders, "Memorandum in Opposition to Defendants' Cross Motion for Summary Judgment and Reply," *Goodridge v. Department of Public Health*, No. 01-1647-A, March 4, 2002, 31, https://www.glad.org/wp-content/uploads/2003/11/2002-03 -04-goodridge-plaintiffs-reply.pdf; quoting from Ellen C. Perrin et al., "Technical Report: Coparent or Second-Parent Adoption by Same Sex Parents," *Pediatrics* 109, no. 2 (2002): 341–44.

24. Gay & Lesbian Advocates & Defenders, "Memorandum in Opposition," 31n27; quoting from American Psychological Association, *Lesbian and Gay Parenting: A Resource for Psychologists* (Washington, DC: American Psychological Association, 1995).

25. Gay & Lesbian Advocates & Defenders, "Memorandum in Opposition," 32n28; quoting from Judith Stacy and Timothy J. Biblarz, "(How) Does the Sexual Orientation of Parents Matter," *American Sociological Review* 66, no. 159 (April 2001): 162.

26. *Goodridge v. Department of Public Health*, 331.

27. *Goodridge v. Department of Public Health*, 336.

28. *Goodridge v. Department of Public Health*, 386–87, 394.

29. Engel, *Fragmented Citizenship*, 259–61.

30. *In re Marriage Cases*, 183 P.3d 384 (Cal. 2008).

31. Equality California, "Respondents' Consolidated Answer to Amicus Curiae Briefs," First Appellate District, Division Three Nos. A110449, A110450, A110451, A110463, A110651, A110652 San Francisco Superior Court Nos. JCCP4365, 429539, 429548, 504038 Los Angeles Superior Court No. BC088506 (November 14, 2007).

32. *Equality California et al.*, "Brief," 16, 19.

33. *Equality California et al.*, 17–18, 19.

34. Human Rights Campaign, Human Rights Campaign Foundation, Equal Justice Society, National Center for Lesbian Rights, National Gay and Lesbian Task Force, "Brief for Amicus Curiae," *Kerrigan v. Commissioner of Public Health* (S.C. Connecticut 17716) (January 11, 2007).

35. American Psychological Association, American Psychiatric Association, and the New York State Psychiatric Association, "Brief of Amicus Curiae," No. 1967-04 (State of New York Court of Appeals, April 11, 2006).

36. *Kerrigan v. Commissioner of Public Health*, 957 A.2d 407 (Conn: Supreme Court 2008), at 437.

37. *Jantz v. Muci*, 759 F. Supp. 1543 (D. Kans. 1991), at 1547–48 and fn. 4.

38. *Jantz v. Muci*, 98, citing *Hernandez-Montiel v. I.N.S.* (9th Cir. 2000) 225 F.3d 1084.

39. "Proposition 8: Ban on Same-Sex Marriage," Institute of Governmental Studies, University of California, Berkeley, n.d., https://www.igs.berkeley.edu/library/elections/proposition-8.

40. *Perry v. Hollingsworth*, No.3:09-cv-02292-VRW (N.D. Cal. 2011).

41. Cross-Examination of Gregory Herek, *Perry v. Hollingsworth*, No.3:09-cv-02292-VRW (N.D. Cal. 2011) (January 22, 2010).

42. Cross-Examination of Gregory Herek, 2124, 2282.

43. Cross-Examination of Gregory Herek, 2177, 2258.

44. *Perry v. Hollingsworth*, No.3:09-cv-02292-VRW (N.D. Cal. 2011).

45. *Perry v. Hollingsworth*, 964–65.

46. *Perry v. Hollingsworth*, 962.

47. *Windsor v. United States*, No. 12-2335 (2d Cir. 2012).

48. Donald B. Verrilli Jr., "Supplemental Brief for the United States," *United States v. Windsor*, No. 12-307 (October 2012), http://sblog.s3.amazonaws.com/wp-content/uploads/2012/10/DOMA-12-307-US-supp-brief.pdf; Gay and Lesbian Medical Association, "Amicus Curiae Brief GLMA: Health Professionals Advancing LGBT Equality (Gay and Lesbian Medical Association) Concerning the Immutability of Sexual Orientation in Support of Affirmance on the Merits," *United States v. Windsor*, No. 12-307 (February 26, 2013).

49. Engel, *Fragmented Citizenship*, 277–78; *SmithKline Beecham Corporation v. Abbott Laboratories*, No. 11-17357 (9th Cir. 2014).

50. Brief for the Leadership Conference on Civil and Human Rights, Nos. 14-1341, 3057, 3464, 5291, 5297, 5818, *DeBoer v. Snyder, Obergefell v. Hodges, Henry v. Hodges, Bourke v. Beshear* (6th Circ. 2014) (unknown date); *Baskin v. Bogan*, 766 F.3d 648 (7th Circ. 2014).

51. Richard A. Posner, *Sex and Reason* (Cambridge, MA: Harvard University Press, 1992); Susan McKinnon, *Neo-Liberal Genetics: The Myths and Moral Tales of Evolutionary Psychology* (Chicago: Prickly Paradigm Press, 2005).

52. Posner, *Sex and Reason*, 105n50.

53. Posner's previous opposition to marriage reform was based mostly in his judicial temperance. Richard A. Posner, "Should There Be Homosexual Marriage? If So, Who Should Decide?," *Michigan Law Review* 1578, no. 95 (1997); Richard A. Posner, "Eighteen Years On: A Re-Review [reviewing William N. Eskridge Jr., *The Case for Same-Sex Marriage: From Sexual Liberty to Civilized Commitment* (1996)]," *Yale Law Journal* 125, no. 2 (2015): 533–42.

54. *Baskin v. Bogan*, 766 F.3d 648 (7th Circ. 2014).

55. *Baskin v. Bogan*, 766 F.3d 648 (7th Circ. 2014), 9–10.

56. *Baskin v. Bogan*, 766 F.3d 648 (7th Circ. 2014), 9.

57. *Baskin v. Bogan*, 766 F.3d 648 (7th Circ. 2014), 17.

58. *Baskin v. Bogan*, 766 F.3d 648 (7th Circ. 2014), 28.

59. Brief for the Leadership Conference on Civil and Human Rights, Nos. 14-556, 14-562, 14-571, and 14-574 (U.S. 2015) (filed March 6, 2015), 28.

60. Engel, *Fragmented Citizenship*, 278; Connor Ewing, "With Dignity and Justice for All: The Jurisprudence of 'Equal Dignity' and the Partial Convergence of Liberty and Equality in American Constitutional Law," *International Journal of Constitutional Law* 16, no. 3 (2018): 753–75.

61. Cyril Ghosh, "Marriage Equality and the Injunction to Assimilate: Romantic Love, Children, Monogamy, and Parenting in *Obergefell v. Hodges*," *Polity* 50, no. 2 (2018): 275–99; Nan D. Hunter, "Varieties of Constitutional Experience: Democracy and the Marriage Equality Campaign," *UCLA Law Review* 64, no. 6 (2017): 1662–727; Marie-Amélie George, "Framing Trans Rights," *Northwestern University Law Review* 114, no. 3 (2019): 555–632.

62. Clifford Rosky, "Same-Sex Marriage Litigation and the Children's Right to Be Queer," *GLQ: A Journal of Gay and Lesbian Studies* 22, no. 4 (2016): 541–68; Rollins, *Legally Straight*, 125–28.

63. Evan Gerstmann, *The Constitutional Underclass: Gays, Lesbians, and the Failure of Class-Based Equal Protection* (Chicago: University of Chicago, 1999); Darren Hutchinson, "'Not without Political Power': Gays and Lesbians, Equal Protection, and the Suspect Class Doctrine," *Alabama Law Review* 65, no. 4 (2014): 975–1034.

64. *Obergefell v. Hodges*, 576 U.S. 644 (2015), 4, 8. Jessica Clarke has reasoned that this combination of moral and scientific weight is characteristic of a shift in the meaning of immutability. Whereas immutability was once primarily descriptive in nature (i.e., a trait is not acquired volitionally and, therefore, is owed protection), they are now frontloaded with a normative commitment to the inherent goodness of the trait in question. Jessica A. Clarke, "Against Immutability," *Yale Law Journal* 125, no. 1 (2015): 2–102.

65. Jonathan Goldberg-Hiller, *The Limits to Union: Same-Sex Marriage and the Politics of Civil Rights* (Ann Arbor: University of Michigan Press, 2002), 101–2.

66. *Gonzales v. Carhart*, 550 U.S. 124 (2007). In *Carhart*, Kennedy perceived a lack of medical consensus regarding the safety and effects of this abortion procedure, which led him to defer to the legislature (unlike *Obergefell*, in which he saw a medical consensus as having already formed). For a refutation of Kennedy's evaluation of medical opinion in *Carhart*, see Mary Ziegler, *Abortion and the Law in America: Roe v. Wade to the Present* (New York: Cambridge University Press, 2020).

67. Vernon A. Rosario, "An Interview with Judd Marmor, MD," *Journal of Gay & Lesbian Psychotherapy* 7, no. 4 (2003).

68. Tom Waidzunas, *The Straight Line: How the Fringe Science of Ex-Gay Therapy Reoriented Sexuality* (Minneapolis: University of Minnesota Press, 2015).

69. Truth Wins Out, "Medical Professionals," 2019, https://truthwinsout.org/the-experts/.

70. American Psychological Association Task Force on Appropriate Therapeutic Responses to Sexual Orientation, *Report of the American Psychological Association Task Force on Appropriate Therapeutic Responses to Sexual Orientation* (Washington, DC: American Psychological Association, 2009); American Psychological Association, "Resolution on Appropriate Affirmative Responses to Sexual Orientation Distress and Change Efforts," August 2009 (updated June 2022), https://www.apa.org/about/policy/sexual-orientation.

71. American Psychological Association Task Force on Appropriate Therapeutic Responses to Sexual Orientation, *Report*, 30.

72. American Psychiatric Association, "Position Statement on Conversion Therapy and LGBTQ Patients," 2018, https://www.psychiatry.org/about-apa/Policy-Finder/Position-Statement-on-Conversion-Therapy-and-LGBTQ.

73. American Psychoanalytic Association, "Position Statement on Attempts to Change Sexual Orientation, Gender Identity, or Gender Expression," 2012, https://apsa.org/content/2012-position-statement-attempts-change-sexual-orientation-gender-identity-or-gender.

74. Association for Behavioral and Cognitive Therapies, "ABCT Apology for Behavior Therapy's Contribution to the Development and Practice of Sexual Orientation and Gender Identity and Expression Change Efforts," June 2022, https://www.abct.org/latest-news/abct-apology-for-behavior-therapys-contribution-to-the-development-and-practice-of-sexual-orientation-and-gender-identity-and-expression-change-efforts-history-and-next-steps/.

75. Ruth Leys, *Trauma: A Genealogy* (Chicago: University of Chicago Press, 2000).

76. Karen L. Graves, *And They Were Wonderful Teachers: Florida's Purge of Gay and Lesbian Teachers* (Champaign: University of Illinois Press, 2009).

77. Amy E. Green et al., "Self-Reported Conversion Efforts and Suicidality among US LGBTQ Youths and Young Adults, 2018," *American Journal of Public Health* 110 (2020): 1221–27;

Jack L. Turban, Noor Beckwith, and Sari L. Reisner, "Association between Recalled Exposure to Gender Identity Conversion Efforts and Psychological Distress and Suicide Attempts among Transgender Adults," *JAMA Psychiatry* 77, no. 1 (2020): 68–76.

78. The Trevor Project, "50 Bills 50 States: About Our Campaign," 2019, https://www.thetrevor project.org/get-involved/trevor-advocacy/50-bills-50-states/about-our-campaign/; Human Rights Campaign, "The Lies and Dangers of Efforts to Change Sexual Orientation or Gender Identity," 2020, https://www.hrc.org/resources/the-lies-and-dangers-of-reparative-therapy.

79. Simon LeVay, *Gay, Straight, and the Reason Why: The Science of Sexual Orientation* (New York: Oxford University Press, 2011); A. Lee Beckstead, "Can We Change Sexual Orientation?" *Archives of Sexual Behavior* 41, no. 1 (2012): 122–34.

80. Joe Carter, "California's Latest Threat to Religious Liberty and Free Speech," Ethics and Religious Liberty Commission of the Southern Baptist Convention, April 24, 2018, https://erlc .com/resource-library/articles/californias-latest-threat-to-religious-liberty-and-free-speech.

81. Robert O. Lopez, "On Ministry and Counseling to Lead People from Homosexuality to Heterosexuality," May 21, 2018, https://www.massresistance.org/docs/gen3/18b/MR-TX-SBC -Resolution/images/Lopez-SBC-Resolution.pdf.

82. Council for Biblical Manhood and Womanhood, "Nashville Statement," 2017, https:// cbmw.org/nashville-statement/.

83. Catholic Church, The Catechism of the Catholic Church, https://www.vatican.va/ar chive/ENG0015/_INDEX.HTM.

84. Congregation for Catholic Education, "'Male and Female He Created Them': Towards a Path of Dialogue on the Question of Gender Theory in Education" (Vatican City, 2019), http:// www.educatio.va/content/dam/cec/Documenti/19_0997_INGLESE.pdf.

85. Massachusetts Catholic Conference, "Conversion Therapy," 2019, https://www.macatho lic.org/news-article/conversion-therapy.

86. Peter Sprigg, "California's Effort to Ban 'Conversion Therapy' Failed: Here's a Better Path We Can All Agree On," 2018, Family Research Council, https://www.frc.org/op-eds/californias -effort-to-ban-conversion-therapy-failed-heres-a-better-path-we-can-all-agree-on.

87. Alliance Defending Freedom, "Legal Analysis of California AB 2943," March 8, 2018, https://drive.google.com/file/d/0B9njBaZTrCfSMFJfRGMzX2ZQeFh0R0U3bFVMS2ZYWUl1 M2VF/view.

88. American College of Pediatricians, "Homosexual Parenting: Is It Time for Change?," 2017, https://www.acpeds.org/the-college-speaks/position-statements/parenting-issues/homosexual -parenting-is-it-time-for-change; American Academy of Pediatrics, "About the AAP," 2018, https://www.aap.org/en-us/about-the-aap/Pages/About-the-AAP.aspx.

89. André Van Mol, "Unlawful and Unnecessary—Oppose AB 1779 & AB 2943," 2018, American College of Pediatricians.

90. Association of American Physicians and Surgeons, "AAPS News July 2016—Discrimination," 2016, https://aapsonline.org/aaps-news-july-2016-discrimination/.

91. Association of American Physicians and Surgeons, "California Proposes Bills to Outlaw Self-Determination in Medical Therapy," 2018, https://drive.google.com/file/d/0B9njBaZTrCfSa Vl5cXJ6SUNsdTdiQXRRdVFvMTRzSHF5bEJj/view.

92. Alliance for Therapeutic Choice and Scientific Integrity Training Institute, "Alliance Statement on Sexual Orientation Change," 2012, https://docs.wixstatic.com/ugd/ec16e9_1d610 8cfa05d4a73921e0d0292c0bc91.pdf.

93. Alliance for Therapeutic Choice and Scientific Integrity Training Institute, "Our Mission: Because Values Matter," n.d., https://www.therapeuticchoice.com/our-mission.

94. Reintegrative Therapy Association, "About Us" and "The Science," 2018, https://www.re integrativetherapy.com/reintegrative-therapy/.

95. Aviva Stahl, "Meet the 'Fringe Extremists' Pushing Flawed Science to Target Trans Kids," *Buzzfeed News*, April 16, 2021, https://www.buzzfeednews.com/article/avivastahl/transgender -trans-kids-healthcare-science; Pediatric and Adolescent Gender Dysphoria Working Group, "Who We Are," 2021, https://gdworkinggroup.org/who-we-are/.

96. Lisa Littman, "Correction: Parent Reports of Adolescents and Young Adults Perceived to Show Signs of a Rapid Onset of Gender Dysphoria," *PLoS One*, March 19, 2019, https://doi .org/10.1371/journal.pone.0214157.

97. Michael K. Laidlaw et al., Letter to the Editor: "Endocrine Treatment of Gender-Dysphoric/Gender-Incongruent Persons: An Endocrine Society Clinical Practice Guideline," *Journal of Clinical Endocrinology & Metabolism* 104, no. 3 (2019): 686–87, https://doi.org/10.1210 /jc.2018-01925.

98. Roberto D'Angelo et al., "One Size Does Not Fit All: In Support of Psychotherapy for Gender Dysphoria," *Archives of Sexual Behavior* 50 (2021): 7–16, https://doi.org/10.1007/s10508 -020-01844-2.

99. Heritage Foundation, "The Medical Harms of Hormonal and Surgical Interventions for Gender Dysphoric Children," March 28, 2019, https://www.heritage.org/gender/event /the-medical-harms-hormonal-and-surgical-interventions-gender-dysphoric-children; William J. Malone, Colin M. Wright, and Julia D. Robertson, "No One Is Born in 'The Wrong Body,'" *Quillette*, September 24, 2019, https://quillette.com/2019/09/24/no-one-is-born-in-the-wrong -body/.

100. Mark Joseph Stern, "Trump Judges Block Laws Banning LGBTQ 'Conversion Therapy' for Minors," *Slate*, November 20, 2020, https://slate.com/news-and-politics/2020/11/trump -judges-conversion-therapy-lgbtq.html.

101. Anagha Srikanth, "Wisconsin Bans Taxpayer Money from Funding Conversion Therapy," *The Hill*, June 4, 2021, https://thehill.com/changing-america/respect/equality/556883-wisconsin -bans-taxpayer-money-from-funding-conversion.

102. Southern Poverty Law Center, "New Jersey Excludes Key 'Conversion' Therapy Experts in SPLC Consumer Fraud Case," 2015, http://www.splcenter.org/news/2015/02/05/new-jersey -judge-excludes-key-%E2%80%98conversion%E2%80%99-therapy-experts-splc-consumer -fraud-case.

103. Lambda Legal, "Lambda Legal Applauds Law Banning 'Reparative Therapy' for California Minors," 2012, https://www.lambdalegal.org/news/ca_2012_lambda-legal-applauds-law.

104. Don Frances, "Bill by Torrance Lawmaker Ted Lieu Banning 'Conversion' of Gay Teens Clears Committee," KKPC, May 9, 2012, https://www.scpr.org/blogs/news/2012/05/09/6031/bill -torrance-lawmaker-ted-lieu-banning-conversion/.

105. Patrick McGreevy, "Gov. Jerry Brown Bans Gay-to-Straight Therapy for Minors," *Los Angeles Times*, September 30, 2012, https://latimesblogs.latimes.com/california-politics/2012/09 /governor-jerry-brown-gay-therapy-minors.html.

106. Erik Eckholm, "Clashing Rulings Complicate Path of Gay 'Conversion Therapy' Law," *New York Times*, December 4, 2012, https://www.nytimes.com/2012/12/05/us/judge-blocks-cali fornia-conversion-therapies-law.html?.

107. *David H. Pickup et al. v. Edmund G. Brown Jr. et al.*, No. 12-17681 (9th Cir. 2013). The court also ruled against challenges concerning the law's supposed vagueness and overbroad nature.

108. *David H. Pickup et al. v. Edmund G. Brown Jr. et al.*, 13.

109. *David H. Pickup et al. v. Edmund G. Brown Jr. et al.*, 35; quoting from *National Association for the Advancement of Psychoanalysis v. California Board of Psychology*, 228 F.3d 1043 (9th Cir. 2000). Although both case law and statutory exemptions in the Child Abuse Prevention Treatment Act of 1996 maintain broad carve-outs for religious parents who refuse certain medical treatments for their children, the Ninth Circuit did not find that such a right extends to access to conversion therapy. Child Abuse Prevention Treatment Act of 1996 (P.L. 104-235).

110. *Welch v. Brown*, 834 F.3d 1041 (9th Cir. 2016). This challenge also included a right to privacy claim, which was adjudicated in a manner similar to the parental rights claim in *Pickup et al. v. Brown* (2013).

111. A version of this law was passed by the New York City Council in 2017 and subsequently repealed in 2019 by advocates who feared defending it before the Supreme Court; *Schwartz v. City of New York et al.*, No. 1:2019-cv-00463 (E.D. N.Y., January 23, 2019).

112. *Ferguson v. JONAH, New Jersey Superior Court* No. L-5473-12 (N.J. Super. Ct. Law Div. 2015); United States Federal Trade Commission, *Human Rights Campaign, National Center for Lesbian Rights, and the Southern Poverty Law Center v. People Can Change, Inc.*, "Complaint for Action to Stop False, Deceptive Advertising and Other Business Practices," February 24, 2016, http://www.nclrights.org/wp-content/uploads/2016/02/FTC-Conversion-Therapy-Complaint.pdf.

113. Greg Burt, "New CA Bill Outlaws Helping Anyone with Unwanted Same-Sex Desires or Gender Confusion," California Family Council, March 14, 2018, https://californiafamily.org/2018/new-ca-bill-outlaws-helping-anyone-with-unwanted-same-sex-desires-or-gender-confusion/; J. D. Flynn, "Could a California Bill Ban Christian Teaching on Homosexuality?," *Catholic News Agency*, April 22, 2018, https://www.catholicnewsagency.com/news/could-a-california-bill-ban-christian-teaching-on-homosexuality-59038.

114. California Family Council, "AB 2943," 2018, https://californiafamily.org/oppose-ca-ab-2943-ab-1779-and-ab-2119-reference-materials/.

115. Alliance Defending Freedom, "Legal Analysis," 1, 3–4.

116. Robbie Short, "Emotional Fight over Conversion Therapy: Should California Limit Services Meant to Turn Gay People Straight?" *CALmatters*, June 24, 2018, https://calmatters.org/articles/gay-conversion-therapy-california-bill/.

117. Short.

118. Don Thompson, "California Gay Conversion Therapy Bill Dropped," *VC Star*, August 31, 2018, https://www.vcstar.com/story/news/2018/08/31/california-gay-conversion-therapy-bill-dropped/1163752002/.

119. Matthew S. Bajko, "Low Rules Out Religious Exemption in Conversion Therapy Ban," *Bay Area Reporter*, January 11, 2019, https://www.ebar.com/news/latest_news/270745; *Masterpiece Cakeshop v. Colorado Civil Rights Commission*, 584 U.S. ___ (2018).

120. Therapeutic Fraud Prevention Act, 116th Congress: H.R. 3570; S. 2008 (2019).

121. Austin Mendoza, "Lieu Ready for Another Attempt at Federal Ban on 'Conversion Therapy,'" *Los Angeles Blade*, June 12, 2019, https://www.losangelesblade.com/2019/06/12/lieu-ready-for-another-attempt-at-federal-ban-on-conversion-therapy/.

122. *King v. Governor of NJ*, No. 13-4429 (3d Cir. 2014).

123. *National Institute of Family and Life Advocates v. Becerra*, 585 U.S. ___ (2018), 7–8.

124. *National Institute of Family and Life Advocates v. Becerra*, 8–9.

125. *Otto v. City of Boca Raton*, No. 19-10604 (11th Cir. 2020), 12.

126. *Otto v. City of Boca Raton*, 21.

127. *Otto v. City of Boca Raton*, 21n7.

128. Briana S. Last and Joanna Wuest, "Policy Disputes Over Sexual Orientation and Gender Identity Change Efforts," *Behavior Therapist* 45, no. 8 (2022): 285–97.

129. *Otto v. City of Boca Raton*, 22, 24.

130. *303 Creative LLC v. Elenis*, No. 21-476.

131. Andrew Koppelman, *Gay Rights vs. Religious Liberty? The Unnecessary Conflict* (New York: Oxford University Press, 2020).

132. For a review of these, see Joanna Wuest, "Review of Andrew Koppelman's *Gay Rights vs. Religious Liberty? The Unnecessary Conflict*," *Perspectives on Politics* 19, no. 1 (2021): 264–65.

133. Joanna Wuest and Briana Last, "With Gay Adoption Decision, Will the Supreme Court Erode the Regulatory State?," *Boston Review*, April 15, 2021, http://bostonreview.net/law-justice /joanna-wuest-briana-last-fulton-v-philadelphia-supreme-court-gay-adoption.

134. *Janus v. American Federation of State, County, and Municipal Employees*, Council 31, No. 16-1466, 585 U.S. ___ (2018).

135. Gordon Lafer, *The One Percent Solution: How Corporations Are Remaking America One State at a Time* (Ithaca, NY: Cornell University Press, 2017).

136. Amanda Hollis-Brusky, *Ideas with Consequences: The Federalist Society and the Conservative Counterrevolution* (New York: Oxford University Press, 2015); John Gramlich, "How Trump Compares with Other Recent Presidents in Appointing Federal Judges," *Pew Research Center*, January 13, 2021, https://www.pewresearch.org/fact-tank/2021/01/13/how-trump-compares-with -other-recent-presidents-in-appointing-federal-judges/.

Chapter Seven

1. Jo Wuest, "The Scientific Gaze in American Transgender Politics: Contesting the Meanings of Sex, Gender, and Gender Identity in the Bathroom Rights Cases," *Politics & Gender* 15, no. 2 (June 2019): 336–60.

2. Katy Steinmetz, "The Transgender Tipping Point," *Time*, May 29, 2014, https://time .com/135480/transgender-tipping-point/.

3. Sean Dooley et al., "Bruce Jenner: When Did He Know?" *ABC News*, April 24, 2015, https://abcnews.go.com/Entertainment/bruce-jenner/story?id=30570567.

4. Diane Sawyer, "Bruce Jenner: The Interview," *ABC News*, April 24, 2015, http://abcnews .go.com/2020/fullpage/bruce-jenner-the-interview-30471558.

5. Jessica Herthel and Jazz Jennings, *I Am Jazz* (New York: Penguin, 2014).

6. Joshua Gamson, *Freaks Talk Back: Tabloid Talk Shows and Sexual Nonconformity* (Chicago: University of Chicago Press, 1998).

7. Brynne Tannehill, "Is Research into Gender Identity a Necessary Evil?" *INTO*, June 11, 2018, https://web.archive.org/web/20210121235133/https://www.intomore.com/impact/is-research -into-gender-identity-a-necessary-evil/.

8. Tucker Carlson, "Transgender Bathroom Debate: State or Civil Rights Issue?," *Tucker Carlson Tonight*, February 24, 2017, https://video.foxnews.com/v/5336728640001/#sp=show-clips.

9. Benoit Denizet-Lewis, "The Scientific Quest to Prove Bisexuality Exists," *New York Times Magazine*, March 20, 2014, http://www.nytimes.com/2014/03/23/magazine/the-scientific-quest -to-prove-bisexuality-exists.html?_r=0.

10. Tamsin Osborne, "Bisexuality Passed on by 'Hyper-Heterosexuals,'" *New Scientist*, August 15, 2008, https://www.newscientist.com/article/dn14543-bisexuality-passed-on-by-hyper-heterosexuals/; Lisa M. Diamond, *Sexual Fluidity: Understanding Women's Love and Desire* (Cambridge, MA: Harvard University Press, 2009).

11. Janet Halley, "Sexual Orientation and the Politics of Biology: A Critique of the Argument from Immutability," *Stanford Law Review* 46, no. 3 (February 1994): 511–12; Kenji Yoshino, "The Epistemic Contract of Bisexual Erasure," *Stanford Law Review* 52 (January 2000): 405; Shane Phelan, *Sexual Strangers: Gays, Lesbians, and Dilemmas of Citizenship* (Philadelphia: Temple University Press, 2001), 78; Nancy J. Knauer, "Science, Identity, and the Construction of the Gay Political Narrative," *Law & Sexuality* 12 (2003): 1–87; Emily R. Gill, "Beyond Immutability: Sexuality and Constitutive Choice," *Review of Politics* 76, no. 1 (Winter 2014): 93–117.

12. Roger Lancaster, *The Trouble with Nature: Sex in Science and Pop Culture* (Berkeley: University of California Press, 2003), 19.

13. Jennifer Terry, *An American Obsession: Science, Medicine, and Homosexuality in Modern Science* (Chicago: University of Chicago Press, 1999), 43–50.

14. Steven Angelides, *A History of Bisexuality* (Chicago: University of Chicago Press, 2001), 50–54.

15. Robert Beachy, *Gay Berlin: Birthplace of a Modern Identity* (New York: Viking, 2015).

16. Susan Stryker, *Transgender History: The Roots of Today's Revolution*, 2nd ed. (Berkeley, CA: Seal Press, 2017), 55.

17. David F. Greenberg, "Transformations of Homosexuality-Based Classifications," in *The Gender/Sexuality Reader: Culture, History, and Political Economy*, ed. Micaela di Leonardo and Roger Lancaster (New York: Routledge, 1997), 187.

18. Stryker, *Transgender History*, 56.

19. Joanne Meyerowitz, *How Sex Changed: A History of Transsexuality in the United States* (Cambridge, MA: Harvard University Press, 2004).

20. Allan Bérubé, *Coming Out under Fire: The History of Gay Men and Women in World War II* (New York: Simon & Schuster, 1990).

21. Stryker, *Transgender History*, 62; American Civil Liberties Union, "History of Sodomy Laws and the Strategy That Led Up to Today's Decision," 2003, https://www.aclu.org/other/history-sodomy-laws-and-strategy-led-todays-decision.

22. Mattachine Society of Washington, "Committee on Picketing and Other Lawful Demonstrations: Regulations for Picketing," n.d., Library of Congress, http://www.kamenypapers.org/images/KamenyPicketInstructions.jpg.

23. C. A. Tripp, "Psychiatric Moralists in Unison," January 1966, collection 2007-009, box 4, folder 8, Judd Marmor Papers, ONE National Gay & Lesbian Archives, Los Angeles, CA.

24. Meyerowitz, *How Sex Changed*, 177, 183.

25. Stryker, *Transgender History*, 60–61.

26. Stryker, 64–74.

27. Gay Revolutionary Party Women's Caucus, "Realesbians and Politicalesbians," in *Out of the Closets: Voices of Gay Liberation*, Twentieth Anniversary ed., ed. Karla Kay and Allen Young (New York: New York University Press, 1992), 178. See also Paula C. Rust, *Bisexuality and the Challenge to Lesbian Politics: Sex, Loyalty, and Revolution* (New York: New York University Press, 1995).

28. Thomas Szasz, "Male and Female Created He Them," *New York Times*, June 10, 1979, https://www.nytimes.com/1979/06/10/archives/male-and-female-created-he-them-transsexual.html.

29. Robin Morgan, "Lesbianism and Feminism: Synonyms or Contradictions?," keynote address at the West Coast Lesbian Feminist Conference, Los Angeles, CA, April 14, 1973, https://www.onearchives.org/wp-content/uploads/2015/02/Lesbianism-and-Feminism-Synonyms-or-Contradictions-by-Robin-Morgan-April-14-1973.pdf.

30. Janice G. Raymond, *The Transsexual Empire: The Making of the She-Male*, reissued ed. (New York: Teachers College Press, 1994).

31. Sheila Jeffreys, *Gender Hurts: A Feminist Analysis of the Politics of Transgenderism* (Abingdon, UK: Routledge, 2014).

32. BiNet USA, "A Brief History of the Bisexual Movement," n.d., https://www.binetusa.org/bihistory2.html.

33. Amin Ghaziani, *The Dividends of Dissent: How Conflict and Culture Work in Lesbian and Gay Marches on Washington* (Chicago: University of Chicago Press, 2008), 150.

34. Martin S. Weinberg, Colin J. Williams, and Douglas W. Pryor, *Dual Attraction: Understanding Bisexuality* (New York: Oxford University Press, 1994).

35. Harry Benjamin et al., *The Transsexual Phenomenon* (New York: Ace, 1966).

36. Stryker, *Transgender History*, 96–105.

37. Bernice L. Hausman, *Changing Sex: Transsexualism, Technology, and the Idea of Gender* (Durham, NC: Duke University Press, 1995), 129; Raymond LePage and Caroline Albert, "Fifty Years of Development in the Endocrinology Laboratory," *Clinical Biochemistry* 39, no. 5 (May 2006); Stryker, *Transgender History*, 56. Ironically, the same advancements in hormonal research that were used to feminize and masculinize human bodies beyond their biological trajectories and to conjecture the blend of psychological and physiological necessities for such hormonal interventions were soon applied in studies that investigated homosexuality's possible biological nature.

38. Suzanne Kessler, "The Medical Construction of Gender: Case Management of Intersexed Infants," *Signs* 16, no. 1 (1990): 3–26; Meyerowitz, *How Sex Changed*, 114–19.

39. Tey Meadow, *Trans Kids: Being Gendered in the Twenty-First Century* (Oakland: University of California Press, 2018), 59–63; Sahar Sadjadi, "Deep in the Brain: Identity and Authenticity in Pediatric Gender Transition," *Cultural Anthropology* 32, no. 1 (2019).

40. For an extensive discussion of these clinicians and theorists and citations to their main works, see chapter 4.

41. Hausman, *Changing Sex*, 72; Meadow, *Trans Kids*, 60.

42. Meadow, *Trans Kids*, 61.

43. Meyerowitz, *How Sex Changed*, 115–16.

44. Meyerowitz, 117–18.

45. American Psychiatric Association, *Diagnostic and Statistical Manual of Mental Disorders*, 2nd ed. (Washington, DC: American Psychiatric Press, 1980).

46. American Psychiatric Association, *Diagnostic and Statistical Manual of Mental Disorders*, 5th ed. (Washington, DC: American Psychiatric Press, 2013).

47. Megan Davidson, "Seeking Refuge under the Umbrella: Inclusion, Exclusion, and Organizing within the Category Transgender," *Sexuality Research and Social Policy* 4, no. 4 (2007): 60–80.

48. Phyllis Frye, "Proceedings from the Fourth International Conference on Transgender Law and Employment Policy, TRANSGEN '95, Houston, TX," June 1995, Digital Transgender Archive, https://www.digitaltransgenderarchive.net/files/hm50tr815; Deborah Sontag, "Once a Pariah, Now a Judge: The Early Transgender Journey of Phyllis Frye," *New York Times*,

August 29, 2015, https://www.nytimes.com/2015/08/30/us/transgender-judge-phyllis-fryes-early
-transformative-journey.html.

49. Sandy Stone, "The *Empire* Strikes Back: A Posttranssexual Manifesto," 1987, https://san
dystone.com/empire-strikes-back.pdf; Riki Anne Wilchins, *Read My Lips: Sexual Subversion
and the End of Gender* (Ithaca, NY: Firebrand Books, 1997).

50. Davidson, "Seeking Refuge"; Katrina Karkazis, *Fixing Sex: Intersex, Medical Authority,
and Lived Experience* (Durham, NC: Duke University Press, 2008); Georgiann Davis, *Contesting Intersexuality: The Dubious Diagnosis* (New York: New York University Press, 2015); Regina
Kunzel, "The Rise of Gay Rights and the Disavowal of Disability," in *The Oxford Handbook on
Disability History*, ed. Catherine Kudlick, Kim Nielsen, and Michael A. Rembis (New York: Oxford University Press, 2018), 459–76.

51. Zein Murib, "Transgender: Examining an Emerging Political Identity Using Three Political Processes," *Politics, Groups, and Identities* 3, no. 3 (2015): 381–97.

52. Murib, "Transgender"; Zein Murib, "Rethinking GLBT as a Political Category in U.S.
Politics," in *LGBTQ Politics: A Critical Reader*, ed. Marla Brettschneider, Susan Burgess, and
Christine Keating (New York: New York University Press, 2017), 14–33.

53. Jessica Xavier, "PFLAG Transgender Resource Packet," October 17, 1995, collection 7616,
box 42, folder 35, Parents, Families and Friends of Lesbians and Gays (PFLAG) Records, Division
of Rare and Manuscript Collections, Cornell University Library, Ithaca, NY.

54. Judd Marmor, ed., *Sexual Inversion: The Multiple Roots of Homosexuality* (New York:
Basic Books, 1965).

55. PFLAG, "PFLAG Votes 'Yes' Overwhelmingly to Include Transgender in Mission," 1998,
and "Our Trans Children: A Publication of the Transgender Outreach Networks of Parents,
Families and Friends of Lesbians and Gays (PFLAG), 2nd edition," 1998, collection 7616, box 43,
folder 35, Parents, Families and Friends of Lesbians and Gays (PFLAG) Records, Cornell University Library, Ithaca, NY.

56. PFLAG, "Our Trans Children," 4.

57. Human Rights Campaign, "HRC Releases Ground-Breaking Public Opinion Research
on Transgender Issues," September 30, 2002, collection 7301, box 268, folder 40, National Gay
and Lesbian Task Force Records, 1973–2000, Division of Rare and Manuscript Collections, Cornell University Library, Ithaca, NY.

58. Ghaziani, *Dividends of Dissent*, 177–78.

59. Paisley Currah and Lisa Jean Moore, "'We Won't Know Who You Are': Contesting Sex
Designations in New York City Birth Certificates," *Hypatia* 24, no. 3 (2009): 113–35; Paisley Currah,
Sex Is as Sex Does: Governing Transgender Identity (New York: New York University Press, 2022).

60. *Brown v. Zavaras*, 63 F.3d 967, 971 (10th Cir. 1995).

61. *Brown v. Zavaras*, 971.

62. *Estelle v. Gamble*, 429 U.S. 97 (1976).

63. Jason Pierceson, "Transgender Rights and the Judiciary," in *The Remarkable Rise of
Transgender Rights*, ed. Jami K. Taylor, Daniel C. Lewis, and Donald P. Haider-Markel (Ann Arbor: University of Michigan Press, 2018), 136–60.

64. *Fields v. Smith*, 653 F.3d 550 (7th Cir. 2011).

65. Brief of *Amici Curiae* Medical and Mental Health Professionals: American Medical Association, Mental Health America, National Commission on Correctional Health Care, World
Professional Association for Transgender Health, Dr. Wylie Hembree, and Dr. Loren Schechter
in Support of Plaintiffs-Appellees, *Fields v. Smith*, Nos. 10-2339 and 10-2446, November 29, 2010,

https://www.aclu.org/legal-document/fields-v-smith-brief-amici-curiae-medical-and-mental
-health-professionals.

66. Cole Thaler et al., "Third Amended Complaint for Declaratory and Injunctive Relief,"
Sundstrom et al. v. Franks, No. 06-C-0112 (CNC), December 18, 2006, https://www.aclu.org
/legal-document/sundstrom-v-frank-third-amended-complaint; citing J.-N. Zhou et al., "A Sex
Difference in the Human Brain and Its Relations to Transsexualism," *International Journal of
Transgenderism* 1 (1997).

67. *Fields v. Smith*.

68. *Kosilek v. Spencer* (2012); Pierceson. "Transgender Rights and the Judiciary," 151.

69. *Kosilek v. Spencer*, 774 F.3d 63 (1st Cir. 2014).

70. *Edmo v. Corizon* (9th Cir. 2019).

71. *Edmo v. Corizon*, Case No. 1:17-cv-00151 (U.S. District Id. 2018), 13–14, 28.

72. Aviva Stahl, "Prisoners, Doctors, and the Battle over Trans Medical Care," *Wired*, July 8,
2021, https://www.wired.com/story/inmates-doctors-battle-over-transgender-medical-care/.

73. *Cristina Nichole Iglesias v. Federal Bureau of Prisons*, No. 19-CV-415-NJR, April 18, 2022.

74. Stefan Vogler, *Sorting Sexualities: Expertise and the Politics of Legal Classification* (Chicago: University of Chicago Press, 2021), 114–15.

75. Adena L. Wayne, "Unique Identities and Vulnerabilities: The Case for Transgender Identity as a Basis for Asylum," *Cornell Law Review* 102, no. 1 (2016): 252.

76. Stefan Vogler, "Determining Transgender: Adjudicating Gender Identity in U.S. Asylum Law," *Gender & Society* 33, no. 3 (2019); *Avendano-Hernandez v. Lynch*, 800 F.3d 1072
(9th Cir. 2015).

77. Vogler, "Determining Transgender," 456.

78. Gay and lesbian plaintiffs also made "like sex" arguments using Title VII during this period. *DeSantis v. Pacific Telephone & Telegraph Co.*, 608 F.2d 327 (9th Cir. 1979).

79. Human Rights Campaign, "State Equality Index," 2020, https://www.hrc.org/resources
/state-equality-index.

80. Parker Marie Molloy, "What Barney Frank Still Gets Wrong on ENDA," *Advocate*, October 1, 2014, https://www.advocate.com/commentary/2014/10/01/op-ed-what-barney-frank-still
-gets-wrong-enda.

81. *Holloway v. Arthur Andersen Co.*, 566 F.2d 659 (9th Cir. 1977), 663.

82. *Holloway v. Arthur Andersen Co.*, 661.

83. *Sommers v. Budget Mktg., Inc.*, 667 F.2d 748, 749–50 (8th Cir. 1982); *Ulane v. Eastern Airlines,
Inc.*, 742 F.2d 1081 (7th Cir. 1984); *Etsitty v. Utah Transit Authority*, 502 F.3d 1215 (10th Cir. 2007).

84. *Ulane v. Eastern Airlines*, 1087.

85. *Price Waterhouse v. Hopkins*, 490 U.S. 228 (1989); *Oncale v. Sundowner Offshore Services,
Inc.*, 523 U.S. 75 (1998). By 1998 even Justice Antonin Scalia would agree with sex stereotyping
in principle.

86. Andrew Koppelman, "The Miscegenation Analogy: Sodomy Law as Sex Discrimination," *Yale Law Journal* 98 (1988): 145–64; Mary Anne Case, "Disaggregating Gender from Sex
and Sexual Orientation: The Effeminate Man in the Law and Feminist Jurisprudence," *Yale Law
Journal* 105 (1995): 1–105; Cary Franklin, "The Anti-Stereotyping Principle in Constitutional Sex
Discrimination Law," *New York University Law Review* 85, no. 1 (2010): 83–173.

87. Kimberly Yuracko, *Gender Nonconformity and the Law* (New Haven, CT: Yale University
Press, 2016), 93–97; Jessica A. Clarke, "How the First Forty Years of Circuit Precedent Got Title VII's
Sex Discrimination Provision Wrong," *Texas Law Review Online* 98 (2019): 83–130.

88. *Smith v. City of Salem*, 378 F.3d 566 (6th Cir. 2004). See also *Barnes v. City of Cincinnati*, 401 F.3d 729 (6th Cir. 2005); *Kastle v. Maricopa County Community College District*, 325 Fed. Appendix 492 (9th Cir. 2009).

89. *Schroer v. Billington*, 577 F. Supp. 2d 293 (D.D.C. 2008), 3, 30.

90. Yuracko, *Gender Nonconformity and the Law*, 23–26, 173.

91. *Jespersen v. Harrah's Operating Co.*, 444 F.3d 1104 (9th Cir. Apr. 14, 2006) (en banc). However, some courts have disagreed with the *Jespersen* ruling: *Hayden ex rel. A.H. v. Greensburg Community School Corp.*, 743 F.3d 569 (7th Cir. 2014), 577–79.

92. *Bostock v. Clayton County*, 590 U.S. ___ (2020).

93. Joshua A. Block and Galen Leigh Sherwin, "Alaska Airlines Letter on Behalf of Justin Wetherell," June 4, 2021, ACLU, https://www.aclu.org/letter/alaska-airlines-letter-behalf-justin -wetherell-june-4-2021.

94. Derrick Clifton, "Ted Cruz: Parents Who Let Kids Transition Are 'Child Abusers,'" *Out*, October 24, 2019, https://www.out.com/politics/2019/10/24/ted-cruz-parents-who-let-kids-transition -are-child-abusers.

95. Karl Bryant, "Making Gender Identity Disorder of Childhood: Historical Lessons for Contemporary Debates," *Sexuality Research and Social Policy* 3, no. 1 (2006): 23–39.

96. Shannon Price Minter, "'Déjà vu All Over Again': The Recourse to Biology by Opponents of Transgender Equality," *North Carolina Law Review* 95, no. 4 (2017): 1161–204.

97. Gayle Rubin, "The Traffic in Women: Notes on the 'Political Economy' of Sex," in *Toward an Anthropology of Women*, ed. Rayna Reiter (New York: Monthly Review Press, 1975), 157–210; Gayle Rubin, "Thinking Sex: Notes for a Radical Theory of the Politics of Sexuality," in *Pleasure and Danger: Exploring Female Sexuality*, ed. Carole Vance (Boston: Routledge & Kegan Paul, 1984), 267–319.

98. Kristen Schilt and Laurel Westbrook, "Doing Gender, Determining Gender: Transgender People, Gender Panics, and the Maintenance of the Sex/Gender/Sexuality System," *Gender & Society* 28, no. 1 (2014): 32–57.

99. "An Act to Provide for Single-Sex Multiple Occupancy Bathroom and Changing Facilities in Schools and Public Agencies and to Create Statewide Consistency in Regulation of Employment and Public Accommodations," Session Law 2016-3, House Bill 2, March 23, 2016, http://www.ncleg.net/Sessions/2015E2/Bills/House/PDF/H2v4.pdf; Kristen Schilt and Laurel Westbrook, "Bathroom Battlegrounds and Penis Panics," *Contexts*, August 20, 2015, https://con texts.org/articles/bathroom-battlegrounds-and-penis-panics/.

100. *Macy v. Holder*, EEOC Appeal No. 0120120821 (2012); *Lusardi v. McHugh*, EEOC Appeal No. 0120133395 (2015); Office of the U.S. Attorney General, "Treatment of Transgender Employment Discrimination Claims under Title VII of the Civil Rights Act of 1964," December 15, 2014, https://www.justice.gov/file/188671/download; US Department of Justice, Civil Rights Division, and US Department of Education, Office for Civil Rights, "Dear Colleague Letter on Transgender Students," May 13, 2016, https://www2.ed.gov/about/offices/list/ocr/letters/colleague-201605 -title-ix-transgender.pdf; . As soon as the Trump administration took power, it began rescinding these directives and passing new discriminatory ones: US Department of Justice, Civil Rights Division, and US Department of Education, Office for Civil Rights, "Dear Colleague Letter," February 22, 2017, https://www2.ed.gov/about/offices/list/ocr/letters/colleague-201702 -title-ix.pdf; Katie Keith, "HHS Proposes to Strip Gender Identity, Language Access Protections from ACA Anti-Discrimination Rule," *Health Affairs*, May 25, 2019, http://www.healthaffairs .org/do/10.1377/hblog20190525.831858/full/.

101. Transgender Law Center, "Vice President Joe Biden: Transgender Discrimination 'Civil Rights Issue of Our Time,'" October 31, 2012, https://transgenderlawcenter.org/archives/2312.

102. US Department of Justice, "Attorney General Loretta E. Lynch Delivers Remarks at Press Conference Announcing Complaint against the State of North Carolina to Stop Discrimination against Transgender Individuals," May 9, 2016, https://www.justice.gov/opa/speech/attorney-general-loretta-e-lynch-delivers-remarks-press-conference-announcing-complaint.

103. *United States of America v. State of North Carolina et al.*, No. 1:16-cv-00425 (M.D.N.C. 2016), 7.

104. *Joaquín Carcaño et al. v. North Carolina Governor Patrick McCrory et al.*, No. 1:16-cv-236 (M.D.N.C. 2016), 8.

105. Brief for National Center for Lesbian Rights, GLBTQ Legal Advocates & Defenders, National Center for Transgender Equality, Forge, Transgender Law & Policy Institute, and Trans People of Color Coalition as Amici Curiae Supporting Reversal on Behalf of Plaintiffs-Appellants, *Joaquín Carcaño et al. v. North Carolina Governor Patrick McCrory et al.*, No. 1:16-cv-236 (M.D.N.C. 2016) (October 25, 2016).

106. Aruna Saraswat, Jamie D. Weinand, and Joshua D. Safer, "Evidence Supporting the Biological Nature of Gender Identity," *Endocrine Practice* 21, no. 2 (2015): 202.

107. Defendants' and Intervenor-Defendants' Brief in Opposition to the United States' Motion for Preliminary Injunction, *United States of America v. State of North Carolina et al.*, No.1:16-cv-00425-TDS-JEP (August 17, 2016); Moriah Balingit, "After Trump Administration Rescinds Transgender Student Directive, States Drop Lawsuit Challenging It," *Washington Post*, March 2, 2017, https://www.washingtonpost.com/news/education/wp/2017/03/02/after-trump-administration-rescinded-transgender-student-directive-states-drop-lawsuit-challenging-it/.

108. Dawn Ennis, "Human Rights Campaign Sets Sights on Johns Hopkins after Controversial Trans Report," *NBC News*, September 1, 2016, http://www.nbcnews.com/feature/nbc-out/hrc-sets-sights-johns-hopkins-after-controversial-sexuality-gender-report-n641501/.

109. Amy Ellis Nutt, "Long Shadow Cast by Psychiatrist on Transgender Issues Finally Recedes at Johns Hopkins," *Washington Post*, April 5, 2017, https://www.washingtonpost.com/national/health-science/long-shadow-cast-by-psychiatrist-on-transgender-issues-finally-recedes-at-johns-hopkins/2017/04/05/e851e56e-0d85-11e7-ab07-07d9f521f6b5_story.html.

110. Lawrence S. Mayer and Paul R. McHugh, "Sexuality and Gender Findings from the Biological, Psychological, and Social Sciences," *New Atlantis*, no. 50 (2016): 1–143. It is worth noting that *New Atlantis* is not a respectable peer-review journal, but instead an appendage of the Ethics and Public Policy Center, a conservative Christian think tank that has defended both the Defense of Marriage Act and Don't Ask, Don't Tell.

111. Mayer and McHugh, 13–58.

112. Greg Lacour, "HB2: How North Carolina Go Here (Updated)," *Charlotte Magazine*, March 30, 2017, https://www.charlottemagazine.com/hb2-how-north-carolina-got-here-updated/.

113. Alliance Defending Freedom, "Physical Privacy Policy," n.d., https://adflegal.blob.core.windows.net/web-content-dev/docs/default-source/documents/resources/campaign-resources/marriage/safe-bathrooms/local-student-physical-privacy-policy.pdf?sfvrsn=2; Daniel Bennett, *Defending Faith: The Politics of the Christian Conservative Legal Movement* (Lawrence: University Press of Kansas, 2017).

114. *G. G. v. Gloucester County School Board*, No. 15-2056 (4th Cir. 2016).

115. In this sense, Grimm's case morphed into a fight over the legacy of *Auer v. Robbins*, 519 U.S. 452 (1997).

116. Gavin Grimm, "I'm Transgender and Can't Use the Student Bathroom: The Supreme Court Could Change That," *Washington Post*, October 27, 2016, https://www.washingtonpost .com/opinions/im-transgender-and-cant-use-the-student-bathroom-the-supreme-court-could -change-that/2016/10/27/19d1a3ae-9bc1-11e6-a0ed-ab0774c1eaa5_story.html.

117. Brief in Opposition, *Gloucester County School Board v. G. G., By His Next Friend and Mother, Deirdre Grimm*, No. 16-273 (September 2016), 4.

118. Brief of Respondent, *Gloucester County School Board v. G. G., By His Next Friend and Mother, Deirdre Grimm*, No. 16-273 (February 2017), 3.

119. Brief for Dr. Paul R. McHugh, MD, Dr. Paul Hruz, MD, PhD, and Dr. Lawrence S. Mayer, PhD, as Amici Curiae Supporting Petitioner, *G. G. v. Gloucester County School Board*, No. 16-273 (January 10, 2017), 3–4.

120. Brief for McHugh et al.; Judith Butler, *Gender Trouble: Feminism and the Subversion of Identity* (New York: Routledge, 2016), 6–7.

121. Brief for McHugh et al., 9.

122. Stephanie Brill and Rachel Pepper, *The Transgender Child: A Handbook for Families and Professionals* (San Francisco: Cleis Press, 2018); Meadow, *Trans Kids*; Sadjadi, "Deep in the Brain."

123. *Board of Education of the Highland Local School District v. U.S. Department of Education et al.*, No. 2:16-cv-00524 (S.D. Oh. 2016); *Juliet Evancho et al. v. Pine-Richland School District et al.*, No. 2:16-cv-01537 (W.D. Pa. 2017).

124. Memorandum of Law Supporting Plaintiffs' Motion for Preliminary Injunction, *Juliet Evancho et al. v. Pine-Richland School District et al.*, No. 2:16-cv-01537-MRH (W.D. Pa. 2017) (October 20, 2016), 2–3.

125. *Whitaker v. Kenosha Unified School District No.1 Board of Education*, No. 16-CV-943-PP (E.D. Wi. 2016). The Seventh Circuit in this case has also been receptive to the biopolitical conception of transgender identity as evidenced in its language that "this is not a case where a student has merely announced that he is a different gender. Rather, Ash [the plaintiff] has a medically diagnosed and documented condition"; *Whitaker v. Kenosha Unified School District No.1 Board of Education*, No 16-3522 (2017), 24.

126. Declaration of Dr. R. Nicholas Gorton, M.D. (Exhibit 3), *Whitaker v. Kenosha* (2016).

127. *Juliet Evancho et al. v. Pine-Richland School District*, 8–9.

128. *Whitaker v. Kenosha Unified School District*, No. 16-3522 (7th Cir. 2017), 24.

129. Sahar Sadjadi, "The Vulnerable Child Protection Act and Transgender Children's Health," *Transgender Studies Quarterly* 7, no. 3 (2020): 508–16; Matt Lavietes and Elliott Ramos, "Nearly 240 Anti-LGBTQ Bills Filed in 2022 So Far, Most of Them Targeting Trans People," *NBC News*, March 20, 2022, https://www.nbcnews.com/nbc-out/out-politics-and-policy/nearly-240 -anti-lgbtq-bills-filed-2022-far-targeting-trans-people-rcna20418.

130. Priya Krishnakumar, "This Record-Breaking Year for Anti-Transgender Legislation Would Affect Minors the Most," CNN, April 15, 2021, https://edition.cnn.com/2021/04/15/poli tics/anti-transgender-legislation-2021/index.html.

131. Complaint for *B.P.J. v. West Virginia State Board of Education*, S.D. WV, Case 2:21-cv-11111, May 26, 2021.

132. Complaint for *B.P.J. v. West Virginia State Board of Education*, 2, 8–9. See also Rebecca M. Jordan-Young and Katrina Karkazis, *Testosterone: An Unauthorized Biography* (Cambridge, MA: Harvard University Press, 2019).

133. Complaint for *B.P.J. v. West Virginia State Board of Education*, 5.

134. Declaration of Joshua D. Safer, MD, FACP, FACE, *B.P.J. v. West Virginia State Board of Education*, May 26, 2021, https://www.aclu.org/sites/default/files/field_document/bpj_v_west_virginia_state_board_of_education_-_declaration_of_joshua_d._safer_md.pdf. Safer has also served as an expert witness in a similar case involving Idaho's 2020 anti-trans sports-participation case: Declaration of Joshua D. Safer, MD, FACP, FACE, *Hecox v. Little*, No.1:20-cv-184-CWD, April 30, 2020, https://www.aclu.org/legal-document/hecox-v-little-safer-declaration.

135. Declaration of Safer, *B.P.J. v. West Virginia*, 5; Endocrine Society, "Transgender Health Position Statement," 2021, https://www.endocrine.org/advocacy/position-statements/transgender-health.

136. Declaration of Safer, *B.P.J. v. West Virginia*.

137. Brief of Defendants-Appellants, *Dylan Brandt v. Leslie Rutledge*, No. 21-2875 (November 15, 2021), 5, https://www.aclu.org/legal-document/brandt-et-al-v-rutledge-et-al-brief-defendants-appellants.

138. *Grimm v. Gloucester County School Board*, No. 19-1952 (4th Cir. 2020); *Adams v. School Board of St. Johns County*, 968 F.3d 1286 (11th Cir. 2020).

139. Amy Howe, "Justices Won't Intervene in Dispute over Transgender Rights and Bathrooms," *SCOTUSblog*, June 28, 2021, https://www.scotusblog.com/2021/06/justices-wont-intervene-in-dispute-over-transgender-rights-and-bathrooms/.

140. Joanna Wuest, "A Conservative Right to Privacy: Legal, Ideological, and Coalitional Transformations in U.S. Social Conservatism," *Law & Social Inquiry* 46, no. 4 (2021): 964–92.

141. Jay Greene, "Puberty Blockers, Cross-Sex Hormones, and Youth Suicide," June 13, 2022, Heritage Foundation, https://www.heritage.org/gender/report/puberty-blockers-cross-sex-hormones-and-youth-suicide.

142. Kerith J. Conron and Kathryn K. O'Neill, "Prohibiting Gender-Affirming Medical Care for Youth," UCLA School of Law Williams Institute, March 2022, https://williamsinstitute.law.ucla.edu/publications/bans-trans-youth-health-care/.

143. Jack L. Turban et al., "Legislation to Criminalize Gender-Affirming Medical Care for Transgender Youth," *Journal of the American Medical Association* 325, no. 22 (2021): 2251–52.

144. Mary Ziegler, "The Deviousness of Texas's New Abortion Law," *Atlantic*, September 1, 2021, https://www.theatlantic.com/ideas/archive/2021/09/deviousness-texass-new-abortion-law/619945/.

145. Mary Ziegler, *Abortion and the Law in America: Roe v. Wade to the Present* (New York: Cambridge University Press, 2020).

146. Joanna Wuest, "The Dead End of Corporate Activism," *Boston Review*, May 18, 2022, https://bostonreview.net/articles/the-dead-end-of-corporate-activism/.

147. Liz Scott Lamagdeleine, "What Is Gender-Affirming Medical Care for Transgender Children? Here's What You Need to Know," *Texas Tribune*, August 4, 2021, https://www.texastribune.org/2021/08/04/gender-affirming-care-transgender-texas/.

148. William E. Burleson, *Bi America: Myths, Truths, and Struggles of an Invisible Community* (New York: Harrington Park Press 2005), 21.

149. Tom Waidzunas and Steven Epstein, "'For Men Arousal Is Orientation': Bodily Truthing, Technosexual Scripts, and the Materialization of Sexualities through the Phallometric Test," *Social Studies of Science* 45, no. 2 (April 2015): 187–213.

150. Waidzunas and Epstein, 189.

151. Gerald C. Davison and G. Terence Wilson, "Attitudes of Behavior Therapists toward Homosexuality," *Behavior Therapy* 4 (1973): 686–96.

152. Tom Waidzunas, *The Straight Line: How the Fringe Science of Ex-Gay Therapy Reoriented Sexuality* (Minneapolis: University of Minnesota Press, 2015), 74.

153. Waidzunas, 94–95.

154. Waidzunas, 122.

155. Benedict Carey, "Gay, Straight or Lying? Bisexuality Revisited," *New York Times*, July 5, 2005, http://www.nytimes.com/2005/07/05/health/straight-gay-or-lying-bisexuality-revisited.html.

156. Gerulf Reiger, Meredith L. Chivers, and Michael J. Bailey, "Sexual Arousal Patterns of Bisexual Men," *Psychological Science* 16, no. 8 (August 2005): 579–84.

157. The contradiction here is that a narrow scientific theory and method led to what at least sounds like a queer theory of bisexuality: for these researchers, male bisexuality is not so much defined by arousal than it is by the interpretation of particular desires. Lest proponents of queer theory be too enthused, recall that the baseline assumption here is that orientation and identity for *men* in particular is directly related to how external stimuli directs blood flow to the penis (a decidedly *not* queer theoretical premise).

158. Reiger, Chivers, and Bailey, "Sexual Arousal Patterns of Bisexual Men," 580.

159. Loraine Hutchins, "Sexual Prejudice: The Erasure of Bisexuals in Academia and the Media," *American Sexuality Magazine* 3, no. 4 (2005).

160. National Gay and Lesbian Task Force, "The Problems with 'Gay, Straight or Lying,'" July 2005, https://studylib.net/doc/8200124/the-problems-with--gay--straight-or-lying-.

161. National Gay and Lesbian Task Force, "The Problems with 'Gay, Straight or Lying.'" The statement also noted that Bailey had recently come under fire for endorsing Ray Blanchard's widely condemned theory that many trans women suffer from *autogynephilia*, a condition wherein a person assigned male at birth medically transitions to fulfill an erotic wish to become a woman. Michael Bailey, *The Man Who Would Be Queen: The Science of Gender-Bending and Transsexualism* (Washington, DC: Joseph Henry Press, 2003).

162. Andy Humm, "Firestorm over Bisexuality in Times," *Gay City News* July 20, 2005, https://gaycitynews.com/firestorm-over-bisexuality-in-times/.

163. Fritz Klein, *The Bisexual Option: A Concept of One Hundred Percent Intimacy* (New York: Harrington Park Press, 1978).

164. American Institute of Bisexuality, "About Fritz Klein," n.d., http://www.americaninstituteofbisexuality.org/fritz-klein/.

165. Denizet-Lewis, "The Scientific Quest to Prove Bisexuality Exists."

166. Allen M. Rosenthal et al., "Sexual Arousal Patterns in Bisexual Men Revisited," *Biological Psychology* 88, no. 1 (September 2011): 112–15. That same year, Kinsey Institute researchers published a similar study: Jerome A. Cerny and Erick Janssen, "Patterns of Sexual Arousal in Homosexual, Bisexual, and Heterosexual Men," *Archives of Sexual Behavior* 40, no. 4 (August 2011): 687–97.

167. American Institute of Bisexuality, "Controversy over Professor Bailey and the Existence of Bisexuality," 2010, BiBrain.org; Gerulf Reiger and Ritch Savins-Williams, "The Eyes Have It: Sex and Sexual Orientation Differences in Pupil Dilation Patterns," *PLOS One*, August 3, 2012, https://doi.org/10.1371/journal.pone.0040256. Additionally, AIB has funded research by psychologists Ritch Savins-Williams and Gerulf Reiger, who use pupil dilators to measure bisexual arousal and sexual curiosity.

168. David Tuller, "No Surprise for Bisexual Men: Report Indicates They Exist," *New York Times*, August 22, 2011, http://www.nytimes.com/2011/08/23/health/23bisexual.html.

169. Faith Cheltenham, "Real to Everyone: Bisexual Study Sponsored by AIB Makes the News," *BiNet USA Blog*, August 25, 2011, http://binetusa.blogspot.com/2011/08/just-this-week -journal-of-biological.html.

170. Truth Wins Out, "Bisexuality," LGBTScience.org, n.d., http://www.lgbtscience.org/bi sexuality/.

171. Adam Polaski, "Bi Activist Adrienne Williams Honored by White House," Bilerico Report on LGBTQ Nation, June 27, 2011, http://bilerico.lgbtqnation.com/2011/06/bi_activist_adri enne_williams_honored_by_white_hou.php.

172. Adrienne Williams, "The American Institute of Bisexuality on Bi Men, Part 1," *Bi Talk*, August 30, 2011, https://archive.org/details/podcast_bi-talk_the-american-institute-bise _1000332797220.

173. Denizet-Lewis, "The Scientific Quest to Prove Bisexuality Exists."

174. Tuller, "No Surprise for Bisexual Men.".

175. Rachel Nolan, "Beyond the Cover Story: Benoit Denizet-Lewis on Bisexuality and the Seven Dimensions of Sexual Orientation, *The 6th Floor* (blog), *New York Times*, March 24, 2014, http://6thfloor.blogs.nytimes.com/2014/03/24/behind-the-cover-story-benoit-denizet-lewis -on-bisexuality-and-the-seven-dimensions-of-sexual-orientation/?_r=0.

176. Nicole Kristal, "Bisexuals Lack Support—and It's Literally Killing Us," *Advocate*, April 1, 2016, http://www.advocate.com/commentary/2016/4/01/bisexuals-lack-support-and-its-literally-killing -us; Bisexual Resource Center, "Past Campaigns," 2021, https://bihealthmonth.org/past-campaigns/; Human Rights Campaign, "Living into Equity This Bisexual+ Health Awareness Month," March 1, 2021, https://www.hrc.org/news/living-into-equity-this-bisexual-health-awareness-month.

177. Adolph Reed Jr. and Merlin Chowkwanyun, "Race, Class, Crisis: The Discourse of Racial Disparity and Its Analytical Discontents," *Socialist Register* 48 (2012), https://socialistregister .com/index.php/srv/article/view/15650.

178. Lori E. Ross et al., "Prevalence of Depression and Anxiety among Bisexual People Compared to Gay, Lesbian, and Heterosexual Individuals: A Systematic Review and Meta-Analysis," *Journal of Sex Research* 55, nos. 4–5 (2017): 435–56; Emilie E. Doan Van et al., "Perceived Discrimination, Coping Mechanisms, and Effects on Health in Bisexual and Other Non-Monosexual Adults," *Archives of Sexual Behavior* 48, no. 1 (2019): 159–74.

179. Williams Institute, "LGBT Poverty in the United States," UCLA School of Law, October 2019, https://williamsinstitute.law.ucla.edu/publications/lgbt-poverty-us/.

180. Florence Ashley, "Simpson's Paradox in LGBTQ+ Policy: A Case Study," *Sexuality Research and Social Policy* (2020), https://doi.org/10.1007/s13178-020-00500-7.

181. Dani Blum, "The 'Double Closet': Why Some Bisexual People Struggle with Mental Health," *New York Times*, June 30, 2021, https://www.nytimes.com/2021/06/30/well/bisexual -mental-health-lgbt.html.

182. Aaron Safron et al., "Neural Correlates of Sexual Orientation in Heterosexual, Bisexual, and Homosexual Men," *Scientific Reports* 7, no. 41314 (2017), https://doi.org/10.1038/srep41314.

183. Jeremy Jabbour, "Robust Evidence for Bisexual Orientation among Men," *Proceedings of the National Academy of Sciences of the United States of America* 117, no. 31 (2020): 18369–77.

184. Hannah Thomasy, "Researchers Revisit Male Bisexuality—and Draw Critics," *Undark*, August 17, 2020, https://undark.org/2020/08/17/bisexuality-paper-draws-critics/.

185. Josh Milton, "Scientist Who Denied Bisexual Men Exist Finally Comes to His Senses and Discovers, Yes, Bi Guys Are Telling the Truth," *Pink News*, July 21, 2021, https://www.pink

news.co.uk/2020/07/21/bisexuality-bisexual-j-michael-bailey-gerulf-rieger-northwestern
-essex-university-biphobia/.

186. David Artavia, "Male Bisexuality Is Real, a New Study Confirms Once and for All," *Advocate*, July 21, 2021, https://www.advocate.com/bisexual/2020/7/21/male-bisexuality-real-new
-study-confirms-once-and-all.

187. Complaint for Declaratory and Injunctive Relief, *D.N. v. DeSantis*, Case 0:21-cv-61344-
XXXX, June 29, 2021, 10, https://hrc-prod-requests.s3-us-west-2.amazonaws.com/Litigation.pdf
?mtime=20210630085703&focal=none.

Conclusion

1. Oreo Cookie, July 29, 2021, https://twitter.com/Oreo/status/1409875226423398400.

2. Rachel Shatto, "Oreo & PFLAG Have Teamed Up Again to Create Limited-Edition Pride
Cookies," *Advocate*, June 22, 2021, https://www.advocate.com/business/2021/6/22/oreo-pflag
-have-teamed-create-limited-edition-pride-cookies.

3. Stephen Vider, *The Queerness of Home: Gender, Sexuality, and the Politics of Domesticity
after World War II* (Chicago: University of Chicago Press, 2021).

4. Lisa Duggan, "The New Homonormativity: The Sexual Politics of Neoliberalism," in *Materializing Democracy: Toward a Revitalized Cultural Politics*, ed. Russ Castronovo and Dana D.
Nelson (Durham, NC: Duke University Press, 2002), 179.

5. Human Rights Campaign, "Sexual Orientation and Gender Identity Definitions," 2021,
https://www.hrc.org/resources/sexual-orientation-and-gender-identity-terminology-and
-definitions; Dear Abby, "Friend Finds Gender Fluidity a Hard Concept to Swallow," *Stamford
Advocate*, June 20, 2017, https://www.stamfordadvocate.com/entertainment/article/Dear-Abby
-Friend-finds-gender-fluidity-a-hard-11226682.php.

6. *Bostock v. Clayton County*, 590 U.S. ___ (2020), 33.

7. Jim Dalrymple II, "How 'Black' NAACP Leader Rachel Dolezal Was Outed as a White
Woman," *Buzzfeed News*, June 13, 2015, https://www.buzzfeednews.com/article/jimdalrympleii
/heres-how-black-naacp-leader-rachel-dolezal-was-outted-as-a; "A Summary of Cases Relating
to Rachel Dolezal," *New York Times*, June 16, 2015, https://www.nytimes.com/interactive/2015
/06/16/us/document-rachel-dolezal-cases.html.

8. Rogers Brubaker, *Trans: Gender and Race in an Age of Unsettled Identities* (Princeton, NJ:
Princeton University Press, 2016).

9. Patrick R. Grzanka, "Amy Coney Barrett Was Criticized for Using the Term 'Sexual Preference.' Should We Care?," *Washington Post*, October 20, 2021, https://www.washingtonpost
.com/nation/2020/10/20/amy-coney-barrett-was-criticized-using-term-sexual-preference
-should-we-care/.

10. Kimberly Yuracko, *Gender Nonconformity and the Law* (New Haven, CT: Yale University Press, 2016).

11. Rogers Brubaker, "The Dolezal Affair: Race, Gender, and the Micropolitics of Identity,"
Ethnic and Racial Studies 39, no. 3 (2016): 415.

12. Andrea Ganna et al., "Large-Scale GWAS Reveals Insights into the Genetic Architecture of Same-Sex Sexual Behavior," *Science* 365, no. 6456 (2019), https://doi.org/10.1126/science
.aat7693; Joanna Wuest, "The New Genomics of Sexuality Moves Us Beyond 'Born This Way,'"
Psyche, February 24, 2021, https://psyche.co/ideas/the-new-genomics-of-sexuality-moves-us-be
yond-born-this-way.

13. Lindsey Bever, "There's No 'Gay Gene,'" *Washington Post*, August 29, 2019, https://www.washingtonpost.com/health/2019/08/29/theres-no-gay-gene-genetics-are-linked-same-sex-behavior-new-study-says/.

14. Sarah S. Richardson and Hallam Stevens, eds., *Postgenomics: Perspectives on Biology after the Genome* (Durham, NC: Duke University Press, 2015).

15. A. Maxmen, "Controversial 'Gay Gene' App Provokes Fears of a Genetic Wild West," *Nature*, October 29, 2019, https://www.nature.com/articles/d41586-019-03282-0.

16. Ganna et al., "Large-Scale GWAS," 4.

17. Brendan P. Zietsch and Morgan J. Sidari, "The Kinsey Scale Is Ill-Suited to Most Sexuality Research Because It Does Not Measure a Single Construct," *Proceedings of the National Academy of Sciences* 117, no. 44 (2020): DOI: 10.1073/pnas.2015820117.

18. Ganna et al., "Large-Scale GWAS."

19. E. O. Wilson, *Sociobiology: The New Synthesis* (Cambridge, MA: Harvard University Press, 1975).

20. Michael Warner, *The Trouble with Normal: Sex, Politics, and the Ethics of Queer Life* (Cambridge, MA: Harvard University Press, 1999).

21. Jeffrey M. Jones, "LGBT Identification Rises to 5.6% in Latest U.S. Estimate," *Gallup*, February 24, 2021, https://news.gallup.com/poll/329708/lgbt-identification-rises-latest-estimate.aspx.

22. GLAAD, "Accelerating Acceptance 2017," 2017, https://www.glaad.org/files/aa/2017_GLAAD_Accelerating_Acceptance.pdf.

23. Kacie M. Kidd et al., "Prevalence of Gender-Diverse Youth in an Urban School District," *Pediatrics* 147, no. 6 (2021), https://doi.org/10.1542/peds.2020-049823.

24. Pam Belluck, "Many Genes Influence Same-Sex Sexuality, Not a Single 'Gay Gene,'" *New York Times*, August 29, 2019, https://www.nytimes.com/2019/08/29/science/gay-gene-sex.html.

25. Brendan P. Zietsch et al., "Genomic Evidence Consistent with Antagonistic Pleiotropy May Help Explain the Evolutionary Maintenance of Same-Sex Sexual Behaviour in Humans," *Nature Human Behaviour*, August 23, 2021, https://doi.org/10.1038/s41562-021-01168-8.

26. Robert Carlson, "Estimating the Biotech Sector's Contribution to the US Economy," *Nature Biotechnology* 34, no. 3 (2016): 247–55; Kean Birch, "Rethinking Value in the Bio-Economy: Finance, Assetization, and the Management of Value," *Science, Technology, and Human Values* 42, no. 3 (2017): 460–90.

27. Steven Peter Vallas and Daniel Lee Kleinman, "Contradiction, Convergence and the Knowledge Economy: The Confluence of Academic and Commercial Biotechnology," *Socio-Economic Review* 6, no. 2 (2008): 283–311; Editors, "The Service-Based Bioeconomy," *Nature Biotechnology* 32, no. 597 (2014), https://doi-org.ezproxy.princeton.edu/10.1038/nbt.2961.

28. Clive Cookson, "German Biotech Smashes European Fundraising Record," *Financial Times*, July 9, 2019, https://www.ft.com/content/14f62204-a188-11e9-a282-2df48f366f7d; Riley Griffin and Drew Armstrong, "Pfizer Vaccine's Funding Came from Berlin, Not Washington." *Bloomberg*, November 9, 2020, https://www.bloomberg.com/news/articles/2020-11-09/pfizer-vaccine-s-funding-came-from-berlin-not-washington.

29. Clare Elwell, "How 500,000 Britons Are Critical to Assessing Global Disease Risk," *Financial Times*, August 22, 2018, https://www.ft.com/content/80c82a0a-a48f-11e8-8ecf-a7ae1beff35b.

30. Bennett McIntosh, "There's (Still) No Gay Gene," *Harvard Magazine*, August 29, 2019, https://www.harvardmagazine.com/2019/08/there-s-still-no-gay-gene.

31. Nadia Abu El-Haj, "The Genetic Reinscription of Race," *Annual Review of Anthropology* 36 (2007): 283–300; Duana Fullwiley, "The Molecularization of Race: Institutionalizing

Human Difference in Pharmacogenetics Practice," *Science as Culture* 16, no. 1 (2007): 1–30; Jonathan Kahn, *Race in a Bottle: The Story of BiDil and Racialized Medicine in a Post-Genomic Age* (New York: Columbia University Press, 2012).

32. Aaron Panofsky and Catherine Bliss, "Ambiguity and Scientific Authority: Population Classification in Genomic Science," *American Sociological Review* 82, no. 1 (2017): 59–87.

33. David Reich, "How Genetics Is Changing Our Understanding of 'Race,'" *New York Times*, March 23, 2018, https://www.nytimes.com/2018/03/23/opinion/sunday/genetics-race.html.

34. Jonathan Kahn et al., "How Not to Talk about Race and Genetics," *BuzzFeed News*, March 30, 2018, https://www.buzzfeed.com/bfopinion/race-genetics-david-reich?utm_term=.cq RPRLLG5#.inyj6ppDV.

35. Nicholas Wade, *A Troublesome Inheritance: Genes, Race and Human History* (New York: Penguin, 2014).

36. Robert Plomin, *Blueprint: How DNA Makes Us Who We Are* (London: Penguin Random House, 2018).

37. Nathaniel Comfort, "Genetic Determinism Rides Again," *Nature*, September 25, 2018, https://www.nature.com/articles/d41586-018-06784-5.

38. Kathryn Paige Harden, "The Science of Terrible Men," *Aeon*, March 11, 2021, https://aeon .co/essays/what-do-we-do-with-the-science-of-terrible-men; M. W. Feldman and Jessica Riskin, "Why Biology Is Not Destiny," *New York Review of Books*, April 21, 2022, https://www.nybooks .com/articles/2022/04/21/why-biology-is-not-destiny-genetic-lottery-kathryn-harden/.

39. Carino Gurjao, "Opinion: Unintended, but Not Unanticipated: The Consequences of Human Behavioral Genetics," August 29, 2019, *Broadminded Blog*, Broad Institute, https://www .broadinstitute.org/blog/opinion-unintended-not-unanticipated-consequences-human-beha vioral-genetics.

40. Stephanie Clare, "Biological Sex and the 'Overrepresentation of Man,'" in "Gay Genes in the Post-Genomic Era: A Roundtable," Stephanie Claire, Patrick Grzanka, and Joanna Wuest, *GLQ* (forthcoming).

41. Alice Popejoy and Stephanie Fulington, "Genomics Is Failing on Diversity," *Nature* 538, no. 7624 (2016): 161–64.

42. Gina Colata, "'Nothing to Do with Genes': Racial Gaps in Pandemic Stem from Social Inequities, Studies Find," *New York Times*, December 9, 2020, https://www.nytimes.com/2020 /12/09/world/nothing-to-do-with-genes-racial-gaps-in-pandemic-stem-from-social-ineq uities-studies-find.html.

43. Dorothy Roberts, *Killing the Black Body: Race, Reproduction, and the Meaning of Liberty* (New York: Vintage, 1998).

44. Gbenga Ogedegbe, et al., "Assessment of Racial/Ethnic Disparities in Hospitalization and Mortality in Patients with COVID-19 in New York City," *JAMA Network Open* 3, no. 12 (2020), https://doi.org/10.1001/jamanetworkopen.2020.26881.

45. Akinyemi Oni-Orisan, "Embracing Genetic Diversity to Improve Black Health," *New England Journal of Medicine* 384 (2021): 1163–67; citing from M. Nei and A. K. Roychoudhury, "Genic Variation within and between the Three Major Races of Man, Caucasoids, Negroids, and Mongoloids," *American Journal of Human Genetics* 26, no. 4 (1974): 421–43. For more on the problems with the "pandemic of racism" and treating racism itself as a biomedical problem, see Briana Last, "Is Racism a Disease?" *nonsite*, no. 33 (2020), https://nonsite.org/is-racism-a-disease/.

46. Joanna Wuest, "The Dead End of Corporate Activism," *Boston Review*, May 18, 2022, https://bostonreview.net/articles/the-dead-end-of-corporate-activism/.

47. Heritage Foundation, "The Heritage Foundation Supports the Promise to America's Children," February 22, 2021, https://www.heritage.org/press/the-heritage-foundation-supports-the-promise-americas-children.

48. Heritage Foundation, "The Equality Act in the Senate," March 21, 2021, https://www.heritage.org/gender/heritage-explains/the-equality-act-the-senate.

49. Abigail Shrier, *Irreversible Damage: The Transgender Craze Seducing Our Daughters* (Washington, DC: Regnery, 2020).

50. Committee on the Judiciary, "The Equality Act: LGBTQ Rights Are Human Rights," March 17, 2021, https://www.judiciary.senate.gov/meetings/the-equality-act-lgbtq-rights-are-human-rights.

51. Roger N. Lancaster, *Sex Panic and the Punitive State* (Berkeley: University of California Press 2011).

52. Michael Bailey, *The Man Who Would Be Queen: The Science of Gender-Bending and Transsexualism* (Washington, DC: Joseph Henry Press, 2003); Michael Bailey, "How to Ruin Sex Research," *Archives of Sex Behavior* 48 (2019), 1007–11, https://doi-org.ezproxy.princeton.edu/10.1007/s10508-019-1420-y.

53. Michael Bailey, "The Minority Stress Model Deserves Reconsideration, Not Just Extension," *Archives of Sexual Behavior* 49 no. 7 (2020): 2265–68, https://doi.org/10.1007/s10508-019-01606-9.

54. Ilan H. Meyer, John E. Pachankis, and Daniel N. Klein, "Do Genes Explain Sexual Minority Mental Health Disparities?," *Archives of Sexual Behavior* 50, no. 3 (2021): 731–37, https://doi.org/10.1007/s10508-020-01909-2.

55. "The Pioneering Psychologist Who Proved That Being Gay Isn't a Mental Illness," *Aeon*, October 20, 2020, https://aeon.co/videos/the-pioneering-psychologist-who-proved-that-being-gay-isnt-a-mental-illness.

56. Michael Bailey et al., "Sexual Orientation, Controversy, and Science," *Psychological Science in the Public Interest* 17, no. 2 (2016): 45–101.

57. Michael Bailey, "How to Ruin Sex Research," *Archives of Sexual Behavior* 48 (2019): 1007–11.

58. Economic Policy Institute, "The Productivity-Pay Gap," July 2019, https://www.epi.org/productivity-pay-gap/; Carter C. Price and Kathryn A. Edwards, "Trends in Income from 1975 to 2018," Rand Corporation, 2020, https://www.rand.org/pubs/working_papers/WRA516-1.html.

59. Colin Crouch, *Post-Democracy after the Crises* (Cambridge: Polity, 2020).

60. Phillip M. Ayoub, "Attacking LGBT Life Helped the Right-Wing Polish President Win Reelection—Barely," *Washington Post*, July 21, 2020, https://www.washingtonpost.com/politics/2020/07/21/attacking-lgbt-life-helped-right-wing-polish-president-win-reelection-barely/.

61. Zoltán Kovács, "PM Orbán at CPAC: Here's Hungary's 12-Point Recipe for Christian Conservative Success," *About Hungary*, May 9, 2022, https://abouthungary.hu/blog/pm-orban-at-cpac-heres-hungarys-12-point-recipe-for-christian-conservative-success.

62. Ryan Conrad, ed., *Against Equality: Queer Revolution, Not Mere Inclusion* (Oakland, CA: AK Press, 2014).

63. As scholars of mass incarceration, the carceral state, and sex panics have shown, one apparent scapegoat appears to be the amorphous figure of the sex offender (notably, which right-wing politicians have no qualms equating with law-abiding LGBTQ+ people). Lancaster, *Sex Panic and the Punitive State*; Marie Gottschalk, *Caught: The Prison State and the Lockdown of American Politics, Revised Edition* (Princeton, NJ: Princeton University Press, 2016); JoAnn Wypijewski, *What We Don't Talk About: Sex and the Mess of Life* (New York: Verso Books, 2021).

64. W. David Hill et al., "Genome-Wide Analysis Identifies Molecular Systems and 149 Genetic Loci Associated with Income," *Nature Communications* 10, no. 5741 (2019), https://doi.org/10.1038/s41467-019-13585-5; Daniel Barth, Nicholas W. Papageorge, and Kevin Thom, "Genetic Endowments and Wealth Inequality," *Journal of Political Economy* 128, no. 4 (2020), https://doi.org/10.1086/705415; Andries T. Marees, "Genetic Correlates of Socio-Economic Status Influence the Pattern of Shared Heritability across Mental Health Traits," *Nature Human Behaviour* 5 (2021): 1065–73, https://doi.org/10.1038/s41562-021-01053-4.

65. Abdel Abdellaoui et al., "Genetic Correlates of Social Stratification in Great Britain," *Nature Human Behaviour* 3 (2019): 1332–42.

66. Karen E. Fields and Barbara J. Fields, *Racecraft: Soul of Inequality in American Life* (London: Verso, 2012).

67. Diana C. Mutz, "Status Threat, Not Economic Hardship, Explains the 2016 Presidential Vote," *Proceedings of the National Academy of Sciences of the United States of America* 115, no. 19 (May 8, 2018), https://www.pnas.org/content/115/19/E4330; Tehama Lopez Bunyasi, "The Role of Whiteness in the 2016 Presidential Primaries," *Perspectives on Politics* 17, no. 3 (September 2019): 679–98.

68. Anne Case and Angus Deaton, *Deaths of Despair and the Future of Capitalism* (Princeton, NJ: Princeton University Press, 2020); Angus Deaton, "Is Capitalism Killing America?," *The Demand Side* (podcast), August 2021, https://podcasts.apple.com/us/podcast/the-demand-side/id1538150328?i=1000533854941.

69. Adolph Reed Jr., *Stirrings in the Jug: Black Politics in the Post-Segregation Era* (Minneapolis: University of Minnesota Press, 1999), 179–96; Chris Maisano, "The New 'Culture of Poverty,'" *Catalyst* 1, no. 2 (2017).

70. Troy Duster, *Backdoor to Eugenics*, 2nd ed. (New York: Routledge, 2003).

71. Sarah McBride, "HRC & Trans People of Color Coalition Release Report on Violence against the Transgender Community," Human Rights Campaign, November 17, 2017, https://www.hrc.org/news/hrc-trans-people-of-color-coalition-release-report-on-violence-against-the.

72. Libby Adler, *Gay Priori: A Queer Critical Legal Studies Approach to Law Reform* (Durham, NC: Duke University Press, 2018); Joanna Wuest, "After Liberation: Sex, Social Movements, and Capital since the New Left," *Polity* 54, no. 3 (July 2022).

73. Allan Bérubé, "The Story of the Marine Cooks and Stewards Union," 2016, outhistory.org, https://outhistory.org/exhibits/show/no-baiting/red-race-queen.

74. Michael Ward and Mark Freeman, "Defending Gay Rights: The Campaign against the Briggs Initiative in California," *Radical America* 13, no. 4 (1979): 11–26.

75. Karl Marx and Friedrich Engels, *The Communist Manifesto* (New York: Penguin, 2002); Marshall Berman, *All That Is Solid Melts into Air: The Experience of Modernity*, new ed. (London: Verso Books, 2010).

Index

abortion, 17, 97, 147
Abzug, Bella, 120
Acanfora, Joe, 92–96, 240n9, 240n14
ACT UP, 25, 128–30, 133
Ad-Hoc Task Force to Challenge Sodomy
 Bans, 102–4. *See also* Gay Rights Litigators'
 Roundtable
Aetna, 16
African Americans, 196
agency, 182–83, 203
age-of-consent laws, 76
Aid to Dependent Children, 74
Alaska Airlines, 175
Alcoholic Beverage Control (ABC), 45
Alito, Samuel, 181
Alliance Defending Freedom (ADF), 19, 137, 151,
 155, 158, 178, 181, 198, 218n86
Alliance for Therapeutic Choice and Scientific
 Integrity (ATCSI) Training Institute, 151–52
Altman, Dennis, 54–55, 68, 227–28n12
Alvarez, Walter, 42–43
American Academy of Pediatrics, 140, 151
American Anthropological Association (AAA),
 99
American Bar Association (ABA), 99
American Civil Liberties Union (ACLU), 19, 25,
 47–48, 72–73, 91, 96–98, 102, 110, 122, 126, 138,
 141, 144, 146, 171, 174–75, 177–80, 240n8, 241n24;
 Gay and Lesbian Rights, 121
American College of Pediatricians (ACP), 153;
 Committee on Adolescent Sexuality, 151
American Educational Gender Information
 Service, 168
American Federation of Teachers, 204
American Foundation for Equal Rights (AFER),
 142

American Institute of Bisexuality (AIB), 161, 163,
 184–87
American Law Institute (ALI), Moral Penal Code,
 48
American Medical Association (AMA), 52, 63–64,
 171
American Psychiatric Association (APA), 8, 24,
 42, 53, 68, 70, 72, 82, 85–86, 91, 97, 99, 101, 109,
 117, 142, 147–48, 157, 159, 167, 174; Committee on Nomenclature, 64–66; Council on
 Research and Development and Reference,
 66; homosexuality, declassifying of, 6–7, 52,
 147; homosexuality, demedicalizing of, 92;
 homosexuality, as sociopathic personality
 disturbance, 36–37; "Lifestyles of Non-Patient
 Homosexuals," 64–65; reform of, 51–52, 65–67,
 77–78; "Stop It, You're Making Me Sick!," 65–66
American Psychoanalytic Association, 67, 80, 148;
 as homophobic, 110
American Psychological Association (APA),
 67–68, 99, 123, 140, 142, 149; Task Force on
 Appropriate Therapeutic Responses to Sexual
 Orientation (SOCE), 148, 154–55
American Public Health Association, 67–68
Americans for Prosperity (AFP), 19, 158
Anderson, Erica, 18
Angier, Natalie, 109
Anglo-Saxon race suicide, 33
*Answers to a Parent's Questions about Homosexu-
 ality* (National Gay Task Force), 85
Anthem, 16
anthropology, 48, 57, 87, 98
antidiscrimination, 15, 72, 116, 128; laws, 14, 67,
 71, 75–76, 115, 119–22, 125–26, 170, 191, 201;
 wounded attachments, 216n62
Apuzzo, Virginia, 82

Aqueno, Tom, 130
Arkansas, 180–81
Association for the Advancement of Behavioral
    Therapies (AABT), 61, 65–67, 232n93
Association of American Physicians and Surgeons
    (AAPS), 151
Association for Behavioral and Cognitive Thera-
    pies (ABCT), 148
Atlanta, GA, 116–17
Auer v. Robbins, 265n115

Baehr v. Miike, 139–40
Bailey, Michael, 110–14, 116, 123, 127, 129, 161, 184–
    88, 199, 268n161
Baker, Donald F., 98–102
Baker, Jack, 65
Baker v. Wade, 100–103, 241n40
Barber, James, 99
Barlow, David, 67, 148
Baron, Miron, 110–11
Barrett, Amy Coney, 122; sexual preference, use
    of, 191
Baskin v. Bogan, 146; biological immutability,
    144–45
bathroom ban policies, 11
Bawer, Bruce, 128
Bayh-Dole Act, 78
Bazelon, David, 46–48
Beach, Frank A., 57
Beck, Aaron T., 61, 230n56
Becket Fund for Religious Liberty, 19, 137
behavioral genetics, 3, 8, 70, 83–84, 110
behavioral psychology, 61
Being Homosexual (Isay), 80
Bell, Alan P., 80–82, 87–88
Bell, Arthur, 71
Bell Curve, The (Murray), 129, 202, 221n126
Benjamin, Harry, 48, 164, 166–68, 170
Ben-Shalom, Miriam, 123
Berlin, 164
Berman, Marshall, 204–5
Besen, Warren, 183–84
Bezos, Jeff, 14
Biden, Joe, 176
BiDil heart medication, 196
Bieber, Irving, 42, 61–63, 66, 79, 81, 86
Bi-Net USA, 184, 185, 186
biodeterminism, 99, 112, 114, 132, 136, 145, 149, 152,
    199–200
bioessentialism, 4, 9, 10, 13, 20–21, 23, 25–26, 89,
    109, 112–13, 115–17, 119, 123, 127–28, 132–34, 143,
    146, 150, 152, 159, 162, 195, 197–98, 200, 204;
    adaptive nature of, 17; critics of, 11, 16
biologically linked fate, 14
BioNTech, 195
biopolitics, 5, 27, 182–83, 186–87

bioreductivism, 8, 84, 89, 195–96, 201–2
biotech, 195
Bipartisan Legal Advisory Group (BFLAG),
    143–44
biphobia, 187
Bisexual Health Awareness Month, 186–87
bisexual identity, 58–59
bisexuality, 26, 58, 88, 116, 161–64, 166, 182; biologi-
    cal narrative, 169; denial of, 199; double closet,
    187; identity of, 186; phallometric device, 183;
    promiscuity, association with, 169–70; queer
    theory of, 268n157; rates of poverty, 187; social
    stigma against, 187; study of, 184–88; suspicion
    toward, 166; as threat, 59
Bisexual Option, The (Klein), 185
Bisexual Organizing Project, 186
Bisexual Research Center, 184, 186–87
Bi Social Network, 186
Bi Talk (podcast), 186
Black Cat Café, 44
Blanchard, Ray, 268n161
"blue denim elitism," 72
Blueprint: How DNA Makes Us Who We Are
    (Plomin), 196
Bolsheviks, 34
"Born Perfect" campaign, 135, 149
born this way, 101, 192; critics of, as homonorma-
    tive, 20; era of, 71; evolution of, 5, 8; frame,
    43; idea of, 138, 194; ideological appeal of, 147;
    ideology, 2–5, 23–25, 188; logic, 4, 10–11, 168,
    170; narrative, 9, 20, 91, 127–28; politics, 3, 17,
    32, 159; thesis, adaptability of, 22
Born This Way (Lady Gaga), 1, 135
Bostock v. Clayton County, 174–75, 181, 191–92
Boutilier, Clive Michael, 48–49
Bowers v. Hardwick, 91, 103–4, 122–23, 125–26,
    133
Bowers, Marci, 18
Bowman, Karl, 165
Bradley Foundation, 19, 137
Bray, Robert, 118
Brewster, Lee, 59
Briggs, John, 75, 77
Bristol Myers Squibb, 16
Broad Institute, 197
Brown, Dr. Howard, 71, 110
Brown, Jerry, 154
Brown, Wendy, 216n62, 216n63
Brown v. Zavaras, 170
Brubaker, Rogers, 7, 192
Bryant, Anita, 70, 75–77
Buchmeyer, Jerry, 99–102
Budapest, 200
Burns, Ken, 37
Burr, Chandler, 115, 125
Bush, George H. W., 119

Bush, George W., 138
Butler, Judith, 11; theory of performativity, 179

California, 19, 36, 43–44, 75, 96, 141, 153–57, 165, 204; Proposition 8, 142–43
California Board of Equalization, 44
California Business and Professions Code, 44–45
California Family Council, 155–56
Cameron, Paul, 100
Canaday, Margot, 49
Canby, William, 124
capitalism, 12, 57, 71–72
Carlson, Tucker, 161
Carter, Jimmy, 71
Carter, Joe, 150
Case, Anne, 202
Center for American Progress, 142
Center for the Study of Partisanship and Ideology, 18
Center for Transgender Medicine, 177
Charlotte, NC, 176
Chicago Gay Liberation Front, 64
child abuse, 18, 72–73, 153, 175
Child Abuse Prevention Treatment Act, 258n109
Christianity, 241n40
Citizens for Good Public Policy, 176
citizenship, 19, 25, 36, 137, 159; biopolitical character of, 3, 5, 178–79; denial of, 48
Civil Rights Act: Title VII, 111, 20, 173–76, 181, 191, 263n78; Title IX, 11, 175–76, 178, 181, 191
civil service, security clearance, 45
Civil Service Commission (CSC), 39, 45–46, 49
Clarke, Jessica, 255n64
Clinton, Bill, 119, 138; Don't Ask, Don't Tell (DADT), 124–25
"clone," 108
cognitive behavioral therapy, 52–53
Cold War, 33–34, 137
Colorado, 112, 121, 126, 133
Colorado Legal Initiatives Project, 126
Combahee River Collective, 55
Come Out! (newspaper), 55, 58
Committee for Concerned Psychiatry (CCP), 64–65
Communist Party of the United States (CPUSA), 34
Connecticut, 141–42, 155
Conrad, Florence, 31–32, 38
Conservative Political Action Committee, 200
Consumer Legal Remedies Act, 155
conversion therapy, 10, 22, 25–26, 67, 100, 135–36, 148, 183, 258n109; bans, 147, 150–57, 159, 171; as consumer fraud, 156; discrediting of, 80; for minors, 156–59
Coors, Joseph, 70
Cordy, Robert J., 140–41

Cory, Donald Webster, 37
Council for Biblical Manhood and Womanhood, "Nashville Statement," 150
Counter-Psychiatric Group, 58
COVID-19 pandemic, 19; race gap, as class gap, 197; racial disparities, 197; vaccine, 195
Creative LLC v. Elenis, 158
critical race theory, 19
Crouch, Colin, 19
Culinary Workers, 204

Dade County, FL, 76
Dahl v. Secretary of United States Navy, 123
Dallas, TX, 98
Dallas Doctors Against AIDS, 101
dark money, 19–20
Darwin, Charles, 3; Darwinian paradox, 195
Daughters of Bilitis (DOB), 6, 38–40, 54, 71
Davenport, Charles, 33
Davison, Gerald, 61, 66, 183
"Dear Abby" column, 86–87
Deaths of Despair (Case and Deaton), 202
Deaton, Angus, 202
defeminization, 114
Defense of Marriage Act (DOMA), 1, 138, 143, 265n110
D'Emilio, John, 127–28, 249n139
Democratic Party, 15, 71–72, 119, 168
Derrida, Jacques, 128
DeSantis, Ron, 188
detransition, 18
DeVos family, 19
Dewees, Curtis, 37
Diagnostic and Statistical Manual of Mental Disorders (DSM), 11, 24, 60, 62–65, 96, 147, 157, 199; changes to, 97, 99; first edition of, 36–37; gender identity disorder, 167; homosexuality, declassification of, 77, 165; third edition, 66, 167; revising of, 6–7, 66–67
disruptive identities thesis, 16–17
diversity, 15–16
DNA, 202; double-helix form, 78; home-testing firms, 195–96; recombinant, 78
Dobson, James, 118
Dobzhansky, Theodosius, 8
Doe v. Commonwealth's Attorney of Richmond, 97, 241n31
Dolezal, Rachel, as transracial, 191
Don't Ask, Don't Tell (DADT), 10, 119, 124–25, 135, 138, 265n110; repeal of, 1
Dörner, Günter, 236–37n71; sex-hormone hypothesis, 82
Douglas, William O., 49, 59, 97
drag persona, 59
Drag Queens, 59
Drake, Arnold, 131

Duberman, Martin, 71
Dubofsky, Jean, 126–27
Dupree, 241n31
dysphoria, 153; gender, 178, 198

East Coast Homophile Organizations, 39–40
East Germany, 236–37n71. *See also* Germany
EDK Associates, 116–17
Ehrenreich, Barbara, 75
Ehrensaft, Diane, 179–80
Ehrhardt, Harryette, 241n40
Eighth Amendment, 171
Eisenhower, Dwight D., Executive Order 10450, 45
Ellis, Albert, 37
Ellis, Havelock, 163–64
Ellis, Lee, 88
Employment Non-Discrimination Act, 11, 173
Endocrine Society, 153, 180
endocrinology, 3, 68, 81, 84, 166; sex hormones, focus on, 82
Engels, Friedrich, 34–35, 204–5
Enslin, Eugene, 97, 99
Environmental Protection Agency (EPA), 19
Equal Employment Opportunity Commission (EEOC), 133, 176
equality, 17, 55, 76, 137–38, 146, 156, 200, 203; economic, 16; queer, 155; sexual, 204; women's, 198; workplace, 14
Equality Act, 11, 173, 198
Equality California, 141, 154
Equality Foundation of Greater Cincinnati Inc., 126
Equality Non-Discrimination Act (ENDA), 121
equal protection clause, 11, 25, 90–91, 95, 97, 99, 102–4, 112, 122, 124, 126, 139, 141, 143–44, 146, 173, 175, 177–78
Erickson, Reed, 166
Eros and Civilization (Marcuse), 54
essentialism, 17, 150, 195; genetic, 123; queer cultural, 192
establishment clause, 98
Estelle v. Gamble, 171
Ethics and Public Policy Center, 265n110
etiology, 3, 38, 42, 79, 82, 90, 92, 133, 150, 169, 191, 239n110; biology, 188–89; biosocial, 200; etiological theory, 4; trans, 179
Ettelbrick, Paula, 111
Ettner, Randi, 172
eugenics, 2, 4, 22–23, 33, 44, 77–78, 130, 153, 196–97
Europe, 166, 195, 200
European Union (EU), gender studies programs, 200
evolutionary psychology, 23, 83, 144
ex-gay movement, 67, 118–19, 148, 183–84
Eysenck, Hans, 61, 230n54

Fairness for All Act, 181
Falwell, Jerry, 70
Family Policy Alliance, 198
Family Research Council, 25, 155; Policy Studies, 150–51
family values, 7–8, 70, 73, 75
Fausto-Sterling, Anne, 243n12
Federal Bureau of Prisons, 172
Federalist Society, 19
Federal Trade Commission (FTC), 155–56
Feldblum, Chai, 133
feminization, 113–14
fetal pain research, 19
fetishism, 62
Fidesz, 200
Fifth Order, 36
Fight Repression of Erotic Expression (FREE), 58
Firestone, Shulamith, 53–55, 57
First Amendment, 17, 43, 91, 98, 125, 136–37, 153–57, 159
Fleuti, George, 48
Florida, 43, 45, 76, 115, 123, 157; Criminal Psychopath bill, 42
Focus on the Family: Family Research Council, 118; Love Won Out campaign, 118–19, 148
Ford, Clellan S., 57
Fordism, 74
Fortas, Abe, 49
Foucault, Michel, 5, 32, 41, 128, 136, 217n82
Fouratt, Jim, 55
Fourteenth Amendment, equal protection clause, 11, 90–91, 95, 99, 102, 104, 139, 141, 144, 146, 173, 175, 177
France, 200
Frankfurt school, 53, 89
Freedman, Alfred, 65–66
Freedom for All Americans, 15
Freud, Sigmund, 16, 33, 49, 54, 56, 58–60, 62–63, 89, 164, 227–28n12; neo-Freudianism, 80
Freund, Kurt, 183–84
Friedman, Richard C., 80
Friedman, Stanford, 93–94
Frontiero, Sharron, 90
Frontiero v. Richardson, 90, 95–96, 99, 103, 173
Fryer, John: Nixon mask, 65
Fulton v. City of Philadelphia, 158
Furnish, Victor, 241n40
futurity, 10

Gainesville, FL, 176
Gainesville Area Human Rights Campaign, 115
Ganna, Andrea, 192–94, 196
Gay Academic Union, 128
Gay Activists Alliance (GAA), 65–67, 71, 73, 76–77, 120
gay bar scene, 44–45

"gayborhood," 15

gay brain, 107–8, 132, 144–45, 149

Gay Community (newspaper), 55

gay gene, 2–3, 9, 23, 25, 43, 83–84, 89, 104, 107–8, 112, 118–19, 131–33, 135, 161, 192, 195, 199; efficacy of, 117; eugenic potential, 129–30; hype, 114; narrative of, 128; queer theory critics of, 128; racial character of, 20; skeptics of, 127; social stability, 129

gay genomania, 134

gay identity, 94, 102, 113, 132; and science, 191

Gay & Lesbian Advocates & Defenders (GLAD), 140

Gay and Lesbian Alliance Against Defamation (GLAAD), 21–22, 114, 121–22, 184, 194

gay and lesbian identities, 58–59, 143

gay and lesbian movement, 26; born this way logic, success with, 170; marriage equality, 161

gay and lesbian rights social movement, 70–71; and assimilation, 69

Gaylesta, 154

gay liberation, 51–53, 58, 60, 64, 68, 75, 77, 165; newspapers, 55

Gay Liberation Front (GLF), 51, 54–55, 63, 71, 77; "A Brief Essay on Bullshit Expertise," 57; mental health profession, denouncement of, 56–57. *See also individual branches*

Gay Liberation Front–Bay Area (GLF–Bay Area), 64

Gay Liberation Front–Chicago (GLF-Chicago), 64

Gay Liberation Front, London chapter, 55

Gay Liberation Front–Los Angeles (GLF-LA), 63–64; Red Butterfly caucus, 56–57, 59; "Statement of Purpose," 56

Gay Liberation Front–St. Louis (GLF–St. Louis), 57–58

Gaylord v. Tacoma School District, 240n8

Gay National Rights Lobby (GNRL), 120

GAYPA, 64–66

gay politics, 38–39

gay rights, 92, 102, 122

gay rights advocacy, 70, 83, 122, 127, 183; orientation, as term, 120; science's role in, 31–32

gay rights litigation, 91, 98, 122

Gay Rights Litigators' Roundtable, 102. *See also* Ad-Hoc Task Force to Challenge Sodomy Bans

gay rights movement, 69–70, 76–79; equal protection clause, 104

Gay Rights National Lobby, 69

gay rights organizations, rise of nonprofits, 68

gays and lesbians, rational basis test, 144

Gay Women's Liberation, 58

Gay World, The (Hoffman), 41

Gay Youth Caucus, 76

Gebhard, Paul, 42–43, 72–73

gender: as biological, 175, 194–95; as fluid concept, 179; gender dysphoria, 178, 198; gender fluidity,

11–12; as performative genre, 168; reorientation over affirmation, 171; and sex, 34–35; and sexuality, 5, 170, 190, 194, 204–5; sexual preference, 167; as socially constructed, 179; as term, 166

gender identity, 4, 11, 14, 81, 87–88, 94, 127, 150, 198; biological basis of, 178–80, 191; biomedical theory of, 179–80; clinics, 167; immutability of, 177, 179–80; as medical concept, 178; as sex itself, 170–71, 173–74, 177, 179; and sexuality, 167; sexual orientation, 169, 172, 174–75, 191, 203; as social construct, 177; Title VII protections, 173–74

gender nonconformity, 87, 162, 165–67, 175; homosexuality, link between, 82, 88

Gender Trouble (Butler), 179

Generation Z, 194

genetic essentialism, 123

genetics, 4, 42–43, 68, 79, 84, 170; gene editing, 197; and hormones, 194–95

genomania, 9, 25, 122

genome-wide association studies (GWAS), 26, 194–96, 199, 201; racially skewed, criticism of, 197; single nucleotide polymorphisms (SNPs), 192–93

genomics, 110, 195, 201; nature over nature, rejection of, 192

Georgia, sodomy law, 102–4

German Society for Sex Research, 236–37n71

Germany, 32, 164, 170, 200, 236–37n71. *See also* East Germany

Gilded Age, 22

Gittings, Barbara, 39, 65, 71, 86

Gladue, Brian, 82–83

Gloucester County School Board v. G. G., 178, 181, 265n115

Gold, Ronald, 65–66, 71–72, 131

Gonzales, Mark, 130

Gonzales v. Carhart, 171, 255n66

Goodridge v. Department of Public Health, 140

Gorsuch, Neil, 191

Gorton, R. Nicholas, 179–80

Gould, Stephen Jay, 22–23

Graber, Susan P., 154–56

Grant, Madison, 4, 33, 197

Grassley, Chuck, 198

"Great Awakening," 18

Greeks, 213n30

Green, Richard, 82–83, 87, 123, 126–27, 166–67

Grigson, James, 100

Grimm, Gavin, 178–79, 181, 265n115

Griswold v. Connecticut, 43

Hagel, Nina, 11

Hamer, Dean, 107, 108, 111–12, 116, 126–27, 129–33, 161; sissy thesis, dispelling of, 113–14

Hamer, Marion, 131

Hammersmith, Sue Kiefer, 80–82
Hampson, Joan, 166–67
Hampson, John, 166–67
Hanson, Craig, 57
Haraway, Donna, 237n80
Harden, Kathryn Paige, 196
Hardwick, Michael, 102–3
Harry Benjamin International Gender Dysphoria
    Association, 168, 172. *See also* World Profes-
    sional Association for Transgender Health
    (WPATH)
Hawaii, 139–40, 253n20; pro-marriage equality
    ruling, 138
Hawley, Josh, 22
Hawley, Peter, 112–13
Hay, Harry, 34–36
Hayes, Steve, 67
Heald, Felix P., 93
Hellman, Ronald, 82–83
Herdt, Gilbert, 87
Herek, Gregory, 123, 143
Heritage Foundation, 19, 25, 153, 181, 198, 218n86
Hernandez-Montiel, Geovanni, 172
Herrnstein, Richard J., 221n126
heterosexism, 53–54, 55, 133–34
heterosexuality, 16, 24, 39–41, 51, 56, 74, 89, 143,
    145, 150, 183, 191, 230n49, 240n8; causes of, 88;
    exclusive, 60, 83; exclusivity, as abnormal, 57; as
    normative ideal, 137–38
*High Tech Gays v. Defense Industrial Security
    Clearance Office*, 124
Hill, Danny, 101–2
Hillbilly Elegy (Vance), 202
Hirschfeld, Magnus, 129–30, 164, 170
Hitler, Adolf, 129–30
HIV/AIDS, 101, 119, 166, 182, 243n12; advocacy, 128
Hobby Lobby, 19
Hoffman, Martin, 41
Holloway, Ramona, 173
Holloway v. Arthur Andersen Company, 173
Holt, Lee, 101
homonormativity, 190
homophile movement, 7, 34, 41–42, 49–52, 58–59,
    63–65, 71, 75, 112, 183, 193, 199; "gay is good"
    slogan, 39–40, 165; homophile, as term, 6, 35;
    legal fights of, 43–47; organizations, 24, 91–92,
    122; pluralism of, 40, 60
homophobia, 110, 116, 128–29, 203, 204
Homo sapiens, 83
homosexuality, 16, 24, 41, 46–47, 54–55, 61, 66, 70,
    73, 114, 137, 143–45, 154, 167, 182–83, 191, 196–97,
    240n16; as abnormal, 93; adaptationists, 60;
    as adaptive trait, 193–94; American troops,
    33; in animal kingdom, 83; antidiscrimination
    backlash, 126; antidiscrimination cases, 125;

behaviorist perspective, 152; as benign variant
of normal, 91, 147; biodeterministic conceptions
of, 80; biological basis of, 57, 77–88, 90, 99, 103–
4, 109, 111, 115, 261n37; "blame," concept of, 69;
causality, question of, 42–43; causes of, 38, 73,
77, 79–80, 85–86, 88, 91, 110, 230n56; children,
effect on, 91–95, 97; as choice, 9, 85–86; classification of, 62–63; as contagion, 36, 44, 94, 117;
as continuum, 56, 163–64; declassification of, 7,
52–53, 68, 77, 147, 165; demedicalizing of, 78, 92;
denouncing of, 22; discrimination against, 99,
191–92; as disorder, 157; equal protection clause,
97–99, 124; as evolutionary adaptation, 83, 89;
exclusive, 60, 83; exclusivity, as abnormal, 57;
fixed nature of, 123; gender nonconformity, 82,
88; genetic link to, 112, 118; genomic marker, 111;
"homosexual panics," 93; immigration, 47–49;
as immoral "choice," 7–8; immutability, 123–26;
as infectious, 93; as innate, 86, 116–17; as legal
status, 49; as maladaptation, and modernity,
36; male castration, 165; mental illness model,
62–64, 199; multiple-causes thesis, 79–80, 85,
100, 107; as natural and benign, 32, 35–36; nature v. nurture debate, 107–8, 111–12, 118–19; as
oppressed cultural minority, 34; as orientation,
39; as pathological disorder, 39; pathological
model, 77, 79, 101, 109, 147; pathology school,
62, 67–68; percentage of population, 57–58; as
person's constitution, 86; as protected status,
122; as psychogenic maladaptation, 33; psychopathology, equated with, 33–34; rational nexus
test, 46; reclassifying of, 62; "sick citizens," 37;
as sociopathic personality disturbance, 36–37,
60; as status v. behavior, 44; surveillance tactics,
96; as threat, 33; transgressive gender identities,
conflating with, 42; transitional, 93; as trauma-
based response, 60; twins study, 79, 110; vice
squads, 44. *See also* sexual orientation
*Homosexuality: A Psychoanalytic Study of Male
    Homosexuals* (Bieber), 61
Homosexual: Oppression and Liberation (Altman),
    54
Homosexual Law Reform Society (HLRS), 47–48
Hooker, Evelyn, 41, 47, 62–63, 79, 86–87, 112, 199,
    228–29n29
Hoover, J. Edgar, 45
Hopkins, Anne, 174
Hormones and Brain Differentiation (Dörner),
    82
House Subcommittee on the Employment of
    Homosexuals and Other Sex Perverts in
    Government, 45
Houston, TX, 116–17
"How Gay Are You? (app), 193
Hruz, Paul, 179

Hubbard, Ruth, 110, 116
Hudson, Sam, 97
human difference, 3–4, 27, 195; biological theories
 of, 21, 77, 84
human genome, 104, 192, 193
Human Genome Project (HGP), 107, 132, 192, 196;
 "gay gene" studies, 89; sequencing efforts, 9
Human Rights Campaign (HRC), 7, 14, 19, 21–
 22, 108, 114, 132–33, 141–42, 155, 161, 168–69,
 173, 182–83, 186, 190, 203; antidiscrimination
 legislation, support of, 115; "Just as They Are,"
 149
Human Rights Campaign Fund, 113
Humm, Andrew J., 109
Hungary, 200
hunter-gatherer societies, 83

Idaho, 267n134
"Ideas of Gay Liberation" (Weeks), 55
identity politics, 3, 16, 120, 162–63
immigration, and homosexuality, 47–49
Immigration and Naturalization Services (INS),
 48–49, 226n111
immutability, 90–91, 112, 143, 147; biological,
 144–46, 179–80; "born that way," 175; equal
 protection clause, 25, 126–27, 141, 144; of gender
 identity, 177, 179–80; of homosexuality, 123–26;
 and identity, 170; legal claims, 99, 103, 112,
 123–24, 142, 146; theories of, 175; thesis, 149;
 transsexuality, 173
Indiana, 144
Indiana University, 6, 42
inequality, 4, 15–16, 23, 129, 198, 200–204
Inman, Richard, 42–43
Inmate Sex Change Prevention Act, 171
In re Marriage case, 141
Institute for Sexual Science, 164
International Foundation for Gender Education,
 168
intersex rights movement, 168
intersexuality, 94
Irreversible Damage: The Transgender Craze
 Seducing Our Daughters (Shrier), 198
Isay, Richard, 80
"I Was Born This Way" (song), 1

Jacksonville, FL, 97
Jaffy, Florence. See Conrad, Florence
Janus Society of Philadelphia, 39–40
Janus v. AFSCME, 158
Jenner, Caitlyn, 160, 191
Jennings, Dale, 35–36
Jennings, Jazz, 160
Jerry Springer Show, The, 160
Johns Hopkins University, 167

Johnson, Marsha P., 51, 59, 166
Jorgensen, Christine, 160, 164–65

Kallmann, Franz, 62, 79
Kameny, Frank, 31–32, 39–40, 42, 45–47, 49, 65, 71,
 92, 241n31
Kansas, 125
Karpman, Benjamin, 46
Kaufman, Benjamin, 148
Keller, Jonathan, 156
Kellogg, Jim, 103
Kennedy, Anthony, 1, 133, 144, 191, 255n66;
 immutability, invoking of, 146–47; scientific
 authority, and dignity, 147
Killian, Mary Lou, 121
King, Gregory, 113
King, Martin Luther, Jr., 39
Kingdon, Kirsten, 13, 131
Kinsey, Alfred, 6, 36, 42, 48–49, 56, 58–61, 79, 96,
 104, 164; influence of, 35
Kinsey Institute, 6, 12, 24, 42, 47, 57–58, 63, 70, 72,
 80–81, 83, 87, 97, 99, 103–4, 108, 109, 113, 117,
 120–21, 152
Kinsey Institute for Research in Sex, Gender and
 Reproduction, 87. See also Kinsey Institute
Kinsey scale, 185, 193; sexuality, degree of, 182
Kinsey studies, 45, 81
Kirtzer, Sheeri, 184
Klassen, Albert, Jr., 97–98
Klein, Fritz, 185
Koch, Charles, 19
Koch brothers, 137
Koppelman, Andrew, 218n86
Kosinski, Michal, 22; "gaydar," 21
Krafft-Ebing, Richard von, 33, 129–30,
 163
Kuhn, Thomas, "normal scientists," 63

Ladder, The (journal), 31, 38–39, 42
Lady Gaga, 1, 135
Lafer, Gordon, 159
Laing, R. D., 56
Lambda Legal, 7, 25, 69, 96–98, 102–3, 111, 126,
 138–41, 144, 146, 154, 171, 179; Defense and
 Education Fund, 91; Defense Fund, 109
Lancaster, Roger, 26–27, 162, 243n12
Landers, Ann, 86
Larsen, Jim, 186
Lavender Scare, 33–35, 45
LaVere, Alice, 38
Lawrence v. Texas, 104, 133
Leadership Conference on Civil and Human
 Rights, 146–47
Lesbian Avengers, 128
Lesbian Feminist Liberation, 71

lesbianism, 62; as impediment to happiness, 38; lesbian feminists, 58; lesbian organizations, 24

LeVay, Simon, 110, 112, 114–16, 118, 123, 129, 134, 152, 161, 243n12; bioessentialism, commitment to, 109; gay brain study, 108, 144–45, 149; immutability thesis, 149

Lewis, Oscar, 202

Lewontin, Richard, 13, 23, 89

LGBT, 168; as biopolitical construction, 163; Generation Z, identification with, 194

LGBTQ+, 1–3, 5, 9–13, 16, 20, 22, 114, 132–34, 136, 163, 178, 187–88, 199, 201, 204; adoption, 151; advocates, 18–19, 21, 108, 137, 146, 153, 184–85, 192–93, 198, 200, 203; anti-LGBTQ+ bills, 198; biomedical technologies, investment in, 21; bisexual health disparities, 26; community, 155–56; identities, 14, 17, 150; minors, 158–59; opponents of, 17; people, 273n63; personhood, 158–59; right-wing threats to, 198, 200; suicide prevention, 149; Victory Fund, 15

liberationists, 51–53, 58–59, 63, 70; consciousness-raising activities, favoring of, 54–56

Liberty Counsel, 137, 157

Library of Congress, 174

Lieu, Ted, 154, 156

life sciences, liberal turn of, 78

Littlejohn, Larry, 64–65

Lombroso, Cesare, 21

Los Angeles, 34, 41

Los Angeles Police Department (LAPD), police entrapment, 96

Lourie, Reginald Spencer, 93

Louisiana, 103

Low, Evan, 155–56

Lvovsky, 225n80

Lynch, Loretta, 176–77

Mackenzie, Jeanne, 245n45

Macy, John, Jr., 46

Maher, Bill, 18

Male Homosexuality (Friedman), 80

Manford, Jeanne, 73

Manford, Morty, 73

March on Washington for Lesbian, Gay, and Bi Equal Rights and Liberation, 169–70

Marcuse, Herbert, 53, 227–28n12; desublimation, warnings against, 54

marginality, 16

Marine Cooks and Stewards Union, 204

Marmor, Judd, 42, 65, 67, 78, 85–88, 96, 99, 101–4, 120, 126–27; multiple-causes thesis, 79–80, 100

marriage equality, 10, 26, 135–36, 147. *See also* same-sex marriage

Martin, Del, 65

Marx, Karl, 204–5

masochism, 62

Massachusetts, 140, 172

mass incarceration, 273n63

Masterpiece Cakeshop case, 156, 158

Masters and Johnson, 58–59, 103

Mattachine Foundation, 40–41

Mattachine Review (journal), 37–38

Mattachine Society, 6, 34, 35, 37–38, 44, 51, 56, 63–64, 81, 199; Florida chapter, 42, 45; Mattachine Society of Washington (MSW), 39–40, 45–46, 71; New York City Mattachine Society (MSNY), 39–40; tensions within, 36

Mattox, Jim, 101

Mayer, Lawrence, 177, 179

McCarron-Walter Act, 48

McCarthy, Joseph, 33, 36

McCarthyism, 34, 45

McConnell, Mitch, 159

McCrory, Pat, 176–77

McFeeley, Timothy, 113

McHugh, Paul, 177, 179

Mead, Margaret, 48

Medicare for All, 187

Medvedev, Dmitry, 21

Mental Health America of Northern California, 154

meritocracy, 196

Mexico, 172

Michaels, Walter Benn, 13

Michigan, 155

Michigan Womyn's Music Festival, 166

Millett, Kate, 53, 59

Minneapolis–St. Paul, MN, 119

Minnesota, 120

minority stress model, 199

Mixner, David, 119

modernity, 36, 165, 199, 204–5

Money, John, 48, 87–88, 93, 95, 103, 166–67, 240n16; gender acquisition, 94

Moore, Leonard Page, 48–49

Moral Majority, 70

moral panics, 2

Moynihan, Daniel Patrick, 202

Mucciaroni, Gary, 121

Mueller, Kimberly J., 154

Murray, Charles, 4, 130, 202, 221n126

Murray, Heather, 73

Nabisco, Oreo cookie, 190

National Association for the Advancement of Colored People (NAACP), 19

National Association for Mental Health, 63

National Association for Research and Therapy of Homosexuality (NARTH), 118, 148, 151, 154

National Bisexual Network, 184

National Center for Lesbian Rights (NCLR), 1, 127, 141, 154–55, 172, 177, 179; Born Perfect campaign, 149

National Council of Alcoholism, 37
National Education Association, 240n9
National Family Council on Drug Addiction, 37
National Gay and Lesbian Task Force, 7, 67–69,
    71–75, 77, 82, 84–86, 89, 91–92, 96–97, 99,
    108–10, 117–18, 120, 133, 141, 146, 169, 182, 184–85,
    249n139; Families Project, 111; Military Free-
    dom Initiative, 125; Policy Institute, 127
National Gay Rights Advocates (NGRA), 96, 102
National Institute of Mental Health (NIMH) Task
    Force, 95, 97
National Institute of Mental Health Task Force on
    Homosexuality, 47
National Institutes of Health (NIH), 78, 110
National LGBTQ Task Force, 190
National Organization for Women (NOW), 53,
    72–73
National Policy Roundtable, 133
National Rally, 200
National Science Foundation (NSF), 78
National Student Gay Liberation Conference, 76
National Transsexual Counseling Center, 59
Nazism, 41, 164
neoliberalism, 23, 200
neuroendocrinology, 8, 70
neurology, 84
neuroplasticity, 152
neuroscience, 3, 68
New Atlantis (journal), 177, 265n110
New Deal, 33, 74, 200–201
New Jersey, 43, 45, 141, 153
New Left, 24, 51–57, 62, 64, 128, 165
Newman, Pauline, 245n45
New York, 43, 141–42
New York City, 43, 71, 73, 258n111; Human Rights
    Commission, 109
New York City Gay Pride Parade, 129
New York Times, 18, 107, 109, 111, 113, 161, 163,
    184–87, 195–97
Nicolosi, Joseph, Jr., 152
Nicolosi, Joseph, Sr., 148, 151–52
Niemöller, Martin, 199
NIFLA v. Becerra, 157–58
Nixon, Richard M., 47, 65
Norris, William A., 123–24
North American Conference of Homophile Orga-
    nizations (NACHO), 40, 63
North American Man/Boy Love Association
    (NAMBLA), 76–77
North Carolina, 97–98; House Bill (HB) 2, 176–78, 180
Northwestern University, 184
Norton, Clifford, 46
Norton v. Macy, 46–48

Obama, Barack, 1, 133, 143, 176–77, 186
Obergefell v. Hodges, 1, 146, 255n66

Ochs, Robyn, 186
O'Leary, Jean, 71
One-Dimensional Man (Marcuse), 54
ONE Inc., 37, 43
ontology, 2, 17, 92
Orbán, Viktor, 200
Oregon, 22, 121
Oregon Speaks Out Project, 115
Otto v. City of Boca Raton, 157

Panofsky, Aaron, 84
pansexuality, Pansexual Flag, 190
pansy shows, 33
Papua New Guinea, 87
Parents and Friends of Ex-Gays and Gays, 118
Parents and Friends of Lesbians and Gays
    (PFLAG), 7, 73, 76–77, 84, 88–89, 108, 112–13,
    118, 130–31, 141, 182, 190; advocacy literature,
    87; bioessentialist theory, commitment to, 115,
    117; conference workshops, 115; family values,
    appeal to, 75; ideology of, 74; popular advice
    columnists, hounding of, 86–87; "Project
    Open Mind," 116–17; trans right rhetoric, early
    adapter of, 169
Parents of Gays (POG), 70, 73
Parkland Junior High School, 92
Partial-Birth Abortion Ban Act, 171
patriarchy, 53, 71
pederasty, 77
Pediatric and Adolescent Gender Dysphoria
    Working Group, 152–53
pedophilia, 62, 73, 183
Penn State University, 92
Pennsylvania, 179, 180
personhood, 9, 91, 119, 131–32, 138, 142, 147, 158–59;
    bisexual, 186; genomic, 196; trans, 167, 175
Pfizer, 195
phallometric testing, 183–85
Phillips, Jack, 156
physiognomy, 21–22
Pickup et al. v. Brown, 258n110
Pillard, Richard, 84, 87, 110–14, 116, 123, 127, 134
Place at the Table, A (Bawer), 128
Plomin, Robert, 196
PLoS One study, 153
pluralism, 17, 13, 26, 40, 55, 127
Polak, Clark, 40
Poland, 200
Pomeroy, Wardell, 37, 45, 58
population genetics, 21
Posner, Richard, 144–45, 147, 254n53
Postal Workers, 204
post-Fordism, 74
post-genomic age, 196, 202–3
poverty, gays and lesbians, 243n10
Premarin, luteinizing hormone (LM) levels, 82

Price Waterhouse, 174
Price Waterhouse case, 174
Pride Month, 1, 190
Prince, Virginia, 165
privacy, 99–100, 122, 133, 181, 188; claims, 91, 101–4
Progressive Era, 5, 32, 212n19
Prohibition, repeal of, 43–44
pro-life advocates, heartbeat bills, 182
"Promise of America's Children, The," 198
Pruett, Kyle, 139
pseudoscience, 4
psychiatry, 3, 26, 32, 36, 41, 52–53, 60, 63–64, 67, 78, 81, 92, 97, 109–10, 139; psychodynamic theories within, 62
psychoanalysis, 26, 36, 52–53, 61–63, 81–82, 230n56, 232n93
psychology, 3, 32, 52, 60, 78, 81, 84, 92, 97, 139; evolutionary, 23, 83, 144
public goods, 203
public health, 197
Public Health Services (PHS), 48–49
public spaces, 75
Puerto Rico, 10, 153
Putin, Vladimir, 21

QAnon, 22
Quayle, Dan, 119
Queens Liberation Front (QLF), 59
Queer by Choice, 130–31
queer family, 138
queer identity, 136; as multifaceted, 200
Queer Nation, 25, 128–29
queer people, 23; special rights, 22
queer politics, 134
queer rights movement, 136–37; homonormative nature of, 20
queer theory, 3, 26–27, 128, 200

race, 20
race science, 4, 21, 129; IQ-based, 230n54; as misnomer, 23
Racial Integrity Act, 129
racial justice, 16
racism, 72
Radecic, Peri Jude, 118
radical lesbian feminism, 166
Radicalesbians, 58, 165
Rado, Sandor, 60–62
Raleigh, NC, 176
Rather, Dan, 76
Raymond, Janice, 166
Reagan, Ronald, 9, 171–72, 195
"Refugees from Amerika: A Gay Manifesto" (Wittman), 56, 59
Reich, David, 196
Reich, Wilhelm, 66

Reinisch, June, 87–88
Reintegrative Therapy Association (RTA), 152
rejection sensitivity, 199
religious liberty, 155
religious right, 9, 70, 75, 118; competing rights language, 158, 188
reparative therapy, 38, 148, 179
Republican Party, 2, 70, 119, 158, 171, 177, 181, 188; trans identity, denying of, 189; "woke capitalists," decrying of, 182
Rieger, Marilyn, 36
Right Wing of the Republic, 200
Rivera, Sylvia, 59, 166
Robinson, Kent, 64–65
Rockefellers, 6
Rockhill, Nathalie, 71
Roe v. Wade, 19, 97, 100, 104
Roman Catholic Church, behavior v. orientation, 150
Romer v. Evans, 126–27, 133, 144
Roosevelt, Theodore, 33
Rosenthal, Allen, 185
Rove, Karl, 138
Rubenfeld, Abby, 102–4
Ruitenbeek, Hendrik, 41–42, 49
Russell, Sten, 38
Ruthstrom, Ellyn, 186

sadism, 62
Safer, Joshua, 177–78, 180, 267n134
Sagarin, Edward, 37
same-sex marriage, 1, 10, 104, 143–44, 151, 158; adoption, 252n13; bans, striking down of, 146; biology, as savior, 145; and children, 139–40; as social imperative, 138. *See also* marriage equality
San Diego, CA, 76
San Francisco, CA, 38, 72, 76; same-sex couples, marriage licenses, 141
Sathirapongsasuti, Fah, 196
"Save Adolescents from Experimentation Act," 18
Save Our Children, 76
Sawyer, Diane, 160–61
Schattschneider, E. E., 20
schizophrenia, 78
Schroer, Diane, 174
Schwartz, Pepper, 139
science, and politics, 2, 3
Science of Desire, The (Hamer), 112, 132
Scientific-Humanitarian Committee, 164
scientism, 4
Scott, Bruce, 46
Scott v. Macy, 46–47
Second Behavior Modification Conference, 64
Second Industrial Revolution, 5
secular liberalism, conservatives, casualties of, 17

Seidenberg, Robert, 65
selfhood, 14, 75–76
sex: as biology, 181; as gender, 176; right-wing reactions to, 175–76; and sexuality, 144
Sex and Reason (Posner), 144
sex discrimination, 90, 139, 173–74, 177, 191
sexism, 54–55, 71–72
sex panics, 22, 33–35, 73, 201
sexology, 32–33, 115, 199, 236–37n71
"Sexual Arousal Patterns in Bisexual Men Revisited" (AIB study), 185
Sexual Brain, The (LeVay), 114
sexual contagion, fears of, 198
sexual difference, gender nonconformity, 77–78
sexual fluidity, 26, 194
Sexual Freedom League, 59
sexual identity, 14, 55, 70–71, 82, 119, 121, 123–25, 131–32, 141, 143, 161, 172–73; immutable nature of, 138
Sexual Inversion: The Multiple Roots of Homosexuality (Marmor), 42, 79
sexuality, 54, 56, 78, 87–88, 90–91, 95–96, 107, 110, 112, 115, 128, 133, 148, 150, 152, 192; bio-based theories of, 8; biology, 84–85; causes of, 143; of children, 84, 94; clinical study of, 32; as continuum, 60, 143; "deviant," 193; directionality, 81; and gender, 32, 51, 113–14, 170, 204–5; gender awareness, 94; gender identity, 167; science of, 8, 114; social and cultural factors, shaping of, 193
Sexuality Information and Education Council of the United States (SIECUS), 121
sexual orientation, 4, 14, 25, 82–83, 90, 94, 97–98, 100, 104, 111, 115, 118–21, 123, 125, 131, 140, 149, 186, 196; behavior, changing of, 150–51; biological aspects of, 114, 169, 192–93; causes of, 92; of children, 85, 92, 95; discrimination, 139; etiology, 92; gender identity, 169, 174–75, 191, 203; as immutable, 102, 126–27, 141–47, 152, 170
sexual orientation and gender identity change efforts (SOGICE), 10, 135
sexual preference, 81, 87, 120–22
Sexual Preference: Its Development in Men and Women (Bell, Weinberg, and Hammersmith), 80–82, 87
sexual revolution, 31, 40, 138
sex work, 76
Shelley, Martha, 54–55, 59
Shrier, Abigail, 18, 198
Shubb, William B., 154
Silverman, Jessica Haggett, 187
Silverstein, Charles, 66
Simon, William, 99–101
Smith, Jean, 74–76, 86, 103–4
Socarides, Charles, 62–63, 66, 80, 148
social categories, 7

social contagion, 24; fear of, 199
social Darwinism, 60
social hygiene, 5, 77–78
social justice, 190
social media contagion hypothesis, 18
social sciences, 84
social welfare state, 14
Society for Evidence-based Gender Medicine (SEGM), 152–53
Society for Human Rights, 34
Society for Individual Rights (SIR), 44, 63–64, 75
sociobiology, 8, 23, 70, 83–84, 144; helper in the nest theory, 145
Sociobiology: The New Synthesis (Wilson), 83
sociology, 97–98, 139
sodomy, 104, 241n24; criminalization of, 97; entrapment, 97; state prohibitions against, 96, 98, 101–3
Southern Baptist Convention, Ethics & Liberty Commission, 150
Soviet Union, 41
speech act, 183
Spencer, Herbert, 60
Spiegel, John Patrick, 65
Spitzer, Robert, 65–66, 183
Sprigg, Peter, 150–51
Stalin, Joseph, 34, 41
Starbucks, born this way-branded charity drinks, 15
Starr, Adele, 73, 86–87
Starr, Lawrence, 86
State University of New York (SUNY), 82
Stayton, William, 93–95
Steffan, Joseph, 123
Stein, Arlene, 22
Stoller, Robert, 68, 166–67
Stonewall Riots, 24, 51, 54, 108, 120, 165; "Stonewall generation," 76
Street Transvestite Action Organization, 59
suicidality, 149; gender-affirming medical care, 181
Sullivan, Andrew, 128
Sylla, John, 161, 185, 187–88
Szasz, Thomas, 56, 165; "Legal and Moral Aspects of Homosexuality," 41

Teamsters, 204
Technology Transfer Act, 78
Texas, 98–99, 102–3, 133, 182
Texas Human Rights Foundation, 98
Texas Republican Party, 22
Thatcher, Margaret, 234n23
them (magazine), 12–13
theology, 97
Therapeutic Fraud Prevention Act, 156
Third Reich, 129
third sex, 163

Third World Gay Revolution, 55
Thomas, Clarence, 157–58, 181
Thompson, Clara, 47
Thorstad, David, 76–77
tolerance, 10, 17, 32, 41, 75, 92, 95, 97, 116–17, 158, 216n63; social, 7–8, 14, 16, 94
Traditional Values Coalition, 121
trans, and trender, distinction between, 18
trans advocates, 178
trans assimilation, 170
trans bathroom panic, 176
trans etiology, 179
transgender, 161, 174, 178, 198; asylum seekers, 170, 172–73; bathroom access, 26, 151, 180–81; biological basis of, 180–81; brain, 3; identity, organic basis of, 177; social contagions, 26; as term, 168; visibility and rights, 160; youth, 19, 181
transgender identity, 18, 163, 266n125; as cultural boogeyman, 161; denying of, 189
Transgender Law Center, 179
Transgender Legal Defense & Education Fund, 161
Transgender Nation, 128
trans healthcare, 18, 167–68, 171–72, 175, 182, 201; anti-trans athlete law, 188; criminalization of, 188; sex-segregated sports programs, 180–81
trans identification: rise in, 18; social influence, 18
trans identity, sexual orientation, 173
trans inmates, prisoners' rights, 26, 170–72
trans legal advocacy, 170
trans military ban, 161
transphobia, 203–4
trans politics, 166
trans population, 3; accommodation and balancing, 181
trans rights, 13, 26, 159, 169–70, 175; national debate over, 176
Transsexual Empire, The (Raymond), 166
transsexuality, 26, 59, 67, 94, 113–14, 116, 167, 169, 240n16; and genetics, 170; immutability, 173
Transsexual Phenomenon, The (Benjamin), 166
transsexuals, 162, 165, 167, 170
trans sports, 26
trans trending, 198, 203
transvestites, 42, 165
transvestitism, 62, 164, 167
trans visibility, conservative reaction to, 18
trans women, 17; as autogynephilia, 199, 268n161; of color, 20, 203
trans youth, 2, 17, 22, 26, 175, 180–81, 188, 198–99
Trevor Project, 16, 149, 156
Tribe, Laurence, 103
Tripp, C. A., 42, 81
Trump, Donald, 133, 137, 153, 156–57, 159, 161, 175–76, 191, 202, 264n100
Truth Wins Out, 148, 183–84, 186

Tulsa, OK, 116–17
Twenty-First Amendment, 43–44
Twenty Questions about Homosexuality (National Gay Task Force), 85–86
23andMe, 21, 192, 196–97
twin-study methodology, 84

UK Biobank, 192, 195, 197
Ulrichs, Karl Heinrich, 33, 163
underclass, 202
United Auto Workers (UAW), 204
United States, 1, 32–34, 70–72, 74, 76, 84, 148, 164, 170, 172, 236–37n71
United States v. Bhagat Singh Thind, 226n111
United States Professional Association for Transgender Health, 177
United Steelworkers, 204
University of California, Los Angeles (UCLA), 167
University of Western Ontario, 132
US Public Health Service, 67–68

Vallerga v. Department of Alcoholic Beverage Control, 44–45
Vance, J. D., 202
Van Mol, André, 151
ventriloquism, 14
Vera, Tony, 161
Vermont, 141
Verrilli, Donald, Jr., 144
Vincenz, Lilli, 65
Virginia, 97, 129, 178
Virginia v. Loving, 97
Voeller, Bruce, 67, 71–73, 97, 99, 120
Vogler, Stefan, 172

Wade, Henry, 101
Wade, Nicholas, 196
Wald, Elijah, 110
Walker, Vaughn, 143
Walker, Whitman, 112–13
Wang, Yilun, 21
Washington, DC, 10, 76, 127, 153, 168, 240n9
Washington Gay Activists Alliance (GAA), 92–93, 240n9
Washington Post, 107, 195
Watkins v. U.S. Army, 123
Weeks, Jeffrey, 55
Weimer Republic, 129–30
Weinberg, Martin S., 80–81, 82, 87–88, 103–4, 110, 121
Weinrich, James, 84, 87, 112–13
Weiss, Jillian, 161
West Virginia, 18, 180
We Will Not Protect You (ACT UP), 129
Weyrich, Paul, 70
Whitaker, Ash, 180, 266n125

"Why Ask Why" Addressing the Research on Homo-
sexuality and Biology (PFLAG), 115–16, 131
Why Is My Child Gay? (PFLAG), 87–88
Wilbur, Cornelia, 62–63
Willerman, Lee, 110
Williams, Adrienne, 186
Williams, Richard, 140
Williams Institute on Sexual Orientation and
Gender Identity Law and Public Policy report,
136; LGBT Poverty Study, 187
Wilson, E. O., 84, 193–94, 237n80, 237n83, 237n84;
macaques, study of, 83
Wilson, Robin Fretwell, 218n86
Wilson, Woodrow, 33
Windsor v. U.S., 143–44
Wisconsin, 145, 153, 171, 179–80
Wittman, Carl, 56; "A Gay Manifesto," 76

Wolf, Mark, 172
Wolfson, Evan, 103–4
women's liberation movement, 53, 57
women's rights movement, 165
Woodward v. United States, 122
Workers Conference to Defeat the Briggs Initia-
tive, 204
working class, 202
World League for Sexual Reform, 164
World Professional Association for Transgender
Health (WPATH), 18, 168. *See also* Harry
Benjamin International Gender Dysphoria
Association
World War II, 2, 33, 36, 43, 78

Young, Ivy, 111
Young, J. H., 95